Palestine and the Palestinians

Palestine and the Palestinians

Samih K. Farsoun

with

Christina E. Zacharia

WestviewPress

A Division of HarperCollins*Publishers*

Copyright © 1997 by Westview Press, A Division of HarperCollins Publishers, Inc.

Published in 1997 in the United States of America by Westview Press, 5500 Central
Avenue, Boulder, Colorado 80301-2877, and in the United Kingdom by Westview
Press, 12 Hid's Copse Road, Cumnor Hill, Oxford OX2 9JJ

Library of Congress Cataloging-in-Publication Data
Farsoun, Samih K.
  Palestine and the Palestinians / Samih K. Farsoun with Christina
E. Zacharia.
    p. cm.
  Includes bibliographical references and index.
  ISBN 0-8133-0340-0
  1. Palestinian Arabs—Economic conditions.   2. Palestinian Arabs—
Social conditions.   3. Palestinian Arabs—Politics and government.
4. Israel-Arab conflicts.   I. Zacharia, Christina E.   II. Title.
DS119.7.F336   1997
956.9405'4—dc21   97-21954
                                                                        CIP

The paper used in this publication meets the requirements of the American National
Standard for Permanence of Paper for Printed Library Materials Z39.48-1984.

10   9   8   7   6   5   4   3   2   1

For my brother, David Farsoun,
and my colleague and friend Naseer Aruri
—Samih Farsoun

For my family
—Christina Zacharia

Contents

Tables and Illustrations

Figures

Maps

Appendixes

Preface and Acknowledgments

The Palestine question and the Arab-Israeli conflict have generated an enormous amount of literature over the years. Most of it, often partisan and polemical, has been concerned with political history, international relations, and current developments in the conflict. More recent studies deal with the Palestinians themselves, especially the politics and internal dynamics of the Palestine Liberation Organization (PLO). The Palestinian uprising (intifada) against the Israeli occupation of the West Bank and Gaza Strip also generated many worthwhile analyses, and there have been numerous studies on the social organization, political economy, and varied social aspects of different periods of Palestine's history and of the occupied territories. Far fewer studies have focused on the varied diaspora Palestinian communities. Together, the extensive published and unpublished works (in the form of reports, doctoral dissertations, and master's theses) provide us with a relatively comprehensive if not truly complete overview of Palestine and the Palestinians.

Nevertheless, we believed that a single volume that tied together the various strands of knowledge about Palestine and the Palestinians historically and in the present was still missing. This book is a political economy of Palestine prior to the catastrophe (*al-Nakbah* in Arabic) of the destruction of Palestinian society in 1948 and, since then, of the Palestinian communities, their institutions, and their national liberation movement and the intifada of those under occupation. It also offers an assessment of the Israel-PLO accords and their consequences for the Palestinian future.

However, an important caveat must be noted at the outset. In the post-1948 era, the Palestinian people and its patrimony were dismembered, and three Palestinian population groupings, vastly unequal in size and varied in structure, emerged. The largest is the diaspora, or refugee communities; the second is made up of the Palestinians in the Israeli-occupied areas of Palestine called the West Bank and Gaza Strip; the third and smallest is the Palestinian community that remained on its land inside Israel after Israel emerged. These Palestinians with Israeli citizenship are what Israel and many Western scholars call the "Israeli Arabs." More than three-quarters of a million people (out of a total Palestinian population of 6.8 million in 1996), about 17 percent of the population of Israel, these Palestinians have come to play an increasingly important role both inside 1948–1967 Israel and with regard to their Palestinian compatriots outside its borders. Because of space considerations, we do not analyze the structure, dynamics, and influence of the Palestinian community in Israel.

In writing this overview of the political economy of Palestine and the Palestinians, we have relied on a large number of historical and contemporary source materials. Christina Zacharia reserached and wrote Chapter 6, "Palestinian Resistance to Israeli Occupation: The Intifada." In addition, she helped in revising and editing much of the manuscript and in preparing tables. She has been a keen critic and an untiring coworker.

This work would not have been possible without the help of many institutions and individuals. The American University in Washington, D.C.; the School of Oriental and African Studies (SOAS) in London; and the Institute for Palestine Studies (IPS) and the Center for Policy Analysis on Palestine (CPAP), both in Washington, D.C., offered invaluable research facilities and sources. We wish to thank Naomi Baron and the Mellon Grant Program of the College of Arts and Sciences of the American University and especially Ramzi A. Dalloul of London for research funds.

We are also grateful to the numerous individuals who assisted with or contributed to this project in one way or another, in particular Anita De-Pree, Heidi Shoup, Georgina Copty, Michael F. Brown, Helen Koustenis, Michael Webb, Greg Welsh, Kyu Bum Lee, Katherine Zacharia, Philip Mattar, Heather Henyon, George Abed, and Bill Vornberger; Barbara Ellington and Laura Parsons of Westview Press; as well as copyeditor Alice Colwell. Naseer Aruri of the University of Massachusetts at Dartmouth provided us with many important materials, commented on a number of chapters, and has offered much encouragement and support over the years of our friendship. Naji 'Allush kindly allowed us to use two of his tables. Special thanks also go to Katha Kissman for her extensive help.

We wish to thank the following publishers and institutions for permission to reprint or reproduce tables and maps: Addison, Wesley, Longman, Harlow, UK; Americans for Middle East Understanding, Inc., New York; Cambridge University Press, New York; the Center for Policy Analysis on Palestine, Washington, D.C.; Foundation for Middle East Peace, Washington, D.C.; Indiana University Press, Bloomington; Institute for Palestine Studies, Washington, D.C.; International and Area Studies, University of California, Berkeley; Magnes Press, Jerusalem; Princeton University Press, Princeton; Routledge, London; UNESCO, Paris; UNRWA, United Nations, New York; World Bank, New York; Yale University Press, New Haven, Connecticut; and Zed Books, London.

Finally, to many others we cannot name here, we extend our gratitude. Named or unnamed, of course, those who helped us bear no blame for any errors, omissions, interpretations, or conclusions of this book. Those remain our responsibility.

Samih K. Farsoun
Christina E. Zacharia

Acronyms

AHC	Arab Higher Committee
ALF	Arab Liberation Front
ALNL	Arab League for National Liberation
CA	Civil Administration
CPRS	Center for Palestine Research and Studies
DFLP	Democratic Front for the Liberation of Palestine
EU	European Union
FATU	Federation of Arab Trade Unions
GDP	gross domestic product
GNP	gross national product
GUPS	General Union of Palestinian Students
GUPT	General Union of Palestinian Teachers
GUPW	General Union of Palestinian Workers
GUPWom	General Union of Palestinian Women
ICA	Jewish Colonization Association
ICRC	International Committee of the Red Cross
IDF	Israeli Defense Forces
IMF	International Monetary Fund
IPC	Iraq Petroleum Company
JMCC	Jerusalem Media and Communication Center
JNF	Jewish National Fund
LNM	Lebanese National Movement
MAN	Movement of Arab Nationalists (also called Arab Nationalist Movement, ANM)
NGC	National Guidance Committee
NGO	nongovernmental organization
OAU	Organization of African Unity
OETA	Occupied Enemy Territory Administration
PA	Palestinian Authority
PANU	Palestine Arab National Union
PAWS	Palestine Arab Workers Society
PCP	Palestine Communist Party
PDP	Palestinian Development Programme
PECDAR	Palestine Economic Council for Development and Reconstruction

PFLP	Popular Front for the Liberation of Palestine
PICA	Palestine Jewish Colonization Association
PISGA	Palestinian Interim Self-Governing Authority
PLA	Palestine Liberation Army
PLDC	Palestine Land Development Company
PLO	Palestine Liberation Organization
PNA	Palestinian National Authority
PNC	Palestine National Council
PNF	Palestine National Front
PPP	Palestine People's Party
PRCS	Palestine Red Crescent Society
PRM	Palestinian Resistance Movement
PSF	Palestinian Security Forces
UN	United Nations
UNESCWA	United Nations Economic and Social Commission for West Asia
UNLU	Unified National Leadership of the Uprising
UNRWA	United Nations Relief and Works Agency
VAT	value-added tax
WZO	World Zionist Organization

Palestine and the Palestinians

ONE

The Question of Palestine
and the Palestinians

Palestine is a small territory, and the Palestinians—the indigenous Arab people of Palestine—are a relatively small population, numbering 6.8 million in 1996. Yet the Palestinian problem has loomed large on the international scene for at least fifty years, with tangled roots nearly a century old. Since 1948, the Arab-Israeli conflict has been punctuated by a major war nearly every decade and countless invasions, incursions, clashes, and skirmishes, producing regional and global tensions and even threatening world peace during the cold war. Indeed, since the advent of the nuclear age, the only known nuclear war alert was issued by the United States during the fourth major Israeli-Arab war, the October War of 1973.

The question of Palestine and the Palestinians continues to be central in international affairs, as the United States, the Pacific Rim, and the European Union (EU) compete for economic domination in the emerging world order. The hegemony of industrialization depends upon oil, a commodity entangled in the volatile conflict over Palestine. The 1973 Arab oil embargo, a result of the Arab-Israeli war of that year, is a potent reminder of the political and economic linkages of the issue, as is the 1991 Gulf War. Middle Eastern oil, which consists of the largest reserves and productive capacity on earth, and the derivative "military hardware" market are a lucrative prize for contemporary rival economic powers. As Simon Bromley argues, control of world oil has been pivotal in the United States' post–World War II global hegemony.[1] Thus the problem of Palestine has been a hidden side of the global political economy.

At the political level, the question of Palestine manifests itself in the United Nations (the Palestinian conflict is the single issue that has generated the largest number of resolutions) and in international organizations such as the Organization of African Unity (OAU), the Movement of the Non-Aligned States, and the Islamic Conference. Lord Caradon, the British

1

ambassador to the United Nations and architect of UN Security Council
Resolution 242 (see Appendix 1), which spelled out the conditions for
peace in the Middle East after the June 1967 War, stated: "The future of the
Middle East depends on the Palestinians. They have advanced to the center
of the world stage. . . . The future and the fate of . . . Palestinians increasingly dominate the search for peace."[2] Nearly all Third World states in
Africa and Asia and some in Latin America severed diplomatic relations
with Israel after the Israeli-Arab war of October 1973. Earlier, in 1967, the
former Soviet bloc countries cut diplomatic ties with Israel as a consequence of the June War of that year. Indeed, many Third World governments expelled the Israeli diplomatic missions from their capitals and
offered their premises to the Palestine Liberation Organization, internationally recognized in 1974 as the legitimate representative of the Palestinian people. Since the end of the cold war, most countries have restored
diplomatic relations with Israel. New nations born out of the collapse of
the Soviet Union fostered relations with Israel and the PLO alike.

Only Israel, the United States, and a few U.S. allies, clients, and depen-
dencies continued to deny recognition to the Palestinians as a people and
the PLO as their legitimate representative. The long-held minority position
of the United States and Israel, combined with the rise in international influence of the Palestinians since 1967, often placed the U.S. government in
an untenable position. That was before the collapse of the Soviet Union, the
Palestinian intifada against Israeli occupation that exploded in December
1987, and the Gulf War of 1991.

After these dramatic changes, the United States, as the remaining superpower, launched a more sustained "peace process" in 1991, after the Gulf
War. This effort, spearheaded by Secretary of State James Baker, culminated
in the 1991 Madrid peace conference, which brought to the negotiating
table Israel, the surrounding Arab states, and representatives of the Palestinians under occupation in the West Bank and the Gaza Strip (but not the
PLO, because of both Israeli and U.S. objections). The Madrid peace conference, followed by eleven rounds of bilateral and multilateral negotiations in Washington, D.C., and elsewhere, reached an impasse that lasted
until September 13, 1993, when the Israel-PLO Declaration of Principles
(the Oslo Accords) were signed. The handshake between Yasser 'Arafat,
chairman of the Executive Committee of the PLO, and Yitzhak Rabin,
prime minister of Israel, following the signing initiated a new reality that
would change the nature of the Arab-Israeli conflict and the future of the
Palestinians and the Middle East for generations to come.

Palestine Within the Arab Context

Significant as it is in the international context, the question of Palestine is
far more critical in the Middle East and Arab regions. In their history, cul-

ture, and religion, Palestine and the Palestinians have long been an integral part of the Arab and Islamic worlds. For centuries, the country and the people have been the geographical and social bridge connecting the Mashreq (the Arab East) to Egypt and the Maghreb (the Arab West). Palestinians are related by kinship, economic, religious, and political ties to the people of Lebanon and Syria to the north, Jordan and Iraq to the east, Saudi Arabia to the southeast, and Egypt to the west. Since the destruction of Palestine in 1948 and the forceful dispersal of its people into the surrounding Arab states, the Palestinian question has influenced the political and economic dynamics of the eastern Arab world, including, of course, matters involving oil. It has been a formative issue not only in relation to conflicts between states in the region but also between contending political groups and between regimes and the people within many states. The cause of Palestine became central to both secular (nationalist, radical) and religious political and ideological movements buffeting the region.

One of the most powerful ideological concerns regarding Palestine involves religion. Islam holds Palestine sacred; the Qur'an refers to the country as "al-Ard al-Muqaddasah" (the Holy Land). Al-Khalil (Hebron) and Al-Quds (Jerusalem) are sacred cities. The Ibrahimi Mosque in Al-Khalil is the site of the grave of the prophet Abraham (Ibrahim, in Arabic). Al-Quds is the site of al-Haram al-Sharif (the Noble Sanctuary) upon Temple Mount, the third holiest shrine of Islam, after Mecca and Medina. The Noble Sanctuary includes al-Masjed al-Aqsa and the Qubbat al-Sakhra (Dome of the Rock) mosques. It is from the Dome of the Rock during the night of al-Mi'raj that the prophet Muhammad miraculously ascended to heaven upon the winged stallion al-Buraq. Al-Quds and al-Ard al-Muqaddasah of Filastin (Palestine) are powerful symbols of identity for Muslim individuals and the entire Islamic *umma*, the nation or community of believers. Al-Ard al-Muqaddasah is part of the Muslim umma lands as much as it is part of Arab patrimony. Islamic fundamentalists, traditionalists, and modernizers do not waver from this perception.

The significance of Al-Quds and Palestine to Muslim Arabs should not be construed as less important than its significance to Christian Arabs, who are an integral part of the Arab and Islamic world. In the modern history of the region, Christian Arabs were leaders in the Arab cultural renaissance, the struggle for Palestine, and the movement to free the Arab world from European domination.[3] The founders of two of the most important pan-Arab political movements in the post–World War II period—George Habash, a Palestinian who launched the Movement of Arab Nationalists, and Michel 'Aflaq, a Syrian who established the Ba'ath Party—are Christians, as are many leaders and activists of several other influential political groups throughout the Arab Mashreq. In short, Palestine and its people, Muslims and Christians, are interwoven into the complex human social and political network of the region.

In modern times, until the 1980s, Arab nationalism mobilized the Arab peoples. Developed among the elites in the Mashreq, Arab nationalism became the rallying ideology in the effort to win independence, which began in the latter period of Ottoman Turkish rule, in the second half of the nineteenth century. At war with the Ottomans during World War I, the British, and to a lesser extent the French, encouraged Arab nationalists to launch a revolt against the Ottoman Turks, help defeat their armies, and liberate Arab lands from 400 years of Ottoman dominion. Through deception and collusion, however, the British and French undermined efforts to establish an independent Arab kingdom in the Mashreq areas liberated from the Turks. After the Allied victory, the British and the French, with the approval of the League of Nations (the organization they founded and controlled), divided the Arab Mashreq into a group of small states according to their own interests, without any indigenous economic or political rationale.

Most threatening for Palestine and the Palestinians and other Arabs was the 1917 Balfour Declaration by the British government, which promised the European Zionists a Jewish homeland in Palestine (see Appendix 2).[4] Zionism was from the start a Western imperialist project, and Arab nationalists opposed both Zionism and Western imperialism. Arab nationalists of the 1950s and 1960s viewed the emergence of Israel as a direct threat and a tool of Western, by then principally U.S., imperialism to divide, dominate, and exploit the Arabs. Similarly, the politically renascent Muslim revivalists of the last two decades of the twentieth century consider Zionism, Israel, and Western (especially U.S.) hegemony in the region as a threat to Islam and the Islamic community. Many politically active Muslims believe that Western and Israeli hegemony in the region must be resisted resolutely.

Since World War I, especially after 1948, Palestine stood as the emotional and ideological symbol of both secular Arab nationalism and political Islam, embodying concern for kinspeople and fellow believers as well as resentment against foreign domination. The threats of Zionism and Israel and the struggle against them have historically resonated among all sectors of the Palestinian and Arab populations: Muslim and Christian; religious and secular; modern and traditional; rural and urban; elite and mass; bourgeois, worker, and peasant. This made the Palestine question a powerful *domestic* issue in Mashreq Arab states and among the pan-Arab and Islamic movements since the turn of the twentieth century.

For Arab states, Palestine is not simply a foreign policy issue; it is a principal source of the legitimizing ideology of the post–World War II Arab political culture and regimes.[5] Of course the question of Palestine is not the only issue over which Arab leaderships rise and fall but is intertwined with domestic economic, ideological, class, ethnic, and other political issues. The Palestine question (and since 1967 the organized Palestinian movement under the PLO) has shaped Mashreq Arab politics in four broad historical phases: before the destruction of Palestine in 1948 and continuing until the war of 1967; the reemergence of the Palestinian movement since 1967; the 1991 Gulf War and its aftermath; and the repercussions of 1993 Oslo Accords between Israel and the PLO.

Before 1948 the peoples and governments of the Mashreq strongly supported the beleaguered Palestinians in conflict with the British Mandate authorities and European Zionist Jewish settlers. The Palestinian revolt of 1936–1939 against the British Mandate profoundly affected the opinions of Arab intellectuals, politicians, activists, and youths in surrounding countries. Military officers in Syria, Egypt, and later Iraq justified the takeovers of the established civil governments in part because of the 1948 defeat. They argued that the loss of Palestine was due to the negligence, corruption, and treachery of those governments.[6] The Palestine question and the threat of Israel provided these new, modernizing military rulers of the 1950s and 1960s with the ideological legitimacy to acquire and exercise full control over their nascent states, under the banner of *ma'arakat al-massir* (the battle of destiny)—the confrontation with both Israel and its overseas European and U.S. supporters. For these regimes, the Palestine question was the focus of national solidarity and consensus, the liberation of Palestine justifying the dramatic changes in the traditional social, economic, and political order.[7]

The defeat of the Arab nationalist states by Israel in six days in the June 1967 War discredited these regimes and ushered in another period of internal change. Palestine and Palestinian rights were reduced to secondary (if not rhetorical) status as Arab states redefined the Arab-Israeli conflict as the struggle to regain only the territories occupied by Israel. This was codified in the Arab states' acceptance of UN Security Council Resolution 242, which confirmed the inadmissibility of the acquisition of territory by force and the withdrawal of Israel from Arab territory in return for peace but referred to Palestine and the Palestinians only indirectly as refugees. By 1973, regional Arab political leadership shifted to the more conservative oil-exporting states (particularly Saudi Arabia), as did the national Arab responsibility for Palestine.[8] The cause of Palestine served the rulers of the oil states by appeasing popular sentiment. As Mohammad al-Rumayhi observed: "The tension born from extremely rapid social change, the need for foreign and [expatriate] Arab labour force, the over-conspicuous alliance with the US, all worked together to destroy the old consensus and reveal the anachronism of state structures. In order to legitimise their hold on power, the Gulf countries seem to be forced to prove the positive use of their power . . . for tangible results in Palestine."[9]

The oil-exporting states of the Arabian peninsula supported the Palestinian cause (and the PLO) financially and diplomatically in all international fora, including the United Nations. During the 1970s, the level of Arab support grew as Arab control of oil and financial power increased. By 1981, at the high point of Arab oil power, King Fahd of Saudi Arabia spearheaded an Arab League plan for the political settlement of the Palestine question and the Arab-Israeli conflict: recognition of Israel in return for establishment of a Palestinian state in the West Bank and Gaza.

After the 1967 war, however, Palestinian guerrilla organizations emerged and engaged in armed struggle against Israel; under the umbrella of the PLO, they linked together the exiled Palestinian communities. Through the PLO, Palestinians regained control of their cause from the guardianship of Arab states. But the growth and power of the guerrilla organizations politically destabilized the countries in which they had significant demographic presence, particularly Jordan and Lebanon. This was due in part to the disruption of the domestic balance of political power and in part to the punitive Israeli attacks, which the host governments tried to avoid by controlling Palestinian activity.[10]

Nonetheless, until the 1991 Gulf War, the Palestinian cause continued to provide legitimacy for Arab leaders. The authenticity of their regimes was measured by their lip service or active commitment to Palestine and the Palestinians. President Anwar Sadat of Egypt, for example, justified his stunning trip to Jerusalem in 1977 and the 1979 Israeli-Egyptian peace treaty by claiming that they would bring both peace between Arabs and Israelis *and* solve the problem of Palestine. Similarly, in the name of serving the cause of Palestine, the Syrian government in 1976 sent troops to Lebanon to contain the militarily ascendent Palestinian guerrillas and their secular and leftist Lebanese allies. In 1986 King Hussein of Jordan said his involvement in the U.S.-initiated "peace process" was only intended to help achieve a political settlement to the question of Palestine. Also in 1986 King Hassan of Morocco, in an extraordinary move, met with the Israeli prime minister, Shimon Peres, to explore, as the king stated, advancing Arab (League) demands regarding Palestinian rights.

Except among oppositional movements of political Islam and secular Arab nationalists and leftists, the ideological importance of the Palestinian cause in domestic Arab politics receded sharply as a result of the PLO's affiliation with Iraq during the 1991 Gulf War. Even popular support for Palestine and the Palestinians among the Arab host populations declined. The expulsion of over 350,000 Palestinian civilians from Kuwait after it was liberated from Iraqi occupation did not create a political crisis for that regime or major reverberations in pan-Arab politics. In short, the political capital and goodwill afforded to the PLO within most official Arab circles was spent by 1991. The oil-exporting states ostracized and ceased providing funds to the PLO. The Gulf War therefore left the organization politically and diplomatically isolated and financially weakened. Without the direct financial support of Arab states, Palestinian institutions and people both under occupation and in exile suffered severely. With the exception of Jordan and Syria, the Arab world (especially the oil-exporting states) disengaged further from the Palestinian cause by redefining it as the sole responsibility of the PLO, a declining and increasingly less influential organization.

Although Israelis and the Western media, intellectuals, and politicians may charge Arab politicians and their opponents with opportunism, the latter do not use the Palestine cause merely for partisan purposes.[11] The Palestinian cause has always retained popular support among the mainstream Mashreq Arab public, has remained crucial for domestic legitimacy (even stability), and is rarely underestimated by Arab political leaders. Already by 1993, Arab financial support for the PLO and Palestinian institutions under occupation resumed, albeit not at the same level as before. Yet for Palestinians and other Arabs, the 1991 Gulf War underscored the U.S. government's double standard: The United States would not tolerate the Iraqi invasion of Kuwait but turned a blind eye toward Israeli occupation of Palestinian and other Arab territories. The United States could not continue to ignore the issue indefinitely; this obvious contradiction in policy and other imperial imperatives to ensure international control over oil led U.S. policymakers to resuscitate the "peace process" shortly afterward.[12]

The incongruity in U.S. foreign policy aggravated the political predicament of Arab rulers allied with the United States or dependent on U.S. protection. Since 1948, Arab political leaders, particularly government officials, have been faced with a persistent dilemma: the discrepancy between their strong public rhetorical posture in support of the Palestine question and political pragmatism regarding the conflict. Since the 1970s this dilemma has become more intense and complex because of three factors. The first is the increasing integration into and dependence of the Mashreq states, especially oil-exporters, on the West (in particular the United States), which does not share the Arab view of Palestine and actively works against it. The second is the rise of Palestinians who recaptured their cause in the 1960s, mobilized their dispersed people, and influenced both domestic and inter-Arab politics. The third is the spread of politicized Islam, which also militantly adopted the cause of Palestine, accenting its domestic and foreign policy differences with the pro-Western regimes of the Arab countries. The interpenetration of the domestic, pan-Arab, foreign policy, and Palestinian issues had long propelled the PLO into regional interstate Arab politics, popular pan-Arab and Islamic movements, and domestic oppositional and factional politics. Conversely, this interpenetration encouraged the countervailing intervention of Arab states, parties, and political movements into Palestinian politics. In the context of growing Arab economic and political interdependence with the West, the interlocking of Palestinian and Arab issues heightened the Arab leaders' political dilemma, emphasizing the gap between the image and the reality of their support of Palestine and the Palestinians. As this issue became entangled in political and economic relations with the United States, Israel's superpower patron, Arab governments were all the more eager to contain the destabilizing contradiction if not eliminate it altogether by solving the Palestine problem.

The Question of Palestine and the Palestinians

In the West the most misunderstood element within the question of Palestine is the Palestinian people. It is their unceasing, persistent activism that keeps the cause of Palestine at the fore. Despite dispersal and the absence of a stable territorial base, Palestinians have been the founders, leaders, and untiring activists not only of Palestinian but also of pan-Arab political movements. They have been the engineers, designers, teachers, professionals, consultants, advisers, and diplomats to the peoples and governments of the oil-exporting states. They intermarry with and are the colleagues, comrades, friends, and business partners of other Arabs. After their diaspora, the Palestinians entered the social, economic, and political fabric of Mashreq Arab societies. In many respects, they have become the political conscience of the Arab world.

In general, neither Palestinian exilic life since 1948 nor Palestinian life under occupation since 1967 has been secure. Yet out of a nation largely of rural peasants, the Palestinians have become urban, skilled, educated, and cosmopolitan. In nearly two generations after the destruction of their society in 1948, the exiles achieved the highest educational rates in the Middle East.[13] Despite the trauma of dispossession and dispersal, many have flourished economically. A nation of demoralized, leaderless refugees turned into a nation of revolutionaries.[14] Palestinians under occupation in the West Bank and the Gaza Strip tenaciously resisted Israeli domination and eventually launched a spectacular intifada in 1987.

The experience of the Palestinians is unique and remarkable: After dispossession, destitution, and dispersal; during a national struggle that has spanned more than eight decades, they have become a productive people politically and economically as well as in academe, science and engineering, medicine, journalism, literature, poetry, art, and music. Although Palestine was a diverse society prior to 1948, the catastrophe that divided the people physically kept them united socially and politically. Since then, they articulated common aspirations for the restitution of their political rights and a vision for building a humane and democratic society in a liberated, independent Palestine. This book therefore concentrates on the Palestinian people, society, and culture; the Palestinians' communal structures and economic roles, their political culture and dynamics, and their future.

Perceptions of Palestinians

Palestinians and the West

The Palestinian image in Western Europe and the United States has metamorphosed considerably over the twentieth century. The transformation proceeded in four distinct stages. Once seen as insignificant, the Palestinians were perceived after 1948 as miserable, idle "Arab refugees" who irrationally begrudged Israelis their homeland. Following 1967 the Palestinians were portrayed as violent terrorists. With the eruption of the intifada in 1987, the image began to shift to that of youthful rebels resisting, under great odds, the Israeli military occupation of the West Bank and Gaza Strip. Sensational television footage of Palestinian youths being beaten mercilessly by Israeli soldiers contributed to the change in image. For the first time, the long-cherished Western perception of a little, beleaguered Israel facing the Arab Goliath was reversed. Having been portrayed dramatically on television screens worldwide, Israel's harsh policies toward Palestinians elicited widespread criticism. In the United States, not only congresspeople and local politicians but also church leaders, Jewish community leaders, and the public in general were repulsed by Israel's practices, expressed sympathy for the plight of the Palestinians, and demanded a resolution to the conflict.[15] Fearing a potential threat to its interests and allies in the Middle East, the U.S. government undertook yet another peace initiative in 1988 (the Schultz initiative), which formally opened negotiations with the PLO in Tunisia.

Long demonized by Israel and its supporters, Palestinians under occupation suddenly became humanized, and the intifada restructured the parameters of the Palestine question and the Arab-Israeli conflict. This change in image and context was further reinforced by the vision of articulate and dignified Palestinian negotiators in the 1991 Madrid peace conference and the follow-up formal negotiations in Washington. The image of the diaspora Palestinians and the PLO, however, remained unchanged. Finally, after the 1993 signing of the secretly negotiated Oslo Accords in Washington, D.C., both the overall Palestinian and PLO images were transformed significantly to those of partners to Israel in the process of peacemaking in the Middle East. Nonetheless, in the West and Israel and often even among officials of the Palestinian Authority in the West Bank and Gaza Strip, Palestinian opponents of the terms of the so-called Oslo peace agreements continue to be labeled as terrorists, whether they commit acts of violence or not. Palestinian trauma, suffering, dispossession, and destitution were rarely portrayed in Western media or academic tomes and tended to be seen as inconsequential or, as Edward Said once put it, as an "offstage catastrophe."

Western ideological views of Palestinians are remarkably deep-rooted and persistent, inspired as they were by the political culture of nineteenth-century European imperialism.[16] Imperialism was premised on the right of conquest, on the right of the "superior," white Europeans to rule over "inferior" nonwhites in Africa and Asia. British and Continental attitudes toward the colonized world of Asia and Africa were characterized at best by noblesse oblige and at worst by arrogance, racism, and disregard for indigenous peoples.

Indigenous Palestinians were presumed alternatively as either nonexistent or disposable. The powerful image created by European Jewish Zionists is reflected in a slogan that declared Palestine a "land without people for a people without land."[17] Coined by Israel Zangwill in the early 1900s, it sought to generate popular support for the Zionist project in Palestine by denying the existence of the natives. On November 2, 1917, with its army at the gates of the southern Palestinian city of Gaza, imperial Britain issued the Balfour Declaration (named after Lord Arthur James Balfour, the foreign secretary), which promised the European Zionist movement support for "the establishment in Palestine of a national home for the Jewish people" (see Appendix 2). It ignored the indigenous Palestinians except as "the existing non-Jewish communities." The declaration qualified that Britain would facilitate the achievement of the Zionist project so long as "nothing shall be done which may prejudice the civil and religious rights" of non-Jews.[18] This backhanded provision failed to refer to the *national* or *political* rights of the Palestinian Arabs. Two years after the declaration, Lord Balfour explained: "In Palestine we do not propose even to go through the form of consulting the wishes of the present inhabitants of the country. Zionism, be it right or wrong, good or bad, is rooted in age-old traditions, in present needs, in future hopes of far profounder import than the desires and prejudices of the 700,000 Arabs who now inhabit that ancient land."[19]

Such imperial British disregard for the indigenous peoples parallels Zionist and continuing Israeli attitudes. Israelis tended to dismiss the existence of the Palestinians, but in those rare instances when they acknowledged them, they typically dehumanized them. Consider, for example, the statement of the Israeli prime minister Golda Meir, who said in 1969 that "Palestinians do not exist"; or consider a remark by her successor, Levi Eshkol, who said: "What are Palestinians? When I came here [to Palestine] there were 250,000 non-Jews, mainly Arabs and Bedouins. It was desert, more than underdeveloped. Nothing."[20] During the 1982 Israeli invasion of Lebanon—principally a war against the Palestinians and the PLO— Prime Minister Menachem Begin of Israel called the Palestinians "two-legged beasts," a remark widely reported in the U.S. media.

After the 1967 occupation of the West Bank and the Gaza Strip by Israel, Palestinian existence could no longer be denied. Who and how many Palestinians are there? What is their geographic distribution? And where is their homeland? These emerged as charged political and polemical questions.[21] One notorious answer was offered by the Israeli political Right: "Jordan is Palestine," and there should not and could not be a "second Palestinian state between Jordan and Israel." The Israelis, as did many of their Western supporters, labeled the Palestinians under occupation merely the "inhabitants" of Judea and Samaria or of the administered (not occupied) territories and claimed they thus had no political rights. Indeed those among them who resisted the occupation were called terrorists.

This epithet became especially popular in the West after the political reemergence of the Palestinians in 1967. Beginning in the 1970s, Palestinians seemed to confirm this perception with a series of airplane highjackings and acts of violence by groups of militant, often renegade Palestinians and their allies. Starting in the mandate period, the British and Jewish Zionist settlers called Palestinian militants and resistance fighters of all kinds simply terrorists.[22] U.S. politicians up to the time of President Ronald Reagan referred to the PLO as a "gang of terrorists." Only the administration of George Bush avoided this epithet upon embarking on the new peace process after the 1991 Gulf War.

The intifada of 1987 undermined that pejorative rhetoric. But while the West became more sympathetic to the plight of the Palestinians in general, the PLO remained nefarious. During the negotiations leading up to the 1991 Madrid peace conference and the peace process, both the United States and Israel rejected the PLO as a participant.[23] But as Israeli and U.S. politicians and the media well knew, the Palestinian negotiators were in fact appointed by the organization, received instructions from it, and reported directly to its leadership for decisions. Only after the signing of the secretly negotiated Oslo Accords in 1993 was the pretense of PLO nonparticipation dropped. Thus, for most Palestinians and other Arabs, the Israel-PLO Declaration of Principles (as we show in Chapter 7) was deeply flawed and unfair. One observer described the drama and bitter irony of the signing ceremony: "It would take the pen of Swift to evoke the nauseating scenes of hypocrisy, bad faith and self-delusion on the White House lawn on September 13, crammed as it was with people who for long years were complicit in the butchery and torture of Palestinians and the denial of their rights, now applauding the 'symbolic handshake' that in fact ratified further abnegation of those same rights."[24]

By 1994, then, the image of the Palestinians was dramatically transformed. The "terrorist" epithet is now used principally by Israel, its supporters in the West, and Western conservatives to describe Islamic Palestinian militants and others who object to the terms of the Oslo Accords. Yet even though the image of the PLO and the Palestinians in the West has brightened, in practice Israel and the United States continue to resist acceptance of their internationally codified political and civil rights. Both governments vigorously reject Palestinian national rights, including the right of return, and establishment of an independent sovereign state on the West Bank and Gaza Strip.[25]

Palestinian Self-Image

In contrast to Israel and the West, the Third World views the Palestinians positively because the Palestinians were able to promote their own image there. Although in some cases they were relegated to awkward political and diplomatic statuses, they were rarely degraded, as Third World governments, nongovernmental organizations, media, and intellectuals respected the Palestinian perspective. In most of the world—the non-Western world—the Palestinians were viewed as a dispossessed people who have struggled to regain their inalienable national rights. The PLO was recognized as a national liberation movement that solely and legitimately represented the Palestinian people and provided the organizational framework for mobilizing them and serving their needs.

This perspective is derived from the Palestinian self-image.[26] They consider themselves the indigenous people of Palestine who have inalienable national rights. Pre-1948 Palestinians constitute *al-Sha'ab al-Filastini* (the Palestinian people), part of the greater Arab umma whose *watan* (homeland) is Filastin. They see themselves, however, as divided into two great segments: those in *al-dakhel* (literally, "inside" historic Palestine, both citizens of Israel and those under occupation in the West Bank and Gaza) and those in *al-manfa* (exile) or *al-ghourba* (estrangement) dispersed in the Arab states, Europe, the Americas, and elsewhere.[27]

In their own view, a child born of Palestinian parents, either in al-dakhel or al-manfa, is automatically a new member of al-Sha'ab al-Filastini, and by virtue of descent never forfeits the political right to Palestine no matter what travel document or passport he or she carries. The person is both Palestinian and Arab just as someone may be Syrian and Arab or Egyptian and Arab. Although similar to the Egyptian Arab or Syrian Arab in identity, the Palestinian Arab has lost his or her watan. He or she believes that the Palestinian people has been dispossessed of its homeland of Palestine, dispersed physically, and denied elemental political rights of return, self-determination, and statehood. Thus in the consciousness of the Palestinians, they are a stateless nation struggling to regain their rights to statehood in Palestine.

A Stateless Nation

Ironically, not unlike the diaspora Jews who perceived themselves as a nation, the Palestinians are in this sense the mirror image of those who dispossessed and dispersed them. The conditions that shaped the modern Palestinian identity are complex and deep; they began forming in the last years of Ottoman rule but have much earlier roots. The Greek, Roman, and Arab designation of Philistia, Palaestina, and Filastin, respectively, continued to exist until the Mongolian invasion of the thirteenth century. In the following two centuries, however, under Mamluk rule from Cairo, the territory was divided into districts named after the major cities from which they were administered. Similarly, during their 400-year-long rule (1516–1917), the Ottomans divided that same territory into three *sanjaks* (subdistricts) under the *wilaya* (governorate) of Damascus. During the late Ottoman period, a larger autonomous sanjak of Al-Quds covered most of Palestine. Historically, the administrative integrity of Palestine has been continually reaffirmed.

Over the centuries, the governmental administrative base lent cohesion to Palestine as a province, as did its religious institutions. Both Muslim and Christian organizations were long based in Al-Quds and jurisdictionally covered Jund Filastin (the military district of Palestine, under Muslim Arab rule) and often outlying areas. The Arab Christian Orthodox Patriarchate (Greek rite) of Jerusalem existed uninterrupted since the Byzantine era. Similarly, the Muslim high *shari'a* (Islamic law) courts and legal institutions, centered in Al-Quds, performed parallel functions. Finally, the nationwide Qays and Yaman rival familial alliances and the Nabi Musa (Prophet Moses) and other national celebrations created bonds among the people and fostered a distinctive identity.

Sponsored and encouraged by the European powers during the late Ottoman period in Palestine, Zionism—the colonial project to settle and Judaize Palestine—posed a threat to Palestinians. Arab intellectuals, writers, journalists, and educators were especially alert to the dangers of European Zionist ideology. The Arab press of the pre–World War I period in Palestine and elsewhere is full of articles debating the Zionist historical claims and asserting Arab rights to Palestine.[28] Intellectual life was also concerned with the history of the Arabs and Palestine; it attempted to define the place and significance of Palestine in the Arab world.[29] With the defeat of the Ottomans in World War I, the victorious British, under the auspices of the League of Nations, established the Mandate of Palestine. Unlike the Ottoman rulers, the League of Nations trusteeships were to prepare the natives for self-rule. Thus came into formal being the modern country of Palestine and the legal identity of modern Palestinians. With the establishment of the British Mandate over Palestine and its declared intent of fostering a "national home" for Jews, Zionism presented a clear and present threat. Palestinian response to both the Zionist/British action and ideology furthered Palestinians' identity and consciousness of their historic rights to the land. During that period the cultural climate in Palestine was heavily charged with questions of nationhood, self-determination, and communal reform.[30]

As Arab countries began to negotiate their independence from British and French rule, the volume and intensity of Palestinian rhetoric and polemic increased. Even the titles of the newspapers established in Palestine during the mandate period express a nationalist bent: *Filastin* (Palestine), *Al-Karmel* (Carmel, after Mount Carmel, which overlooks the coastal city of Haifa), and *Al-Defa'a* (Defense). Palestinian historiography of the time was especially concerned with documenting Arab history and presence in Palestine, as if the writers sought to "repeople the terrain with the thick presence of ancestors."[31] 'Arif al-'Arif, one of the most prolific historians of the period, portrayed continuous Arab presence in Palestine since before Islamic and Hebraic times: "We must consider Gaza to have been an Arab city all through the ages . . . and the Muslim conquest . . . to have been merely a new consolidation of the Arab conquest that preceded it."[32]

Overall, Palestinian Arabs perceived Zionism as a new European crusade. Palestinian Arab rights that had been challenged nearly a millennium before were challenged again. This unique sense of Arab Palestinianism was strengthened during the mandate period in the struggles—ideological, political, and armed—against both the British colonial authorities and Jewish Zionist settlers. By the time in 1948 that Palestine was shattered as a society, partitioned as a country, and destroyed as a nation, modern Palestinian identity was consolidated.

The trauma of the destruction of their society and of dispossession and dispersal—*al-Nakbah* (the catastrophe), as they call it—solidified Palestinian self-consciousness, creating among them a psychological bond, a strong feeling of identity and unity, of mutual care and responsibility. No matter where they meet, Palestinians quickly recognize each other through their Arabic dialect, sometimes through their family or clan names. Even those born outside Palestine after 1948 identify themselves as coming from the city or village where their Palestinian parents were born. Thus Palestinians after 1948, inside historic Palestine and as refugees outside, clung to their identity as Palestinians and their self-conception as rightfully belonging to the country. The Palestinian identity belied all the Western plans of the 1950s and early 1960s to resettle the Palestinians in surrounding Arab countries. Numerous formal Western missions that proposed solutions to the Middle East conflict assumed that with sufficient material inducements, Palestinian refugees would accept resettlement and relinquish claims to their homes, villages, and homeland. Western analysts and politicians also assumed that the new generation of Palestinians born in exile would have no attachment to Palestine.[33] They were wrong.

The rise of the PLO in 1967 gave Palestinians an institutional framework, a stronger sense of resolve, and greater unity around the announced goals of the movement. These were the liberation of Palestine and the return of the refugees to their homes. Palestinian political consensus and commitment escalated even higher with the intifada. However, this unity of purpose and goals, the consensus over the means of achieving such goals, the style and method of decisionmaking by the leadership, the character and powers of the leaders, the structure and function of the organization, and indeed Palestinian identity seem to have been shattered by the Oslo Accords.[34] Although the consequences of these recent divisions in Palestinian ranks are serious and contribute to new and different political dynamics among them, we can assess them conclusively (as we see in Chapters 7 and 8) only after the implementation of the provisions of the accords, and perhaps not until the results of the "final status" negotiations.

On Studying Palestine and the Palestinians

The question of Palestine has generated a jungle of literature, heavily polemical, but there are few studies of Palestine as a society and Palestinians as a people. Recent studies of the social and economic history of the nineteenth century and mandatory Palestine, many of which are excellent, point out more of the gaps in our knowledge than they provide us with a comprehensive overview of the country's and the diaspora communities' structure and dynamics. These historical studies have generated different paradigms, each of which yields insights but the implications of which have not been fully developed or resolved. Roger Owen, an economic historian, identifies some of these conceptual problems. They concern whether Palestine in the nineteenth century was a single economic entity, the corollary questions of interregional variations, and the differential impact of European influence. A second problem revolves around the land tenure system, especially the role of *musha'a* (communal) land, its various forms, and its varied social consequences. And finally, there is the issue of the socioeconomic impact of European religious—Christian and Jewish—activity on the country.[35] In short, the nature, structure, and dynamics of Palestinian society and the impact of Europe on it are not conclusively documented or analyzed.

This problem becomes more intractable with the attempt to analyze the socioeconomic transformation of Palestine during the British Mandate period, 1917–1948. To begin with, Palestine was subjected to abrupt changes of regime: in 1917 with the British invasion, in 1948 with the destruction of the country and the creation of Israel, and in 1967 with the Israeli occupation of the rest of historic Palestine, the West Bank, and Gaza Strip. Each wrenching event had consequences for the socioeconomic structure and political dynamics of the society that need to be examined as a whole, not as separate processes. While the problem of reliable data is acute, the frame of reference to situate the data also poses sticky questions. Three competing paradigms can be discerned: twentieth-century Palestine as a typical European colony; Palestine as two separate, coexisting communities, Arab and Jewish, each with its own social, economic, and political arrangements; and Palestine as two sectors, the capitalist (principally Jewish) progressively dominating the precapitalist (primarily Arab).[36]

Problematic as it is to conceive of mandatory Palestine, the question of how to conceptualize Palestinian society after 1948 is even more challenging. Since 1948 the Palestinians as a people came to be divided into three broad segments: those in Israel who remained on the land after the formation of the state of Israel (the smallest segment); those in the West Bank and Gaza Strip who came under Israeli military occupation after the 1967 June War (a larger segment); and those dispersed communities in exile from 1948 until the present (the largest segment). Yet they have developed one nuanced collective identity as Palestinians. A study of the post-1948 Palestinian people, then, would by necessity have to contain these three segments, the different conditions and factors that shaped their varied communal structures and histories, those others that drew them closer or pushed them apart, and the interlocking and overarching dynamics that sustained this unique, postdismemberment syncretic society.

For a number of reasons, the analysis of such a unique syncretic social formation cannot follow a conventional analytical method. First, there are no reliable systematic data on the Palestinians in the three segments in terms of numbers, communal structures, or dynamics. Further, the Palestinians, especially those in exile and to a lesser extent those in the West Bank and Gaza Strip, have engaged in social and physical mobility extensively within the host countries and across their borders. The latter movements, some of which were voluntary and individual (involving a search for a job or education) and others forced and collective, disrupted individual life plans, their communal structure, their institutional orders, and their political dynamics. These changes are not detailed in every case, nor are their social, economic, political, or psychological impacts assessed. There are enormous gaps in our knowledge of the three segments of post-1948 Palestinian social structure. Above all, there is no general or comprehensive social history of the Palestinian people.

What exists for the post-1948 period are disparate studies of isolated aspects of the Palestinian people. And many, although not all, of these studies are framed by narrowly or pseudo-objective theoretical frameworks derived from adversarial or unsympathetic political concerns.[37] Studies of the Palestinian Arabs in Israel are a prime example. Khalil Nakhleh notes:

> the questions most of these studies raised . . . often related to undefined sociological processes which Western social science has generated (e.g., modernization), rather than to the basic ideological underpinnings of the State of Israel which created the minority status of the [Palestinian] Arab population . . . Such a persistent avoidance is purposeful, and it can be understood mainly in terms of an *a priori* adherence on the part of these researchers to the major ideological construct of political Zionism.[38]

The thrust of Nakhleh's critique is (1) that (Zionist) ideology supersedes evidence and influences the direction of interpretation of the research on the Palestinian "Arabs of Israel"; (2) that they are conceptualized as isolated fragments, their nationalism as an aberration, not a natural response to their oppressed collective status; (3) that Israeli Arab social structure is stagnant, locked into traditional relationships as if the Arabs were still living in Ottoman times; and (4) that the methodological dichotomy, comparing traditional versus modern social structure, masks contradictory ideologies and moral judgments. Nakhleh therefore calls for an examination of the presuppositions of such research in order to understand the status and contradictions of the life of the Palestinian minority inside Israel. A more trenchant and specific critique is by Talal Asad, who deconstructs the Orientalist foundations of Israeli anthropology and articulates an alternative perspective of political economy for understanding the history, structure, and dynamics of Palestinian village society under Israeli rule.[39]

Studies of Palestinian society have long been informed by modern politics. G. W. Bowersock, author of *Roman Arabia*, an exceptional study of the Middle East region in Roman times, during which Palestine was at the center, makes a similar point. Historical research on Roman and early Byzantine eras in the Middle East is subtly deflected because of an Israeli reluctance "to confront the fact of an Arabian state and subsequently an even more extensive Palestinian state in the Middle East. These states were part of an international community of Rome and Byzantium but without the sacrifice of their cultural or economic independence."[40] The modern politics of archeology is everywhere as ideological; Israeli scholar-archeologists engage in "the manipulation of the ancient history for present purposes [which] is an unusually bold deception . . . especially where the facts are known."[41]

Elia Zureik, author of a major study on the Palestinians in Israel, concurs.[42] He points out that Israeli social scientists ignore Zionist practices in the process of proletarianization of Palestinian peasantry as they do in interpreting the structure and change generally. Zureik proposes that the study of the post-1948 Palestinian social history draw largely upon the sociology of the minorities and, for those still in historic Palestine, on the sociology of settler regimes that best characterizes the history of the country.[43]

Zureik has formulated a schematic outline of Palestinian social transformation since the beginning of the twentieth century. His stages of twentieth-century Palestinian history include: first, a dual society characterized by asymmetrical power favoring Zionist settlers and Zionist colonization of the country in the pre-1948 period; second, internal colonization of Palestinian patrimony and the proletarianization and segregation of the remaining Palestinians between 1948 and 1967; third and simultaneous to the second, political and economic dependency of the West Bank and Gaza Strip on Jordan and Egypt, respectively (1948–1967); fourth, accelerated forms of internal colonialism inside Israel and colonial dependency of the occupied territories of the West Bank and Gaza Strip, including land (and resource) confiscation, proletarianization of the work force, and denial of rights (1967–present); and fifth, total control by Israel in the future with policies of Zionization and Palestinian depopulation.[44] This is a useful guide to the transformation of Palestinian society in historic Palestine. It lacks, however, a conceptualization of the commensurate structural transformation of Palestinian communities in exile, as, for example, analyzed briefly by Pamela Ann Smith[45] and others. The integration of these works into the schema will provide a more comprehensive picture of Palestinian society since al-Nakbah. Also absent from Zureik's schema is a theoretical formulation that explains the reasons for or causes of the shifts from one stage to the other and that also accounts for the different characteristics of the historical stages he correctly identifies.

One final point needs to be made: The socioeconomic transformations of Palestinian communities in exile do *not* take place in isolation from the dynamics of change in the specific countries in which they reside or the political economy of the region as a whole. The region has become far more integrated, albeit differentially, into the world market since 1948. Thus the transformations of the region including Palestine and the post-1948 Palestinian communities are directly related to the changes of the global political economy. A more comprehensive formulation that ties Palestine, the Palestinian communities, and the region to the world political economy is needed. This will allow for identification of both general and specific structural factors and conditions responsible for shaping Palestinian society in the nineteenth century, during the mandate period, in the post-1948 era, and in the post-Oslo era, as well as the probable future direction of change. The purpose of this book is to provide a more general and comprehensive formulation of Palestine and the post-1948 Palestinian communities that links their social transformation to regional and global restructuring.

Notes

1. S. Bromley, *American Hegemony and World Oil* (University Park: Pennsylvania State University Press, 1991).

2. Lord Caradon, "The Palestinians: Their Place in the Middle East," paper presented at the annual conference of the Middle East Institute, Washington, D.C., September 30–October 1, 1977, 1.

3. G. Antonius, *The Arab Awakening: The Story of the Arab National Movement* (New York: Capricorn Books, 1965). See also H. Sharabi, *Arab Intellectuals and the West: The Formative Years, 1875–1914* (Baltimore: Johns Hopkins University Press, 1970).

4. See the text of the Balfour Declaration and many other important documents in United Nations, *The Origins and Evolution of the Palestine Problem, 1917–1988* (New York: United Nations, 1990).

5. For a fuller discussion, see M. C. Hudson, *Arab Politics* (New Haven: Yale University Press, 1989), 118.

6. Ibid., 302; see also H. Sharabi, *Nationalism and Revolution in the Arab World* (Princeton: Van Nostrand, 1966).

7. The manner and degree of support for the Palestine cause emerged as one of the key issues in the Arab cold war between the Egypt of Gamal 'Abdul-Nasser (leader of the nationalist camp) and Saudi Arabia (leader of the conservative camp). See M. H. Kerr, *The Arab Cold War* (New York: Oxford University Press, 1971).

8. W. Kazziha, "The Impact of Palestine on Arab Politics," in G. Luciani, ed., *The Arab State* (Berkeley: University of California Press, 1990), 306–309.

9. M. Al-Rumayhi, "Factors of Social and Economic Development in the Gulf in the Eighties," in R. Khalidi and C. Mansour, eds., *Palestine and the Gulf* (Beirut: Institute for Palestine Studies, 1982); cited in Kazziha, "The Impact of Palestine on Arab Politics," 310.

10. N. Chomsky, "Middle East Terrorism and the American Ideological System," in E. W. Said and C. Hitchens, eds., *Blaming the Victims* (London: Verso, 1988), 97–147, especially 106; see also N. Chomsky, *The Fateful Triangle: The United States, Israel and the Palestinians* (Boston: South End Press, 1983).

11. E. W. Said, *The Question of Palestine* (New York: Vintage Books, 1980), 6.

12. S. K. Farsoun, "Palestine and America's Imperial Imperative," *Middle East International,* 7 August 1992, 16–17.

13. A. Zahlan and R. S. Zahlan, "The Palestinian Future: Education and Manpower," *Journal of Palestine Studies* 6, 4 (Summer 1977): 103–112. See also I. Abu-

Lughod, "Educating a Community in Exile: The Palestinian Experience," *Journal of Palestine Studies* 2, 3 (Spring 1973): 94–111; N. Badran, "The Means of Survival: Education and the Palestinian Community, 1948–67," *Journal of Palestine Studies* 10, 4 (Summer 1980): 44–74. A comprehensive study of the educational experiences and attainments of the varied Palestinian population segments was produced by S. Graham-Brown, *Education, Repression and Liberation: Palestinians* (London: World University Service UK, 1984).

14. R. Sayigh, *Palestinians: From Peasants to Revolutionaries* (London: Zed Press, 1979).

15. The intifada propelled the Palestine issue directly into the U.S. presidential campaign when supporters of the candidate Jesse Jackson brought the issue to the floor of the 1988 Democratic Party convention in Atlanta.

16. Said, *The Question of Palestine*, 73–82.

17. United Nations, *The Emergence of the Palestine Problem, 1917–1988*, 10.

18. Ibid., 8.

19. Quoted in L. Jenkins, "Palestine Exiled," *Rolling Stone*, 9 June 1983, 32.

20. Quoted in *Newsweek*, 17 February 1969, p. 53.

21. See N. G. Finkelstein, "Disinformation and the Palestine Question: The Not-So-Strange Case of Joan Peters' *From Time Immemorial*," in E. W. Said and C. Hitchens, eds., *Blaming the Victims* (London: Verso, 1988), 33–69. Only recently, as a result of revisionist scholarship, did Israeli academics produce literature that challenged to a degree established Zionist myths and facts. See S. Flapan, *The Birth of Israel: Myths and Realities* (New York: Pantheon, 1987); B. Morris, *The Birth of the Palestine Refugee Problem, 1947–1949* (Cambridge: Cambridge University Press, 1987); A. Shlaim, *The Politics of Partition: King Abdullah, the Zionists and Palestine, 1921–1951* (New York: Columbia University Press, 1990); B. Kimmerling and J. S. Migdal, *Palestinians: The Making of a People* (New York: Free Press, 1993); see also a critique of Israeli social science conceptual framework in B. Kimmerling, "Sociology, Ideology and Nation Building: The Palestinians in Israeli Sociology," *American Sociological Review* 57 (August 1992): 446–460.

22. N. Bethell, *The Palestine Triangle* (London: Andre Deutsch, 1979), 20–75. See the original documents of the British Mandate authorities, prepared in December 1945 and January 1946 for the information of the Anglo-American Committee of Inquiry, in *A Survey of Palestine*, vol. 1 (Washington, DC: Institute for Palestine Studies, 1991), 35–56.

23. Israel then insisted and the United States acceded to the demand that Israel approve the names of all the Palestinian negotiators—a remarkable development in the annals of international relations, where one party is not permitted to freely name its own negotiators.

24. A. Cockburn, "Why Say No?," *Nation*, 4 October 1993, 342.

25. For some time, public opinion polls in the United States have shown that official government policy toward the Middle East is at variance with public attitudes. Public opinion favors a Palestinian state as a solution to the Middle East conflict. See F. Moughrabi, *American Public Opinion and the Palestine Question*, Occasional Paper 4 (Washington, DC: International Center for Research and Public Policy, 1986).

26. See N. H. Aruri, "Dialectics of Dispossession," in N. H. Aruri, ed., *Occupation: Israel over Palestine*, 2nd ed. (Belmont: Association of Arab-American Univer-

sity Graduates, 1989), 3–28; and E. W. Said, *The Politics of Dispossession: The Struggle for Palestinian Self-Determination, 1969–1994* (New York: Pantheon, 1994).

27. Sayigh, *Palestinians: From Peasants to Revolutionaries*, 8.

28. Y. Khoury, *Arab Press in Palestine: 1876–1948* (in Arabic) (Beirut: Institute for Palestine Studies, 1976); R. Khalidi, "The Role of the Press in the Early Arab Reaction to Zionism," *Peuples Méditerranéens/ Mediterranean Peoples,* July-September 1982, 102–124. See also Sharabi, *Arab Intellectuals and the West*; and A. Abu-Ghazaleh, *Arab Cultural Nationalism in Palestine* (Beirut: Institute for Palestine Studies, 1973).

29. M. Buheiry, ed., *Intellectual Life in the Arab East: 1890–1939* (Beirut: American University of Beirut Press, 1981).

30. Abu-Ghazaleh, *Arab Cultural Nationalism in Palestine.*

31. T. Khalidi, "Palestinian Historiography: 1900–1948," *Journal of Palestine Studies* 10, 3 (Spring 1981): 61.

32. 'A. al-'Arif, *History of Gaza* (in Arabic) (Al-Quds: Matba'at Dar al-Aytam al-Islamiyya, 1943), 114.

33. D. Hirst, *The Gun and the Olive Branch* (London: Futura, 1977), 264–266.

34. E. W. Said, introduction and epilogue to *The Politics of Dispossession*, xiii–xlviii, 413–420. See also N. H. Aruri, "Oslo and the Crises in Palestinian Politics," *Middle East International,* 21 January 1994, 16–17; and Cockburn, "Why Say No?" 342–343.

35. R. Owen, introduction to R. Owen, ed., *Studies in the Economic History of Palestine in the Nineteenth and Twentieth Centuries* (Carbondale: Southern Illinois University Press, 1982), 2–3.

36. Ibid., 4.

37. Kimmerling, "Sociology, Ideology and Nation Building."

38. K. Nakhleh, "Anthropological and Sociological Studies on the Arabs in Israel: A Critique," *Journal of Palestine Studies* 6, 4 (Summer 1977): 61–62.

39. T. Asad, "Anthropological Texts and Ideological Problems: An Analysis of Cohen on Arab Border Villages in Israel," *Review of Middle East Studies* 1 (1975): 1–40.

40. G. W. Bowersock, "Palestine: Ancient History and Modern Politics," *Journal of Palestine Studies* 14, 4 (Summer 1985): 51. See also N. Abu El-Haj, "Excavating the Land, Creating the Homeland: Archaeology, the State and the Making of History in Modern Jewish Nationalism," Ph.D. dissertation, Duke University, 1995.

41. Bowersock, "Palestine: Ancient History and Modern Politics," 56.

42. E. Zureik, *The Palestinians in Israel, a Study in Internal Colonialism* (London: Routledge and Kegan Paul, 1978).

43. E. Zureik, "Toward a Sociology of the Palestinians," *Journal of Palestine Studies* 6, 4 (Summer 1977): 3–6.

44. See E. W. Said, I. Abu-Lughod, J. L. Abu-Lughod, M. Hallaj, and E. Zureik, "A Profile of the Palestinian People," in E. W. Said and C. Hitchens, eds., *Blaming the Victims* (London: Verso, 1988).

45. P. A. Smith, *Palestine and the Palestinians, 1876–1983* (London: St. Martin's Press, 1984); and R. Sayigh, *Too Many Enemies: The Palestinian Experience in Lebanon* (London: Zed, 1994).

TWO

Before al-Nakbah: The Modern Social History of Palestine

The modern history of Palestine before al-Nakbah—Palestine's catastrophic destruction—begins around 1800 and ends in 1948. It is divided into two main historical periods: The first covers the nineteenth century and World War I (1914–1917), and the second begins after WWI with the establishment of the British Mandate of Palestine under the auspices of the League of Nations. The transforming forces of the nineteenth and twentieth centuries affected the social history of the entire Arab Mashreq and the whole Middle East. Their particular configuration in Palestine, however, had consequences far more devastating for the indigenous Arab population of the country. Together, these powerful forces may be summarized in one phrase: European interventionism. This chapter concentrates on the structure and transformation of Palestinian society during the first period. It identifies the major social, economic, and political factors and trends that transformed Palestine *and* that, we believe, continue to shape attitudes and events in the region, Israel, the occupied territories of the West Bank and Gaza Strip, and among the Palestinians in exile.

European intervention in Palestine encouraged the process of European settlement in the country, transformed the economy, created new social classes, and rearranged power relations among existing social groups, including the recent Jewish immigrant settlers. This process of intervention started slowly in the early nineteenth century but intensified and accelerated in the second half of the century after the conclusion of the Crimean War (1853–1856), which hastened the opening of the Ottoman Empire, especially Palestine. Although the consequences of European intervention

21

were initially small and incremental, they later became large and wrenching. Over the 150 years, economic activity and productivity in trade, agriculture, industry, and services expanded substantially but became more
closely linked to and dependent on Europe, especially Britain, the emergent
hegemonic colonial power. European interventionism accelerated all the indigenous processes in place since the eighteenth century and propelled
Palestine from a largely subsistence and semifeudal, tribute-paying mode of
existence into a market economy and finally, before its destruction, into dependent capitalist underdevelopment. Most significant, it created the conditions for the destruction of Palestine and the dispossession of its people in
1948, the year of al-Nakbah.

The nineteenth century thus saw not only a new emphasis on monetary
relations over the whole of Palestine with the expansion of the market but
also the initiation of capitalist social relationships of production and exchange.[1] Accompanying these shifts were structural changes in the land
tenure and ownership systems, the development of industrial/artisanal and
service activity, labor force transformation, population redistribution, and
commensurate urban growth. The Ottoman authorities introduced administrative, legal, and governmental reform (rationalization) and centralization, which also contributed to the process of transformation. No less significant was the new "peaceful crusade"[2] of religiously inspired European
immigration, investment, and institutional development. Just as important,
modern education expanded and increased in scope, and social values,
norms, and life-styles changed. Arab and Palestinian nationalism and Islamist consciousness awoke. And all of this occurred in the context of a
rapidly increasing population, both because of natural increase and (to a
lesser extent) because of the immigration of European Christians and Jews,
which restructured the demographic composition of the country. This latter
aspect, which began in earnest only in the 1880s, became a critical factor in
Palestine by the mid-twentieth century.

Social and Economic Organization

Conventional history suggests that the severe conditions and tyranny under
Ahmad al-Jazzar (1775–1804), the Ottoman *vali* (governor) of 'Akka
(Acre), led to the depopulation of Palestine. Cotton production, which
thrived in the eighteenth century, went down, and Palestine's economy became depressed. The declines in population and agriculture forced some
peasants to revert to nomadic life; along with nomadic bedouin pastoralists
from the nearby Arabian and Syrian deserts, they grazed their flocks further
into the plains of Palestine. The combination of exorbitant taxation, the de-
cay of the Ottoman feudal tax-farming system, and especially nomadic en-
croachment discouraged investment and recovery in the area. Village and
agricultural life retreated increasingly to the hill areas of the central spine of

the country, where peasants, relatively safe over the centuries, developed the land's agricultural potential by labor-intensive terracing.

This standard view of the destructive activity of the nomadic bedouin pastoralists throughout the period of Ottoman Palestine is challenged by Beshara Doumani in reference to the nineteenth century:

> This view completely ignores the multitude of economic, political, and cultural connections that linked the Bedouin with the settled regions. The Bani Sakhr and Huwaytat tribes, for example, have for generations sent thousands of camel loads annually to Nablus, supplying the city's merchants and soap manufacturers with *qilli*, a raw material crucial to the city's soap industry. They also provided raw wool, *samn* (clarified butter), horses, camels, and other primary products in return for iron, textiles, and other manufactured items. A network of political agreements further tied the Bedouin to the urban centers, which were keen on safeguarding the *hajj* procession and routes of trade.[3]

Palestinian peasants clung to their land, their villages, their families, their *hamula*s (patrilineal clans or lineages), and their identity. During the more secure periods, peasants tended to return to the low-lying plains, under the influence or control of bedouin pastoralists or semisettled bedouins, to rebuild their villages, establish new ones, and repair the infrastructure. Population density in the plains surrounding and bisecting the mountainous central spine of Palestine continuously fluctuated throughout the centuries. While the plains were accessible to the military arms of the central authorities (Ottoman or Egyptian) and vulnerable to the periodic raids of nomadic bedouins, the central hills of Palestine provided natural barriers. Because of its ruggedness and the difficulty of conquering and holding it, the hill country afforded the Palestinian people—peasants, town dwellers, and local political lords—a measure of autonomy that allowed the development of an indigenous political economy and unique social formations. This occurred not only in the hills of Palestine but also in Mount Lebanon and in the Nusayriyyah hills of northwestern Syria.

In the eighteenth century, Palestinians raised cotton in the western plains and some of the flat areas of higher elevation, but most of the terraced hills of central Palestine were planted with olive trees, which are well suited to the climate and soil. Other agricultural products—wheat, corn, barley, and sesame in particular—were grown in the valleys and nearby plains. Oil extracted from olives was and continues to be a primary material in cooking and soap making, and prior to the twentieth century it was also used for paying taxes and as fuel for lamps. Olive oil, soap, textiles, grain, and sesame seeds were important export commodities to the regional market.

In one sense, the four hill regions of Palestine—Al-Jaleel (Galilee), Jabal Nablus, Jabal al-Quds (Jerusalem), and Jabal al-Khalil (Hebron)—had more or less distinct socioeconomic formations, although they were differentially interconnected to each other and to the surrounding regions. For example, the city of Nablus, the administrative, commercial, manufacturing, and cultural center of Jabal Nablus district, was connected by trade, especially in textiles, olive oil, and soap, to the rest of Palestine, to the hajj caravans east of the Jordan River, to Damascus, and to Cairo and Damietta in Egypt.[4]

The hill regions, which always had the highest population densities and autonomy in Palestine, shared a number of important social organizational features. Palestinian peasants lived in a large number of small villages surrounding the principal cities. As Doumani describes the situation:

> Virtually every adult male peasant had access to land he could call his own, and the size of the landholding did not differ substantially from one peasant to another. In theory, all lands outside the immediate confines of the village formally belonged to the state, and could not be bought and sold as private property. Peasants had usufruct rights to agricultural lands, and in return for its use they paid taxes, called miri (taxes), which were levied both in cash and in kind. In actual practice, however, peasants had de facto ownership of miri land. Over the centuries each clan and village became identified with particular lands they considered their own, and each adult male member passed on his share to his male children through inheritance.[5]

All the hill country in Palestine and other mountainous regions of the eastern Mediterranean were, up to the nineteenth century, characterized by a highly autonomous peasantry, resistant to externally imposed authority, organized in patrilineal clans, surviving by farming small plots of land, and living by norms, customs, and values anchored in their Islamic civilization (except of course for the native Christian communities). Peasants were typically armed, and the Ottoman authorities did not have a direct military presence in or control over the hill regions. They relied on indigenous leaders, often rural *shaykh*s, for control, administration, and taxation until the centralization drive of the mid-nineteenth century. Thus the hilly regions of Palestine collectively developed a unique and distinctive political economy and social formation: the musha'a land use system and the hamula structure of social organization.

The land-equalizing musha'a village had four basic features:

> The cultivated land was divided into several sections, each of which was fairly homogeneous with regard to soil type, terrain, access from the village and other advantages [in other word, equalization was according to quality, not value]. Each share was entitled to an equal portion of the common cultivated land as a whole, and of each of those sections. Finally, all of the common arable land was periodically redistributed, usually by lot in proportion to the number of shares held by each titleholder.[6]

Of course each of these features was subject to variation. By the nineteenth century, however, redistribution progressively ceased. Ya'akov Firestone argues that the musha'a system was not a system of communal ownership, involving a legal entity that owned the land, but rather a system of co-owner-ship, a relationship among individual members that allowed the cessation of redistribution or reapportionment in the modern era and the relatively easy privatization and adjustment to an exchange economy. Further, the co-ownership in the musha'a system did not contradict the 1858 reformative Ottoman land codes, nor was its dissolution required. The musha'a system provided the peasantry with subsistence and a surplus with which to pay taxes. Its slow change in the modern era of exchange or market economy was due to the lack of cash, which became available only as the peasant earnings increased over the late nineteenth and early twentieth centuries. Of course cash was available to the peasant patrons and protectors—the shaykhs and notables—who were in good positions to acquire such land.[7]

In the context of a precarious existence and absence of direct central con-trol, the hamula system organized peasant life socially, economically, and politically. Based on kinship, hamulas involved numerous mutual social obligations that provided social and physical security. The hamulas regu-lated and guaranteed access to productive lands and the rights of the indi-vidual over them. They also acted as an important credible mechanism for the assessment of taxes and the distribution of the tax burden among the villagers. The hamulas protected the individual and kin from both external attack and internal feuds. Led by their own shaykhs, the hamulas therefore provided the individual within the nuclear family collective protection in all aspects of his or her life.

Hamulas varied in size, power, and influence. Over the years some hamu-las grew and split into several segments. Others declined and disappeared or were incorporated into more powerful hamulas. Hamulas could extend over one or more villages, and villages typically had residents from more than one hamula. During much of the Ottoman period, groups of villages were organized into subdistricts called *nahiya*s, each under the control of a shaykh, who typically belonged to the strongest family of the most power-ful hamula in the area. Nahiya shaykhs represented first and foremost their own hamulas but also the lesser ones in the district in relation to Ottoman authority. This was basically an informal system of patron-client relation-ships. As long as the hamula shaykhs appropriately performed their tax-collecting function, they were confirmed as tax farmers and political leaders by the provincial Ottoman governors. When feuds and conflicts emerged within or among the hamulas or clans (groups of hamulas), district officials or urban notables (*wujaha* and *a'yan*) with tax-farming interests would ex-ploit such divisions and manipulate the hamula shaykhs to their advantage. In such situations, nahiya shaykhs would often lose much of their auton-omy. Nonetheless, the staying power of these hamulas and the leading fam-ilies within them is remarkable. For example, in the Nablus nahiyas the eighteenth- and nineteenth-century hamulas and most of their leading fam-ilies—those of Jayyusi, Jarrar, Qasim, Rayyan, Tuqan, 'Abdul-Hadi, and the segment that split from the latter, the al-Masri—continue to be the principal hamulas. Similarly, in the nahiyas of Jabal Al-Quds, the Bargouthi, 'Urayqat (Erikat), Abu-Gowsh, Lahham, Simhan, and other hamulas still dominate the district now as they did in the past.

The Palestinian rural political economy was not isolated. Rural surplus not only was appropriated as tax by the Ottomans and local leaders but also was part of a larger economic system of trade, exchange, or barter with the nearby city or commercial center. Besides being commercial centers, the cities of nineteenth-century Palestine were also loci of manufacture, crafts and artisanal work, administrative offices, and religious and judicial activity. They were populated by Ottoman officials (Turkish and local Arab), local merchants, craftsmen, artisans, shopkeepers, innkeepers, laborers, 'ulama (theologians), and qadis (judges) of the shari'a courts. In the city of Nablus, textile, soap, and other manufactures gave the city a central role in Palestine as the Ottoman period progressed. Artisans and craftsmen were organized into guildlike groups that regulated the process of production, pricing, and standards. The political economy of the Nablus included bedouins who supplied it with an important resource, qilli, an alkaline powder made from burning certain desert plants and used in the production of soap. Doumani estimates that the population of Nablus increased from 4,000 or 5,000 in the late sixteenth century to 20,000 by the mid-nineteenth century.[8] Although soap manufacturing made Nablus famous in the nineteenth century, soap was exported throughout the region already by the end of the eighteenth century.

Peasant, pastoral nomadic, and urban social formations coexisted and interlocked in a complex political economy. It was not feudal as was Europe, nor even as was Mount Lebanon, with its autonomous emir and its authority structure characterized by parceled sovereignties held together by networks of loyalties and obligations. Each Lebanese feudal lord, or muqata'aji, autonomously exercised economic, judicial, social, and political control over the peasantry, which was dependent on him for protection. In contrast, the hamula chiefs and nahiya shaykhs of Palestine were principally appointed or recognized as de facto Ottoman authorities (tax-collecting officials), not autonomous muqata'ajis.

Further, unlike Mount Lebanon's long-established feudal and clan lords, the successive nahiya shaykhs were often of recent bedouin origin. Palestine was close and open to the great Syrian and Arabian deserts, and its highlands were less rugged and more accessible to the nomadic pastoralist bedouins and their conquering chieftains than Lebanon's high mountain ranges. These geographical features lent themselves to differences in social organization; Palestine tended to be more tribal and less feudal in structure than Mount Lebanon. Thus Palestinian peasants' obligations to their shaykhs were more tributary than feudal in character. The land tenure system also reflected this structure. Although a communal landholding (musha'a) system existed, much property—olive groves, vineyards, and other orchards—was private, individual, inheritable, and not redistributed as musha'a. In short, rather than feudal lords, Palestine was ruled by what Alexander Schölch simply calls "local lords," shaykhs, who were Ottoman tax farmers, collecting the rural surplus as tribute to the Turkish overlords.[9]

During periods of Ottoman decentralization or of weakness of central authority, the local Palestinian lords gained a greater measure of autonomy, which perhaps allowed for a process of some feudalization. Ottoman-appointed or -confirmed nahiya shaykhs ruled the Palestinian countryside next to urban notables, and the Ottoman religious or administrative officials. In Jerusalem the notables included the Husseinis and the Khalidis, whose descendants remained important Palestinian leaders into the twentieth century. The families of some of these rural shaykhs and urban notables remained influential into the twentieth century not because their official positions sustained them but (as we see in the next chapter) because they were able to accommodate and adapt these positions and material bases of power to the changing economic situation. The drive for reform (the Tanzimat), administrative reorganization, and centralization by the Ottoman authorities in the middle of the nineteenth century disempowered the rural nahiya shaykhs. The whole of Palestine came under direct Ottoman control based in the major cities, which privileged the urban notables over the rural shaykhs.

European Penetration: The Prelude

While the economic conditions of Palestine during the first three centuries of Ottoman rule vacillated between the extremes of depression and prosperity, the social and political structures remained essentially unchanged. Ottoman functionaries came and went as officials, but no Turkish colonization or Turkification took place. Palestine's Arab character remained intact, and many of the ethnic minorities and remnants of invaders became Arabized over the years. The Ottoman Turkish administrators themselves were always a tiny numerical minority who relied heavily in their bureaucratic apparatuses on local Arabs, who typically were their coreligionists. With respect to the Christian and the tiny Jewish minorities in Palestine, the Ottomans abided by the old covenant of the caliph 'Umar, the second successor after the Prophet Muhammad, and formalized it into the *millet* (sectarian) system. The social (including family) and religious affairs and courts of the "People of the Book," the Christians and Jews, were completely autonomous, though they had to pay a poll tax. A chief cleric of each sect (millet) was assigned to represent the sect before the Sublime Porte in Istanbul.

Of greater significance to the future of Palestine and the Arab Mashreq was Ottoman encouragement of the export-import trade with Europe. The

Ottomans allowed European merchants, missionaries, and consuls to reside in the territory. As a result, the value of British and French trade with the Arab coastal cities rose during most of the nineteenth century. Palestinian and Arab Mashreq primary agricultural commodities were exchanged for manufactured European goods—a pattern of trade that became the hallmark of underdevelopment in the twentieth century.

European missionary and cultural activity in Palestine and the region resumed after a long absence since the Crusades. Through concessions by the Sublime Porte to France, French (and Italian) Catholic missionary activity intensified but came into conflict with local Christian churches—the Orthodox, Coptic, Armenian, and Abyssinian. The Ottomans treated European merchants and other European residents in their domains, including Palestine, as another Christian millet and allowed them extraterritorial judicial, religious, cultural, and social autonomy. Contrary to the Arab millets, who were subject to the sultan's authority, the European Christian millets had the backing of the powerful and rising European states.

As the central Ottoman authorities weakened in the nineteenth century, European states extended their protection to the local Arab Christians and other minorities. France claimed protection over all the Catholics—eastern and western—of the Ottoman domains. Eastern Catholic ranks had swelled as the Maronite church of Mount Lebanon united with Rome and as Orthodox churches splintered, some of these factions uniting with Rome as well. These sects became known as the Uniate churches. Not to be outdone, imperial Russia claimed protection over all the Orthodox churches. The British joined the trend by claiming protection over the tiny minorities of Jews, the Druze (a unique, independent splinter sect from Shi'a Ismailism), and the newly recruited local Protestants. The European claims of protection emerged as one of the most powerful forms of leverage on the weakened Ottoman Empire. European economic, political, and cultural intervention in Ottoman Palestine and the Arab Mashreq became the overwhelming force that shaped the economic, social, cultural, and political history of Palestine and the region ever since.

Opening to the West:
Egyptian Occupation, Palestinian Revolt

Napoleon Bonaparte's invasion of Egypt and Palestine in 1798–1799 both symbolizes and signals intensive European intervention in the region. Napoleon's march into Palestine was unsuccessful. He was stopped at the gates of 'Akka by the allied forces of the Ottoman governor, Ahmad al-Jazzar, and local Arabs. In his retreat from Palestine, Napoleon unleashed a scorched earth policy, his troops destroying and burning the coastal area of Palestine. His depredations followed upon the disasters of the plague, the locust, the tax farmer, and the heavy-handed repression of al-Jazzar in the last quarter of the eighteenth century. Palestine thus began its modern period in an inauspicious condition.

Within the region the Ottomans were challenged by Muhammad Ali, the ruler of Egypt, nominally their subordinate and victor over Napoleon. In a military campaign by Ibrahim Pasha, Muhammad Ali's son, Egypt wrested control of Palestine and Syria from central Ottoman authority. The Egyptian occupation (1831–1840) introduced reforms that led to the dismantling of the old order. The Egyptian policy of centralized control rapidly came into conflict with the system of local notables and rural shaykhs who had established themselves as autonomous tax farmers and political brokers during Ottoman rule. Secularization of the judicial system also deprived the 'ulama of their influential position. Commercial and administrative activity came under the control of the newly created local councils (*majalis*; *majlis* in the singular). Further, the Egyptian ruler attempted to disarm the population, institute military conscription and corvée labor, increase the rate of taxation, impose a capitation tax (*ferde*, Turkish for "individual," from the Arabic *fard*), and establish trade monopolies.

These policies accompanied improved material conditions, increased rural security, the attempted settlement of bedouin tribes (especially in southern Palestine and the Jordan valley), the draining of marshes, concessions to cultivate new lands, as well as greater protection and equality for Christian and Jewish minorities.[10] The Egyptian administration in Syria and Palestine failed to monopolize the international trade because the British opposed the policy. As a result, during Egyptian rule over Syria and Palestine, Ibrahim Pasha monopolized only internal trade, and accordingly derived lesser revenues. And because the Egyptians were unable to establish a system of direct tax collection, they were forced to revert to tax farming. Tax farms were auctioned off to the highest bidder at much larger sums than ever before and collected more taxes in money, not in kind.

Egyptian policies became burdensome to the Palestinian population, which consequently rebelled.[11] The revolt of peasants, urban notables (including the religious functionaries), and rural shaykhs started in Nablus and spread to Safad, Tabariyya (Tiberius), Al-Khalil, Gaza, and Al-Quds. The rebellion began when the notables informed Ibrahim Pasha's governors that they would not supply his army with a quota of conscripts. This represented but one of several larger grievances: The peasants resisted heavier taxes and conscription, while the notables resisted Egyptian centralization of tax collection, the basis of their long-standing power and autonomy.

Determined to quell the rebellion, Ibrahim Pasha ordered attacks on the cities and leaders of the revolt. Parts of several towns and many villages were destroyed; rape and mass killings were perpetrated. It is estimated that Ibrahim Pasha forcefully conscripted 10,000 men to serve in Egypt.

The population was disarmed and an iron rule reimposed. In the six more years of Egyptian rule following the rebellion, until 1840, governmental control in local affairs increasingly tightened. In the course of these events, some of the old social-political leaders were eliminated, and new social classes, both economically and politically based, replaced them by the second half of the century.[12] At the very least, rural shaykhs gave way to urban notables—for the most part Christian in the coastal towns and Muslim in the interior. Ironically, Ibrahim's process of centralization facilitated the nearly nationwide revolt against his rule and further integrated the country. From then on, but especially after the end of the Crimean War in 1856, varied processes and factors progressively gave the area of Palestine social, economic, administrative, and political coherence, which culminated in the twentieth-century (Mandate of) Palestine.[13] If a modern state is defined by its monopoly over the use of violence and the regulation of both national and local affairs, then the Egyptian administration of Palestine in the 1830s formed the first such entity in the region, and the resurgent Ottoman Empire, which reconquered Syria and Palestine in 1840, continued the process.

The Egyptian era initiated other important social developments that accelerated in pace and widened in scope during the Ottoman period that followed. For example, the Egyptians lifted economic and other restrictions on Christians (and the small minority of Jews), and European Christian missionaries flowed into the country. Egyptian rule thus opened Palestine to Western intervention on a larger scale and encouraged the emergence of local urban notables, who inserted themselves as intermediaries on behalf of the Western European capitalist economies.

Egyptian rule in Palestine ended not because Palestinians managed to overthrow the occupiers. Rather, Ibrahim Pasha was defeated by the combined forces of the Ottoman sultan, the British navy, and troops raised locally (Syrian, Lebanese, and Palestinian). Europe, especially Britain, feared the end of the Ottoman Empire—the so-called sick man of Europe—as it was being challenged and replaced by the new rising power of Muhammad Ali's Egypt. The British thus conspired against Muhammad Ali with his erstwhile French allies by agreeing to the French conquest of northern Africa, helping rearm and resupply the Ottoman army and some local forces and directly engaging in naval attacks against Egyptian forces. The Ottoman sultan reimposed his authority over Syria and Palestine, and Muhammad Ali was reduced to a mere and weakened local monarch under the nominal sovereignty of the sultan.

The price the Ottomans paid for regaining Syria and Palestine was high; the British acquired strategic power in the whole Near East. Perhaps as an act of goodwill, or pressure, the Ottoman authorities agreed to the Anglo-Turkish commercial convention of 1838[14]—reduction of import duties, abolition of prohibitions and duties on exports, and in general the elimination of trade barriers—and in 1839 issued the famous Hatt-i Sherif of Gulhane. This was one of several generations of famous edicts of reform the Ottoman authorities issued during the nineteenth century that are collectively known as the Tanzimat (rationalization and reorganization). The commercial convention and reforms gave the British and the other Europeans much greater leverage in penetrating the Ottoman domains, including Palestine.

After the exit of the Egyptian army in 1840, Ottoman authority did not control the rivalry and power struggles of the local Palestinian notables. Palestine lapsed into some disorder as notables and their factional allies, some of whom had profited and emerged stronger from the Egyptian occupation, struggled for power. In part this was a consequence of their restored autonomous status; bedouin tribes and rural populations rearmed themselves and resisted tax payments. The local balance of power, restructured and realigned during the Egyptian occupation, was disturbed again as a result of Ottoman restoration. Some previously pro-Egyptian notables lost out in the restored Ottoman order, while others became sufficiently strong to make a bid for greater power and influence. "In Jabal Nablus, for instance . . . families like the 'Abdul-Hadis had gained enough power during the Egyptian period to challenge the older groups, often bringing in their peasant clients and bedouin allies for those ritual trials of strength designed to improve their position as tax-collectors and surplus appropriators."[15]

Sputtering feuding and intermittent Ottoman campaigns against rural shaykhs' power, especially in central and northern Palestine, intensified into the 1850s, occasionally fostered by the Ottomans as a tactic of divide and rule. For their part, European consuls and their agents tried to undermine Ottoman authority by encouraging factionalism, often under the guise of protecting their citizens or their local protégés. By the 1860s, however, the Ottomans became determined to impose their policy of centralization, direct control, and reform. To this end, they launched a systematic military campaign to subjugate and break the power of the local lords. The rural shaykhs succumbed or were defeated militarily by Ottoman armies; some were sent into exile. A new order was emerging in the second half of the nineteenth century. The shaykhs and notables tried to protect their sociopolitical positions by integrating themselves into the new structures of the resurgent Ottoman administration, especially the urban political-administrative consultative majalis, which supervised tax farming, the commercial boards, the courts of law, and so forth. Social, economic, and political power shifted from rural shaykhs to the urban notables in these councils.

From Subsistence to Market Economy

Although the feuds of the notables during the decades of the 1840s and the 1850s were at times economically destructive,[16] economic activity generally increased throughout the first half of the nineteenth century. As an example, and perhaps as a measure of improved economic conditions, trade between Palestinian districts and the rest of the Middle Eastern region and Europe grew substantially. Available figures indicate that British exports to Syria and Palestine rose from an annual average of £119,753 between 1836 and 1839 to a high of £303,254 in 1850.[17] The majority of imports were cotton goods. Palestine exported cereals to Britain from Gaza and Jaffa. Trade between the Middle East and France in 1836–1838 amounted to 4 million francs in exports and 3.8 million francs in imports.

During this period Palestine was also involved in trade with other parts of the eastern Ottoman domains. Syrian and Palestinian exports to Egypt and Turkey rose from £250,504 in 1836 to £359,732 in 1838, while imports rose from £197,272 to £296,996 for the same years. This process of increased commercialization (or, to be more correct, the transition from subsistence to market economy) in the course of the disintegration of quasi-feudal relations in Syria, Palestine, and Lebanon in the mid-nineteenth century is detailed in the works of many scholars, especially I. M. Smilianskaya, Roger Owen, and Beshara Doumani.[18] Smilianskaya, in a general work on the whole Levant, shows that the largely barter economy of seventeenth-century Palestine gave way in the middle of the nineteenth century to increased commercialization in the form of a commodity-money nexus and agricultural and urban artisan and industrial specialization. Agricultural specialization involved cash crops that supplied regional and foreign markets. Urban specialization occurred as the relatively autonomous home industries of the peasant household declined; exchange between the country and the city increased and became diversified to include peasant tools, utensils, thread, and clothing.[19] Agricultural specialization, craft and industrial production, and the transformation of regional cities into commercial centers indicate "the evolution of a common market which for the time being was confined to Syria, Lebanon and Palestine."[20] However, while both Owen and Charles Issawi stress the relative importance of the European over the regional trade sector, Doumani disputes that conclusion, arguing that the impetus for the development of a market economy in Palestine came as well from the indigenous regional dynamics of agricultural specialization.[21]

Indigenous Commercialization: The Case of Nablus

The major industrial regional centers and internationally linked commercial cities such as Aleppo and Damascus in Syria experienced sharp decline as a result of the direct European economic onslaught, whereas the religiously significant city of Al-Quds (Jerusalem) started its steep economic, demographic, and institutional ascendance. Nablus, however, a smaller, inland, and relatively autonomous urban center, underwent a process of commercialization and transformation that was more a result of indigenous investment activity than of foreign capital.

Commercialization and privatization of agricultural land in the Nablus region antedated the 1858 land code and other Ottoman reforms. Nabulsi merchant capital contributed to rural commercialization and the development of a market in agricultural land in areas other than those of cotton. Nablus had long manufactured and traded, locally and regionally, in textiles and soap. Both industries relied on locally grown agricultural products: cotton and olive oil. Textile manufacturing and the expansion of soap production began in the 1820s—before the emergence of competition from machine-made European textiles. As Owen, Haim Gerber, and Doumani point out, European goods did not cut into the Nablus textile market until the 1850s, because the industry supplied the poorer and more traditional peasants.[22] By then the textile industry of Nablus was put at a disadvantage by imports from Damascus and Cairo.

Not so, however, the soap industry. Olive oil was always in demand as a cash crop and was disentangled from the politically instituted cotton trade monopolies. Produced by independent small farmers, it was less subject to competition and price fluctuation than cotton. Indeed oil came to be more valued than Ottoman currency. But unlike the currency, the value of oil was limited by its perishability; cotton was not, and therefore was in higher demand in the international markets. As the regional and local demand for soap increased, the merchants of Nablus actively sought and encouraged olive oil production.[23]

The principal mechanism for the Nabulsi merchant appropriation of the olive oil surplus of the countryside was the *salam* (futures purchase) contract and moneylending system, which was legitimate under the shari'a as interpreted by the Hanafi school of Islamic jurisprudence.[24] The salam system encouraged trade, provided liquid capital to the rural population, intensified monetization of the economy, and increased the levels of investment and production. Without political positions or power (as tax farmers or large landowners), the Nablus merchants and financiers had only moneylending to access the rural surplus. By the mid-nineteenth century, the Nablus merchants replaced landlords and rural shaykhs as the prime agents of moneylending to the rural population. They also acted as mercantile middlemen in the supply of cash crops to European traders and entered into alliances with the existing elites—landowners, rural shaykhs, and religious and administrative officials.

Most important for the Palestinian peasantry, usurious moneylending (involving 15–35 percent interest rates) was extended to individuals and entire villages. This led to the massive indebtedness of the peasantry—who were increasingly forced to pay taxes in cash rather than in kind—and the commercialization and alienation of agricultural land. By the second half of the century, a growing number of peasants lost their land and became sharecroppers and tenant farmers on land that their ancestors had tilled for centuries. The sale of state or miri land by indebted peasants with usufruct

rights (inheritable use rights over land treated as private) had been normal-
ized by midcentury, prior to the Ottoman land law of 1858.[25] As a result,
usurious merchants transformed themselves into large landlords. Further, a
growing differentiation among the peasantry led to new patterns of stratification: the emergence of both landless and rich peasants.[26]

Changes in class structure and relations were not limited to the Nablus
countryside. The city itself also changed as a consequence of the capitalization and consolidation of the soap industry and the reorganization of the
process of soap production. The process was complex, involving merchant
moneylenders, factory owners, artisans, laborers, and bedouins. The Ottoman state, whose main concern was taxation, was also part of the
process. Because soap production was a capital-intensive industry, it favored single merchants, partners, or joint owners with concentrated wealth
who came increasingly to finance every stage of production. Many individuals simultaneously became soap manufacturers, oil merchants, moneylenders, entrepreneurs, and landowners.[27]

In short, by midcentury a new composite ruling class, based principally
on the expropriation of the rural surplus (from peasants who had been disarmed, left indebted, and abandoned by their traditional rural leaders), was
composed of merchants, tax-farming urban notables, religious functionaries, and urbanized landowners. In contrast to these powerful notables and
families, the peasantry began a long process of dispossession and emergence as a proletarianized mass.

Palestine at Mid-Nineteenth Century

The commercialization of cotton in the eighteenth century strengthened
traditional oppressive rulers who monopolized trade and undermined the
position of the urban commercial and financial bourgeoisie. Olive oil and
soap production did the exact opposite in Nablus in the nineteenth century.
As this development coincided with the elimination of internal and external
trade barriers, the soap industry created indigenous market capitalism
based on traditional products, organization, and processes of production.
Palestinian cities and their surrounding areas during this period can be divided into two types: those directly impacted by the Western thrust into
Palestine, which included Jerusalem, Bethlehem, Nazareth, Jaffa, and
Haifa, and those that were less directly affected, such as Nablus, Gaza, Al-
Khalil, Safad, Tabariyya, and 'Akka.

Except for the demographic decline of 'Akka, available data indicate that
the latter cities and their districts generally experienced economic and sociopolitical developments similar to those of Nablus.[28] For example, by the
1850s the older tetrapolis of Al-Khalil (Hebron) merged into a single city as
a consequence of its economic and demographic growth. Hebron was

known for its glassware, colorful jewelry, leather tanning, and water bags. Although these were important, the city relied mostly on viticulture, sheep and goat herding, trade with the bedouins, and the sale of grapes, raisins, and *dibs* (molasses made from carob) within Palestine and for export to the region. Imported Bohemian and other European glassware did not have an immediate impact in the local market, as Hebron glass was sold to poorer peasants and nomads. In urban centers, such as Jerusalem, shops stocked both Hebron and European glassware. The market for glassware was similar to that for pottery, soap, and fabrics produced in Gaza. Although the black pottery of Gaza was a conspicuous product, the city's weaving industry was no less significant. The Gazans turned wool from the bedouins and flax and cotton from Egypt into textiles. Gaza, however, relied less on handicrafts and industry than on agriculture and trade.

In the 1850s Gaza was an important trade entrepôt, a node in the regional trade routes between Egypt, Arabia, and the Fertile Crescent but also with Europe. During the boom years in international grain demand of the period (especially around the Crimean War), Gaza and Jaffa were vital grain-exporting centers. Similar to Nablus and Hebron, Gaza was also directly linked to the annual hajj caravan from Damascus and the north. Gaza began to decline as a regional trade center only after the opening of the Suez Canal in 1869. The secondary cities of Palestine did not undergo a fundamental economic restructuring during this period, although they shared in the general economic upswing. They also felt the processes of commercialization and, to a lesser extent, capitalization.[29]

The experience of Nablus, Gaza, and Hebron—substantially different from the major cities of Jerusalem, Jaffa, and Haifa—indicates that the development of capitalism in the mid-nineteenth century was slow and uneven. It was also based largely on the production and manufacture of goods from agricultural crops. However, capital accumulation increasingly shifted from a base of regional trade to export-oriented agriculture and import trade in manufactured goods, which placed Palestine at a disadvantage in relation to industrializing Europe. The development of capitalism in Palestine was slow despite the presence of a money-commodity nexus. Nevertheless, wage labor appeared in the form of farm workers and urban artisan-industrial labor, construction, and service workers. Reports collected by Smilianskaya indicate that some peasants spent up to two-thirds of the farming season working as farmhands and that "there already existed in the mid-nineteenth century a standard rate ... and a common market ... for hired labor in the varied regions of Syria and Lebanon," and Palestine as well.[30]

As in Jabal Nablus, rural wage labor, albeit on a small scale, signified labor and social differentiation of the peasantry throughout Palestine at midcentury. Most significant, however, was the dispossession of the peasantry and its "transformation from owners of allotments and small proprietors to *metayers* (tenant farmers)."[31] Large-scale farming did not yet appear, and the peasant-metayer was economically exploited by semifeudal conditions imposed by the usurer merchants and landlords. This class of landlords and merchants did not reinvest in agriculture but in trade, usury, real estate in the urban areas, and to a much lesser extent in manufactories such as spinning mills. The Palestine-wide composite class of interlocked urbanized notables, together with the emergent coastal comprador bourgeoisie (agents of foreign firms), commanded an important role in the second half of the nineteenth and the first half of the twentieth centuries.

The comprador bourgeoisie in particular and the merchants and landed gentry connected to it by trade and money operations were the indigenous social classes that facilitated the European penetration of Palestine and the rest of the Mashreq. Owen outlines the institutional supports for this European connection within the Ottoman domain; among them were the growing number of resident European merchants, regular credit links with European banking houses, the presence of local intermediaries (often Christians), as well as the regular routing of steamships (a new and more reliable transport system). Neither roads nor railways existed yet in the hinterland; commercial transport continued to rely on animal power, especially camels, far into the century. Perhaps as significant, European governments supported and protected their national merchants and local agents. Both France and Britain forced Ottoman authorities to establish mixed tribunals to arbitrate commercial conflicts among Europeans and locals in Syria and Palestine. The merchant councils of the coastal towns also became dominated by the Europeans. The 1850 Ottoman commercial code, based on a French system, further favored the Europeans over the local merchants.

The economic effects of market and capital expansion in Palestine were numerous. The integration of different Palestinian districts into European capitalist economies varied during this period. Similarly, the commensurate expansion of monetary transactions and the involvement of the peasants and artisans in exchange relations and in capitalist relations of production differed by region. This greater involvement was expressed in cash-crop production, agricultural specialization, and industrial manufacture. Above all, the expansion of trade, especially with Europe, enlarged the scope and areas of capital accumulation.[32]

The effects on industry were mixed. While M. A. Ubicini provides evidence of a general decline in Ottoman (including Arab regional) industry in the 1840s,[33] Owen, Doumani, and Schölch dispute his claims. According to Owen, for example, European trade in manufactured goods with Syria and Palestine produced varied results. Some artisan occupations did disappear, but others for a time continued to produce affordable traditional household goods and fabrics. This is in part because the demands of an increasing population and the poor peasantry could not be satisfied by the more expensive European imports.

In short, the development of a market economy and the advancement of capitalism in mid-nineteenth-century Palestine was primarily based on agricultural specialization in the context of increasing population and trade. As a result, villages sprang up on the plains, and the population shifted westward. Coastal urban centers began their rapid growth, and Christian merchants profited most from the European connection. Most important, the old subsistence and semifeudal order died and the new market economy based on money and commodities triggered deep and qualitative social structural change that set the stage for greater transformation in the second half of the nineteenth century.

Integration of Palestine into the World Economy: 1856–1914

After the Crimean War, Palestine became more intensively and extensively integrated into the world economy, laying the foundations for its capitalist peripheralization. This period advanced the destruction of the old subsistence, pastoral, semifeudal, and commercial society as agrarian production, agrarian landownership, agricultural export trade, urbanization, and urban economic development expanded. In addition to the penetration of foreign capital, the combined and mutually reinforcing factors of Ottoman reform and the growing link between indigenous commercial and finance capital and European markets impelled the change.

Ottoman Reform

Administrative and legal reforms were part of a general Ottoman policy of modernizing and centralizing the state against the European threat. The Ottomans also renewed their interest in the Arab provinces as they lost their eastern European territories. With respect to Palestine, the administrative reorganization linked the territory directly to Istanbul. Nevertheless, the Ottomans popularly and often formally referred to the country as Arz-i Filistin (Land of Palestine), not unlike the Arabic name its indigenous inhabitants used.[34] Ottoman reform and reorganization began, as we noted in an earlier section, in 1839 with the Hatt-i Sherif of Gulhane (the Noble Rescript).[35] The Hatt guaranteed the security of life, honor, and fortune for Ottoman subjects regardless of their religion. It called for the establishment of systems of assessing, fixing, and levying taxes and of raising troops by conscription and the creation of salaried government bureaucracy. The assurance of free possession, utilization, and inheritance of property and guarantees against arbitrary confiscation was noteworthy. In effect, this decree created the minimal conditions for the development of private property, a market, and bourgeois social relations and culture.[36]

The weakness of central Ottoman authorities and their involvement in
major border wars, however, discouraged full implementation of the Hatt-i
Sherif Tanzimat. Social and political upheavals of the 1850s and 1860s led
both the Ottomans and the leading Europeans powers to formulate new
political and administrative structures that would produce a more secure
framework for the expansion of commercial agriculture and growth of
trade.[37] Accordingly, in 1856 the Ottoman sultan 'Abdul-Majid issued a
new decree, the Hatt-i Humayun (the Imperial Rescript). As was the first
edict, this one was issued in response to pressure from European powers.
Both these edicts and the formulation of subsequent laws liberalizing economic activity smacked of foreign diktats.[38]

The new edict reaffirmed the principles of the Hatt-i Sherif of Gulhane,
including equal rights for non-Muslims. It also specified the rationalization
of administration, taxation, and justice. Most important for the economy
of the empire, the Tanzimat produced new land and penal codes in 1858, a
reorganization of the legal system in 1860, and new maritime and commercial codes in 1861. Perhaps most relevant were the *tapu* (Arabic *tabu*) land
registration laws of 1861 that formally allowed state miri land to be sold as
mulk, or private property, and that gave foreigners the right to own landed
property. As a consequence, Christian and Jewish Europeans bought land,
and the process of colonization commenced.

The expenditures for the Crimean War and the corruption and extravagance of the ruling class contributed to an Ottoman financial crisis, forcing
the government to obtain loans from European banks and eventually leading to Ottoman bankruptcy. In 1881 the Muharram Decree (named after
the Muslim month in which it was issued) consolidated European financial
control over the empire. In a parallel development, the Egyptian government also went bankrupt, and Britain occupied Egypt and took control of
its finances in 1882. Overall, these events intensified European influence in
the Ottoman Empire and Egypt and accelerated the development of distorted and dependent capitalism in the whole region, including Palestine.

The Expansion and Consolidation of Private Property

The consequences of the Ottoman reforms on landownership in Palestine
were complex and in some instances contradictory. Schölch believes that in
spite of the privatization of much communal land (miri and musha'a), the
musha'a system may have actually increased with the expansion of cultivation in the coastal and inland plains.[39] Yet the profitability of cash-crop
agriculture and the tax revenues accrued may have encouraged the Ottoman authorities to codify informal private landownership patterns in the

land law of 1858 and the tabu land registration law of 1861. It led to the rise of extensive landed estates privately owned by urban notables from Palestine and Lebanon. For the peasantry, the ownership of private property was more of a short-term liability than an asset. Because peasants feared that the tabu law would increase taxation and extortion and the conscription of the owner and family members into the military, many registered their land in the names of their clan chiefs or urban a'yan. Often the tabu law confirmed the de jure right of rural and urban tax farmers to lands they had managed to appropriate de facto. Over the years, a greater number of peasants lost the legal rights to their land and became mere sharecroppers, tenant farmers, and rural wage laborers. Furthermore, in the late 1860s the Ottoman authorities carried out land sale campaigns, especially in northern Palestine.[40]

Privatization of landholding in Palestine thus contributed to the decline of small and medium-sized properties, the rise of huge landed estates, and the increase in land prices. The arable land of Palestine amounts to 8.76 million *dunum*s (4 dunums to 1 acre), that is, 33 percent of the total land area. By the beginning of the twentieth century, only 20 percent of the land of Galilee and 50 percent of Jabal al-Quds were in peasant hands.[41] "According to official data for 1909, 16,910 families worked 785,000 dunums in the sanjaks of Jerusalem, Nablus and Acre, or an average of 46 dunums each. A register from the second decade of this century listed 144 large landed proprietors in Palestine owning 3,130,000 dunums, or an average of 22,000 dunums each."[42] This, according to Abraham Granott, represented one-third of all cultivable land. Naji 'Allush notes that 250 large landlords owned 4.143 million dunums, representing nearly half of the agricultural land of Palestine.[43] Table 2.1 provides a breakdown of such large landholding.

Schölch identifies three principal groups who acquired the land: the urban a'yan, members of the coastal commercial and financial bourgeoisie (most of them Europeans and European protégés, including those of Beirut), and European colonists (German Christian Templars and Jews). For example, in the Jabal Nablus area, the 'Abdul-Hadis acquired 60,000 dunums of land and seventeen villages in the Jenin and 'Arraba areas, the Jayyusis of Tulkarem twenty-four villages and their lands, the Husseinis of Jerusalem 50,000 dunums, the Bargouthis thirty-nine villages and their lands, the Abu-Khadras 30,000 dunums, and the al-Taji al-Farouqis 50,000 dunums. These notable Palestinian hamulas still play pivotal economic and political roles in the West Bank today. Perhaps more dramatic because of its future impact was the case of the Sursoqs, a rich Beirut merchant family. In 1869 the Sursoq brothers bought the lands of seventeen villages in the central Marj Ibn 'Amer valley; their total holdings there and near Nazareth came to 230,000 dunums. Other merchant families from Lebanon included Bustrus, Tuwayni, Farah, and Salaam.[44] *Awqaf* lands (untaxable religious

TABLE 2.1 Large Landholdings in Palestine by District, Early Twentieth Century

	Number of Landlords	Area[a] (in thousands of dunums)
Jerusalem and Hebron	26	240
Jaffa	45	162
Nablus and Tulkaren	5	121
Jenin	6	114
Haifa	15	141
Nazareth	8	123
'Akka	5	157
Tabariyya	6	73

[a]1 dunum = 919 square meters, or roughly 0.25 acre.
SOURCE: N. 'Allush, *Arab Resistance in Palestine (1917–1948)* (in Arabic) (Beirut: Dar al-Tali'a, 1975), 15.

properties) were also extensive, estimated at 100,000 dunums. Of the European Jews, the most notable was Melville Bergheim, a German merchant, banker, industrialist, and landowner who acquired 20,000 dunums near the village of Abu-Sush.[45] The German Pietistic Protestant colonists, the Templars, started somewhat ahead of the European Jews; however, Jewish colonization, which began after 1882, surpassed the Templars quickly as Jews acquired large land areas by World War I.

Trade and Agriculture

From midcentury until World War I, Palestine tremendously increased agricultural production and exports. The growing trade volume also reflected the extension of cultivation to nearly all land previously used for pasturage. James Reilly quotes two European observers who described these regions: The Jordan valley had "inexhaustible granaries. . . . Year after year, without artificial manuring, crops are raised," and in 1859 the southern coastal plain was planted with "wheat, wheat, a very ocean of wheat."[46] Schölch provides similar figures for land used for grain production in northern Palestine; his data show that 49 percent of the land was devoted to wheat and barley, 13 percent to sesame, and the rest to other grains and olives.[47]

During this same period, agricultural production and export shifted. Starting in the early 1850s, demand for sesame (from France, which used the oil in the manufacture of soap and perfume) increased production sharply. While sesame replaced cotton and grains in the more hilly regions of Palestine, the production of oranges in western coastal areas leapt significantly, especially around Jaffa. Orange production was capital intensive, and much of the profit was reinvested in expanding the area of the groves. By 1873 there were 420 orange groves on the coastal plain around Jaffa

TABLE 2.2 Average Yearly Exports of the Main Goods from Jaffa, Haifa, and 'Akka, 1872–1882 (in millions of kiles, oqqas, and units)

Export Goods	Jaffa (1873–1877 and 1879–1882)	Haifa (1872–1880)	'Akka
Wheat (kiles)[a]	0.279	0.429	1.2911
Barley (kiles)	0.102	0.111	0.203
Durra (kiles)	0.062	0.233	0.625
Sesame (oqqas)[b]	2.059	0.800	1.000
Olive oil (oqqas)	1.027	0.053	0.260
Soap (oqqas)	0.904	–	–
Wool (oqqas)	0.115	–	–
Oranges units)	19.650	–	–

[a] 1 kiles = 36 liters.
[b] 1 oqqa = 1.28 kilograms.
SOURCE: A. Schölch, *Palestine in Transformation, 1856–1882: Studies in Social, Economic and Political Development,* translated by W. C. Young and M. C. Gerrity (Washington, DC: Institute for Palestine Studies, 1993), 82.

and in the 1880s about 500 (each between 2 and 6 acres), for a total of around 800,000 trees.[48] Between 1850 and 1880 alone, the orange grove areas of Jaffa quadrupled in size,[49] and the orange harvest increased from 20 million units in the mid-1850s to 36 million in 1880. Orange groves were the most profitable form of capital investment of the period.

Beside grains, sesame, and oranges, Palestine exported olive oil and *durra* (maize) as well as soap and other minor products. Table 2.2 provides data on average yearly export values between 1872 and 1882. The table shows that oranges and sesame, and secondarily wheat, became the principal exports of Palestine. Seaborne trade from Jaffa increased from £156,000 in 1857 to £336,000 in 1881 and £1,361,000 in 1908. Cereal export climbed from £84,000 in 1873 to £156,000 in 1881; orange export rose from 6 million oranges in 1857 to 26.25 million in 1879. Sesame production and export also increased: from 503,000 *oqqas* (or okes, an oke equaling 1.28 kilograms) to 4 million between 1857 and 1880. Olive oil exports also rose from 20,500 oqqas in 1857 to 3.85 million in 1876 and 5.30 million by 1880.

The prosperity of Palestine continued to grow in the first decade of the twentieth century. The value of production and export fluctuated throughout the nineteenth century, however, as a result of weather, market demands, and the political and security conditions in Palestine, the region, Europe, and the United States. As examples, a boom in cotton prices occurred during the first half of the 1860s as a result of the American Civil War, and grain prices surged in the mid-1850s as a result of the Crimean

War. In contrast, in 1877–1879 Palestine was hit by drought and locusts in addition to heavy Ottoman conscription, factors that led to depressed levels of production and the importation of grain and flour.[50] Table 2.3 gives the total values of exports from Jaffa for the period of 1885 up to the early twentieth century.

In Jaffa there was a consistent rise in orange and soap exports as well as exports of wines and spirits.[51] Initially exported to Egypt and Asia Minor, oranges were exported in large quantities to Europe and Russia after 1875. Jaffa oranges became famous because their thick skins kept the fruit unbruised, sweet, and juicy even after the long journey to Europe. Between 1880 and 1910, the land area planted with orange orchards around Jaffa alone increased from 4,000 dunums to 30,000.[52] Orange exports rose from 290,000 cases in 1897 to 1.6 million in 1913.[53] The French demand for sesame continued relatively strong. In its best years (1889–1897), the value of sesame exports was nearly equivalent to orange exports. While most agricultural products were exported to Europe, soap was exported to Egypt, Yemen, and the Hijaz.[54] This indicates the involvement of Palestine in regional Arab and Middle Eastern (including Turkish and Greek) markets. Yet figures on the scope, structure, and direction of that trade are unavailable because the Ottomans kept few if any relevant records.[55]

Owen provides data on the value of imports through Jaffa, Gaza, and Haifa/'Akka: Annual averages for imports into Jaffa were only £264,000 in 1883–1887 and rose to £1.37 million for 1908–1912. M. Y. al-Husseini reports similar data: Imports to Jaffa, Haifa, and Gaza rose from £1.13 million in 1908 to £1.95 million in 1913. He contrasts them with the decline in exports from £1.13 million to £906,520 for the same years.[56] Except for soap, Palestine exported cash crops and imported manufactured goods, including some luxury items. Both the increase and content of imports into Palestine reflected the demand of the growing number of European residents and settlers and probably the changing tastes of the new Palestinian middle and bourgeois classes.[57]

During most of the second half of the nineteenth century, Palestine showed an export surplus that helped offset the larger Syrian/Ottoman balance-of-trade deficits.[58] This pattern reversed in the early years of the twentieth century, during which the value of imports exceeded that of exports. Still, Palestine did not develop a deficit because of the flow of capital into the country from varied sources: immigrant Palestinians in the Americas who sent remittances; European interests that sought to build up and support the increasing number of Christian settlers and institutions in the country; Jewish settlers and institutions; and European companies and entrepreneurs who invested especially in infrastructure and railways. This "invisible" capital inflow helped to redress the early-twentieth-century balance-of-trade deficit and stimulated steady economic growth, uneven prosperity, and expansion of the market economy.

TABLE 2.3 Total Value of Exports from Jaffa, 1885–1905 (in thousands of pounds sterling)

	Wheat	Maize	Olive Oil	Sesame	Soap	Wool	Oranges	Colocynth	Hides	Wines and Spirits	Water-melon	Handi-crafts	Other Articles
1885	3.60	7.87	5.26	32.00	13.72	2.40	26.50	0.80	0.64	–	–	–	19.77
1886	3.32	9.00	–	45.53	8.96	3.70	22.40	2.15	0.54	–	–	–	18.93
1887	15.00	21.00	7.55	42.50	38.40	3.60	36.00	1.60	1.00	–	–	–	19.72
1888	7.80	16.96	20.62	28.12	45.00	2.00	55.00	2.00	0.75	–	–	–	26.06
1889	16.95	18.20	26.43	62.66	33.60	2.30	51.20	1.80	–	–	–	–	30.40
1890	19.92	111.24	75.08	109.32	44.70	4.56	83.12	2.20	7.62	–	–	–	89.62
1891	3.30	17.30	20.70	30.80	124.00	4.30	108.40	3.80	8.60	–	–	–	79.33
1892	–	0.42	1.35	69.35	46.80	5.55	62.00	2.58	7.10	–	–	–	63.30
1893	–	2.58	13.84	54.94	112.00	2.40	69.50	0.95	4.07	–	–	–	73.34
1894	–	2.00	9.05	42.15	114.00	0.40	51.00	0.8	1.20	–	–	–	65.00
1895	3.56	3.20	2.60	42.75	93.24	2.70	65.00	1.40	3.80	–	–	–	65.37
1896	1.92	14.17	6.05	59.80	113.11	5.32	72.60	2.50	14.27	–	–	–	83.69
1897	–	8.45	3.50	40.00	81.90	4.00	75.80	1.00	9.80	–	26.00	–	58.93
1898	14.00	3.00	4.50	28.00	62.00	3.36	82.50	1.40	8.10	–	24.85	–	75.07
1899	–	1.22	11.35	21.00	125.75	1.75	77.00	1.30	10.25	2.90	26.10	–	47.52
1900	–	2.95	9.11	30.56	44.55	1.36	74.21	1.88	1.16	21.84	24.50	–	52.37
1901	–	0.12	11.50	25.20	57.00	2.15	86.52	2.19	3.45	35.35	21.75	–	42.40
1902	–	1.45	–	29.26	18.76	1.32	86.50	1.45	2.98	18.40	17.65	4.85	20.77
1903	–	–	5.33	30.04	77.56	4.50	93.43	3.70	4.00	30.35	19.00	7.10	47.23
1904	–	–	0.95	23.35	62.00	7.93	103.95	3.65	6.00	37.86	11.00	9.00	29.61
1905	11.0	–	–	13.82	56.91	4.54	114.65	3.37	8.11	47.02	18.80	12.58	77.01
Total	100.37	141.13	234.77	861.15	1374.05	70.51	1504.28	42.52	102.81	193.72	189.65	33.53	1085.44

SOURCE: M. Buheiry, "The Agricultural Exports of Southern Palestine, 1885–1914," *Journal of Palestine Studies* 10, 4 (Summer 1981): 70.

Jerusalem and Coastal Urban Development

Beginning with the end of the Crimean War, commercial activity in Jerusalem and the coastal urban centers of Jaffa and Haifa rose rapidly. This in turn triggered growth in the size of the urban population, the spatial areas of the cities, productivity, monetization and capitalization of the economy, and social differentiation. In general, the development of commercial exchange and growth in the market were greater in the coastal area than in the hinterland. There were, however, two exceptions: Jerusalem, an interior city, was much more integrated into the European economy, while Nablus, also a city in the interior, was more integrated into the local and regional markets. Jerusalem became an important center of religious activity for European Christians and Jews. Europeans built and maintained Christian schools, hospitals, convents, monasteries, churches, and charitable institutions, which may have stimulated local Arab Christians to do the same. Similarly, Jewish immigration and charitable activity grew, although settler colonies were not established until 1882. In 1845 about 5,000 European pilgrims visited the Holy Land; in the month of February 1858 the number reached 9,854 and in March of the same year there had been 13,475 pilgrims. Between 1850 and 1859, the Franciscans registered 55,763 pilgrims and 229,346 overnight travelers in their Palestinian hostels. During the 1870s Jerusalem supported an average of 10,000 to 20,000 pilgrims a year during the pilgrimage seasons.[59] Jerusalem's growth,[60] as that of Jaffa and Haifa, triggered a construction boom that both signified and furthered the general economic expansion. The resurgence of European Christian religious interest in Jerusalem and Bethlehem also led to a sharp rise in the production of devotional artifacts sold to pilgrims and exported to Europe.

Nablus, in contrast, grew as a regional manufacture and trade center unconnected to European pilgrimage. Its main industries, as we noted earlier in the chapter, were the manufacture of soap, olive oil, and cotton textiles. Between 1860 and 1882, the number of soap factories increased from fifteen to thirty.[61] Nablus textiles supplied the local and regional markets, and its trade was connected to the hajj caravans to Mecca. Although not directly linked to European trade and pilgrimage, Nablus shared in the general market expansion and economic growth of the period.

Of the coastal cities, 'Akka declined as the nearby port of Haifa naturally acquired a favored position for European steamship trade.[62] Haifa and Jaffa grew in economic activity, population, and social heterogeneity. Between 1841 and 1917, the built-up areas of Haifa and Jaffa expanded dramatically—from 123 dunums to 1,201 and from 98 to 1,280, respectively, although population densities actually declined.[63] Haifa and Jaffa also benefited from the construction of roads and a railway connecting them to the interior in the late Ottoman era.

The most important port city during the last days of Ottoman control of Palestine was Jaffa. It was the principal port for the export of agricultural products and the nearest seaport to Jerusalem.[64] Although Jaffa had no harbor for large seagoing vessels, it processed 80,000 passengers annually during the 1890s.[65] A road connecting Jaffa and Jerusalem opened in 1868, a railway in 1892; both furthered commercial activity along the coast. Jaffa was also a center of manufacture (soap, olive oil, and sesame oil), although orange production was the most important source of seasonal wage labor. Already in 1879, 5,000 persons were daily employed in picking and packing oranges in the Jaffa area. In short, Jaffa, like all Palestinian towns, grew rapidly, engaging in economic exchange with the surrounding areas, relying less on subsistence farming and production for use, and creating more wage labor.

Handicrafts and Industry.   Urban centers were the loci of relatively vigorous industrial and handicraft production. According to Schölch, except for soap, Palestinian industry was not threatened by European mass production between 1856 and 1882.[66] Overall figures for soap production in Palestine are unavailable. However, one index of its significance are the figures for export from the seaport of Jaffa. Jaffa alone exported 43,000 tons (at £1.4 million) in 1885, which rose to 525,000 tons (at £12.6 million) in 1899 and then declined to 227,500 tons (at £5.7 million) in 1905.[67] Of course these figures exclude the amount of olive oil consumed locally and transported overland or exported from other coastal towns for the soap industry and food consumption. In the period just before World War I, there were over 300 olive oil presses in Palestine. Of these, thirty were hydraulic presses in the Jaffa-'Akka coastal area.[68] In 1901 a French firm established a huge factory in Jaffa equipped with six hydraulic presses and a refinery for extracting first-grade oils.

Similar to olive oil, sesame oil extraction was vital to trade and local consumption. It is estimated that toward the end of the nineteenth century between thirty and forty presses existed in the Ramleh, Jaffa, and Jerusalem triangle. Moreover, spinning and weaving were important to cities such as Safad, Nazareth, Nablus, Beit Jala, Al-Khalil, and Gaza and continued to expand despite the increase in imported manufactured cotton goods throughout most of the nineteenth century.[69] Reports from around the turn of the twentieth century, however, indicate a decline in those activities. Nevertheless, Christian devotional artifacts and souvenirs produced in Bethlehem, Jerusalem, and Nazareth destined for the pilgrims and export rose sharply. Except for soap and souvenirs, the major share of manufactured products were destined for the local and regional markets, another index of the expanding integrative capitalist market of Palestine. Regular weekly market (*souq*) days—Fridays in Al-Quds, Jaffa, Al-Khalil, Majdal, Gaza, and elsewhere—were important in furthering rural-urban exchange.

In general, industrial and craft production in Palestine during this period was labor intensive and technologically primitive. For example, soap making remained almost unchanged throughout the period. Soap was produced in huge brass cooking vats surrounded by containers for storing oil and trays for pouring out, leveling, and cutting the soap into cakes. Skilled soap workers were organized into guilds, supervised by a shaykh who maintained standards, regulated trade, and appropriated the taxes due to the authorities.[70] The master and the workmen were paid in kind, but by the turn of the century some were paid a wage. Also by the turn of the century more modern industry began to appear. Data from the first industrial census of Palestine conducted by the British Mandate authorities indicate that there were 1,236 factories and workshops before World War I.[71] Of these, 925 were Palestinian owned and 300 were Jewish owned.[72] The latter figure reflects the emergent economic impact of Jewish immigrants two decades before the war.

Banking and Credit Systems. Perhaps one of the most important mechanisms of the penetration of European capital, the growth of a market economy, and the integration of Palestine into the world economy was banking and other systems of credit, necessitated by the rise of the export-import trade. The first bank, the Imperial Ottoman Bank, a joint British-French venture, opened in 1885 in Jerusalem and Jaffa. Other banks followed shortly thereafter: Crédit Lyonnais in Jaffa and Jerusalem; the Anglo-Palestine Company (a Jewish bank) and the Deutsche Palästina Bank in Haifa, Jaffa, and Jerusalem; and the Palestinian Commercial Bank.[73] These banks were pivotal in the financing of infrastructure late in the Ottoman era; projects included the port facilities in Jaffa and Haifa, highways and railways, as well as telegraph and other facilities. They were also crucial in processing the capital flows from Europe and the Americas and in the building of factories just prior to World War I.

Communication and Transportation. Besides banking and credit systems, another factor in facilitating the development of an internal market in Palestine and of integration of the country into European markets was the newly developed communications and transport network. Prior to the building of the Jaffa-Jerusalem carriageway in 1868, all transport depended on animal power: horses, mules, donkeys, and camels. With the paving of roads, the volume of traffic in goods and people rose considerably. By 1913 Palestine had the highest ratio of length of railways to population in the region: more than 600 kilometers per million people.[74] The material, fuel, and skills necessary for railway construction and maintenance came from outside Palestine and thus did not have a strong multiplier effect on the economy except to increase the export, import, and to some degree internal trade.[75]

The railroad and the paved highways between major cities contrasted dramatically with the transport system in the rest of Palestine. Nonetheless, the market expanded into nearly all parts of the country. Besides paved roads and railways, the Ottomans established a postal service and allowed the foreign powers—Austria, Germany, France, and Russia—to do the same in Palestinian cities. In addition, a telegraph network, established in 1865, connected Palestinian towns with the region. Although humble, these facilities and services laid the foundations for the expansion of the market in Palestine and the country's greater integration into the European economies.

European Immigration and Colonial Settlement: The Beginnings

European colonists settled in Palestine, accelerating the integration of the country into Europe. Initially, however, immigrants in small numbers were Muslims from formerly held Ottoman territories: Maghrebis who were defeated by the French colonization of North Africa, Bosnians fleeing Austrian repression in Yugoslavia, and Circassian refugees from the Russian Caucasus.[76] They arrived in relatively small numbers and assimilated quickly into the culture and society of Arab Palestine.

Unlike the Muslim immigrants, who were refugees, the Christian and Jewish settlers were religiously and ideologically motivated. European Christian settlement began in 1868. The most successful were the Tempelgesellschaft (Association of Templars), an offshoot of a Protestant Pietistic religious movement in the German kingdom of Württemberg. Its leaders preached the creation of "the people of God" to rescue humankind from the anti-Christian spirit, to assemble in Jerusalem, and to regain control of Palestine as heirs to the Promised Land.[77] After their arrival in Palestine, the Templars' ideology shifted to improving the Holy Land and setting a good example for the Arab natives. By World War I, the German Templars established seven urban and agricultural settlements in Haifa, Jaffa, Sarouna, Jerusalem, Wilhelma, Galilean Bethlehem, and Waldheim. In addition to their agricultural, trade, and tourist activities, the German colonists organized a carriage service between Jaffa and Jerusalem and Haifa and Nazareth.

Templar numbers and impact on Palestine remained minimal compared to that of the Jewish immigrants. Small numbers of Jews lived in Palestine prior to 1882. They were Sephardic, originating from Spain, North Africa, and other parts of the Ottoman domains, and spoke Turkish or Arabic and often Ladino (a mixture of Spanish and Hebrew). Over the years they became acculturated and similar to the local Palestinian Arabs in most aspects of their life except religion. Following the pogroms in eastern Europe and Russia, however, Jewish immigration gained momentum: Approximately 50,000 European Jews migrated to Palestine between 1882 and the beginning of World War I. While the majority of Jewish migrants clustered in Palestinian cities, some attempted to establish themselves in agricultural settlements. "By 1908 there were twenty-six such colonies with 10,000 members and 400,000 dunums (100,000 acres) of land."[78] Most of this land was purchased from two sources: the Ottoman government or large estate owners. Few Palestinian peasants sold their land, which they had long cultivated under the traditional land tenure system. Instead, they found themselves either evicted or employed as laborers. So began a process of dispossession and peasant disaffection that would culminate in violent conflicts late in the nineteenth and early twentieth centuries.[79]

European Jewish agricultural settlements at first produced specialized cash crops, such as grapes for wine and spirits. Later, using poorly paid Palestinian labor, the settlements entered into citrus fruit and grape production and established marketing cooperatives. By 1913, Jewish orange production was 15 percent of total Palestinian export for that year.[80] Shortly after the new century began, Jewish settlements stopped employing Palestinian Arab workers, instead relying exclusively on Jewish labor. In 1909, at Degania, the first kibbutz, an agricultural cooperative based on mixed farming with limited or no use of Arab labor, became an effective instrument for Jewish colonization of Palestine.[81]

Transformation of the Social Structure

Western intervention, the development of the market, and the initiation of European settlement in Palestine triggered profound social structural transformations during the last years of Ottoman rule. We analyze these social changes in terms of three broad areas: (1) population structure, distribution, and change; (2) reorganization in rural and urban class structure and commensurate changes in ethnic ties, religion, values, and social consciousness; and (3) the development of political consciousness and movements. The capitulation agreements (accords that privileged the European merchants), the Tanzimat reforms, and the intrusive European presence combined to wrest Palestine from Ottoman authority in all but a nominal sense. Thus the economic and commensurate demographic, social, and political transformation occurred spontaneously, without authoritative or central control, planning, or direction.

Population Change: Size and Distribution

Throughout the nineteenth century until roughly 1875, the population of Palestine steadily increased as epidemics subsided with advances in nutrition, hygiene, and public health. Using the Ottoman census of 1849, Schölch gives an estimate of 365,224 people in the Jerusalem province that included the central and southern districts of Palestine.[82] Two-thirds of the population lived in 657 villages and one-third in thirteen major cities and towns.[83] Roughly 85 percent of the population was Muslim, 11 percent Christian (who lived principally in the major cities and villages around Jerusalem), and less than 4 percent Jewish (who lived primarily in the cities of Jerusalem, Hebron, Safad, and Tabariyya). From 1865 to 1866, a cholera epidemic struck the population, and the massive Ottoman conscription levies of Palestinian men for the Ottoman wars of 1876–1878 in the Balkans further depopulated the country. It was reported that 10,000 Palestinians were killed in those wars. During the campaigns of conscription, many Palestinians fled east, taking refuge among the bedouins of the desert in order to avoid the Ottomans. After the epidemics, the country grew rapidly: from roughly half a million to over 700,000 between 1880 and 1913.[84]

This high rate of natural increase was accompanied by two other demographic processes. The first was the immigration of European Jews and Christians. As noted in the previous section, 50,000 Jews immigrated to Palestine during this period. On the eve of World War I, the ratio of Jews in the total population had risen to nearly 10 percent, the majority of them European (Ashkenazi) rather than Sephardic Jews. The influx of European Christians raised the total Christian population from 11 to 16 percent by 1914.[85] Most European immigrants settled in the cities, especially Haifa, Jaffa, and Jerusalem.

The process of Palestinian urbanization, the second demographic process, escalated throughout the century but received a significant push three decades before 1914. The settlement of European Jews and Christians in the coastal cities and Jerusalem coincided with the migration of Palestinians from the rural areas, from the smaller outlying villages to the economically vigorous urban centers, particularly those located along the principal arteries of transportation.

Recent investigations dispute the low population statistics previously accepted. For example, Ben-Arieh's estimate of 9,500 people for Nablus in 1860 has come under fire by Doumani, who believes the city's population in 1850 was closer to 20,000.[86] Contrary to the pattern of growth indicated by Ben-Arieh, Doumani holds that Nablus grew significantly during the eighteenth and first half of the nineteenth centuries but stagnated in the second half, during the period of Ottoman modernization.[87] This finding leads Doumani to have "serious doubt about the veracity of hitherto commonly accepted population figures, most of them based on contemporary estimates by Western observers, for the various regions of Palestine during the first three-quarters of the 19th century."[88] Palestinian population estimates for the whole era before the British Mandate are also likely to be undercounts.

The urbanization process, instead of integrating the rural migrants into the urban community, seemed to increase the cultural divide between the *madaniyyin* (urbanites) and *fallahin* (peasants). A polarization in terms of income, education, and Westernization (in dress, use of consumer goods, taste, and behavior patterns) was superimposed on an existent attitude of superiority on the part of the urban-based rulers, religious clerics, administrators, merchants, and landlords toward the peasant producers and taxpayers. The Palestinian *madani-fallah* dichotomy at the end of the Ottoman era represented the opposing social processes of proletarianization and bourgeoisification. Besides indicating the emergent variations in Palestinian life-styles, this dichotomy had profound political implications during the period of conflict under the British Mandate.

Social Class Changes: The Rural Structure

Private property and capitalist relations of production in the context of an expanding market economy transformed class structure. In the rural areas, a complex process of social differentiation and stratification occurred, characterized by inequalities in landholding and new social relationships of production and distribution.[89] There were shifts in what was produced, how, by whom, and under what conditions. With regard to the three primary inputs of agrarian production—land, labor, and capital—the patterns varied. The landlord who resided in the village provided land, tools, seeds, and capital, and the tenant provided labor; the absentee landlord who resided in the city, in contrast, provided land and collected rent.[90]

Collective village work was progressively disappearing, a phenomenon that paralleled the erosion of communal rights and collective taxation. Toward the end of the Ottoman period, the greater mobility of peasants in search of jobs and the experience of wage labor for some displaced villagers created new sexual divisions of labor and began to generate conflicting cultural outlooks in the village.[91] Traditional rural institutions also underwent important change as the autonomous hamula elders and shaykhs gave way to officially appointed village selectmen, *mukhtars*, the Ottoman state's representatives in the villages. All matters of personal and economic affairs came to require the written confirmation of the mukhtar, at first paid in kind and later salaried. With the decline of the corporate village socioeconomic institutions, social relations became increasingly individualized and village solidarity began to disintegrate.

Earlier in the chapter, we discussed the rise of huge private estates owned by rural notables and (even more likely) by absentee urban landlords. This process of large- and medium-scale privatization of agricultural land inevitably led to the eviction of some peasants, who composed a stratum of landless peasants or "free" laborers. They, along with the hired plowmen, formed the bottom rural social class. Often seasonal workers, they sought wage employment in the unskilled construction jobs in neighboring towns and cities. Their numbers and distribution are difficult to estimate, but initially they must have been a small group, their numbers increasing as the orange and other such plantations expanded. By 1914 the class of unskilled workers had expanded considerably. Pamela Smith cites the diary of a Jewish Zionist immigrant-settler: "Hundreds of Arabs are gathering in the wide market square. . . . They are seasonal workers. Among them are a number of full time Arab workers, who live on the settler's farm and go straight to the orange grove. There are about 1,500 of them altogether, everyday."[92] Other peasants became sharecroppers, especially on the estates of absentee landlords. Their material conditions were better than the wage laborers', as they combined sharecropping with rural wage labor.

Above the landless sharecroppers and wage laborers came the small landowners who also worked as sharecroppers. Often the land they owned, small gardens (*hawakir*), allowed them to live above the subsistence level. Between the stratified lower peasantry and the large landlords existed a middle class of peasants, especially in the highlands of Jabal al-Quds, Jabal Nablus, and the Galilee. Over the years these relatively independent farmers became differentiated into a new class of peasants and, by virtue of the fragmentation of their inherited landholdings, even landowners. But peasant indebtedness also led to evictions from the land, as reported by European travelers.[93] The loss of land or its fragmentation shunted many peasants into a variety of economic activities. The market or money economy in the countryside forced Palestinians to pursue *several* sources of income, a practice that blurred class lines, inhibited the consolidation of social class consciousness, and both constrained and encouraged the rupture of traditional social relations. The increasing disaggregation of the village structure paralleled the earlier disintegration of the Ottoman nahiyas and marked the demise of self-governing rural society.

The Urban Class Structure

By the start of the twentieth century, as we have seen, Palestinian cities underwent some industrialization, escalating the expansion of commerce and tourist services. Beginning with the enlargement of the export and import trade, economic activities had a multiplier effect on urban economic life that transformed the urban and ethnic social class structure. Five broad classes emerged: the *ashraf* (nobility), the merchants, retail traders, artisans, and the nucleus of an urban proletariat.[94] The ashraf were descendants of Hijazi families, either from the prophet or Muhammad's companions and the Arab Islamic military commanders who conquered Palestine in the seventh century. Among these families (who continue to play an important role in contemporary Palestinian affairs) were the Tamimis, who, like the Dajanis (Daoudis), were entrusted with awqaf, and the Nusseibahs, whom the second Caliph 'Umar gave the keys to the city of Al-Quds. Other families such as the Husseinis, Khalidis, Alamis, and Nashashibis were bestowed with similar trusts. Waqf trustees kept a share of the waqf revenue for their own use. The ashraf were recognized as a corporate body with their own elected leader (the *naqib*), were exempted from paying taxes, and could be prosecuted only by their own council, not Ottoman authorities. Because they were literate, they often occupied Ottoman governmental posts and so were in an excellent position to take advantage of the changes brought forth by the Ottoman administrative and economic reforms. Much peasant land was registered in their names, and they eventually converted it into private property. This, in addition to the increase in their revenues, especially from management and control of religious waqfs, allowed them to accumulate capital rapidly and engage in other economic activities, sometimes competing with the non-ashraf urban merchants.

The emergent commercial bourgeoisie, especially the import-export merchants, tended to be Christian minorities rather than the ashraf, a result of the capitulations system that began centuries earlier. Favored by the European powers, the Palestinian and Lebanese Christian Arabs, and to a much lesser extent the Jewish minority, were able to take advantage of the expansion of the import-export trade. With the rapid increase in urban population and demand, these merchants accumulated vast wealth and diversified their economic activity into banking, credit services, real estate, some industry, and agricultural estates. While the Christian Palestinian urban merchants became important economic movers in the country, the Muslim notables were politically more powerful in late Ottoman times. As educated Muslims, they were considered natural leaders of the Palestinian people, who were expressing a nascent patriotism. They came to dominate the political life of Palestine.

Palestine's rapid and differentiated urbanization also brought forth a petite bourgeoisie of small (retail) merchants and shopkeepers and the beginnings of a new "middle class" of white-collar functionaries: civil servants, police, teachers, and clerks. Modern professionals such as journalists, lawyers, medical doctors, and engineers also began to appear in small numbers. Relative to their overall proportion in the population, Christians were overrepresented in the emerging intelligentsia and professional classes largely because of the education they received from European missionaries. This overrepresentation of certain religious groups in different occupations gave Western observers the impression of ethnic specialization in economic activity. Although we believe that the thesis of ethnic division of labor in late Ottoman Palestine is overstated, Western sources note that Muslims dominated in the milling of wheat and other grains and the production of meat, sweets, glass, and wool; Orthodox Christians tended to be gold jewelers, makers of brass and copper utensils, and sellers of wines and spirits;

TABLE 2.4 Workers in Major Industries, Palestine, Circa 1912

Industry	Location	Number
Devotion articles (mother-of-pearl)	Jerusalem	259
Textiles	Gaza, Majdal, Jerusalem	467
Tanning	Al-Khalil, Jaffa, Jerusalem	82
Mats and carpets	Jaffa, Jerusalem	156
Glass	Al-Khalil	39
Soap	Nablus	600
Total		1,603

SOURCE: M. al-Sharif and N. Badran, "Emergence and Evolution of the Palestinian Working Class" (in Arabic), *Samed al-Iqtisadi* 27 (April 1981): 45.

Latins (local Roman Catholics) specialized in carpentry, blacksmithing, and barbering and Jews in the production of wines and spirits, repair of clocks and watches, the sale of perfumes, and banking and money changing. Other crafts and economic activity were common to all.[95]

Artisans were variously affected by the market development in the cities. Many of the goods imported did not directly compete with locally produced crafts or products. They reflected the needs of the European settlers and the acquired tastes of the new Westernized, bourgeoisified Palestinians. Those artisans who produced for the bulk of the unmodernized population were not initially affected adversely. By World War I the demand structure for artisan goods changed as changing tastes, impoverishment of the peasantry, and price inflation decreased in some established crafts such as textiles but increased in new ones such as roof tiles and metal and wood frames for construction purposes. Studies suggest that 10–15 percent of the labor force was involved in artisan production. Tables 2.4 and 2.5 show the number of workers in major Palestinian industries and the numbers of types of industries. The low numbers in Table 2.4 indicate that most artisans were in workshops usually not exceeding five workers or at home in cottage industries. Some worked as wage laborers for small merchants who supplied them with the raw materials and working capital; others worked for payment in kind.

Finally, although increasing numbers of people found themselves earning wages for their labor, a genuine, industrial proletariat had not yet appeared. The traditional clientelist, patriarchal values and norms governing the social relations of production, including the urban guilds, were indeed decaying, but an absolute rupture with the past culture had not yet occurred. In an effort to further liberalize the economy, guilds were abolished outright by the Young Turks in control of the Ottoman Empire in 1912. More people were cast out of the corporate fold before new, more modern collective structures could smooth the transition. However, the restructur-

TABLE 2.5 Major Industries in Palestine, Circa 1918

Industry	Number
Metalwork	101
Jewelry	20
Weaving	168
Garments	166
Food processing	178
Chemical	390
Paper and printing	27
Leather	29
Wood	90
Mother-of-pearl	52
Other	10
Total	1,236

SOURCE: N. 'Allush, *Arab Resistance in Palestine (1917–1948)* (in Arabic) (Beirut: Dar al-Tali'a, 1975), 9–10.

ing of the modes of production and of sociopolitical relations, especially vis-à-vis the newly arriving foreign settlers and residents, triggered a process of indigenous political mobilization.

Political and Cultural Reactions

The structural transformations of Palestinian (as well as Syrian, Egyptian, and Iraqi) society during the nineteenth century encouraged the reemergence of an Arab rather than simply Islamic consciousness and set the population on a collision course with the Turkish Ottoman overlords. For example, in the 1840s and 1850s, Western consuls reported that large segments of the Palestinian Arab population disliked or hated the Ottoman Turkish authorities. They "regarded the Turkish Caliphate as a fraud and distorted (as a political pun) the (honorific Turkish) title of *khan* into *kha'in* (traitor, in Arabic)."[96] The Ottoman Turks were also seen as responsible for the European economic and cultural assault on Palestine, especially during and after the Crimean War. A general social crisis erupted in the 1860s; in Lebanon it turned into a civil war between Christians and Druze. Although minor Muslim-Christian tension developed in Palestine, the spontaneous expression of "popular rage" targeted the consular and missionary buildings.[97] Schölch cites the British consul, who in 1858 reported much Palestinian talk of independence, "not the independent action of central Ottoman dominion in reference to European and other Powers, but independence from Turkish control over them."[98] In Palestine the reemergence and consolidation of Arab consciousness were accompanied by the emergence of Palestinian consciousness—the ideological side of the structural transformation of Palestinian society. These two identities, Arab and Palestinian, were mutually reinforcing.

Reflecting the Ottoman administrative divisions of Palestine into subdistricts of larger units based in Damascus and Sidon (later Beirut), the political economy of the country was also segmented in the latter half of the nineteenth century. Both the economy of the hills (traditionally semifeudal, provincial, and subsistence based) and economy of the plains (tribal, pastoral, and semisettled) were, as we have seen above, being differentially and differently transformed by monetization and capitalization. And yet the countrywide "party" or factional alliances of Qays and Yaman[99] (ancient Arab names for a binary political division that existed as well in much of the rest of the Fertile Crescent) politically interlocked the Palestinians across religious, clan (hamula), and district divides. In short, although segments of Palestinian society were structurally (that is, physically and economically) isolated, they were nevertheless interconnected politically. The embryonic factors of capitalist development, such as the expansion of trade, the expansion and monetization of internal markets in both commodities and labor, and the extension of the communication infrastructure, overcame the structural isolation. Most visibly, subsistence farming and geographic isolation began to disappear as people increasingly came into contact with one another and with more intrusive governmental authorities. The administrative reorganization, which elevated the *mutasariffiyya* (subdistrict) of Jerusalem into an independent unit directly linked to Istanbul and referred to the historic territory (including the northern districts of Nablus, 'Akka, and Galilee) as Arz-i Filistin, reflected Palestine's emergence as a single entity.

Religious Institutional Foundations

Palestine's status as a Christian Holy Land was upheld in the administrative institutions of three principal Christian denominations. The jurisdiction of the Greek Orthodox patriarchate of Jerusalem extended over the three ancient Roman districts of Palestine. So did the Latin (Roman Catholic) patriarchate and Anglican (British Protestant) bishopric of Jerusalem. Each held authority throughout Palestine. It is therefore not surprising that Christians fostered the concept of Filastin as a country.[100] Greek Orthodox Palestinians in particular advanced Palestinian consciousness. For example, in the first decade of the twentieth century, two brothers who were leaders of *al-nahda al-orthodoksiyya* (the orthodox renaissance) published a newspaper in Jaffa called *Filastin*. In general, local Arab Christian activism, including the establishment of social service institutions (schools, hospitals, orphanages, etc.), became all the more assertive as European and American missionary groups targeted them for proselytization. The emergent Palestinian intelligentsia included a strong Christian component, evident through their newspapers (*Filastin and Al-Karmel* in Haifa), books and pamphlets, cultural clubs, and auxiliary church groups for both men and women. Rather than reinforcing their differences from their Muslim neighbors, then, Christians in Palestine tended to affirm their sense of belonging to a larger Arab and Palestinian community.

The informal or popular religion of the common and mostly illiterate people encouraged a "national" Palestinian consciousness. Almost every village had its tomb of a saint (*wali*) or sacred sanctuary (*maqam*).[101] These popular religious practices, often contrary to the teachings and principles of established religion, gave meaning, hope, and comfort to peasants whose existence depended on natural and political forces much beyond their control. Two of the most important expressions of folk religion, those most "national" in character, were the maqams and festivals of Nabi Saleh (the prophet Saleh) and Nabi Musa (the prophet Moses). Held after the spring harvests, these festivals drew thousands of people from villages all over Palestine not only to celebrate the holiday but also to exchange information, commercial products, and political news; resolve feuds; and arrange marriages. In short, these festivals, attended by native Christians and Muslims alike, reasserted shared values and norms and encouraged a common Palestinian identity.

The Role of Modern Education and Values

Arab consciousness in Palestine was strengthened with the spread of literacy and formal education. Ottoman reforms included the establishment of schools for training modern cadres in administrative and military skills. The study of Arabic language and literature was secondary to the study of Turkish in these schools. The missionary and local private and religious schools, however, stressed Arabic, competing missionary educators thus distinguishing their missions from the Ottoman authorities in order to ingratiate themselves with the indigenous Palestinian people.[102] At the same time, a growing intelligentsia was introduced to modern secular and scientific thought, which, in the context of an expansive market economy, stimulated new sociopolitical values, spurred an Arabic literary and language renaissance, encouraged wider intellectual horizons, and furthered Arab (as distinct from Ottoman or Islamic) consciousness.

The traditional sources of values in Palestinian society stem from the ideologies of Islam and Christianity, the semifeudal system, and tribal social organization. In sum, these fostered a sense of fatalism, dependency on a superior power, and social corporateness allied with the insignificance of the individual. The semifeudal order emphasized absoluteness in rule, social ascription, and status distinction, whereas the tribal organization taught strong corporate loyalty, independence of action, and egalitarianism. Though in many ways contradictory systems, both highlighted a narrowness of identity, of loyalty, and of sociopolitical consciousness. In addition, they were patriarchal, relegating women to an inferior status and circumscribed conditions. This narrowness, ascription, and absolutism conflicted with values of secularism, liberalism, and new concepts regarding the value of the individual. The emergence of a modern, secular, and educated intelligentsia brought a new social division to the country (and the region): modernist versus traditionalist. The intelligentsia's debates inadvertently integrated the traditional tribal and semifeudal segments of society, as the elites from both competed for the leadership of "the people."

The new intelligentsia became agitators who articulated the fears and aspirations of the coalescing Palestinian people. We noted above the establishment of several newspapers; the intellectuals also published books such as Najib 'Azoury's *Awakening of the Arab Nation in Turkish Asia* (1905) and Najib Nassar's *Zionism: Its History, Object and Importance* (1911) and founded sociopolitical organizations (underground before 1908 and public thereafter), economic and business societies, and rhetoric clubs.

Palestinian Response to Pre-WWI Jewish Colonization

Unlike the Palestinian Jews (Sephardic and Oriental), who were culturally assimilated, the European Jews (Ashkenazim) tended to live in separate quarters in the cities of Jerusalem, Al-Khalil, Tabariyya, and Safad. The new immigrant Ashkenazim rapidly became the majority of Jewish residents of Palestine: In 1845 32 percent of Jews were Ashkenazim; by 1916 they made up 59 percent. Perhaps much more important for Palestine and the Palestinians is the rapid increase of the total Jewish population after 1882 and the establishment of agricultural colonies. Jewish population in agricultural colonies increased from 500 in 1882 to 11,990 in 1914, while in the urban areas it increased from 23,500 to 73,010 for the same period.[103]

Jewish agricultural land settlement in Ottoman Palestine went through two broad phases. The first (1870–1900) was unsystematic and dependent on the purchase of land and direct financial support of wealthy European Jews. Most notably, the French Jewish banker Baron Edmund de Rothschild purchased land for seven settlements, the earliest of which were Migve Yisra'el (1870) and Petah Tiqva (1878) south and east of Jaffa, respectively. Unorganized settlements between 1876 and 1900 numbered twenty-two, with a land area of 167,073 dunums. The second phase of organized settlements began when Rothschild turned over control and financing of the settlements to the Jewish Colonization Association (ICA). This came after the establishment of the World Zionist Organization (WZO) in Basel, Switzerland, in 1897. Between 1900 and 1914, twenty-five settlements were established with a land area of 163,984 dunums.[104]

Spontaneous and intermittent Jewish settlement activity became systematic and expansive with the formal launching of the Zionist movement. Although early Palestinian reaction to Jewish settlement and land purchases was localized and impulsive, it became more conscious, political, and sustained with the second and later phases. The early responses were attacks by peasants and bedouins who were shut off from their communal or grazing land by Jewish settler-colonists.[105] For example, at the end of the century the ICA, with the forceful intervention of the Ottoman troops, was able to expel the peasants from and take control of more than 60,000 dunums of land in the Tabariyya area. This and another case, in 'Afula, generated a great deal of newspaper coverage and agitation warning of the threat of dispossession by Zionism.

In general, urban Jewish immigration increased rapidly. Jerusalem's Jewish population nearly doubled between 1881 (13,920) and 1891 (25,322).[106] In Jaffa, Haifa, and other cities, it grew at an even faster pace, alarming urban Palestinians and creating some ill will among them, according to Jewish sources of the period. The first formally recorded act of Palestinian opposition and protest occurred in 1891. A telegram signed by a number of Palestinian notables, sent from Jerusalem to Istanbul, urged the Ottoman authorities to prohibit Russian Jews from entering Palestine and acquiring land.[107] Opposition by native Palestinian Arabs to foreign immigration thus preceded the foundation of the Zionist movement. Jewish sources of the time observed that the declared aim of the Zionist Congress to establish a home in Palestine quickly affected relations between Palestinian Arabs and the Jewish immigrants.[108]

Unofficial opposition to Zionism began to express itself more spontaneously, directly, and forcefully. In 1908 clashes between Palestinian Arabs and Zionist immigrant Jews occurred in Jaffa, and peasants attacked Zionist Jewish settlers in the district of Tabariyya. From every city, including Haifa, signed statements were sent to Ottoman authorities protesting the sale of land to Zionist settlers. Najib Nassar, the editor of Haifa's newspaper *Al-Karmel*, was tried for "disturbing the peace" as a result of articles he wrote opposing the sale of land to Zionist Jewish immigrant-settlers. He was found innocent, but his attitude reflected the growing Palestinian fear and discontent with Ottoman policies. By 1910, Palestinian newspapers and the public raised a clamor over the sale of land totaling 2,400 dunums between Nazareth and Jenin by the rich merchant Emile Sursoq of Beirut to the Zionist ICA. The governor of Nazareth district attempted to stop the sale but failed. In 1913 the Sursoqs sold another 22,000 dunums in Marj Ibn 'Amer to the ICA, which displaced hundreds if not thousands of peasant families.

One of the earliest written documents in opposition to Zionism was a booklet by Najib 'Azoury. 'Azoury wrote prophetically,

Two important phenomena, of identical character but nevertheless opposed, which till now have not attracted attention, are now making their appearance in Asian Turkey: these are the awakening of the Arab nation and the latent efforts of the Jews to re-establish, on an extremely large scale, the ancient kingdom of Israel. These two movements are destined to struggle continuously with one another, until one prevails over the other. The fate of the entire world depends on the result of this struggle between the two peoples, which represent two contradictory principles.[109]

With the appearance of Arabic newspapers, opposition to Zionism was articulated more frequently and popularly. Nassar's agitation, which included the convening in Nablus of an "anti-Zionist conference" against Jewish colonization, inspired other Arabic papers and editors even in cities outside Palestine: Beirut, Damascus, and Cairo. They all joined in protest of Zionist immigration and land acquisition and exposed the threat of Zionism to the Arabs.

With the introduction of parliamentary life in the Ottoman Empire (1908–1912), Istanbul became a platform for rhetoric against Zionism; leading the oratory were Palestinian representatives such as Rouhi al-Khalidi and Said al-Husseini, two Jerusalem notables. Another Jerusalem notable, Raghib al-Nashashibi, a candidate for the 1914 elections to the parliament, declared, "If I am elected as a representative I shall devote all my strength day and night to doing away with the damage and threat of the Zionists and Zionism."[110] He was elected by an overwhelming majority. In short, mainstream Palestinian public opinion sensed the threat of Zionism and coalesced against it.

Alarmed Palestinians joined political organizations aimed at stopping the implementation of the Zionist project in Palestine. Associations to end immigration and the sale of land to the Zionist immigrant-settler Jews emerged, especially in the cities of Haifa and Jaffa. The Patriotic Ottoman Party (Hizb al-Watan al-Uthmani) was formed by the southern notable and landlord Shaykh Suleiman al-Taji al-Farouqi. A party member wrote: "The country is in danger and . . . a flood threatens to engulf it and has almost put an end to its political and economic life, and that threat is the Zionist Organization."[111] Other nationalist and anti-Zionist groups included the Nablus Youth Society (Jam'iyyat al-Shabiba al-Nabulsiyya), established in 1914, as were the Jaffa Youth Society and many associations of expatriate Palestinians and Palestinian students in Beirut and Istanbul.

Political events during that period moved swiftly in the region. In 1908 the Young Turks' revolution inside the Ottoman Empire effectively removed the sultan from power. Their attempt to centralize control of the empire more firmly and to emphasize Turkification (and their ideology of pan-Turanism) reawakened Arab consciousness and rekindled open Arab opposition to Turkish rule. The nascent Arab consciousness and its politicization into pan-Arabism reinforced Palestinian identity. On the eve of World War I, the Palestinian Arabs were on the verge of coalescing as a nation. But Palestinian consciousness did not yet transform itself into an all-Palestinian, nationalist movement or develop an independent, centralized political organization. The Palestine Arabs were thus unable to act decisively on their own behalf either against the Ottoman Turks before WWI or, as we see in Chapter 3, against the British authorities during the mandate period between the two world wars.

Notes

1. R. Owen, *The Middle East in the World Economy: 1800–1914* (London: Methuen, 1981); see also B. B. Doumani, "Merchants, Socioeconomic Change and the State in Ottoman Palestine: The Nablus Region, 1800–1869," Ph.D. dissertation, Georgetown University, 1990, subsequently published as *Rediscovering Palestine: Merchants and Peasants in Jabal Nablus, 1700–1900* (Berkeley: University of California Press, 1995).

2. A. Schölch, "European Penetration and the Economic Development of Palestine, 1856–1882," in R. Owen, ed., *Studies in the Economic and Social History of Palestine in the Nineteenth and Twentieth Centuries* (Carbondale: Southern Illinois University Press, 1982), 11. See also A. Schölch, "Britain in Palestine, 1838–1882: The Roots of the Balfour Policy," *Journal of Palestine Studies* 22, 1 (Autumn 1992): 39–56; and A. Schölch, *Palestine in Transformation, 1856–1882: Studies in Social, Economic and Political Development,* translated by W. C. Young and M. C. Gerrity (Washington, DC: Institute for Palestine Studies, 1993), 48–75.

3. B. B. Doumani, "Rediscovering Ottoman Palestine: Writing Palestinians into History," *Journal of Palestine Studies* 21, 2 (Winter 1992): 20. See also M. Sharon, "The Political Role of the Bedouins in Palestine in the Sixteenth and Seventeenth Centuries," in M. Ma'oz, ed., *Studies on Palestine During the Ottoman Period* (Jerusalem: Magnes Press, 1975), 11–30.

4. Doumani, "Merchants, Socioeconomic Change and the State in Ottoman Palestine," 33.

5. Ibid., 36–37.

6. Y. Firestone, "The Land-equalizing *Musha'* Village: A Reassessment," in G. G. Gilbar, ed., *Ottoman Palestine, 1800–1914: Studies in Economic and Social History* (Leiden: E. J. Brill, 1990), 92.

7. Ibid., 96–101; see also Y. Firestone, "Production and Trade in an Islamic Context: Sharika Contracts in the Transitional Economy of Northern Samaria, 1853–1943," *International Journal of Middle East Studies* 4 (April 1975): 308–324.

8. B. B. Doumani, "The Political Economy of Population Counts in Ottoman Palestine: Nablus Circa 1850," *International Journal of Middle East Studies* 26, 1 (February 1994): 1–17.

9. Schölch, *Palestine in Transformation,* 181–190.

10. Owen, *The Middle East in the World Economy*; see also M. Ma'oz, *Ottoman Reform in Syria and Palestine, 1840–1861: The Impact of the Tanzimat on Politics and Society* (Oxford: Oxford University Press, 1968), 12–16; S. Shamir, "Egyptian

Rule (1832–1840) and the Beginning of the Modern Period in the History of Palestine," in A. Cohen and G. Baer, eds., *Egypt and Palestine—A Millennium of Association (868–1948)* (New York: St. Martin's Press, 1984), 214–231; A. Hourani, *A History of the Arab Peoples* (Cambridge: Harvard University Press, 1991), 265–278; and B. Kimmerling and J. Migdal, *Palestinians: The Making of a People* (New York: Free Press, 1993), 3–12.

11. A. J. Rustum, *The Royal Archives of Egypt and the Disturbances in Palestine, 1834* (Beirut: American University of Beirut, 1938); O. Barghouthi and K. Tawtah, *History of Palestine* (in Arabic) (Jerusalem, 1923); and Kimmerling and Migdal, *Palestinians*, 6–12.

12. Ma'oz, *Ottoman Reform*, 14–15; see also A. Hourani, "Ottoman Reform and the Politics of Notables," in A. Hourani, P. Khoury, and M. C. Wilson, eds., *The Modern Middle East: A Reader* (London: I. B. Tauris, 1993), 83–109.

13. Schölch, "Britain in Palestine," 39–56; and Schölch, *Palestine in Transformation*, 9–17.

14. "Anglo-Turkish Commercial Convention of 1838," in C. Issawi, ed., *The Economic History of the Middle East, 1800–1914* (Chicago: University of Chicago Press, 1966), 38–40.

15. Owen, *The Middle East in the World Economy*, 230.

16. Just as significant, rural security, especially in the plains, declined. N. Badran cites an English traveler, W. M. Thomson, on the condition of two villages, Al-'Afula and Fula, which were prosperous until 1859, then became ruins; see N. Badran, "The Palestinian Countryside Before World War I" (in Arabic), *Palestine Affairs* 7 (March 1972): 118.

17. Owen, *The Middle East in the World Economy*, 85. We give figures in either British pounds sterling (£) or Palestinian pounds (£P), depending both on our sources and on the period we are discussing. The Palestinian pound, in use during the mandate period, was tied to British currency; its value, of course, fluctuated.

18. I. M. Smilianskaya, "From Subsistence to Market Economy," in Issawi, *The Economic History of the Middle East*, 226–247; Owen, *Studies in the Economic and Social History of Palestine*; and Doumani, "Merchants, Socioeconomic Change and the State in Ottoman Palestine."

19. Smilianskaya, "From Subsistence to Market Economy," 230.

20. Ibid., 231.

21. See Doumani's critique of this thesis in "Merchants, Socioeconomic Change and the State in Ottoman Palestine."

22. Owen, *The Middle East in the World Economy*; H. Gerber, "Modernization in Nineteenth Century Palestine: The Role of Foreign Trade," *Middle East Studies* 18 (July 1982): 250–264.

23. Doumani details the structure, dynamics, mechanics, and consequences of the olive oil and soap industries as an example of the role of local mercantile and finance capital in commercializing and transforming the Palestinian countryside prior to the penetration of European capital. See Doumani, "Merchants, Socioeconomic Change and the State in Ottoman Palestine," 389–390.

24. This section is based on chapter 7, "The Political Economy of Olive Oil" and chapter 8, "Soap, Class and the State," in ibid., 252–382.

25. Ibid., 269; see also P. Sluglett and M. Farouk-Sluglett, "The Application of the 1858 Land Code in Greater Syria: Some Preliminary Observations," in T. Khalidi, ed., *Land Tenure and Social Transformation in the Middle East* (Beirut: American University of Beirut, 1984), 409–421.

26. Doumani provides evidence for the emergence of an alliance between the rural elite (including the newly rich peasants) and the urban elite against the peasantry. The peasantry, aware of the disadvantages in such an alliance, took a position against it. See Doumani, "Merchants, Socioeconomic Change and the State in Ottoman Palestine," 275–285.

27. Ibid., 381. The economic and legal mechanisms of capital accumulation and concentration, which involved the use of Islamic *waqf*s, need not be detailed here.

28. See the description of the economic bases and social trends in Palestinian cities from early in the nineteenth century until 1882 in Schölch, *Palestine in Transformation*, 110–117 and 118–168.

29. Ibid., 112.

30. Smilianskaya, "From Subsistence to Market Economy," 235, 238.

31. Ibid., 236.

32. Owen, *The Middle East in the World Economy*, 91–92.

33. M. A. Ubicini, "Decline of Ottoman Industry in the 1840's," in Issawi, *The Economic History of the Middle East*, 41–45.

34. Even European Jews and the organized Zionist movement referred to this land as Palestine. N. Mandel, *The Arabs and Zionism Before World War I* (Berkeley: University of California Press, 1976).

35. Ma'oz, *Ottoman Reform*, 21–29.

36. V. Lutsky, *Modern History of the Arab Countries* (Moscow: Progress House, 1971).

37. Owen, *The Middle East in the World Economy*, 153.

38. Ma'oz, *Ottoman Reform*, 27.

39. Schölch, "European Penetration and the Economic Development of Palestine," 22.

40. Schölch, *Palestine in Transformation*, 111.

41. Cited in ibid., 113.

42. Schölch, "European Penetration and the Economic Development of Palestine," 24. See also A. Granott, *The Land System in Palestine*, translated by M. Simion (London: Eyre and Spottiswoode, 1952), 38.

43. Granott, *The Land System in Palestine*, 38–39. N. 'Allush, *Arab Resistance in Palestine (1917–1948)* (in Arabic) (Beirut: Dar al-Tali'a, 1975), 15.

44. Badran, "The Palestinian Countryside Before World War I," 118; I. al-Jawahry, "Land Tenure in Palestine in the Nineteenth Century" (in Arabic), *Journal of the Center of Palestine Studies* 29 (July/August 1978): 5–24; Schölch, "European Penetration and the Economic Development of Palestine," 24; Granott, *The Land System in Palestine*, 81–82; and 'Allush, *Arab Resistance in Palestine*, 15.

45. P. A. Smith, *Palestine and the Palestinians, 1876–1983* (New York: St. Martin's Press, 1984), 13; and Schölch, "European Penetration and the Economic Development of Palestine," 25.

46. J. Reilly, "The Peasantry of Late Ottoman Palestine," *Journal of Palestine Studies* 10, 4 (Summer 1981): 84.

47. Schölch, "European Penetration and the Economic Development of Palestine," 61.

48. Owen, *The Middle East in the World Economy*, 178.

49. Schölch, *Palestine in Transformation*, 92.

50. Ibid., 90.

51. Soap was produced from olive oil. The use of local olive oil in soap production explains the decline in the value of export of raw olive oil.

52. Owen, *The Middle East in the World Economy*, 265.

53. M. Buheiry, "The Agricultural Exports of Southern Palestine, 1885–1914," *Journal of Palestine Studies* 10, 4 (Summer 1981): 79–80.

54. Ibid., 80.

55. The value of Palestine's exports to Europe via the seaports is available from many sources, especially European consular reports of the period. Although foreign trade was quite important in Palestine's economic growth, especially in certain commercial agriculture products, it may be overestimated because of the absence of data on local and regional trade.

56. M. Y. al-Husseini, *Socioeconomic Development in Arab Palestine* (in Arabic) (Jaffa: Al-Taher Bros., 1946), 146.

57. Schölch, "European Penetration and the Economic Development of Palestine," 19–20.

58. See the table in Schölch, *Palestine in Transformation*, 93 and 106–109.

59. Schölch, "European Penetration and the Economic Development of Palestine," 27.

60. Y. Ben-Arieh, "The Growth of Jerusalem in the Nineteenth Century," *Annals of the Association of American Geographers* 65 (1975); see also Y. Ben-Arieh, "The Population of the Large Towns in Palestine During the First Eighty Years of the Nineteenth Century, According to Western Sources," in Ma'oz, *Studies on Palestine*, 49–69. Additionally, see R. Kark, "The Contribution of the Ottoman Regime to the Development of Jerusalem and Jaffa, 1840–1917," in D. Kushner, ed., *Palestine in the Late Ottoman Period: Political, Social and Economic Transformation* (Jerusalem: Yad Izhak Ben Zvi, 1986), 30–45.

61. A. Rabay'ah, "Palestine Industry in Modern Times," paper presented at the third international conference on Levantine history, Amman, 1980.

62. R. Kark, "The Rise and Decline of Coastal Towns in Palestine," in Gilbar, *Ottoman Palestine*, 69–90.

63. Ibid., 84.

64. Schölch, "European Penetration and the Economic Development of Palestine," 34; see also Kark, "The Rise and Decline of Coastal Towns in Palestine."

65. Schölch, *Palestine in Transformation*, 38.

66. Ibid., 12.

67. Buheiry, "The Agricultural Exports of Southern Palestine," 69–70.

68. M. al-Sharif and N. Badran, "Emergence and Evolution of the Palestinian Working Class" (in Arabic), *Samed al-Iqtisadi* 27 (April 1981): 42.

69. Owen, *The Middle East in the World Economy*, 9, 93–94, 266.

70. A. al-Ramini, *Nablus in the Nineteenth Century* (in Arabic) (Amman: Dar al-Sha'ab, 1979), 110–114.

71. S. B. Himadeh, ed., *Economic Organization of Palestine* (Beirut: American University of Beirut, 1938), cited by Owen, *The Middle East in the World Economy*, 266.

72. Ibid..

73. E. Weakley, "Report on the Conditions and Prospects of British Trade in Syria," 279, and N. T. Gross, "The Anglo-Palestine Company: The Formative Years, 1903–1914," both in Gilbar, *Ottoman Palestine*, 219–253.

74. G. Baer, "The Impact of Economic Change on Traditional Society in Nineteenth Century Palestine," in Ma'oz, *Studies on Palestine*, 497.

75. Ibid.

76. Smith, *Palestine and the Palestinians*, 15.

77. A. Carmel, "The German Settlers in Palestine and Their Relations with the Local Arab Population and the Jewish Community, 1868–1918," in Ma'oz, *Studies on Palestine*, 442–444.

78. Owen, *The Middle East in the World Economy*, 446; Schölch, "European Penetration and the Economic Development of Palestine," 45.

79. R. Khalidi, "Palestinian Peasant Resistance to Zionism Before World War I," in E. W. Said and C. Hitchens, eds., *Blaming the Victims* (London: Verso, 1988), 207–233.

80. Owen, *The Middle East in the World Economy*, 271.

81. Ibid., 272.

82. Schölch, *Palestine in Transformation*, 29, 31, 42.

83. Ibid., 284.

84. J. B. Barron, *Palestine: Report and General Abstracts of the Census of 1922* (Jerusalem: Government of Palestine, 1923), 3.

85. Smith, *Palestine and the Palestinians*, 21, citing Mandel, *Arabs and Zionism Before World War I*, xxi.

86. Ben-Arieh, "The Population of the Large Towns in Palestine"; Doumani, "The Political Economy of Population Counts," 1–17.

87. Ibid., 1.

88. Ibid.

89. See Badran, "The Palestinian Countryside Before World War I," 118ff.

90. Owen, *The Middle East in the World Economy*, 268.

91. Badran, "The Palestinian Countryside Before World War I," 118ff.

92. Smith, *Palestine and the Palestinians*, 35.

93. Granott, *The Land System in Palestine*, 294.

94. The following is based on I. al-Nimr, *History of Jabal Nablus and al-Balqa*, vol. 1 (in Arabic) (Nablus: N.p., 1936); Barghouthi and Tawtah, *History of Palestine*; M. al-Sharif and N. Badran, "Emergence and Evolution of the Palestinian Working Class," 34–48; M. al-Sharif, "A Contribution to the Study of the Process of the Emergence of the Arab Labor Movement in Palestine" (in Arabic), *Samed al-Iqtisadi* 18 (July 1980): 50–77; N. Badran, *Education and Modernization in Palestinian Arab Society* (in Arabic) (Beirut: PLO Research Center, 1978), 18–58; Smith, *Palestine and the Palestinians*, 18–31.

95. A. Awad, *Introduction to the Modern History of Palestine, 1831–1914* (in Arabic) (Beirut: Arab Institution for Studies and Publishing, 1983), 104.

96. Y. Porath, "The Political Awakening of the Palestinian Arabs and Their Leadership Toward the End of the Ottoman Period," in Ma'oz, *Ottoman Reform in*

Syria and Palestine, 371, citing J. Finn, *Stirring Times*, 2 vols. (London: Kegan Paul, 1978).

97. Schölch, *Palestine in Transformation*, 270–272.

98. Ibid., 273.

99. Ibid., 191–196; see also M. Hoexter, "The Role of Qays and Yaman Factions in Local Political Divisions: Jabal Nablus Compared with the Judean Hills in the First Half of the Nineteenth Century," *Asian and African Studies* 9 (Fall 1973): 249–311.

100. Porath, "The Political Awakening," 359.

101. T. Canaan, *Mohammadan Saints and Sanctuaries in Palestine* (London: N.p., 1927); see also Reilly, "The Peasantry of Late Ottoman Palestine," 94–97.

102. G. Antonius, *The Arab Awakening: The Story of the Arab National Movement* (New York: Capricorn Books, 1965); A. Hourani, *Arabic Thought in the Liberal Age: 1798–1939* (Oxford: Oxford University Press, 1970).

103. Jewish Agency, *Statistical Abstract of Palestine, 1944–1945* (Jerusalem: Jewish Agency, 1946), 234.

104. Data are from N. Sokolow, *History of Zionism*, vol. 2 (London: Longmans, 1919), 329–331.

105. Khalidi, "Palestinian Peasant Resistance to Zionism," 207–233.

106. Mandel, *The Arabs and Zionism*, 38.

107. Awad, *Introduction to the History of Palestine, 1831–1914*, 132; Mandel, *The Arabs and Zionism*, 39–40; Porath, "The Political Awakening," 376.

108. Mandel, *The Arabs and Zionism*, 41.

109. N. 'Azoury, "Le Réveil de la nation arabe," cited in Hourani, *Arabic Thought in the Liberal Age*, 279; and Mandel, *The Arabs and Zionism*, 52.

110. Porath, "The Political Awakening," 377.

111. *Filastin*, 20 September 1911, cited in ibid., 379.

THREE

The Road to al-Nakbah: The Palestine Mandate, 1917–1948

In the mid-nineteenth century, the traditional subsistence, semifeudal, and tribute-paying economy of Palestine was eroding under a regime of clan-based local notables subject to Ottoman suzerainty. The old order gave way to a new order of commercial agriculture, a monetized economy, and the beginnings of an indigenous market linked by trade to the region and Europe under a more centralized Ottoman control. Social change accompanied this new political-economic order: increased population, urbanization and westward (to the coast) migration, the domination of urban over rural notables, the rise of Palestinian Christian and Muslim merchants, and the beginnings of new forms of social organization and consciousness. In the second half of the nineteenth century and the early twentieth century before World War I, however, this new order was itself restructured and reoriented toward dependent peripheral market capitalism as a result of both European intervention and the active participation of native landed and comprador classes. This transformation was similar to that of the surrounding Arab region except in one major respect: the arrival in the country of European colonial settlers and immigrants, principally Jewish, which eventually led to the dispossession of Palestine's native people.

The process of settler colonialism in Palestine was similar to earlier ones in Algeria, South Africa, and the Western Hemisphere.[1] Gershon Shafir, an Israeli sociologist, identifies three broad types of settler colonies: mixed colonies, which incorporate natives; plantation or extractive colonies, which incorporate slaves and indentured labor (such as the Caribbean colonies and New World colonies in general); and pure settler colonies, which reject native labor in favor of poor white settler-workers.[2] According to Shafir, Jewish settlement in Palestine was of the pure settler colony variety, although populated Palestine was ill suited for such a colony. Establishing a pure settler colony, which in this case had its ideological basis in Zionist exclusivism had several implications for Palestine and its people, for example, a separate "exclusive Jewish economy," which Shafir and others argue was nevertheless "integrally linked" with the Palestinian economy.[3] Unlike America or the New World in general, Palestine was relatively heavily populated, with a thriving agrarian-based society. It did not have "free territory," that is, it had a low or no degree of "frontierity" available to immigrant-settlers, as Baruch Kimmerling, another Israeli sociologist, points out.[4] Accordingly, European (Jewish Zionist and some Christian) settlers had to purchase land from the indigenous owners. But as Shafir argues, "in the first stage of Zionist settlement, the only way open for the acquisition of land was ownership—the exchange of capital for land. When the Jewish collectivity achieved sovereignty and became militarily powerful, the *conquest* of land replaced buying it."[5]

In this chapter we analyze the impact on Palestine and the Palestinians of the process, under British auspices, of the creation of a European Jewish collectivity in the country, its achievement of sovereignty, and its conquest of the land, which together resulted in al-Nakbah. Two structural processes—rapid settler colonialism and colonial capitalist transformation—combined during the British Mandate period to subjugate the Palestinian people and destroy Palestinian society. While the emergent Palestinian bourgeoisie participated in a minor way in the latter process, it was the European Jewish settlers, with the help and protection of the British authorities, who were the principal agents of the dual processes.

World War I: Britain and Zionism

The Palestinian struggle had been part of the nationalist Arab resistance, first to Turkish rule in the late nineteenth century and second to British and French colonialism over the region in the wake of World War I.[6] Combined with the legacy of a long, exploitative Ottoman rule, the consequences of European colonialism on the region—political balkanization, economic dependency and underdevelopment, retardation of institutional development, and the Zionist Jewish colonial settlement in Palestine—initiated Arab protest and established the parameters of Arab nationalist (and now Islamist) politics. Thus in the Middle East World War I was a watershed that, along with the collapse of the Ottoman Empire, directed the twentieth-century destiny of the Arab Mashreq, including Palestine.

Starting in 1915, Britain entered into three pivotal and contradictory agreements with three different parties—the French government; the leader of the Arab revolt against the Ottoman Turks, Sharif Hussein of Mecca; and the leader of the Zionist movement in Britain, Lord Rothschild—within two years. These were the secret Sykes-Picot agreement, the McMahon-Hussein agreements (Appendix 3), and the Balfour Declaration (Appendix 2). Together these agreements transformed the Arab Mashreq and Palestine forever.

The Sykes-Picot agreement of May 16, 1916, divided the former Ottoman dominions in the Arab east between Britain and France as administered territories and zones of influence: what emerged as Syria and Lebanon under the French, Transjordan and Iraq under the British. Palestine was to be internationalized.[7] This British-French compact contradicted the British agreement with Sharif Hussein of October 24, 1915. According to this agreement, in return for launching an Arab revolt against the Ottoman Turks, "Great Britain [was] prepared to recognize and support the independence of the Arabs in all the regions within the limits demanded by the Sharif of Mecca."[8] The Arab leaders and rebels viewed this agreement as the basis for a united Arab kingdom in the former domains of the Ottoman Empire in the Arab east including Palestine.[9] The Balfour Declaration of November 2, 1917, a letter from the British foreign minister, Lord Balfour, to the Zionist leader Lord Rothschild, stated that "His Majesty's Government view with favour the establishment in Palestine of a national home for the Jewish people . . . it being clearly understood that nothing shall be done which may prejudice the civil and religious rights of existing non-Jewish communities in Palestine."[10] These contradictory commitments were complicated further by the Anglo-French declaration of November 7, 1918, which called for "the complete and definite emancipation of the [Arab] peoples so long oppressed by the Turks and the establishment of national governments and administrations deriving their authority from the initiative and free choice of the indigenous populations."[11]

Zionism, a modern Jewish political movement, dates from the nineteenth century.[12] Prior to that the theology and mystique of the Holy Land of the Old Testament had been kept alive among Jews since their Diaspora. However, in the context of the European age of imperialism, secular nationalism, and anti-Semitism, especially in Russia and eastern Europe, Zionism, a movement of secular Jewish nationalism rather than Jewish religious identity, took hold among key segments of European Jewry. A principal cause was the sharp rise in anti-Semitism, leading to pogroms and the flight of Jews from Russia and eastern Europe, when Jews by and large were emancipated and assimilated into western Europe. In Russia the escalation of anti-Jewish prejudice and pogroms led to Jewish flight not only to western Europe but also to other countries, including Palestine, where Jews established agricultural settlements on land purchased and supported by the Jewish philanthropists Baron Rothschild and to a lesser extent Sir Moses Montefiore. This organized movement—especially Hovevei Zion (Lovers of Zion)—inspired Y. L.

Pinsker to write a book calling on Jewish autoemancipation as a solution to Russian and east European anti-Semitism. This movement envisioned the restoration of Eretz Israel (the land of Israel) in Palestine.[13]

In western Europe, despite the Enlightenment-inspired processes of liberalization and Jewish assimilation, the arrival of Jewish refugees in increasing numbers forced the reemergence of the "Jewish question." But the more immediate catalyst in the minds of western European Jews was the Dreyfus affair, the celebrated trial and sentencing of a Jewish French military officer falsely accused of treason. Strongly affected by this cause célèbre, Theodor Herzl, a Viennese journalist who had lived in Paris in the 1890s, proposed a solution to the European Jewish question in a book entitled *Der Judenstaat* (The Jewish state). Herzl's solution, like that of Pinsker earlier, was the creation of a separate Jewish state—not in Europe but in some colonial domain. The colonial Jewish state would absorb all of European Jewry and end anti-Semitism on the Continent. This was a precise formulation of the idea of restoration of the Jewish nation long espoused by British religious and secular writers.[14] In 1897 in a meeting in Basel, Switzerland, Herzl organized and became head of the World Zionist Organization, the political arm of the Zionist movement. The WZO declared its program as "the creation of a home for the Jewish people in Palestine"[15] and outlined a strategy to achieve this.[16] It was the WZO's British leaders who received the 1917 Balfour Declaration.

Zionism was a colonial project of European settlers much like those of Algeria, South Africa, Rhodesia, Uganda, Kenya, and elsewhere. The Zionist movement, however, differed in several respects: its religious-ideological justification for the project; the recruitment of Jewish settlers from all, not just one, European countries; and perhaps most important, the absence of imperial backing. Eventually, however, the WZO did acquire the support of Great Britain, the imperial European power necessary for its colonial enterprise in Palestine. At the insistence of the British government, the Balfour Declaration, vague as to the meaning of a "national home" for the Jews (always defined as an independent state by the Zionists) and contradictory as to the rights of Palestinians, was incorporated into the articles of the Mandate of Palestine by the League of Nations, itself a creation of the victorious allies of WWI. The disposition of the former Arab domains of the Ottoman Empire followed the outlines of the Sykes-Picot agreement and the Balfour Declaration far more than it did the McMahon-Hussein understanding.

Palestine Under British Military Administration

Palestine first came under British control in December 1917 in the course of the war against Ottoman Turkey, which had joined World War I on the side of Germany against the Allies. Invading from the Egyptian Sinai, British troops under General Edmund Allenby conquered Palestine and established a military administration that was called the Occupied Enemy Territory Administration (OETA). The British OETA lasted for thirty months, until 1920, when it was replaced by a civilian administration. The administration was bound by and attempted to rule Palestine in accordance with international law, especially the Manual of Military Law, derived from The Hague convention of 1899 and 1907,which obligated conquering armies to maintain the status quo in conquered territories until their future had been determined. Thus none of the senior British military administrators of Palestine was sympathetic to the idea of a "national home" for the Jews. Over this policy the military administration of Palestine quickly clashed with Zionist efforts to change the conditions and privilege the immigrant-settler Jews in Palestine. Although the Zionists had the support of the British Foreign Office and a Foreign Ministry–OETA conflict thus arose, the OETA policy was upheld most of the time.[17]

The Zionist-OETA dispute started within the first month of the occupation when Chaim Weizmann, at the head of the Zionist Commission, requested permission personally to survey Palestine. Major General Gilbert Clayton, political officer of the OETA, objected in large part because of international law and the rising discontent of the Palestinians with Zionism. The visit of the Zionist Commission occurred nonetheless, but even the Foreign Office rejected its proposals, which included a number of requests that raised the fear and hostility of Palestinians and British military administrators alike: participation of Zionist Jews in the military administration of the country; creation of a land authority, to include Zionist Jewish experts, to survey the resources; and formation of an exclusively Jewish military force. Although General Clayton was replaced by Colonel Richard Meinertzhagen, an ardent Zionist, the OETA policy did not change substantially. The reason was clear enough to the political officers and to both Clayton and Meinertzhagen, as it was to the succession of chief military administrators. It was perhaps best stated by chief military administrator General A. W. Money shortly before his departure in 1919: "The Palestinians desire their country for themselves and will resist any general immigration of Jews, however gradual, by every means in their power including active hostilities."[18] In August 1919 Money's successor, Major General H. D. Watson, elaborated further: "The antagonism to Zionism of the majority of the population is deep-rooted—it is fast leading to hatred of the British—and will result, if the Zionist programme is forced upon them, in an outbreak of serious character."[19]

Both Money and Watson were right, as was the report of the King-Crane Commission (see Appendix 4), an unbiased U.S. commission known by the names of its two members, Henry C. King, president of Oberlin College, and Charles Crane, a businessman. At the suggestion of U.S. president

Woodrow Wilson, the Allies in 1919 empowered the King-Crane Commission to inform them of the wishes of the Palestinian and Arab people's for their future. It reported that Arab wishes "were nationalistic, that is to say, they called for a united Syria [including Lebanon and Palestine] under a democratic constitution, making no distinction on the basis of religion."[20] The commission recommended independence for Syria, including Palestine or, failing that, a mandate under the United States (not Britain), in accordance with the wishes of the Arab people. In regard to the Zionist project, the commission recommended "serious modification of the extreme Zionist Program."[21] Because the King-Crane report was unfavorable to Zionism and Anglo-French plans for the area, it was not published until 1922, three years after it was written—after the mandate system was established. The suppression of the King-Crane report and the impending Allied conference in San Remo, Italy, to decide the destiny of the eastern Arab world did not reassure the Palestinians or the other Arabs of the Mashreq.

The Arab and Palestinian people's fears were well founded. The San Remo conference—in direct contradiction with President Wilson's declaration in January 1918 of the principle of self-determination, which had raised Arab hopes—confirmed the Sykes-Picot agreement. Continued foreign rule (now, of course, British and French) of Arab lands reasserted the British intention to pursue the provisions of the Balfour Declaration. Arab and Palestinian discontent triggered demonstrations in Damascus, Baghdad, Haifa, Jaffa, and Jerusalem in February, March, and especially April 1920. Discontent increased as the Damascus Congress of March 1920 came to naught. A gathering of leading Arab nationalists, the meeting had created hope and excitement when it declared Arab lands independent and named Amir Faisal bin Hussein (son of Sharif Hussein of Mecca) king of Syria and Palestine and his brother, Amir Abdullah bin Hussein, king of Mesopotamia (Iraq). In Palestine escalating Palestinian–Zionist Jewish tension exploded in political demonstrations, rioting, and violence that peaked in early April 1920 during a holiday celebrated in all three religions. Five Jews and four Palestinians were killed and scores on both sides were wounded.

The British Commission of Inquiry, appointed to investigate the riots, submitted its report on July 1, 1920, a day after the military administration ended. It "listed as the causes of unrest in the country: British promises to Arabs during the war; the conflict between these promises and the Balfour Declaration; fear of Jewish domination; Zionist overaggressiveness; and foreign propaganda."[22] The commission added that the "Zionists' attitude justifies the description . . . as arrogant, insolent and provocative. . . . If not carefully checked they may easily precipitate a catastrophe, the end of which it is difficult to forecast."[23]

Despite the King-Crane Commission report of 1919, the findings of the British Commission of Inquiry in 1920, and the opinions and dire warnings of the military and civilian administrators of Palestine during the 1817–1920 period, the British political leadership, headed by Prime Minister David Lloyd George, pushed the Jewish national home provision of the Balfour Declaration. By the end of the military administration, on June 30, 1920, Lloyd George appointed Herbert Samuel, a British Zionist Jew, as first civilian high commissioner of Palestine. He was, of course, much more favorable to the building of the Jewish national home than was the OETA of the previous period.

The Palestine Mandate, 1920–1948

Under the direct and powerful influence of Britain and France, the victorious Allies of World War I, the League of Nations created the mandate system and granted Britain mandatory power over Palestine. Map 3.1 shows mandate Palestine and other countries of the region. Formally in place by 1922, the Palestine Mandate came to a close in May 1948 when Britain gave up its authority to the United Nations Organization. The official purpose of the mandate system was to maintain an international trusteeship to prepare former enemy territories for self-rule. However, "the assignment of territory under the mandate system was little more than a thinly disguised title deed, enabling the overseer to promote political, strategic, and economic metropolitan interests."[24]

As the terms of the British Mandate over Palestine included provisions for implementing the Balfour Declaration, it set up irreconcilable and contradictory goals of self-rule for the native Palestinians and a national home (still not specifically defined by Britain) for European Jews, "imperatives that would hamper the development of a unitary state and lead to severe imbalances in communal growth."[25] For the Zionists, the national home meant quite simply a "Palestine . . . as Jewish as England is English, or as Canada is Canadian."[26] In addition to incorporating the whole of the Balfour Declaration, Britain provided for the establishment of a Jewish Agency, to be, in its official language, "recognized as a public body for the purpose of advising and cooperating with the Administration of Palestine in such economic, social and other matters as may affect the establishment of the Jewish population in Palestine," the facilitation of the immigration of Jews to Palestine, and "the close settlement by Jews on the Land," upholding the right of each community to maintain its school system, the use of Hebrew in addition to Arabic and English as official languages, and so on.[27] The mandate agreement was thus framed largely with clauses that favored the Zionist cause over Palestinian self-determination.

While the Zionists were pleased with the mandate provisions, "the [Palestinian] Arabs were especially aroused because, whereas numerous articles of the mandatory agreement referred to the Jewish community by

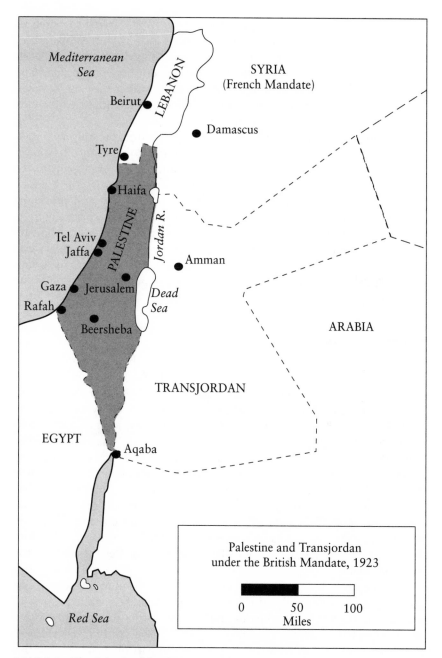

MAP 3.1   The Palestine Mandate
SOURCE: M. Tessler, *A History of the Israeli-Palestinian Conflict* (Bloomington: Indiana University Press, 1994), 166.

name, the Arabs, 90 per cent of the population, were referred to merely as 'the other sections' of the population."[28] The British Mandate government in Palestine undertook to provide the underpinnings of any successful settler movement; to ensure that settlers could numerically expand their base through the right to immigration; to make land available for the new settlers; and to grant the Zionists various forms of preferential treatment or economic concessions in the country.[29]

By the mid-1920s, the British shifted their policy from creating the necessary preconditions for a successful Jewish settler community "to one of sheltering it during difficult times . . . contributing to the development of [a Jewish] enclave economy . . . [and] protectionist toward Jewish industry [and labor]."[30] Under the mandate system, the political and economic frameworks for the colonization of Palestine and the disfranchisement of its people were put into place. Thus the colonial state (the Palestine Mandate government) and the actions of the Jewish settler-colonial community created the historical conditions for the development of classic patterns of capitalism in Palestine: expropriation of the land and proletarianization of the peasantry.

Uniqueness of the Palestine Mandate

Palestine was unique among the mandates created by the League of Nations in that the mandatory power encouraged (European Jewish) immigrants to settle in the country (in accordance with the Balfour Declaration). Otherwise the British treated Palestine as an ordinary colony with the typical links to the metropole in trade, finance, currency, administrative, and defensive policies. Pegged to the sterling area, Palestine was not allowed to have a central bank or to issue its own currency. Its currency was controlled by a Currency Board in London, and the country was administered through "a colonial pattern of revenue and expenditure with particular emphasis on administration and security and very little on government-sponsored development or on welfare services."[31] Palestine, as other colonies, was supposed to pay the costs of its own internal and external security and, in this instance, to guarantee the safety of Jewish colonial settlers against the native Palestinians.

Palestine was a poor country lacking in resources and in investment and growth potential. Britain's main interest in Palestine was strategic, despite the Balfour Declaration's religious and cultural justifications. The country was the key buffer state in the British imperial defense of India, Egypt, and the Suez Canal (the shortest sea route to India); part of the air routes also to India and Iraq; and the principal terminus of the oil pipelines from the Iraqi oil fields (of the British-owned Iraq Petroleum Company, or IPC). However, British and Zionist ideology saw the potential for economic growth of Palestine in the "yeast" of Jewish immigrants with superior education, technological know-how, and capital that would produce an economic "cake" that would be shared with the poor and backward Palestinian Arabs.[32] Indeed, through this Jewish-based development, both the British and the Zionists believed that Palestine would be capable of sustaining a much larger population (including of course the Jewish immigrant-settlers). In this potential the British also saw the resolution of the dual and contradictory obligations they made to the Palestinians (self-determination) and Zionist Jews (a national home) in the mandate agreement.

Implementation of the Zionist Project in Palestine

The Zionist project was fraught with discontinuities, contradictions, and conflicts with the Palestinian natives and occasionally the British Mandate administration, but in the final analysis its implementation was quite successful. By 1948 it achieved an independent Jewish state. In this section we analyze the process in terms of the size, character, and timing of the waves of Jewish settler-immigrants; their land purchases and settlements; their enclave economy; their policies for separate labor; their segregated and exclusivist social institutions; their political organization; and the supportive, preferential, and protectionist British policies.

In-migration and Demographic Transformation. Palestine in 1882 had a small, native migrant religious Jewish community (or *yishuv*, as Israeli and Western Jewish historians call it) of roughly 24,000 among a population of nearly 500,000 Palestinians.[33] The size of the Jewish settler community in Palestine increased, over the period since 1882, through several major waves (called *aliyah*s by Israeli and Jewish historians) of in-migration. The first wave, between 1882 and 1903, totaled about 25,000 Jews, most of Russian origin, and the second, between 1904 and 1914, brought in around 35,000 Jews, most of them eastern Europeans. Although many of these and the earlier settlers emigrated from Palestine soon afterward, the total Jewish population in 1914 reached 85,000. In the 1922 census conducted by the mandate government, the country had a population of 757,182 (perhaps an undercount, as many observers note), with 89 percent Palestinian Arab and 11 percent Jewish. Most Jews lived in the urban areas of new western Jerusalem and the exclusively Jewish Tel Aviv suburb of Jaffa.[34]

The number of Jewish settlers increased with the third and subsequent sporadic waves. The third wave, between 1919 and 1923, brought in 35,000 (again, most of them Russian), whereas the fourth, between 1924 and 1931, added another 85,000 immigrants (most of Polish,[35] middle-class background). Despite this at times heavy in-migration, the relative ratios of the respective ethnic (Palestinian Arab vs. Jewish) representation altered only slightly at the end of this period. The December 1931 British census of the country showed that of the 1.04 million people, 84 percent were Arab and 16 percent Jewish, although the absolute size of the Jewish settler community had doubled since just before World War I. While the increase in the Jewish population was due largely to in-migration, the Palestinian population increased naturally[36] at 2.7 percent per year, a rate that rose to 3.0–3.5 percent by 1948. The fifth wave of Jewish immigration, between 1932 and 1938, may have numbered close to 200,000. Indeed because of the rise of Nazism, 174,000 Jews immigrated to Palestine between 1932 and 1936. After the emigration of 4,000 Jews from Palestine, the 170,000–200,000 in-migrants, added to the 174,000 already residing in Palestine, suddenly raised the Jewish population to an estimated 370,000 in 1936, that is, 28 percent of the total, a dramatic increase from the 16 percent reported in the 1931 census. "It was therefore not surprising that the Arab population should have become alarmed at the rapid rate at which the demographic composition of their country was being altered, without their consent and against their will. . . . This radical change, occurring in the brief span of only five years, must certainly be recognized as an important cause of the [Palestinian] Arab rebellion of 1936."[37]

In the wake of the 1936–1939 Palestinian revolt (discussed in a later section), the British placed a ceiling on new Jewish immigration at 75,000, including 25,000 refugees, to be reached over five years.[38] In addition to this figure, a large, unknown number of illegal immigrants—in contravention of the mandate government ceiling—arrived in Palestine during and after this period. Map 3.2 shows the distribution of population by subdistricts, with percentages of Jews and Palestinians. By the end of 1947, Palestine Mandate government estimates indicate that of a total population of 1.9 million, Jews made up only 31 percent of the population and the rest was Arab (except for the small numbers of British and other Europeans).[39] Thus only a year before "the state of Israel was unilaterally declared and its effective control expanded by force to most of the area contained in the former country of Palestine, the Jewish population still constituted a minority of less than one-third."[40]

Eighty-five percent of the Jewish population remained centered in three major urban centers and their surrounding areas: Jaffa–Tel Aviv, Jerusalem, and Haifa. The Palestinian-Jewish civil war that followed the approval in 1947 of the United Nations partition plan for Palestine led to massive displacement of the Palestinian population from its own country (and thus the birth of the refugee problem). In short, Jewish force of arms accomplished in a little over one year the complete demographic transformation (which could not be achieved in decades of migration) of the part of Palestine that became the state of Israel in 1948.[41] Table 3.1 indicates the rapidly changing size and ratio of the Palestinian and Jewish populations during the mandate period.

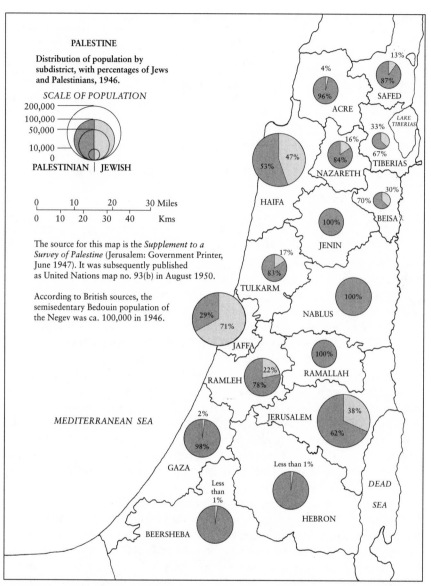

MAP 3.2   Distribution of Population by Subdistrict, with Percentages of Jews and Palestinians, 1946.

SOURCE: W. Khalidi, *Before Their Diaspora* (Washington, DC: Insititute for Palestine Studies, 1984), 239.

TABLE 3.1 Population Distribution in Palestine, 1880–1947

	Arabs		Jews	
	Numbers	%	Numbers	%
1880	300,000	94	24,000	6
1917[a]	504,000	90	56,000	10
1922	666,000	89	84,000	11
1931	850,000	83	174,096	17
1936	916,000	72	384,078	28
1945–1946	1,242,000	69	608,000	31
1947[b]	1,300,000	67	640,298	33

[a]Balfour Declaration.
[b]UN partition.
SOURCE: *Facts and Figures About the Palestinians* (Washington, DC: Center for Policy Analysis on Palestine, 1992), 7.

Land Acquisition. Despite their view that Palestine was a land without people, the Zionists, as early as 1882, discovered that Palestinian land was not uninhabited or readily available.[42] Except for certain swampy areas, Palestine was densely populated and intensively cultivated. Moreover, the land tenure and ownership system was complex and encumbered by varied forms of private and public usufruct rights, despite nineteenth-century Ottoman reforms and liberalization. Available land was expensive and became more so with the rising demand of a population growing as a result of both natural increase and in-migration. With the establishment of the Palestine Mandate, Zionist hopes that state land—perceived as vast and potentially accessible—would serve as a basis for land acquisition also turned out to be largely unrealistic.[43] Nevertheless, by 1947 approximately 195,000 dunums of state land were granted or leased to Jewish settlers by the British Mandate authorities.

The Zionist policy of land acquisition had a political logic: The Zionists looked for quantity and quality, location, and contiguity. Accordingly, they tended to purchase land in large, contiguous areas of the inland and coastal plains. And yet another pattern also derived from this logic: Jews settled on land that was too small for economic profitability but that was necessary to "establish facts" on the ground.[44] These acquisitions were made not by private individuals but by political agencies of the Zionist movement, such as the Jewish National Fund (JNF,[45] also called Keren Kayemeth Leisrael), the Keren Hayesod (or the Palestine Foundation Fund, established in 1920), the Palestine Land Development Company (PLDC), the Palestine Jewish Colonization Association (PICA), and the Jewish Colonization Association.[46] Around 70 percent of all Palestinian land Zionists acquired was purchased

TABLE 3.2 Estimated Jewish Land Purchases in Palestine, 1882–1947
(in thousands of dunums)

	Total Area Owned by Jews	Area Owned by INF	Total Land Purchased
Until 1882	22	–	22
1883–1890	104	–	82
1891–1900	218	–	114
1901–1914	418	16	200
1915–1919	–	25	–
1920–1922	557	72	139
1923–1927	865	197	307
1928–1931	994	298	130
1932–1935	1,232	371	238
1936–1939	1,358	478	126
1940–1941	1,431	566	73
1942–1945	1,606	813	75
1946–1947	1,734	933	622

SOURCE: B. Kimmerling, *Zionism and Territory* (Berkeley: Institute of International and Area Studies, University of California, 1983), 43.

by the PLDC on behalf of the JNF. Collectively owned land was purchased in the name of the Jewish people and reserved for exclusive Jewish use.[47]

The formal establishment of the Palestine Mandate under Britain, and to the north the Lebanon Mandate under the French, created a strong impetus for the sale of vast estates by absentee landlords from Lebanon to the Zionist organizations, which were well endowed with capital. Beirut merchant families found it more convenient and profitable to sell to Jewish organizations than to manage their properties in Palestine. For example, in Marj Ibn 'Amer, the Sursoq family sold to the PLDC 230,000 dunums, including seventeen villages. Granott notes that between 1920 and 1927, 82 percent of all land acquired by the Zionist organizations was purchased from absentee landlords.[48]

During the 1920s Zionist land purchases from non-Palestinian Arab absentee landowners were heaviest. Beginning in the 1930s, land sales by large Palestinian landlords and peasants constituted the greater proportion (89 percent) of the total land purchased by Zionists.[49] Kenneth Stein contends that by 1945, land sales to Jews or Jewish organizations by non-Palestinian absentee Arab landowners constituted 52.6 percent, by large Palestinian owners 24.6 percent, and by peasants 9.4 percent.[50] The area of total land Jews acquired in Palestine by 1945 is officially estimated at 1.59 million out of 7.3 million dunums of arable land.[51] Table 3.2 summarizes data on all Jewish land acquisition in Palestine between 1882 and 1947.

From the data it is possible to discern three periods of intensive land acquisition by Jews and Zionist organizations in Palestine. These were 1923–1927, with an average annual 61,400 dunums of land purchased; 1932–1935, with 59,500 dunums; and 1942–1947, with 61,200 dunums. While in 1922 Jews owned 751,192 dunums, representing 3 percent of the land of Palestine, the total area purchased by Jews by 1947 was 1.73 million dunums,[52] representing nearly 24 percent of all the arable land and 7 percent of the total surface area of Palestine.[53] Most Jews in Palestine, however, lived in cities, as previously discussed. At no time did the percentage of Jews living on the land, that is, on farms, exceed 19.3 percent.[54]

The withdrawal of so much arable land from access or use by Palestinian peasants led not only to their landlessness and proletarianization but also to economic hardship.[55] Thus Palestinian peasant discontent, political activism, and hostility to and violence against the Zionists and the British authorities were highest after periods of high transfer of land, accounting for the 1929 upheaval, the 1936–1939 revolt, and the 1947–1948 internal war. These periods also coincide with heavy waves of Jewish migration into Palestine, particularly the five years before the rebellion of 1936. Map 3.3 indicates Jewish and Palestinian landownership in percentages by subdistrict in 1945. Despite all the land purchases and grants from the British Mandate authorities, the colonist Jews were unable to gain control of more than 7 percent of the land of Palestine except through the 1948 military conquest and again in the 1967 war, when Israel occupied the rest of Palestine.

The British Mandate government had classified Palestinian arable land as good, medium, and poor. After the general armistice of the 1948 war, Israel had captured over 77 percent of Palestine and "more than 95 per cent of the 'good' soil, 64 per cent of the 'medium' and, excluding the Negev, less than 39 per cent of the 'poor.'"[56] The newly sovereign state of Israel also appropriated 80 percent of privately owned Palestinian land and confiscated 40 percent of properties held by Palestinian Arabs who remained on the land and became citizens.[57] The total value of Palestinian losses in 1948 (most appropriated by Israel) is estimated by economist Atif Kubursi to be a staggering £P743,050 million in 1948 prices.[58]

A Separate Jewish Economy.   The roots of Jewish separatism within Palestine extend from the first decade of the mandate.[59] British policy of economic development in Palestine and, specifically, of granting Jewish settlers monopolistic concessions and industrial protectionism facilitated the building of an exclusive Jewish economy, for what the Zionists called the "conquest of land and of labor." In her excellent study of British policy in the 1920s, Barbara Smith shows that even though a part of the British Empire, Palestine was a weak link because of its lack of resources and because the British sought to establish, strengthen, and consolidate a Jewish settler community with wider

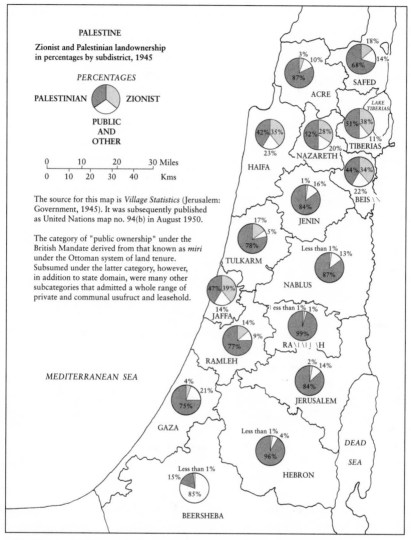

MAP 3.3   Zionist and Palestinian Landownership in Percentages by
Subdistrict, 1945
SOURCE: W. Khalidi, *Before Their Diaspora* (Washington, DC: Institute for
Palestine Studies, 1984), 237.

international links. Although Palestine at large had direct ties to the metropole, the Jewish colonists in Palestine had less connection to the British economy and more to the wider world.[60] And because Britain did not have a privileged economic position vis-à-vis the Jewish settler colonists, British
parliamentary debate often raised the question of benefit to the empire.

Economically, Britain facilitated Jewish land acquisition (except when Palestinian political or violent action caused a reconsideration of policies) and provided for Jewish enterprises in an "incoherent but clearly recognizable" protectionist policy and preferential tariffs that included "the free importation of raw materials already produced in Palestine" by Palestinians.[61] According to article 6 of the mandate charter, Britain promised to facilitate Jewish settlement on state lands and land not required for public purposes.

Besides land for colonies in Athlit, Caesarea, Kabbara, and Beisan, three main national monopolistic concessions were granted to Jewish entrepreneurs in the first decade: the Rutenberg, the Dead Sea salt, and the Athlit Salt Company. The Rutenberg concession was ambitious and controversial:

> Rutenberg was granted exclusive rights to use the waters of the Auja basin and to provide power, electric light, and irrigation using any type of energy in the district of Jaffa ... and exclusive rights ... to carry out a grand hydroelectric and irrigation scheme [based in the Jordan and Yarmouk River basins]. The concession also gave Rutenberg monopolistic rights over the supply of electric power throughout Palestine (excluding Jerusalem) and Trans-Jordan and the possibility of the electrification of the entire railway system.[62]

Opposition to the Rutenberg concession emerged both in Palestine among the Palestinian Arabs, who viewed it as economically privileging Jews, and in Britain among conservative politicians, who detested seeing economic benefits going to a German Jew and to Germany. The Palestine Mandate and the British government ignored these objections and the Jaffa Electric Company and the Palestine Electric Corporation were formed with a majority of Jewish capital in 1921 and 1923. These companies helped electrify a new settlement, Tel Aviv, providing a service crucial to its rapid rise from a suburb of Jaffa to a modern, European-style Jewish city in Palestine.

With regard to the Dead Sea salt concession, the Colonial Office preferred to grant the concession to a British candidate, but given the furor over the Rutenberg concession, it was put up for public tender. In 1930, also after a long controversy in the British Parliament, it went to a team headed by Moses Novomeysky, a Russian Zionist. The Palestine Potash Company, as the concession was called, was clearly a Zionist industrial venture. One final major concession—in addition to several smaller ones—was the Athlit Salt Company, a Jewish enterprise licensed to produce salt. This concession showed special favoritism to the Zionist Jews. The artificially high price placed on salt hurt the Palestinian Arabs in all walks of life.[63] Salt was not just a basic daily food necessity for all, it was a crucial element in the manufacture of soap and leather goods, long established industries of Palestine.

Even before the mandate, Jewish enterprises introduced nonanimal power into production, such as oil presses, flour mills, and power motors in soap manufacturing. In addition, Jewish and German settlers came to dominate the building industry. Also prior to the mandate, the Jewish settlers had laid the foundation for an industrial sector[64] that was more capital intensive and efficient than the Palestinian. This transplanted, rationally organized Jewish industrial sector experienced a new and significant advance during the mandate. While British authorities did not generally support industrialization in the colonies, they encouraged Jewish industry in Palestine. Industrialization took off in the mid-1920s after an urban boom following the wave of migration of middle-class Polish Jews who were sophisticated in industry and business and who settled in cities rather than rural agricultural settlements. This trend was further bolstered and consolidated in the 1930s after the German Jewish immigrants arrived in great numbers in urban centers with even larger capital and technical skills. These developments firmly established Jewish industry in Palestine.[65] During WWII the Jewish industrial base became stronger as the British encouraged it to supply the needs (including military hardware) of Allied forces and the domestic market. By 1939 the *Survey of Palestine* indicated that while Jews composed only 31 percent of the total population, Jewish capital investment in industry was 88 percent of total industrial investment, 90 percent of installed horsepower, and 89 percent of total net industrial output, and Jewish workers represented 79 percent of all industrial workers in Palestine.[66] In short, by 1929 British and Zionist policy brought forth a Jewish industrial sector that had little connection to the Palestinian Arab economy or population.

Zionists in the early 1920s criticized the British authorities for infrastructural, institutional, and financial conditions that discouraged industrialization. It was the Jewish Manufacturers' Association, an interest group, that finally energized the Zionist establishment to push the Palestine Mandate government for more favorable industrial policies. By the mid- to late 1920s, customs regulations were changed and a clear protectionist policy was instituted that included reduced (and sometimes exempted) import duties on raw materials and often on machinery needed for production, as well as the abolition of the 1 percent ad valorem export duty. The Rutenberg concession, the Nesher Cement Company, Shemen (Palestine Oil Industry), and a long list of other Jewish industrial enterprises (in silk, textiles, tanning, confectionery, false teeth, umbrellas, etc.) received *specific* customs concessions despite the tight finances of the Palestine government.[67] Most directly deleterious to Palestinian industry and agriculture was the exemption of import duties on the importation of olive oil and sesame seeds to benefit Shemen. At the same time, import duties on cement were constantly *raised* in order to protect the Jewish-owned Nesher Cement Company. Similarly, import duties on a whole host of items (salt, jelly, jam, cakes, chocolate, etc.) were also specifically raised in order to protect Jewish manufactures.

TABLE 3.3 Source of Food for Jewish Community in Palestine, 1939 and 1944

	1939	1944
Jewish agriculture	26	47
Imports	67	47
Arab agriculture	7	6

SOURCE: Esco Foundation for Palestine, *A Study of Jewish, Arab, and British Policies,* vol. 2 (New Haven, CT: Yale University Press, 1947), 1052.

Such preferential treatment for Jewish industry extended into the World War II period. As in the previous era, British Mandate government policy during the war advantaged Jewish industry at the expense of Palestinian industry, placing orders for military goods with Jewish firms (by 1945 these orders were valued at £P28 million) and nurturing the expansion of nondutiable raw and semifinished goods. Jewish industry was also guaranteed access to Arab consumers in Palestine and the Arab world, further aggravating the Palestinians' predicament.[68] "The result of this situation for Arab industrial development was that Jewish-owned industry grew in those light industries in which Arabs were trying to make headway. Thus, the Jewish sector came into direct competition with [Palestinian] Arab industry."[69] The separate development of the Jewish economy in Palestine is illustrated in Table 3.3, which shows that although Palestine had a primarily agricultural economy, especially in the Palestinian Arab sector, the Jewish community acquired only 7 percent of its food from the Arab sector in 1939 and 6 percent in 1944.

Until the upheaval and riots of 1929, complaints from Palestinian Arabs did little to dissuade the British authorities from making decisions that were harmful to the Palestinian people. In 1930 the British high commissioner received approval from the Foreign Office to raise duties on the importation of products locally produced. These new import duties forced slightly greater Jewish-Palestinian economic exchange and undermined somewhat the Zionist policy of boycotting Palestinian products and of building an exclusive Jewish economy. A Palestinian counterboycott, launched during the 1929 upheaval and again in 1936, however, did not help intercommunal economic integration.[70]

Jewish Labor.   The initial Zionist project of redemption of the land with Jewish agricultural labor[71] quickly transformed during the mandate period into the development of an urban and industrial Jewish economy and a commensurate labor force.[72] As in the development of an exclusive Jewish economy, institutions, and land base, the British colonial government of Palestine contributed to the creation, protection, and unemployment relief of exclusive Jewish labor. The British did not, however, extend this policy to the Palestinian Arab labor force. Further, the British facilitated the creation of a two-tier wage structure for Palestinian Arabs and Jews in both the private and public sectors.[73] These discriminatory labor policies handicapped Palestinian labor in wage levels and working conditions, contributing to Palestinian unemployment, indebtedness, and severe discontent. These factors were important determinants of the sociopolitical upheavals of the Palestinians in 1929, 1936–1939, and 1947–1948.

British colonial economic development policy in Palestine had three basic tenets. The first was a conservative fiscal policy (common to other colonies) by which the colonized people had to pay internal and external security and public expenditures, no matter how narrow its revenue base. The second was a development theory of the Jewish inputs in an undeveloped, resource-poor Palestine that would lead to a structural rise of the whole economy. This idea was predicated on the potential importation of vast Jewish capital and skilled Jewish capitalists into the country. This theory, however, belied the Zionist organizations' labor policies, which encouraged Jewish employers to hire more expensive Jewish workers over the much cheaper Palestinian Arab labor and thus hurt the general growth of all sectors of the Palestinian economy.[74]

According to the third tenet, Britain regulated Jewish migration into Palestine in accordance with the "absorptive capacity" of the country.[75] Early in the mandate period this concept was redefined to mean the absorptive capacity of the Jewish economy only. Although it did not strictly adhere to the policy, the mandate administration found itself supporting the Zionist labor agenda: allowing more Jewish immigration during growth years, favoring Jewish workers in public employment, and providing unemployment relief during periods of economic crisis. The Palestine Mandate government was reluctant to address labor issues, refusing to arbitrate or attempt to resolve labor-management conflicts between Jewish workers and Jewish owners. This resulted in laws that were discriminatory, inadequate, and minimalist in response to pressure from organized Zionists or actual events (e.g., strikes, sociopolitical upheavals, and severe socioeconomic conditions). It left the resolution of such controversies to the Zionist organizations.

The principal means through which the Zionists succeeded in building a separate and privileged Jewish labor force was the Histadrut,[76] the General Federation of Jewish Labor, established in 1920. The Histadrut was like no other union. It owned a construction cooperative (called Solel Boneh), consumer and marketing cooperatives, a bank (Bank Hapoelim), and credit, insurance, and publishing institutions. The great majority of Jewish workers belonged to the Histadrut, and it became one of the largest employers after the establishment of Israel. In contrast to the poorly organized Palestinian workers, organized Jewish labor exerted strong pressure on the Zionist Executive and the British government in Palestine. As a result, the Histadrut was able through the Zionist Executive to gain many concessions from the mandate government.

Separate Social and Political Institutions.   The Histadrut was perhaps one of the most developed Jewish social institutions in Palestine. Among the many activities of this unique union were a health insurance program (the Kupat Holim, or Sick Fund) and training, education, placement, and pension programs. While these were targeted to Jewish workers, the Zionist organizations also extended the wide range of social service institutions to the whole Jewish settler community in Palestine.

Like other practices of the Zionists, the social service institutions were exclusive to Jews. The most important of these were the health and educational sectors. Health services, provided principally by the Kupat Holim of the Labor Federation and by the Haddassah Medical Organization, were coordinated by a Health Council appointed by the Zionist Executive,[77] which worked on health matters with the Department of Health of the Palestine Mandate government. Membership in the Kupat Holim grew from 2,000 in 1920 to tens of thousands by the end of the mandate. More vital was the Haddassah, which established a number of hospitals with clinics, laboratories, and pharmacies in most of the cities of Palestine with heavy Jewish populations (e.g., Jerusalem, Tel Aviv, Haifa, Tabariyya, Safad). Haddassah also established the nurses' training school, the Straus Health Center for All Races and Creeds, infant welfare stations, school hygiene and school lunch programs, and playgrounds, and it developed public health programs for reducing trachoma and malaria among Jews. As a consequence of these raised health standards, the death rate among Jews was less than half that among the majority of the Palestinians. Palestinians' health institutions were comparatively inefficient and fewer, especially in the rural areas. British-instituted public health programs, nevertheless, benefited the entire population, allowing for a rapid rate of natural population increase among the Palestinians.

One of the most important efforts in recreating a Jewish national identity was their educational system. In the mandate agreement, the Zionists won from the British and the League of Nations the recognition of Hebrew as an official language, along with Arabic and English, although Jews represented no more than about 10 percent of the population in Palestine. They also acquired British consent and support (fixed grants-in-aid or bloc grants from the mandate government) for a separate and exclusive private Jewish school system. Zionist authorities, furthermore, gained autonomy over the curriculum, which was imbued with Zionist-inspired Jewish nationalism. This educational system eventually covered kindergarten through secondary schools, vocational schools to technical institutes (e.g., the Technion in Haifa) and major universities (e.g., the Hebrew University in Jerusalem).

While the British authorities allowed the Zionists great autonomy in setting up an educational system, they denied such freedom—and financial support—to the Palestinian Arabs.[78] By 1946 there was a total of 795 schools with 118,335 students for the Palestinians. A little over half, 478 schools, were government schools and the rest private. By the 1940s about 40 percent of the Palestinian schoolchildren attended private schools.[79] Among the rural population, elementary school attendance was only 20 percent, in contrast to 85 percent in the urban centers.[80] Government elementary schools, often to the fourth grade only, were established in less than half of all villages, including a tiny fraction (11 percent) for girls. According to A. L. Tibawi, girls represented 17 percent of all Palestinian students in 1920–1921 and 21 percent in 1945–1946. Despite the apparent advance in education, Palestinian Arabs were disadvantaged relative to the settler-immigrant Jews. Mandate government figures indicate that in 1944 only 32.5 percent of Palestinian Arab children between five and fourteen years old were enrolled in schools; the figure was 97 percent for Jewish children in the same age group.[81] The private and governmental Palestinian school system helped reduce illiteracy substantially yet failed to provide the technical or higher education that the Jewish community provided. Secondary education for urban Palestinians was limited, and unless they attended a teachers' college in Jerusalem, Palestinians had to leave the country to go to a university.

Palestine's educational system for the two communities under the mandate was separate and unequal in terms of quality, financing, levels, and delivery, especially in the rural areas. As the assistant director of education in the mandate government, Jerome Farrell, noted concerning the economizing educational policy: "The natural result of the disparity between the educational facilities offered to Arabs and Jews is to widen the cultural gap between the two races, to prevent social intermixture on equal terms and to tend to reduce the Arabs to a position of permanent inferiority."[82] In order to suppress the rising Palestinian consciousness, British authorities denied the Palestinians the right to teach nationalism.[83] Nationalist sentiment and activity nonetheless surged in the schools, which became locuses of political mobilization during the mandate, as they were later for Palestinians in exile and during occupation in the West Bank and Gaza Strip.[84]

Separation of the two communities was promulgated in 1926 by the British Mandate government's Religious Communities Organization Ordinance. It granted the Jewish settler community in Palestine a juridical personality and the power of taxation for charitable and educational purposes. This ordinance also allowed Jewish religious authorities and courts, as well as

Muslim and Christian ecclesiastical authorities, exclusive jurisdiction over family laws. Similarly, these religious authorities had jurisdiction over waqf, or religious property. Whatever its impetus or justification, this British policy helped the consolidation of a separate Jewish community in Palestine.

A Jewish State-within-a-State. The British authorized the establishment of the Jewish Agency to represent, lead, and negotiate on behalf of the Jewish settler community in Palestine on all aspects of British policy. In turn, the Jewish Agency established various social, economic, and political agencies, institutions, and organizations, including military and intelligence units. Together, these organizations were the nucleus of an emerging autonomous Jewish political authority within the Palestine Mandate government. It was this well-organized, well-financed, and efficient state-within-a-state that mobilized the Jewish population; conducted an effective internal war against the less well organized, mobilized, and financed Palestinians from 1947 to 1948; defeated the Arab armies in the first Arab-Israeli war of 1948; and became the institutional foundation for the state of Israel.

The Palestinian Arabs had no such centralized political agency, nor did the political leaders have the capacity to mobilize the population effectively on a national level. Although the British made numerous proposals for the formation of a parallel Arab Agency, Palestinian Arab leaders flatly rejected the notion because it would have placed the Arab and Jewish agencies on an equal political and moral level at a time when the indigenous people and their leaders were refusing to negotiate their stand on the Zionist settler-colonial project and demanding independence from British rule.

The Economic Transformation of the Palestine Mandate

As Owen noted in his study of economic development in the mandatory period, Palestine became a single economy connected to Britain yet with international borders. Furthermore, Palestine was subject to prevailing economic policies and practices, including a conservative fiscal policy, free trade, little or no governmental economic development policy (therefore making it largely laissez-faire), and a typical colonial attitude of discouraging industrialization in favor of the export of raw materials, minerals, and so on. The expenditures of the Palestine Mandate government in the 1920s and 1930s totaled 60 percent for administration, defense, and security; 12 percent for public works; and 12 percent for welfare. But Palestine was unique compared to other British colonial possessions. As we discussed above, this uniqueness lay in British encouragement of Jewish settler colonialism and in facilitating a modern, industrial economic enclave even at the expense of the economic (but not strategic) interests of the British Empire. Accordingly, the Jewish settlers created in Palestine an enclave society with a European organization and standard of living and demand for European goods and services.

These socioeconomic developments vastly escalated the pace of change and reoriented the structure of Palestinian economy and society. To begin with, the population increased rapidly. As two British censuses (in 1922 and 1931) and subsequent governmental estimates suggest, Palestine's population more than doubled between 1922 and 1946, from 750,000 to 1.8 million (see Table 3.1). The change resulted principally from a natural increase among the Palestinians and from the waves of migration of Jews into the country. The rate of increase of the migrant Jewish population, however, was higher than that of the natural increment among Palestinians, and therefore the Jewish ratio to the total population grew larger: from roughly 11 percent to 31 percent in twenty-four years. While the Palestinian population doubled in size, the Jewish population nearly tripled. Nevertheless, the Palestinian population was still greater by a ratio of two to one.

The population shifted toward urban centers, although the distribution between Jews and Palestinians was uneven. The Palestinian population was still largely rural in the mid-1930s, less so in the 1940s, with roughly 25–35 percent urban; the opposite held for the Jewish population, with roughly 75 percent urban in the same period. Palestinian urbanization between the intercensual years (1922–1931) was highest in Haifa (87 percent), Jaffa (63 percent), Ramleh (43 percent), and Jerusalem (37 percent).[85] Commensurate with this differential geographic distribution of the population was the occupational distribution. Estimates in 1936 indicate that 21 percent of the Jewish labor force worked in agriculture, 20 percent in industry, and 50 percent in services. In contrast, 62 percent of the Palestinian labor force was occupied in agriculture, 8 percent in manufacturing, and 14 percent in services.[86] Owen asserts that although Palestinians outnumbered Jews two to one, both labor forces were roughly the same size as a result of the age distribution (50 percent were below the age of fifteen) and low female participation in wage labor among the Palestinians and because most Jewish migrant-settlers were of the productive age (fifteen to twenty-nine years old). Furthermore, well over 90 percent of the Jews were literate, in contrast to 30 percent of the Palestinians.[87] And the two-tier wage system instituted by the British provided Jewish workers with a wage rate up to three times higher than for the Palestinians. Accordingly, the per capita income for Jews was also nearly three times as high as that for Palestinians: £P44 compared to £P17.

The First Economic Phase, 1920–1939. The structure and dynamics of Palestine's economy during the mandate went through two distinct phases. The first extended from the beginning of the mandate until 1939, and the second, a wartime economy, lasted until 1945, its consequences reaching into 1948, the year of al-Nakbah. In both periods the Jewish and Palestinian communities developed differentially, but during the war the Palestinian economy experienced much greater rates of change and transformation.

The British Palestine Mandate government and the Zionist organizations collected modern economic data from which we are able to assess the performance of Palestine's economy.[88] The data, however, are neither complete nor reliable, especially in Jewish versus Palestinian Arab comparisons. Nevertheless, all available economic data indicate, and all analysts argue, that Palestine's economy during the mandate grew but development differed significantly for Jews and Palestinians. Overall, there are two noteworthy features of Palestine's economy during the mandate period. First, unlike other British colonies, Palestine had high growth rates, which were due in large measure to the immense scale of Jewish migration and to the large amount of their capital transfers.[89] Adding further to these growth rates was the comparatively high economic demand of the Jewish settlers, who had a Western-style standard of living much higher than that of most indigenous Palestinians.

The second feature, which also derives from the scale and timing of Jewish migration into Palestine, was that the Palestine economy did *not* follow the world cycle of economic depression except in the early 1930s. In fact it was countercyclical and grew more rapidly because Jewish migration and capital transfers into Palestine came at the height of the world cycles of depression, when prejudice, anti-Semitism, and repression were greatest in Europe. The sharp worldwide decline in cereal prices in the early 1930s and simultaneous bad harvests, however, devastated Palestinian agriculturalists, especially the Palestinian peasantry, and associated businesses. In general, then, apart from the impact of the cereal crisis, the Palestinian economic cycle coincided with that of the Jewish settler-immigration. It was also severely affected by the Palestinian uprisings against the British authorities and Jewish settler-immigrants, especially between 1936 and 1939. In this latter period, Palestine's economy suffered, as did its people: The national income declined from £P33.8 million in 1936 to £P30.2 million in 1939. During World War II, however, as we see in the next section, the economy rebounded strongly.

Overall agricultural and industrial production rose significantly, along with trade, which value increased severalfold. Government revenue in the same period increased by six times. The greatest growth in agriculture occurred in fruit and vegetable production: Citrus export, for example, rose from 2.4 million cases in 1930/1931 to a peak of 13 million cases in 1938/1939. Land devoted to citrus production increased from 30,000 dunums in 1922 to 300,000 dunums in 1939. Contrary to the beginning of the mandate period, by the 1930s, ownership of citrus groves was evenly divided between Palestinian natives and Jewish settlers largely because Jewish owners had institutional support in credit and marketing. Palestinian landlords also developed banana plantations in the Jordan River valley (the Ghor).

While fruit and vegetables were grown in the irrigated plains and the Jordan River valley, cereals and olives were produced mainly in the rain-fed hills. Unlike citrus fruits, these agricultural goods were produced mostly by Palestinians. The Palestinian Arab economy remained overwhelmingly agrarian. In the plains large tracts of land were devoted to irrigated, export-oriented citrus fruits, while in the hill country cereal, olives, and olive oil were produced for self-consumption, the local market, and, if there was a surplus, for export. The whole Palestinian economy, however, turned more capitalistic as land became alienable, peasants more proletarianized, and wage labor more prevalent. Loss of land to Jewish purchases in the context of population pressure and agricultural stagnation created surplus labor and high unemployment in the countryside. Rural-to-town migration gained momentum, and more Palestinians entered the wage labor market. The Palestinian Arab urban population rose by 85 percent between 1931 and 1944, while the rural population increased by 40 percent in the same period.[90] Shantytowns sprang up around the coastal cities of Haifa and Jaffa, where displaced peasant poverty and insecurity were evident.

Substantial growth in manufacturing also occurred during the first phase. The number of industrial enterprises rose from 1,240 in 1913 to 3,505 in 1927 and about 6,000 in 1936. Industrial workers also grew in number (from 17,955 in 1927 to 48,000 in 1939), while industrial output jumped from £P3.89 million in 1927 to £P9.1 million in 1936.[91] Industrial enterprises, however, remained largely small handicraft workshops. Very few factories employed 100 workers or more, and only a fraction ran on motor power. By European standards, Palestine's industry was backward. Jewish immigrant-settlers owned the majority of Palestine's industry. According to an Esco Foundation study, the number of Jewish industrial enterprises increased from 2,475 in 1929 to 5,606 in 1937, and the number of Jewish workers rose from 10,968 to 29,986 in the same period. Based on a different definition and size of industrial enterprise, the 1939 government census of industry found 13,678 Jewish workers engaged in industry in contrast to only 4,117 "non-Jewish" (Palestinian Arab) workers.[92] Nevertheless, the number of Palestinian wage laborers increased steadily throughout the 1930s as opportunities in public works and private enterprises, including some Jewish ventures, increased (e.g., in citrus groves, the Nesher Cement Company, the Palestine Potash Company). However, much of Palestinian wage labor remained seasonal and itinerant, and a reserve army of labor grew in size and destitution by the end of the 1930s, contributing to the violent explosion of the 1936 revolt.

Capital invested and the value of annual industrial production rose by a factor of nearly fivefold during the 1930s.[93] Following the colonial and

TABLE 3.4 Estimates of Palestine's National Income and Its Sectoral Composition

National Income (£ million)			
	Arabs	*Jewish*	*Total*
1922		1.6	
1936	16.0	17.8	33.8
		23.4 (GDP)	
1939		17.2	30.2
1940		20.6	
1945		88.2	

National Income per Capita (£)		
	Arab	*Jewish*
1923–1924		20
1935		50
1936	17	44
1944	165	

Sectoral Contribution

Output value in agriculture and manufacturing in Palestinian economy (£ million)

	Agriculture	*Manufacturing*
1927		3.89
1936	5.6	5.4
1939	5.59	
1943	19.0	
1944–1945	21.8	

Sectoral distribution of output in the Arab and Jewish economies, 1936 (%)[a]

	Agriculture	*Manufacturing*	*Construction*	*Services*
Arab	25.0	13.0	2.0	60.0
Jewish	9.5	22.0	8.6	59.9

[a]Jewish income measured as NDP.
SOURCE: R. Owen, "Economic Development in Mandatory Palestine (1918–1948)," in G. T. Abed, ed., *The Palestinian Economy: Studies in Development Under Prolonged Occupation* (London: Routledge, 1988), 26.

postcolonial model, both Jews and Palestinians produced more for import substitution and less for export. Unlike the Palestinians, who followed the colonial model of producing textiles, processed foodstuff, cigarettes, and leather goods, the Jewish immigrant-settlers entered as well into the production of metalwork, chemicals, and electrical products along with other, more technically advanced goods. The uneven economic development patterns between Palestinian natives and Jewish immigrant-settlers reflected in estimates of national income, national income per capita, sectoral contribution, and sectoral distribution of output are reflected in Table 3.4. Notably, while the impact of Jewish industrial activity on Palestinian industrial development is difficult to assess, it is possible to argue that it worked to the Palestinians' detriment, especially as the two communities engaged, at different times during the mandate, in one-sided or mutual economic boycotts.

Palestine's external trade climbed during this period from £P5.73 million in imports, £P1.39 million in exports, and an additional £P599,753 in transit and reexport in 1922 to £P14.6 million in imports, £P5.12 million in exports, and £P898,554 in transit and reexport in 1939. Value of trade per capita increased from £P5,732 in 1931 to £P11,345 in 1937. Similar to all dependent colonial economies, the ratio of exports as a percentage of imports ranged from 24 to 37 percent between 1922 and 1939.[94] Palestine consistently carried a trade deficit because the local industry did not grow fast enough to satisfy the high influx of immigrants. The detrimental effects of such an imbalance were offset by the Jewish capital transfers. An important reorientation of external trade also occurred during the mandate period. As in most colonies, Palestine's regional trade declined (from 60 percent of total value to 10 percent in 1939) and increased its trade with Europe.[95]

The consequences of the first two decades of the Palestine Mandate's economic growth and development varied widely between the two communities, the native Palestinians and the Jewish immigrant-settlers, and they were increasingly confronting each other politically and violently. While economic growth strengthened and consolidated the Jewish immigrant-settler community and its political leadership, the uneven, differential, and rapid capitalist economic change polarized the Palestinian people; dispossessed and substantially derogated the well-being of increasing numbers of the peasantry; atomized, displaced, and proletarianized much of it; and fractionalized Palestinian social and political leadership. Communal-based social relations, which had long been on the decline, continued a sharp descent. The increasing impoverishment and declining conditions of the peasantry seemed to generate among them a shared sense not only of dispossession and deprivation but also of oppression. As traditional hamula, kin, religious, and notable-based solidarities waned and were not replaced successfully by more modern, effective, associational ones, the Palestinian nationalist movement resisting Zionist dispossession and seeking independence from Britain faced significant challenges.

The Palestinian War Economy, 1939–1945. During World War II, Palestine became a strategic outpost for the British in the Middle East and eastern Mediterranean region. Palestine became the fortified base of large land, air, and naval military forces; the terminus of oil pipelines from Iraq; and the location of a key oil refinery. The British devised an economic plan—through the Middle East Supply Center (in Cairo), the War Supplies Board, and the Directorate of War Production—to mobilize local and regional agricultural and industrial production for both military and civilian needs in order to reduce dependence on external (European and U.S.) sources of supply. This successful strategy resulted in rapid economic development of nearly all sectors of Palestine's economy, though it was uneven between the Jewish and Palestinian parts. The economy rebounded from the recession and dislocations of the late 1930s, and income levels and standards of living rose. As significant, this effort accelerated the process of social change. In a short period of five years, Palestine had undergone a profound structural transformation.

British mobilization in the agricultural sector produced mixed results, especially as cereal and primarily citrus markets suffered. Citrus export to Britain almost ceased; some orange crops, however, were sold locally and to the military or were juiced. Tremendous increase in potato, olive, and poultry production occurred. Output value in agriculture jumped from £P5.59 million in 1939 to £P21.8 million in 1944–1945.[96] However, export of citrus fruit dropped precipitously during the war: from 15.3 million cases valued at £P4.35 between 1938 and 1939 to 4,594 cases valued at £P3.51 million between 1942 and 1943.[97] Banks made cash/credit advances, some guaranteed by the Palestine Mandate government, to maintain citrus groves. By the end of the war in 1945, citrus production recovered.

Industry also underwent a major expansion. There was a phenomenal increase in industrial capacity, output, and types of products supplied to the military, Palestine's internal market, and the region. One estimate shows that output in Jewish industries jumped by 200 percent, whereas that in Palestinian-owned industry increased by 77 percent.[98] By 1946 the number of industrial enterprises rose to well above 6,000, the majority Jewish owned and only several hundred owned by Palestinians. The *Statistical Abstract of Palestine*, probably using a different definition of industrial enterprise, estimates that in 1939 there were 339 Palestinian Arab industrial establishments employing 4,117 workers, which increased by 1943 to 1,558 enterprises employing 8,804 workers.[99] By 1945 the number of workers in Palestine's industry rose to 70,000–80,000. The percentage increase of workers in industry, most of them Jewish, was 145 percent between 1939 and 1942.[100] The number of Jewish industrial workers jumped from 30,000 in 1936 to 61,000 in 1946, of which 46,000 worked in large industrial establishments.[101] Beside the rise in output and labor, there were sharp increases in capital investment (e.g., from £P11.1 million in 1937 to £P20.5 million in 1943),[102] power use, and wages.

Most remarkable was the production of military and other sophisticated hardware (antitank mines, steel containers, hydraulic jacks, and bodies for military vehicles), especially in the peak years of the Allied North African campaign against German general Erwin Rommel's Afrika Korps. In a report dated April 23, 1943, Sir Douglas Harris, chairman of the Palestine War Supply Board, stated that "the share of the Jewish population in both capital investment and value of production in industry is about 85 percent. The Jewish share in industrial production for the Army, however, exceeds 95 percent of the total."[103] By 1944, after the victory over Rommel, these Jewish factories shifted to the production of civilian goods already in short supply (industrial machinery, diesel engines, fishing trawlers, tools, spare parts for automobiles, electrical and medical equipment, textiles and clothing, home utensils, and pharmaceuticals).[104] Also during this period the Jewish-owned diamond-cutting and -polishing industry (thirty factories employing 3,000 workers) expanded.

Production in small farms and large estates owned by Palestinians increased sharply and was accompanied by the decline, from 180,000 in 1939 to 100,000 in 1944, of rural male laborers who derived a livelihood from agriculture.[105] Delayed British efforts to introduce modern production techniques proved ineffective. Without a comprehensive road network, production in Palestinian Arab agriculture remained largely traditional, especially on the smaller and more remote farms. In industry only a tiny fraction of the Palestinian enterprises were large, powered by electricity or oil (Palestinian industry in 1942 had a total horsepower of 3,812, Jewish industry 57,410), or employed more than 100 workers. The majority of the enterprises were small workshops using human and animal power, employing small amounts of capital and small numbers of workers, and organized along traditional lines. The cultural and technological divide between Palestinians and European settler Jews could not have been more stark. The net national product of the Jewish economy in Palestine nearly doubled during the war, from £P16.7 million to £P29.9 million valued at 1936 prices.[106] Comparable figures for the Palestinian Arab economy are unavailable.

Accompanying the growth and diversification of the Palestinian manufacturing and productive bourgeoisie was the rise of a commercial and professional stratum. The Jerusalem Chamber of Commerce membership list included 118 manufacturing enterprises in 1947 as contrasted with 85 in 1938. In addition, it listed 260 businesses ranging from commission agents to wholesalers of cereals, textiles, and so on. There were also 150 retail and service businesses registered. Jaffa's Chamber of Commerce listed 670 businesses, of which 64 were light manufacturing establishments, 41 small enterprises such as contractors and printers, and nearly 500 retailers and merchants of a vast array of goods and services, including banks, hotels, and bus and taxi companies. Jaffa also had the Palestine Brass Foundry and the Palestine Building and Construction Company.[107] Liberal professionals such as doctors, teachers, and lawyers sharply increased in numbers as well.

The heated economic expansion of the war period generated in Palestine large labor demands; labor shortages developed as early as 1942. Arab workers from Egypt, Transjordan, Syria, and Lebanon were imported by the British but could not ease the strong demand. Rachel Taqqu estimates that "by the 1940's, when labor mobilization reached a wartime peak, the total

TABLE 3.5 Estimated Number Engaged in Each Branch of Production and
Average Output per Head in the Arab Community, 1944

Branch of Production	Number Engaged (thousands)	Total Income (£ million)	Average Income per Person (£)
Agriculture, livestock, etc.	152	20.4	134
Industry and handicrafts	13	3.3	254
Housing	–	2.9	–
Building and construction	20	2.9	145
War department, civilian employment	26	2.7	104
Palestinian troops	2	0.2	121
Transportation and communications	15	3.5	233
Commerce and finance (hotels, etc.)	29	6.9	238
Government and local authorities	32	4.8	150
Other	11	2.0	182
Total	300	49.6	165

SOURCE: P. J. Loftus, *National Income of Palestine*. Cited in R. Taqqu, "Peasants into Workers: Internal Labor Migrations and the Arab Village Under the Mandate," in J. S. Migdal, ed., *Palestinian Society and Politics* (Princeton, NJ: Princeton University Press, 1980), 267.

Arab wage force had expanded to include nearly one third of the entire male [Palestinian] Arab population of working age."[108] According to Taqqu, this was roughly 100,000 workers outside agriculture. In industries other than agriculture, the number of wageworkers in Palestine increased from 169,000 in 1939 to 285,000 (including 23,000 in the armed forces) in 1944.[109]

As a consequence of the demand for labor, average industrial wage earnings rose by 200 percent for Palestinians and 258 percent for Jews; those for unskilled construction workers advanced by 405 percent and 329 percent, respectively. Despite the rise in their wages, the unskilled Palestinian workers remained disadvantaged in comparison to Jewish laborers. Similarly, in the rural areas agricultural wages rose; however, the prices of agricultural inputs shot up sevenfold by 1943. According to one estimate, the index of farm prices rose steadily from 100 in 1938–1939 to 560 in 1943–1944.[110] This dramatic rural economic development quadrupled agricultural income between 1939 and 1944/1945 and provided some segments of the Palestinian peasantry with a "large measure of prosperity," the largest in a very long time.[111] Table 3.5 provides estimates of the number of Palestinian workers in all branches of production. Socioeconomic differentiation and polarization in the population swelled the ranks of both the middle and landless peasantry and also the urban middle class and the city poor. Nearly one-third of Palestine's Arab peasantry was landless by the end of the war, and urban misery increased tremendously. By the end of 1944, 70 percent of Jaffa's Palestinian Arab population lived in slums; the figure for Haifa was 41 percent.[112]

With the rapid formation of the Palestinian wage-earning labor force in the 1940s, working-class organizations sprang up throughout the urban centers.[113] Established in 1925, the Palestine Arab Workers Society (PAWS) grew rapidly during the war: from 2,000 members in 1939 to over 9,000 members in 1943 and 15,000 in 1945. Unions were especially active in the coastal industrial cities of Haifa and Jaffa and in Jerusalem. Another major union, the Federation of Arab Trade Unions (FATU), emerged in 1942 in a split with PAWS. PAWS' political orientation was social democratic, while FATU was communist influenced. FATU concentrated on organizing skilled workers and affiliated worker associations in such large establishments as the British-owned Iraq Petroleum Company, Shell Oil, Consolidated Refineries, the Haifa Harbor, the Royal Depot at Haifa Bay, and the Haifa Public Works Department. Its membership may have reached 4,500. While originally syndicalist, both PAWS and FATU became increasingly politicized by the end of the war. Branches and individuals from both trade union organizations were connected to and influenced by a small leftist Palestinian party, the Arab League for National Liberation (ALNL), founded in 1944 and led by a communist, Emile Tuma. They also were closely linked to the radical and nationalist Arab Intellectuals League, led by Musa Dajani and Mukhlis 'Amr, which boasted 2,000 members.

Palestinian wage labor by the end of the mandate had "scored impressive gains, as witnessed by its growth, activism, and independence. There is no doubt that it had succeeded in forging a relatively strong class consciousness and a working-class culture."[114] The labor movement achieved such accomplishments in the absence of progressive labor laws. While early in the war the British encouraged unionization as part of their labor recruitment policy, by the end of the war the authorities were hostile to the increasingly politicized movement. But neither the labor movement nor the political organizations were sufficiently strong to enable them, along with the more traditional leadership and parties, to succeed in the national political struggle against dispossession in the postwar era.

The Palestinian Struggle Against Dispossession

During the last years of the Ottoman era, Palestinian and other Arab leaders lobbied the Ottoman authorities against the Zionist project. Intellectuals' criticisms of Zionism and peasant resistance to evictions from land purchased by Zionist Jewish agencies indicated concern about the threat of Zionism and presaged the character of the forthcoming resistance. Concern turned into alarm, anger, and hostility when the League of Nations incorporated the Balfour Declaration into the Mandate of Palestine. Discontent spread wider and deeper in Palestinian society as the implementation of the Palestine Mandate's pro-Zionist provisions, especially those of Jewish immigration and land purchases, proceeded. In short, Palestinian actions against both Zionism and the British Mandate of Palestine became highly politicized. Small, seemingly unimportant social and religious incidents quickly erupted into major political confrontations between Palestinians and Jewish immigrant-settlers. Capitalist economic changes that had negative impacts on the peasantry and the urban poor also triggered political uprisings. By the 1930s the clashes and riots targeted the British authorities of the Palestine Mandate government as well.

The process of Jewish empowerment and the commensurate inverse process of Palestinian disenfranchisement, both highly politicized under British auspices, developed through three stages that coincided roughly with the three decades of British colonial rule. The period from 1920 to 1929 culminated in serious rioting, political conflict and violence, and critical British government investigative and policy reports: the Shaw Commission report, the Hope Simpson report, and the Passfield white paper. The period from 1930 to 1939 witnessed a general Palestinian revolt between 1936 and 1939 and forced the British government to issue the 1937 Peel Commission report and the 1939 white paper. The period from 1940 to 1948, a time of dramatic economic transformation and political conflict, saw the establishment of a United Nations partition plan in 1947, an internal Jewish-Palestinian war, the destruction of Palestine, and the rise of Israel as a Jewish state.

The 1920–1929 Decade

The first sign of Palestinian discontent with the new British order arose in April 1920 on the occasion of the Nabi Musa festival. A minor incident led to an assault by Palestinians on a procession of Jews. Although it was investigated by a British-appointed commission, the commission's recommendations were not published. Riots also occurred on May Day 1921 in a charged Palestinian and regional political climate: Arab discontentment with the results of the San Remo (Allied) conference, which awarded the eastern Arab mandates to Britain and France, led to political tension in Palestine, Syria, and Lebanon and a revolt in Iraq.

In Palestine mass Jewish immigration commenced in accordance with the British policy of establishing a Jewish national home. Palestinians perceived the arrival of 10,000 Jewish immigrants between December 1920 and April

1921 as a harbinger of the future. A riot that started in Jaffa between radical leftist and centrist Zionist groups quickly involved the Palestinians, who also attacked the immigration hostel, a symbolic target of their hostility. Forty-eight Palestinians and forty-seven Jews were killed and 219 people wounded. From Jaffa, Palestinian rioting spread to rural areas, fueled by wild rumors of Jews killing Arabs. Several Palestinians were killed by British soldiers in an effort to defend Jewish settlements.

The British appointed a committee to investigate the incident. The Haycraft Commission, led by Sir Thomas Haycraft, chief justice of Palestine, found that the riots were spontaneous and that Palestinian Arabs felt "discontent with and hostility toward" the Jews because of "political and economic causes, especially the issue of Jewish immigration into Palestine."[115] To underscore this point, the commission cited the testimony of David Eder, acting chair of the Zionist Commission, who commented that "there can only be one National Home in Palestine, and that a Jewish one, and no equality in the partnership between Jews and Arabs, but a Jewish predominance as soon as the numbers of that race are sufficiently increased."[116] The immediate result of the riots and the commission report was the suspension of Jewish immigration by the British-appointed high commissioner, or governor, of Palestine. Two months later the British authorities rescinded this order and Jewish immigration into Palestine resumed.

While peasants and the urban poor rioted and used violence against Jewish settlers (but not yet against the British authorities), the Palestinian people in the towns and villages organized themselves into Muslim-Christian associations, Arab literary clubs, the Higher Islamic Council, and other groups in a national effort to resist Zionist designs. The elite launched a movement to unite their political efforts to influence British policy. In December 1920 a Palestine Arab Congress representing, it claimed, "all classes and creeds of the Arab people of Palestine,"[117] was held in Haifa and elected a twenty-four-member leadership called the Palestine Arab Executive. It joined the top leaders of the two competing notable families of Jerusalem who had national stature, the Husseinis and the Nashashibis. The political platform of the congress included condemnation of the Balfour Declaration, the idea of a Jewish national home, and the mandate's support of it; rejection of the principle of mass Jewish immigration into Palestine; and the establishment of a national government in Palestine.[118]

The last point was especially significant because Palestine, like Syria and Iraq, was designated by the League of Nations as a class A mandate, which required the mandatory to establish a national government with legislative and administrative structures. Yet Palestine was treated more like a class B mandate in which these powers were invested in the mandatory. However, diplomatic pressure by the Palestine Arab delegation that lobbied in London and Geneva (at the League of Nations) led the British colonial secretary, Winston Churchill, to clarify the Balfour Declaration. In 1922 the Churchill white paper reasserted British pro-Zionist policy and proposed to allow Jewish immigration only in accordance with the economic "absorptive capacity" of the country and to establish a legislative council. Once again the Palestine Arab Congress countered by proposing the creation of an elected representative legislative council like those in the neighboring class A mandates of Syria and Lebanon, but the British refused.

In October 1923 the British once again offered to create an Arab Agency analogous to the Jewish Agency already established under the provisions of the mandate. The Palestinian leadership again turned down the proposal because they believed that an analogy was unfair given demographic and historical conditions. Further, the Jewish Agency was elected by the whole Jewish community, whereas the proposed Arab Agency would be appointed by the British authorities. Accordingly, the British blocked the Palestinian leadership's quest for an elected parliament for self-rule, leaving the Palestine Arab Executive merely a mouthpiece; unlike the Jewish Agency, the Palestine Arab Executive was not officially recognized by the Palestine Mandate government[119] and therefore had no official advisory or consultative status. The Palestine Arab Congress, which met regularly, remained the principal Palestinian representative, despite the deep fissures in the nationalist ranks, until it was replaced by the Arab Higher Committee (AHC) in 1936. The demands of the congresses (the fifth in 1923 and the sixth in 1924) presented to the British authorities evolved as economic and financial policies came to the fore. An early harbinger, the question of land—the critical issue of the 1929 violent political upheaval—was considered in the 1922 congress, where those assembled demanded protection for small peasants against expropriation, an indication of the fast deteriorating economic conditions of Palestine's peasantry.

Although the Palestine Arab Executive united the rival political clans of the Husseinis and the Nashashibis in an organization that spoke for all Palestinians, their rivalry actually intensified and undermined the unity of the struggle against the settler Zionists and the British. What exacerbated the rivalry was the successful campaign of al-Hajj Amin al-Husseini against the Nashashibi candidate to be appointed mufti in 1921 by Herbert Samuel, as well as elected president of the Supreme Muslim Council, who controlled the Islamic awqaf and their financial resources; shari'a courts and their officialdom; mosques; schools; orphanages; and other institutions to which he could appoint or dismiss many employees. The mandatory government legitimized and recognized the religious leadership of al-Hajj Amin al-Husseini, and by the mufti launched vigorous religious initiatives and an Islamic revival during the 1920s. He expanded welfare and health clinics, built an orphanage, renovated and supported schools, and organized a tree-planting program on waqf lands. Most symbolic, however, was his project of restoring the two mosques—Al-Aqsa and the Dome of the Rock—on the al-Haram al-Sharif in Jerusalem through an international Muslim fund-raising campaign.

To counter the influence of al-Hajj Amin and the ascendant Husseinis' control of the Palestine Arab Executive, the Nashashibis attempted to form an opposing power base. Raghib al-Nashashibi formed national Muslim societies and the National Party (1923) and encouraged the creation of peasant parties (1924). These latter moves were supported by the Zionists as an effort to split Palestinian ranks along social class lines. The National Party countered the Arab Executive by arguing that it failed to change British policy through opposition and thus it would be more productive to work, as it were, in cooperation with the British authorities. These political developments both reflected and fueled the bitter rivalry between the two nationalist factions, which in turn kept the Palestinians from achieving their larger political goals.

The peasant parties or groups were in the vanguard of the violent struggle against the Zionists in the 1920s and the British authorities in the 1930s. The leaders of the peasantry, perhaps more than the elite politicians, demanded immediate social and economic protection against the peasants' worsening situation. The platforms of the rural political groups were noteworthy for their attention to economic matters. They called on the government to adopt specific policies: reduction of taxes; extension of the maturity of debts; provision of long-term loans; building of roads, schools, and the educational system; and the encouragement of agricultural cooperation.

Land purchases and immigration of Jews, along with the infrastructural buildup of the Jewish community under British auspices, created general alarm, but Palestinian diplomacy and political tactics failed to change British policy. Concurrently, during the 1920s a sudden downturn in the economy caused a sharp decline in the well-being of all Palestinians, especially the peasantry. Palestinian concern was reflected in the reunification of the Palestinian nationalist factions in the seventh Palestine Arab Congress, held in 1928. Its resolutions stressed the economic dilemma, calling for tax reform, social welfare for the workers, and increased public expenditure in education. In addition it repeated its abiding political concerns and demands: "The people of Palestine cannot and will not tolerate the present absolute colonial system of government, and urgently insist upon and demand the establishment of a representative body to lay its own Constitution and guarantee the formation of a democratic parliamentary Government."[120]

Although violence had largely subsided by 1921, a combination of factors—Jewish immigration, land purchases, economic privileging and British political stonewalling, economic deterioration for the Palestinians, unemployment, and impoverishment of the peasantry—created a highly charged political situation. As was often the case, a minor religious incident in 1929 at the Western (Wailing) Wall of the ancient Jewish Temple triggered a crisis over rights to the wall and an explosion of violence.[121] Stoked by wild rumor, demonstrations and riots started in Jerusalem and spread to cities such as Haifa, Jaffa, Safad, and Hebron, where Palestinian and Jewish mobs murdered 133 Jews and 116 Palestinians before the violence was suppressed by the British authorities.

The British government response was predictable. It set up a commission, the Shaw Commission, to study the causes of the disturbances; sent another, the Hope Simpson Commission, to conduct a thorough study of the socioeconomic conditions in the country; and issued a policy statement, the Passfield white paper. The Shaw Commission found that the disturbances were spontaneous, perpetrated in the heat of religious and political tension, and were not against British authority. It determined that contributing factors to the disturbances were Palestinian apprehension over Jewish immigration, which it found excessive in 1925–1926, and indiscriminate land sales to Jewish organizations that was leading to the creation of "a landless and discontented class."[122] In short, the Shaw Commission concluded that the basic cause of the disturbances was the Palestinian people's feeling "of disappointment of their political and national aspirations and fear for their economic future."

In his report Sir John Hope Simpson analyzed the land problem and the social and economic conditions of the peasantry in Palestine. He found that the area of arable land was far less than assumed. Substantial growth of the Palestinian Arab population during the decade combined with increased land sales to the Jews created landless Palestinians. For example, in a survey of 104 representative villages, 29.4 percent of the families were landless.[123] The average family holding in these villages totaled 75 dunums, far less than the 130 dunums, the "lot viable," that Hope Simpson determined necessary for adequate income in cereal cultivation. In every village it visited, the commission heard complaints of diminution in the size of landholdings. Despite the numerous protective ordinances passed by the Palestine Mandate government, the most vulnerable in the rural areas (in addition to the landless peasants) were the tenant farmers, who made up 20 percent of the agricultural cultivators.[124] Furthermore, after centuries of use and abuse of land, the yield was low. Thus the majority of the Palestinian population already lived on farms that did not provide a subsistence minimum.[125] As Hope Simpson described the situation: "Evidence from every possible source tends to support the conclusion that the Arab fellah [peasant] cultivator is in a desperate position. He has no capital for his farm. He is, on the contrary, heavily in debt. His rent is rising, he has to pay very heavy taxes, and the rate of interest on his loans is incredibly high."[126]

From mid-1929 into the early 1930s, the prices of agricultural goods fell sharply: Wheat dropped from £P11 to £P6 per ton, barley from £P5 to

£P3, and durra from £P8 to £P4. "The net income of the family . . . has reached vanishing point. . . . It is not an exaggeration to state that the fellah population as a class is hopelessly bankrupt."[127] Indebtedness became widespread, devastating, and punishable by imprisonment. In 1930 Hope Simpson reported that the average indebtedness of the peasant was £P27, on which 30 percent interest was paid, while the average income was between £P25–30 per year.[128] In the urban areas, Hope Simpson also found "serious and general unemployment" among workers and craftsmen as well as a sharp fall in wage rates. Among the skilled artisans, carpenters, and stone dressers, for example, wages fell by 50 percent. Both the rural peasants and the urban workers found themselves in desperate conditions.

Hope Simpson concluded his report with a number of specific and general policy proposals. For immediate relief, he recommended ending imprisonment for debt, exemption from taxation for any peasant making less than £P30 per annum, credit and education for the peasantry, and for the longer term, extensive agricultural development programs. He strongly argued, as did the Shaw Commission, that "there is at the present time and with the present methods of Arab cultivation no margin of land available for agricultural settlement by new immigrants, with the exception of such undeveloped land as the various Jewish Agencies hold in reserve."[129] He urged regulation of land transfer and tight restrictions on immigration. Although he said that Palestinian Arab unemployment was not directly linked to Jewish immigration, he nevertheless stated that the policy of the Palestine government in regard to immigration must be determined by unemployment in Palestine overall, not just in the Jewish community. He recognized that "it is wrong that a Jew from Poland, Lithuania or the Yemen, should be admitted to fill an existing vacancy, while in Palestine there are already workmen capable of filling that vacancy, who are unable to find employment."[130]

The recommendations of Hope Simpson and the Shaw Commission were largely reflected in the Passfield white paper, a policy paper the British government issued in 1930 in an effort to address the causes of the 1929 disturbances. In addition, the Passfield white paper proposed that it was time to develop self-rule institutions in Palestine, although the legislative council it proposed was styled after that in the 1922 Churchill white paper.[131]

Lord Passfield was Sidney Webb, the famous Fabian socialist; he and his white paper came under vigorous attack by the Zionists and pro-Zionists in Britain and Palestine. This political pressure overwhelmed the minority government of Prime Minister Ramsay MacDonald. In a letter the Palestinian Arabs dubbed the "black letter," MacDonald in effect repudiated and reversed the policy changes of the Passfield white paper. This policy reversal kept in place the very social, economic, and institutional processes that the British authorities had determined to be the causes of the disturbances in

Palestine. Indeed these processes picked up momentum in the first five years of the 1930s, leading to a greater Palestinian revolt not only against the Jewish settlers but also directly against British rule.

The 1930s and the 1936–1939 "Arab Revolt"

Through moderate political-diplomatic tactics of petitions, testimonies, delegations, public meetings, congresses, and resolutions with the Palestine Mandate government, elite Palestinian leaders achieved little.[132] According to Philip Mattar, by 1929 the Palestinian people "had become frustrated, more militant, and anti-British."[133] The MacDonald "black letter" added proof of the ineffectiveness of moderate politics. A new tone of militancy imbued newspaper articles, reports, and public speeches that challenged the traditional notables' leadership and unsuccessful methods, and there emerged a new generation of leaders.[134] An all-out revolt was in the making.

The root causes of the revolt remained unchanged: the Palestinians' antipathy toward pro-Zionist British policies and their inability to advance toward self-rule. The new British high commissioner, Sir Arthur Wauchope, pushed his superiors in the Colonial Office in London for the establishment of a Palestinian legislative council. Pro-Zionist politicians defeated this proposal in the British Parliament. The rejection frustrated Palestinian Arabs because neighboring Arab mandates, especially Syria, Iraq, and (earlier) Egypt, had made strides toward sovereignty.

Exacerbating the situation for the peasantry was a land tax, introduced by the British authorities in 1928, based on the value of the higher crop prices of the boom years of 1924–1927. These "crippling tax rates" and a sharp drop in income may have led some peasants and landlords to sell their land.[135] Palestinian land brokers, usurers, and middlemen were especially active in land sales to the Jewish organizations, despite being pilloried and on occasion threatened with physical harm. The difficult economic situation led the mandate government to remit the taxes of the poorest peasants, as recommended by Hope Simpson. Beyond doubt, it was also this economic situation that spurred the peasants to revolt against the British authorities, who in their view created the conditions that continued to jeopardize their place in their homeland.

More alarming for the Palestinians in this economic context was the sudden and spectacular rise of Jewish immigration into the country in the first half of the 1930s. In spite of all the recommendations of various commissions and the consequent governmental decisions to regulate and reduce the number of Jewish immigrants into the country in accordance with the vague concept of "absorptive capacity," tens of thousands of Jews poured into Palestine, the rise of Nazism in Germany having pushed them out of central Europe. Only 4,075 immigrated into Palestine in 1931 and 9,553 in

1932, but the numbers soared to 30,327 in 1933, 42,359 in 1934, and 61,854 in 1935. As noted above, the ratio of Jews within the total population of Palestine jumped from 16 percent in 1931 to 28 percent in 1936.

These contextual factors coincided with the death in 1934 of the head of the Palestine Arab Executive, the organization's demise, and the emergence of more militant groupings, especially the Istiqlal (Independence) Party. These new organizations were pan-Arabist and critical of the moderate Palestinian leadership and its diplomatic methods. They included such articulate and modern men as Awni 'Abdul-Hadi, Akram Zu'ayter, Izzat Darwaza, and Ahmad al-Shuqayri (who became the first chairman of the PLO in 1964). These leaders advocated strong active opposition to the Zionists and, significantly, to the British and the mandate governments; they called for the dismantlement of the mandate and its replacement by a parliamentary Palestinian Arab government. Such views captured the imagination and support of a frustrated and combative public. By 1936 a number of Palestinian political parties reflecting varied socioeconomic and ideological interests had formed.[136] These included the Youth Congress, the National Defense Party (dominated by the Nashashibis), the Palestine Arab Party (dominated by al-Hajj Amin and the Husseinis), the Reform Party, and the National Bloc Party. A Palestine Communist Party had existed since the early 1920s but had little direct influence.[137] It called for an independent Palestine for both Palestinian Arabs and Jews free from British imperialism. Unable to overcome the intercommunal conflict, it split into separate Arab and Jewish parties by the late 1930s.

The activism that produced the new political groupings found a stronger and more militant echo in an underground religious organization led by Sheikh 'Izz ed-Din al-Qassam. Anchored within the rural peasantry, the urban poor, and displaced peasants, this movement was inspired by al-Qassam's concern for social justice and his spirit of direct, revolutionary action. Although a religious cleric, al-Qassam demanded that the mufti supply money for arms, not for mosque renovation and building. Like the Istiqlalis, pan-Arabists, and nationalists, he became convinced that the diplomatic and political tactics of the elite leadership not only were ineffective in securing Palestinian rights but also had brought the country to the edge of disaster.

Nationalists believed the alarmingly high influx of Jewish immigrants was leading to a majority Jewish nation in Palestine. Al-Qassam and his followers took up arms in the countryside as the renewed urban violence and Jewish counterviolence intensified. In November 1935 he and his band of guerrillas were ambushed and killed by British troops. His martyrdom, self-sacrifice, and commitment to the national cause offered the Palestinian people a more honorable and popular model of struggle than that of the elite leadership. A large number of youths throughout Palestine formed guerrilla bands, called themselves Ikhwan al-Qassam (Brothers of al-Qassam), and launched an armed struggle against both the Jewish settlers and the British authorities.

The Ikhwan al-Qassam killing of two Jews in a bus ambush on April 15, 1936, triggered a retaliation by a Jewish militia, the Haganah, who murdered two Palestinians. Counterattacks and further killings in Jaffa led the British to declare a state of emergency. On April 19, 1936, Istiqlal leaders and other nationalists announced a general strike that spread throughout the country and involved middle-class businessmen and professionals in local leadership roles.[138] Organizations of the emergent Palestinian civil society (unions, chambers of commerce, the All-Palestine Conference of Arab Students, etc.) and traditional bedouin and clan leaders supported the strike. To lead the strike, the elite leadership quickly reorganized into the Arab Higher Committee, made up of representatives of the new parties under the chairmanship of the mufti, al-Hajj Amin al-Husseini, who although appointed and beholden to the British authorities, had no alternative but to join the militants. The AHC represented all political factions and social sectors of Palestinian society and announced its goals to be the complete cessation of Jewish immigration, the prohibition of land transfer to Jews, and the establishment of a national government responsible to a representative council.

The strike lasted six months, and before it ended, civil disobedience turned into armed insurrection. In the countryside the revolt was to a considerable extent spontaneously organized, autonomous, and anchored in peasant norms.[139] There was wide variation in the recruitment, organization, leadership, and command structures. Recruitment ranged from voluntary enrollment to selection by hamula or family to selection by village elders to compulsion. Despite coercion in recruitment or in material contributions, such methods did not alienate the villagers.[140] Most peasant families contributed men, money, food, shelter, and materiel enthusiastically. "A *tha'ir* [rebel] was often the whole family's responsibility. It collected money to purchase his rifle and decided which young men would fight and which would stay at home."[141]

The rebels organized themselves into guerrilla bands (*fasa'il*) of a few men with a leader (*qa'id*), on either a temporary or permanent basis. Guerrilla fasa'il often used hit-and-run tactics, at night and principally in their local areas. When called upon, they operated under a regional or national command structure, especially after the arrival of Fawzi al-Qawuqji, a military man of Syrian heritage who also served in the 1947–1948 conflict. Local guerrilla fasa'il became more effective upon integration into nationally coordinated action. Often, however, they responded dramatically and spontaneously (an act they called *faz'a*) in the aid of neighboring village bands or forces under British encirclement or for sounding the alarm upon British troop advance. The local guerrilla bands had the advantage of their small size and knowledge of the terrain to escape the British and hide among their kinspeople and fellow villagers.

In the course of the revolt, the rebels gained control of much of the countryside. They then were faced with administering it. They developed systems of taxation, supply, and armaments. Rebel courts were created to adjudicate village civil conflicts and criminal cases. These replaced traditional institutions; elders and their role in social mediation, conflict resolution, and adjudication; and the British courts. Some rebel leaders codified new regulations in written form and appointed qadis (judges) and other officials.

Both the strike and the armed insurrection were thus a direct challenge to British authority. To counter the revolt, the high commissioner quickly initiated, on April 19, a series of harsh emergency regulations and practices that further hardened Palestinian attitudes. The strike was declared illegal on June 2, 1936, and in late September, after the assassination of a British district commissioner, the British authorities arrested, incarcerated, or deported (to the Seychelles) strike leaders, prominent members of the Higher Arab Committee, union leaders, and others. They censored or closed down newspapers, imposed tough curfews, and meted out collective punishment to villages and city quarters. They also conducted search and seizure operations without warrants in an effort to disarm the populace.[142]

In an early attempt to end the unrest, the British appointed a new commission, the Peel Commission, to investigate Palestinian grievances. Its report lucidly stated that the causes of this revolt were the same as those that had triggered the "disturbances" of 1920, 1921, 1929, and 1933: "the desire of the Arabs for national independence" and "their hatred and fear of the establishment of the Jewish National Home." Its recommendations were therefore to end the mandate and to partition Palestine into a Jewish state, an Arab state, and a British zone in and around Jerusalem.

This proposal outraged the Palestinians, who viewed it as a means to dismember their homeland. The revolt intensified and reached its climax in the summer of 1938. Major Palestinian cities, including Jerusalem, joined the rebellion. With rumors that the war was easing in Europe (because of the 1938 British appeasement pact with Germany), the British launched an all-out campaign to crush the revolt. "With two divisions, squadrons of airplanes, the police force, the Transjordanian frontier forces, and 6000 Jewish auxiliaries, British troops outnumbered the Palestinians ten to one."[143] But they could not defeat the estimated 2,000 Palestinian rebels until 1939, when the Palestinian people became exhausted and wearied. Its political leaders in exile, its military commands contained and segmented, the revolt dwindled. The British government issued a white paper that, for the first time during the mandate, *reversed* its previous policy and responded to Palestinian concerns.

The 1939 white paper capped Jewish immigration at 75,000 over five years, restricted land transfers to limited areas, and proposed to make Palestine independent within ten years if Arab-Jewish relations improved. The Arab Higher Committee was initially divided, but the rebels rejected the white paper, as did, finally, the AHC and the Zionist Jewish leadership. Despite its rejection by both sides, the British implemented the new policy unilaterally. Although it gained important concessions from a British government faced with a new world war, the revolt failed to achieve its principal goal of immediate Palestinian independence.

1940–1948: Palestinian Political and Military Collapse, al-Nakbah

The war in Europe, the Holocaust, the increased Jewish immigration (legal and illegal) to Palestine, sympathy for European Jewry, rising international influence of the Zionist movement (especially in the United States), the weakening of the British Empire, the emergence of the United Nations, the dramatic structural transformation within Palestine, and the defeat of the Palestinian revolt all combined to overwhelm Palestine and the Palestinians during the decade of the 1940s.

The Palestinian Community.   The harsh British suppression of the Palestinian revolt and the reconquest of the country by 1939 decimated Palestinian political and military institutions. Palestinian parties and political activity were made illegal by the British, Palestinian leaders were either in detention camps or exile, Palestinian political activists and fighters in the thousands were in prison or concentration camps, and the community was largely disarmed. Palestinian society was economically devastated, politically and militarily defeated, and psychologically crushed. The collective will to struggle had been broken. The forceful spirit that animated political activism and revolt in the 1930s did not return in full force in the 1940s to resist the ferocious Zionist onslaught of 1947–1948 that resulted in the Palestinian Nakbah.

Several further factors contributed to Palestinian political quietism during the war years: British suppression of political activity and disarming the populace, issuance and implementation of the 1939 white paper policies, and the war-based economic boom. Although released from detention in exile, many Palestinian leaders were prohibited to return to their country. Indeed the British went so far as to authorize in 1941 a Zionist underground terrorist militia, the Irgun Z'vai Leumi, to attempt the assassination of the titular Palestinian leader, al-Hajj Amin al-Husseini, who was in exile in Iraq. It failed. Despite all that, 7,000 Palestinians joined the British army as the threat of the German North Africa Campaign increased by 1943.

The Jewish Community.   In contrast, the Jewish community in the 1940s grew economically strong, became tightly organized politically, and mobilized militarily. With the aid of British training, the Haganah militia, the forces controlled by the Jewish Agency, and other defense militia grew in numbers, skill levels, and sophistication during the 1936–1939 Palestinian revolt. In addition, underground extremist and terrorist Jewish groups, the Irgun and the Lohamei Herut Yisrael (Lehi, or the Stern Gang, as the British called it), also proliferated. Jewish military power was further augmented by the experience and technical skill acquired by the 37,000 volunteers in the Jewish Brigade and other units who served in the British army during World War II. From dependency on British protection since the start of the mandate, the Jewish community by the end of World War II became militarily strong enough to launch a revolt against the British in 1945 and the conquest of Palestine in 1948. There was a decisive shift in the balance of power on the ground between the immigrant-settler Jewish community and the indigenous Palestinians.

Breakdown of the Zionist-British Entente. The Zionists, extremists and centrists, were especially alarmed and antagonized by the 1939 white paper and its unilateral implementation. Unusual in other respects, it was the only British government cabinet policy paper submitted to and approved by the British Parliament.[144] International Zionist organizations along with the Jewish Agency mounted a vigorous diplomatic campaign to undermine the provisions of the white paper. Frustrated with Britain, whose regional political calculations in the context of World War II necessitated placating Arab public opinion and the Arab states, the Zionists turned for support to the United States, the emerging world power. Sympathy for the European Jews suffering brutal Nazi atrocities increased tremendously throughout the world.

In 1942, at a Zionist conference at the Biltmore Hotel in New York, a new Zionist program was announced. In opposition to the white paper, it demanded open immigration into Palestine and settlement of unoccupied land in the country; for the first time, it declared *publicly* the Zionist intention to establish a Jewish commonwealth in Palestine. Zionist policy goals had evolved since 1917 from a Jewish national home to a state in part of Palestine (the 1937 Peel partition proposal) to a state in the whole of Palestine. Shortly after the Biltmore convention, a number of U.S. senators and members of Congress signed a letter to President Franklin Roosevelt supporting Jewish rights to Palestine. And in January 1944, within less than two years, the U.S. Congress passed a joint resolution endorsing the Biltmore program. That same year the opposition Labour Party in Britain recommended that their government encourage Palestinian emigration in order to accommodate European Jews. By August 1945 U.S. president Harry Truman called on the British prime minister to allow 100,000 European Jews to immigrate to Palestine.

International, domestic British, and Zionist pressure escalated throughout the war years, prompting the British government to make several efforts and issue a number of similar policy papers to address the Palestine question. None was feasible or acceptable to the Zionists. In 1944, after the German threat in North Africa subsided, the Stern Gang assassinated Lord Moyne, British resident minister in Egypt, because of his unsympathetic views toward Zionism. This act heightened the tension between the British and the Zionists and drew the special ire and criticism of Prime Minister Churchill, long a supporter of Zionism.

The Zionist Revolt.   The Palestine quandary after World War II led the British and U.S. governments in 1946 to form an investigative commission jointly headed by a Brit and an American. The Anglo-American Commission (also called the Morrison-Grady Commission) recommended the conversion of the Palestine Mandate into a trusteeship divided into two autonomous Jewish and Arab provinces, Jerusalem and the Naqab Desert to remain under British control. The Zionists, the U.S. government, and the Palestinians rejected the plan; the British accepted it. Further, the British resisted U.S. and Zionist pressure to open the gates of Palestine for another 100,000 Jewish immigrants before consideration of the trusteeship proposal in a London roundtable conference planned for September 1946.

Perhaps because of this, the Jewish forces of the Haganah and the Irgun launched a terror campaign and revolt against the British in Palestine. In July 1946, Jewish terrorists blew up the King David Hotel, headquarters of the British Mandate authorities in Jerusalem, killing ninety-one British, Jewish, and Palestinian individuals. The British countered this determined Jewish revolt, which was far more efficient and effective than the earlier Palestinian uprising, with restrained tactics sharply different from those they wielded against the Palestinians: British forces killed thousands of Palestinians in the 1936 rebellion; in contrast, between August 1945 and September 1947, thirty-seven Jewish terrorists and 169 British soldiers died.[145] Whereas the Palestinian leaders in the Arab Higher Committee during the 1936 revolt were arrested, detained, or deported and the committee outlawed for eight years, members of the Jewish Agency were detained for a little over three months in 1946. The failure of the London roundtable, the rejection of Foreign Minister Ernest Bevin's proposals, the Zionist revolt against the British, and attacks against Palestinians by Jewish forces created a tense civil-war-like situation. British control over Palestine began to erode rapidly. It was clear that the British were in retreat and under siege.[146]

United Nations Partition Plan and Descent into War.   The British government decided to withdraw its troops, relinquish control of Palestine, and turn over responsibility for the mandate to the United Nations. After diplomatic machinations in which the Palestinians and the Arab states were at a distinct disadvantage, on November 29, 1947, the UN General Assembly voted Resolution 181 on the Future Government of Palestine (see Appendix 5), which partitioned Palestine into an Arab and a Jewish state. Map 3.4 shows how Palestine was purposely gerrymandered by the United Nations in order to create a Jewish majority in the proposed Jewish state.

The United Nations partition plan was based on the Zionists' own plan endorsed by the United States in August 1946.[147] At a time when the Jewish population of Palestine was around 31 percent of the total, the size of the proposed Jewish state was roughly 55 percent of historic Palestine and included a sizable Palestinian minority of 45 percent. The proposed Palestinian Arab state, in contrast, was awarded 45 percent of the land of Palestine and a negligible Jewish minority. Jerusalem and Bethlehem were supposed to be separate bodies under international auspices. Palestinians and other Arabs were outraged and rejected the United Nations resolution.

Hostilities quickly exploded between the Jewish Zionist forces and the Palestinians. The British set July 31, 1948, for their final withdrawal and secretly informed the Zionist leadership but not the Palestinians. In the event they pulled out by the end of May and left Palestine in disarray. Instead of designing a rational process for transferring the central institutions and functions of government to the majority Palestinians or to the respective Zionist and Palestinian authorities in accordance with the United Nations partition plan, the British in effect simply abandoned everything. This disorderly process added confusion to the rapidly developing internal war between the Jewish forces and the Palestinians.

The self-contained, well-organized, and tightly controlled Jewish community, on the one hand, was well positioned to assume the functions and institutions of government. They, after all, had built parallel autonomous institutions of governance and control in the course of the mandate with the support of the British authorities. After their 1939 defeat, the Palestinians, on the other hand, were unable to rebuild central leadership institutions or the mediating and local civil structures in order to mobilize the exhausted people. When the British abandoned the Arab areas, they left to the unprepared municipal and village authorities the immense responsibility of providing security; policing; defense; electric power; water; and sanitation, medical, educational, and other services. This dilemma was at the same time a product and reflection of the disunity and disorganization among the Palestinian political leadership.

The political reawakening among the Palestinians in 1942 in reaction to the Biltmore program and its support by the U.S. Congress and the British Labour Party was ineffective. Efforts in the postwar period by the titular Palestinian leader, al-Hajj Amin al-Husseini, to unite the weakened political groups and mobilize the fractured polity into a new national movement failed. With Arab public concern for their compatriots in Palestine, the nominally independent Arab states joined to help the beleaguered Palestini-

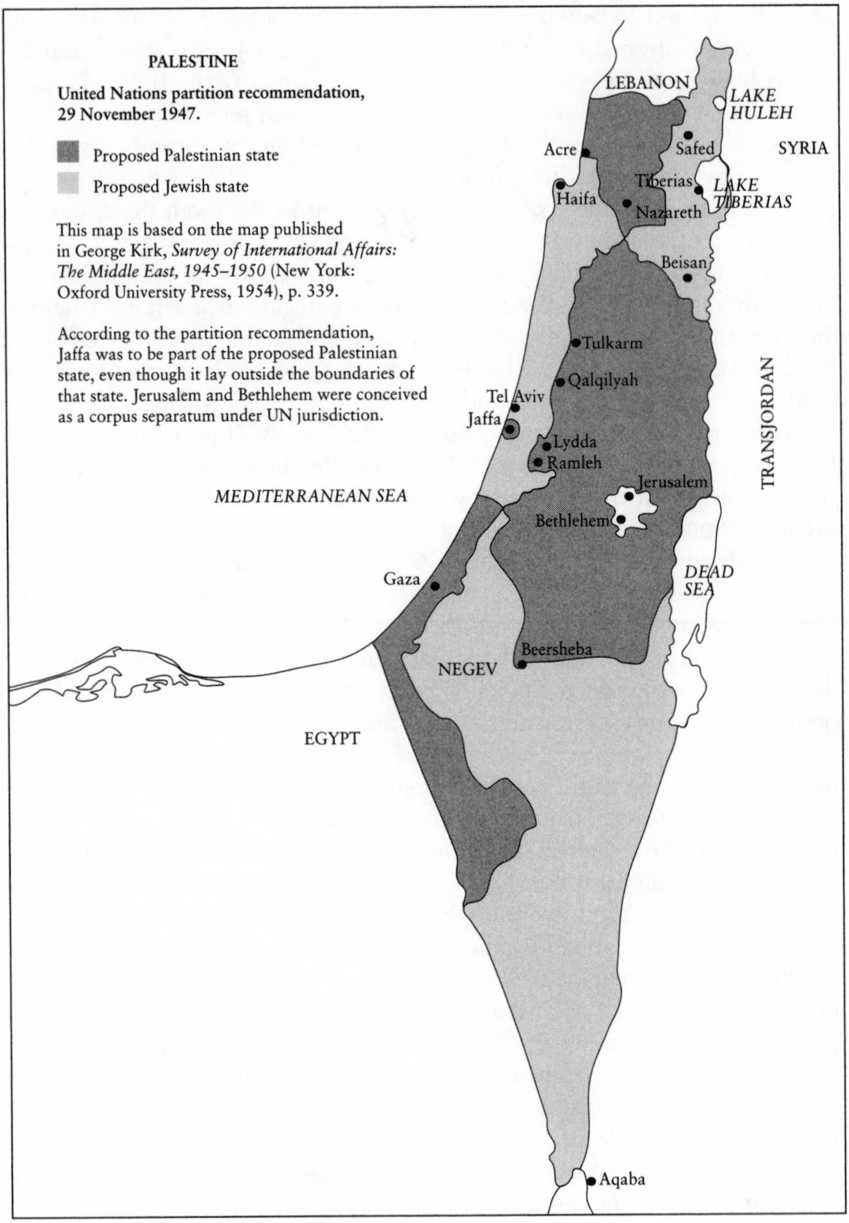
PALESTINE
United Nations partition recommendation, 29 November 1947.
Proposed Palestinian state
Proposed Jewish state
This map is based on the map published in George Kirk, Survey of International Affairs: The Middle East, 1945–1950 (New York: Oxford University Press, 1954), p. 339.
According to the partition recommendation, Jaffa was to be part of the proposed Palestinian state, even though it lay outside the boundaries of that state. Jerusalem and Bethlehem were conceived as a corpus separatum under UN jurisdiction.
LEBANON
LAKE HULEH
SYRIA
Acre
Safed
Tiberias
LAKE TIBERIAS
Haifa
Nazareth
Beisan
Tulkarm
Qalqilyah
Tel Aviv
Jaffa
Lydda
Ramleh
TRANSJORDAN
Jerusalem
Bethlehem
MEDITERRANEAN SEA
Gaza
DEAD SEA
Beersheba
NEGEV
EGYPT
Aqaba

MAP 3.4 United Nations Partition Plan of Palestine
SOURCE: W. Khalidi, *Before Their Diaspora* (Washington, DC: Insititute for Palestine Studies, 1984), 307.

ans. The League of Arab States was founded in part as a mechanism to create a united Arab policy on Palestine and to coordinate aid to the Palestinian people against dispossession by the increasingly evident Zionist threat. The Arab states and public opinion viewed Zionism as a threat not only to Palestine but also to the rest of the Arab world. Thus by 1945–1946 diplomatic policy and decisions regarding the question of Palestine were progressively appropriated from the Palestinian leadership by the Arab states in the framework of the Arab League.

Further compromising the Palestinian cause internationally and its leadership regionally were the machinations of the ambitious Amir Abdullah (son of Sharif Hussein of Mecca), ruler of Transjordan. After World War II, he had set his sights on reuniting and ruling greater Syria (which had been under the control of Vichy France) with the backing of the British. In return, he supported British policy (especially the Peel Commission's recommendation of partition) on Palestine and secretly colluded across the Jordan River with the Zionist leadership for the partition of Palestine.[148] As a participant in Arab League deliberations and decisions on the Palestine question, the Transjordanian government of Amir Abdullah was able to undermine both Palestinian and Arab efforts to save the country. This is most evident in the behavior of his army, the Arab Legion, after its entry into Palestine as part of the Arab League's last-ditch effort to save Palestine from the Zionists in 1948.

The Zionists had planned and organized a Jewish army, not just defensive guards, since 1942—one of the two key decisions of the Biltmore Zionist program—while the Palestinians were being disarmed by the British authorities.[149] Jewish forces numbered roughly 15,000 in early 1948 but swelled to over 60,000 by May 1948. The majority of them were part of Haganah (with World War II experience) and the rest belonged to the terrorist groups, the Irgun and the Stern Gang. For the 1947–1948 hostilities, they recruited a large number of professional military volunteers from all over the world.

The Palestinian leader, al-Hajj Amin al-Husseini, waited to form a volunteer force, al-Jihad al-Muqaddas (the Holy Struggle), until December 1947, after the United Nations partition decision and after hostilities began. By March the irregular force, under two commanders, numbered around 1,600. Some rural-area militias were formed in parts of Palestine, but their total number did not exceed 750. Additionally, towns or town quarters often organized garrisons of defense. Finally, the Futuwwa and Najjadah youth groups had at best a few hundred armed young men. During clashes these forces were on occasion bolstered by faz'a village volunteers. Overall, Palestinian forces in early 1948 may have totaled around 7,000 fighters.

The Arab League, which declared the partition plan illegal, was alarmed by Jewish attacks; because of public pressure, it organized and financially supported a volunteer Arab force, Jaysh al-Inqath (Army of Salvation), under the command of Fawzi al-Qawuqji. With a promised 10,000 rifles, 3,830 Arab men, including 500–1,000 Palestinians, were organized into eight battalions that operated in north central Palestine. Palestinian and Arab fighters were outnumbered, outarmed (by May the Jewish forces had tanks, armored cars, fighter planes, field guns, etc.), and outclassed (in training, technical knowledge, experience, firepower, and mobility) by the armed Jewish regulars and their allied international volunteers. The Palestinians were unprepared politically or militarily to defend the integrity and unity of their country.

The Zionist Conquest of Palestine and al-Nakbah.   The intercommunal Jewish-Palestinian fighting unleashed after the United Nations partition decision was terroristic and defensive. By March 1948 it appeared as if the Palestinians and their volunteer Arab supporters had the upper hand. This was a false impression, as the Zionists had yet to implement their offensive plan. In anticipation, the Zionists began detailed war planning in 1945. The end of the mandate, then set by the British for May 15, 1948, would create a juridical vacuum, and the Zionists had to actualize their Jewish state. Their most ambitious military plan was Plan Dalet, whose objective was conquest and control of the proposed area of the Jewish state and, beyond it, Jerusalem and the Tel Aviv–Jerusalem salient.

In April 1948 the Haganah and its international volunteers launched major operations throughout Palestine. The first was an offensive to capture, occupy, and destroy Palestinian villages along the Jaffa–Tel Aviv–Jerusalem road. A pivotal battle developed a short distance west of Jerusalem, in the hilltop town of Al-Qastal (Castel). The Palestinians fought bravely, and the village changed hands a number of times. The charismatic Palestinian commander 'Abdul-Qader al-Husseini was killed on April 9 defending the town. Simultaneously, Irgun and Stern terrorists attacked and massacred most of the 245 inhabitants of the village of Deir Yassin, 3 miles away from Al-Qastal. These events and the defeat of Qawuqji's diversionary assault on a Jewish colony to the north sent powerful shock waves throughout Palestine and the rest of the Arab world. It led the Arab states, assembled in an Arab League, to consider intervention in Palestine with their regular armies.

Beginning in the second half of April, Jewish military assaults led to the fall of Tabariyya (April 18), Haifa (April 23), Jaffa (April 25), West Jerusalem (April 26), eastern Galilee (April 28), the central plain between Latrun and Ramleh (May 8–9), Safad (May 11–12), Beisan (May 12), and the Naqab villages (May 12). The attacks were brutal. Through terror, psychological warfare, and direct conquests, Palestine was dismembered, many of its villages purposefully destroyed and much of its people expelled as refugees.

As hundreds of thousands of refugees poured into safer areas of Palestine and into neighboring Arab countries, the Arab League could not ignore the tragedy. They ordered their regular armies into battle for Palestine. The

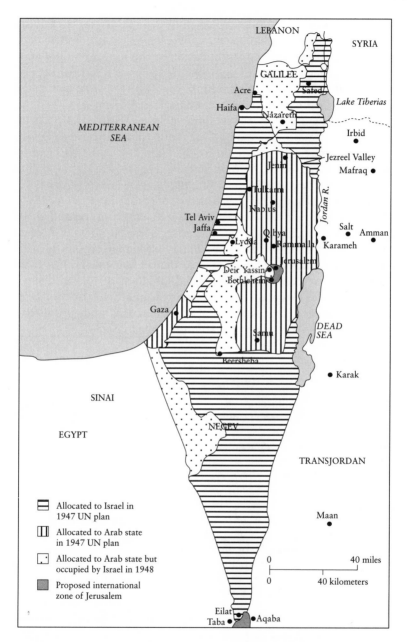

MAP 3.5 Areas of Palestine Conquered by Zionist-Israeli Forces Beyond the Partition Plan

SOURCE: R. Ovendale, *The Longman Companion to the Middle East Since 1914* (London: Longman Group, 1992), 355.

numbers, equipment, and firepower of those regular armies were less than half of what the Arab League's own Military Technical Committee had recommended. As important was the collusion of the King Abdullah with the Zionists: He ordered his British-commanded Arab Legion to secure only the part of Palestine allotted to the Arab state, which he had planned, with the agreement of the Zionists, to annex to Transjordan. Arab state intervention arrived too late and was too little to save Palestine. Map 3.5 shows the areas of Palestine conquered by the Zionist-Israeli forces in 1948–1949, areas allocated to the Jewish state by the United Nations partition plan, and territories allocated to the Arab state. These areas form the state of Israel according to the armistice lines of 1949.

On May 14, 1948, the Zionists declared the State of Israel. Eleven minutes later, the United States recognized Israel. While an expanded Jewish state was forcefully created beyond the area allotted to the Jewish community in the United Nations partition plan, a Palestinian Arab state was not. East central Palestine came under Transjordanian control and was later annexed as the West Bank of the expanded kingdom of Jordan. The Gaza salient came under Egyptian military control. Hundreds of thousands of Palestinians became refugees in the parts of Palestine under Arab control and in neighboring Arab countries. Palestine thus ceased to exist.

Notes

1. B. Kimmerling, *Zionism and Territory* (Berkeley: Institute of International Studies, University of California, 1983), 1–30. See also G. Shafir, *Land, Labor and the Origins of Israeli-Palestinian Conflict, 1882–1914* (Cambridge: Cambridge University Press, 1989).

2. Shafir, *Land, Labor and the Origin of the Israeli-Palestinian Conflict,* 14–17.

3. Ibid., 19.

4. Kimmerling, *Zionism and Territory,* 3.

5. Shafir, *Land Labor and the Origin of the Israeli-Palestinian Conflict,* 21. Emphasis added.

6. M. Y. Muslih, *The Origins of Palestinian Nationalism* (New York: Columbia University Press, 1988). See also W. Abboushi, *The Unmaking of Palestine* (Brattleboro: Amana Books, 1990); Y. Porath, *The Emergence of the Palestinian Arab National Movement, 1918–1929* (London: Frank Cass, 1974); N. Mandel, *The Arabs and Zionism Before World War I* (Berkeley: University of California Press, 1976).

7. F. J. Khouri, *The Arab-Israeli Dilemma,* 3rd ed. (Syracuse: Syracuse University Press, 1985), 8.

8. Second note from Sir Henry McMahon to Sharif Hussein of the Hijaz, 24 October 1915. The note is reprinted in Appendix 3.

9. There was, however, some dispute and lack of clarity in this agreement over the eastern Mediterranean coastal regions of the area. The McMahon note—and it is unclear if Sharif Hussein agreed to this—excluded from the agreement the districts of Mersina and Alexandretta and "portions of Syria lying west of Damascus, Homs, Hama and Aleppo" (see Appendix 3), all regions to the north of Palestine.

10. The Balfour Declaration, 2 November 1917, given in Appendix 2.

11. Anglo-French Declaration, 7 November 1918, cited in appendix A, 6, in Khouri, *The Arab-Israeli Dilemma*, 527.

12. See a sympathetic and concise account in Esco Foundation for Palestine, *Palestine, A Study of Jewish, Arab, and British Policies*, vol. 1 (New Haven: Yale University Press, 1947), part 1, ch. 1, 1–56.

13. See N. G. Finkelstein, *Image and Reality of the Israel-Palestine Conflict* (London: Verso, 1995), ch. 1: "Zionist Orientations," 7–20.

14. A. M. Hyamson, *Palestine Under the Mandate, 1920–1948* (Westport, CT: Greenwood Press, 1950), 1–25.

15. D. Vital, *The Origins of Zionism* (Oxford: Oxford University Press, 1975), 214.

16. Hyamson, *Palestine Under the Mandate*, 29.

17. See the study of the OETA period by J. J. McTague Jr., "The British Military Administration in Palestine, 1917–1920," *Journal of Palestine Studies* 7, 3 (Spring 1978): 55–76.

18. Clayton to Foreign Office (enclosure), 2 May 1919, F.O. 371/2117/68848, cited in ibid., 58.

19. Watson to Allenby, 16 August 1919, F.O. 371/1051/124482, cited in ibid.

20. Quoted in Abboushi, *The Unmaking of Palestine*, 10.

21. Ibid.

22. McTague, "The British Military Administration in Palestine," 70.

23. Quoted in ibid.

24. B. J. Smith, *The Roots of Separatism in Palestine, British Economic Policy, 1920–1929* (Syracuse: Syracuse University Press, 1993), 4. See also Khouri, *The Arab-Israeli Dilemma*, 16–67; J. C. Hurewitz, *The Struggle for Palestine* (New York: W. W. Norton, 1950); H. Frischwasser-Ra'anan, *The Frontiers of a Nation: A Re-examination of the Forces Which Created the Palestine Mandate and Determined Its Territorial Shape* (London: Batchworth Press, 1955); J. Stoyanovsky, *The Mandate for Palestine: A Contribution to the Theory and Practice of International Mandates* (Westport, CT: Hyperion Press, 1976).

25. Y. N. Miller, "Administrative Policy in Rural Palestine: The Impact of British Norms on Arab Community Life, 1920–1948," in J. S. Migdal, ed., *Palestinian Society and Politics* (Princeton: Princeton University Press, 1980), 124.

26. Quoted from *Jewish Chronicle* of 20 May 1921 in Porath, *The Emergence of the Palestinian Arab National Movement*, 56.

27. Quotations from the Mandate for Palestine, 24 July 1922, reproduced in Khouri, *The Arab-Israeli Dilemma*, appendix A, 4, 527–528.

28. Khouri, *The Arab-Israeli Dilemma*, 17.

29. Smith, *The Roots of Separatism*, 6.

30. Ibid., 9.

31. R. Owen, "Economic Development in Mandatory Palestine: 1918–1948," in G. T. Abed, *The Palestinian Economy: Studies in Development Under Prolonged Occupation* (London: Routledge, 1988), 14. Evidence for this statement is clear in the two tables, on revenue and expenditure, that the mandate government of Palestine provides in *A Survey of Palestine*, prepared in December 1945 and January 1946, for the information of the Anglo-American Committee of Inquiry, vol. 1 (reprint, Washington, DC: Institute for Palestine Studies, 1991), 124–125. See also

K. W. Stein, "Legal Protection and Circumvention of Rights for Cultivators in Mandatory Palestine," in Migdal, *Palestinian Society and Politics*, 234.

32. Smith, *The Roots of Separatism*, 7.

33. *A Survey of Palestine*, ch. 6, unnumbered table, 144.

34. J. L. Abu-Lughod, "The Demographic Transformation of Palestine," in I. Abu-Lughod, ed., *The Transformation of Palestine* (Evanston, IL: Northwestern University Press, 1971), 142.

35. *A Survey of Palestine*, ch. 7, tables 2–11, 187–203.

36. See ibid., ch. 6, table 3, 142.

37. Ibid., 150, 151.

38. For the figures on Jewish immigration into Palestine during the mandate, see *A Survey of Palestine*, ch. 6, tables 1–6, 141–144. See also Abu-Lughod, "The Demographic Transformation of Palestine," 143–161; Smith, *The Roots of Separatism*, 10, 76–82; and Owen, "Economic Development in Mandatory Palestine," 32.

39. See the official British estimate for the end of 1944 in *A Survey of Palestine*, ch. 6, table 5, 143: Of an estimated total population of 1.76 million, there were 1.18 million Palestinian Arabs, 554,000 Jews, and 32,000 others.

40. Abu-Lughod, "The Demographic Transformation of Palestine," 152.

41. E. B. Childers, "The Wordless Wish: From Citizens to Refugees," in Abu-Lughod, *The Transformation of Palestine*, 165–202.

42. See J. Ruedy, "Dynamics of Land Alienation," in Abu-Lughod, *The Transformation of Palestine*, 119–138.

43. Kimmerling, *Zionism and Territory*, 37–38.

44. Ibid., 41. Kimmerling here cites the Hebrew edition of a book later translated into English: A. Granott (originally Granovsky), *The Land System of Palestine: History and Structure* (London: Eyre & Spottiswoode, 1952).

45. See W. Lehn and U. Davis, *The Jewish National Fund* (London: Kegan Paul International, 1988).

46. Esco Foundation, *Palestine, A Study of Jewish, Arab, and British Policies*, 331–349.

47. See K. W. Stein, *The Land Question in Palestine* (Chapel Hill: University of North Carolina Press, 1984), 19ff. See also Kimmerling, *Zionism and Territory*; Shafir, *Land, Labor and the Origins of the Israeli-Palestinian Conflict*.

48. Granott, *The Land System of Palestine*. See also Stein, *The Land Question in Palestine*, 226–227, for a list of Jewish land purchases up to 1945 totaling 1.39 million dunums.

49. Y. Porath, *The Palestinian Arab National Movement, from Riots to Rebellion* (London: Frank Cass, 1977), 83–84.

50. Stein, *The Land Question in Palestine*, 226–227.

51. See *A Survey of Palestine*, ch. 8, table 1, 244, for official yearly purchases of land by Jews between 1920 and 1945. See Stein, *The Land Question in Palestine*, 226–227, for the larger estimate.

52. Owen, "Economic Development in Mandatory Palestine," 20.

53. Ruedy, "Dynamics of Land Alienation," 134.

54. Ibid., 127.

55. John Hope Simpson, *Palestine, Report on Immigration, Land Settlement and Development* [the Hope Simpson report] (London: His Majesty's Stationery Office, 1930), 141–143.

56. Ruedy, "Dynamics of Land Alienation," 134–135.

57. D. Peretz, *Israel and the Palestinian Arabs* (Washington, DC: Middle East Institute, 1958), 142.

58. A. Kubursi, "An Economic Assessment of Total Palestinian Losses in 1948," in S. Hadawi, *Palestinian Rights and Losses in 1948: A Comprehensive Study* (London: Saqi Books, 1988), 184. See also A. Kubursi, *Palestinian Losses in 1948: The Quest for Precision* (Washington, DC: Center for Policy Analysis on Palestine, 1996).

59. This section is based largely on Smith, *The Roots of Separatism*, ch. 6, 7, and 8. See also J. Metzer, "Economic Structure and National Goals—The Jewish National Home in Interwar Palestine," *Journal of Economic History* 38 (March 1978): 101–119; N. Halevy and R. Klinov-Malul, *The Economic Development of Israel* (New York: Praeger, 1968); and M. Seikaly, *Haifa: Transformation of an Arab Society, 1918–1939* (London: I. B. Tauris, 1995).

60. See data on origins of imports into Palestine between 1935 and 1944 in *A Survey of Palestine*, ch. 13, 472–473.

61. Smith, *The Roots of Separatism*, 9.

62. Ibid., 119.

63. Ibid., 131.

64. Esco Foundation, *Palestine, A Study of Jewish, Arab and British Policies*, 381–388.

65. Ibid., 696.

66. *A Survey of Palestine*, quoted in Smith, *The Roots of Separatism*, 178. See also M. Seikaly, *Haifa: Transformation of an Arab Society, 1918–1939* (London: I. B. Tauris, 1995).

67. Smith, *The Roots of Separatism*, 164–167.

68. I. Khalaf, *Politics in Palestine* (Albany: State University of New York Press, 1991), 48.

69. Ibid.

70. In 1936 "total intersectoral trade between Jews and [Palestinian] Arabs ... came to only about 7 percent of Palestine's national income." Halevi and Klinov-Malul, *The Economic Development of Israel*, 16–17 and 30. See also R. Szerezewski, *Essays on the Structure of the Jewish Economy in Palestine and Israel* (Jerusalem: Maurice Falk Institute, 1968), table 5; and J. Metzer, "Fiscal Incidence and Resource Transfer Between Jews and Arabs in Mandatory Palestine," *Research in Economic History* 7 (1982): 87–132.

71. Shafir, *Land, Labor and the Origins of the Israeli-Palestinian Conflict*.

72. See the data on the Jewish labor force in *A Survey of Palestine*, vol. 2, 499, 500–502, and 507–509.

73. The actual wage structure in 1928 in the public sector was Arab rural, 120–150 mils per day; Arab urban, 140–170; Jewish nonunion, 150–300; and Jewish union, 280–300. Cited in Smith, *The Roots of Separatism*, 156.

74. See the point of view of J. Metzer and O. Kaplan, "Jointly and Severally: Arab-Jewish Dualism and Economic Growth in Palestine," *Journal of Economic History* 65 (June 1985): 327–345.

75. N. Halevi, "The Political Economy of Absorptive Capacity: Growth and Cycles in Jewish Palestine Under the British Mandate," *Middle Eastern Studies* 19 (October 1983): 456–469. See official regulations and figures on Jewish immigration in *A Survey of Palestine*, ch. 7, 165–224.

76. See Esco Foundation, *Palestine, A Study of Jewish, Arab and British Policies*, 366–369.

77. Ibid., 388–404.

78. A. L. Tibawi, *Arab Education in Mandatory Palestine: A Study of Three Decades of British Administration* (London: Luzac, 1956), 205ff.

79. See A. Abu-Ghazaleh, *Arab Cultural Nationalism in Palestine* (Beirut: Institute for Palestine Studies, 1973), 94. Statistics originally gathered by A. S. al-Khalidi, principal of the Arab College in Jerusalem, and cited in M. F. Abcarius, *Palestine Through the Fog of Propaganda* (London: Hutchinson, 1946), 101–102.

80. A. B. Zahlan and E. Hagopian, "Palestine's Arab Population," *Journal of Palestine Studies* 3, 4 (Summer 1974): 45–46.

81. *A Survey of Palestine*, vol. 2, 638.

82. Cited in Y. N. Miller, *Government and Society in Rural Palestine, 1920–1948* (Austin: University of Texas Press, 1985), 95.

83. See Abu-Ghazaleh, *Arab Cultural Nationalism in Palestine*, for a different viewpoint. See also Miller, *Government and Society in Rural Palestine*, 95–97.

84. Abu-Ghazaleh, *Arab Cultural Nationalism in Palestine*, 19.

85. See the tables of absolute numbers in *A Survey of Palestine*, vol. 1, 147–149.

86. Szereszewski, *Essays on the Structure of the Jewish Economy in Palestine*, table 5, cited in Owen, "Economic Development in Mandatory Palestine," 16.

87. Ibid.

88. These two sections, including the figures, are based on *A Survey of Palestine*; the Esco Foundation, *Palestine, A Study of Jewish, Arab, and British Policies*; and Owen, "Economic Development of Mandatory Palestine," 15–32. Owen summarizes data from numerous studies and reports.

89. The Esco Foundation study claims that "including both public and private sources, it is probable that the Jews brought into Palestine a sum of over £125,000,000 during the last generation. Money was also sent to Palestine through the post office, of which there is no estimate." *Palestine, A Study of Jewish, Arab, and British Policies*, vol. 1, 384–385.

90. See tables 8a and 8b in *A Survey of Palestine*, vol. 1, ch. 6, 150–151.

91. Owen, "Economic Development in Mandatory Palestine," 20–27. See also *A Survey of Palestine*, vol. 1, ch. 13, section 4, "A Survey of Industry," 497–534.

92. *A Survey of Palestine*, vol. 1, 499.

93. Esco Foundation, *Palestine, A Study of Jewish, Arab, and British Policies*, vol. 2, 696.

94. *A Survey of Palestine*, vol. 1., ch. 13, 462–463. Certain years it went above these ratios, especially if the international price of cereals was high or there was a bumper crop in citrus.

95. Owen, "Economic Development in Mandatory Palestine," 19. See the trade figures in *A Survey of Palestine*, vol. 1, ch. 13, 472–473, 479, 481–496.

96. Ibid., 26.

97. Esco Foundation, *Palestine, A Study of Jewish, Arab, and British Policies*, vol. 2, 1056.

98. R. A. Nathan, O. Gass, and D. Creamer, *Palestine: Problem and Promise* (Washington, DC: Middle East Institute, 1946), 150. Cited in Owen, "Economic Development in Mandatory Palestine," 29.

99. *Statistical Abstract of Palestine, 1944–1945* (Jerusalem: Government of Palestine, 1946), 52ff, 58.

100. *A Survey of Palestine*, vol. 1, ch. 13, 507.

101. Esco Foundation, *Palestine, A Study of Jewish, Arab, and British Policies*, vol. 2, 1053.

102. *A Survey of Palestine*, vol. 2, ch. 13, 502.

103. Cited in Esco Foundation, *Palestine, A Study in Jewish, Arab, and British Policies*, vol. 2, 1053.

104. Ibid., 1054–1055.

105. First Interim Report of Employment Committee, 27 October 1944. Cited in Khalaf, *Politics in Palestine*, 36–37.

106. Owen, "Economic Development in Mandatory Palestine," 30.

107. These data are cited in Khalaf, *Politics in Palestine*, 52–53.

108. R. Taqqu, "Peasants into Workmen: Internal Labor Migration and the Arab Village Community under the Mandate," in Migdal, *Palestinian Society and Politics*, 261.

109. First Interim Report of Employment Committee, 27 October 1944. Cited in Khalaf, *Politics in Palestine*, 36.

110. Nathan, Gass, and Creamer, *Palestine: Problem and Promise*, 213.

111. Citing many sources, Owen, "Economic Development in Mandatory Palestine," 30.

112. *A Survey of Palestine*, vol. 2, 694, 696.

113. Data in this part come from Khalaf, *Politics in Palestine*, 38–44.

114. Ibid., 41–42.

115. R. N. Verdery, "Arab 'Disturbances' and the Commissions of Inquiry," in Abu-Lughod, *The Transformation of Palestine*, 281.

116. Ibid., 282.

117. M. E. T. Mogannam, *The Arab Woman and the Palestine Problem* (London, 1937), 125. Cited in D. Waines, "The Failure of the Nationalist Resistance," in Abu-Lughod, *The Transformation of Palestine*, 220.

118. See the text of the resolution in Esco Foundation, *Palestine, A Study in Jewish, Arab, and British Policies*, vol. 1, 475.

119. A. M. Lesch, "The Palestine Arab Nationalist Movement Under the Mandate," in W. B. Quandt, F. Jabber, and A. M. Lesch, *The Politics of Palestinian Nationalism* (Berkeley: University of California Press, 1973), 20–21.

120. League of Nations, Permanent Mandates Commission, *Minutes of the 14th Session*, October-November 1928, annex 9, 246. Cited in Waines, "The Failure of the Nationalist Resistance," 226.

121. See the details in P. Mattar, *The Mufti of Jerusalem* (New York: Columbia University Press, 1992), ch. 3, 33–49.

122. Cited in Verdery, "Arab 'Disturbances' and the Commissions of Inquiry," 290.

123. Hope Simpson, *Palestine, Report on Immigration, Land Settlement and Development*, 26. According to the 1931 census, 22 percent of the total number of families dependent on agriculture were landless. Cited in D. Warriner, *Land and Poverty in the Middle East* (London: Royal Institute of International Affairs, 1948), 63.

124. K. W. Stein, "Legal Protection and Circumvention of Rights for Cultivators in Mandatory Palestine," in Migdal, *Palestinian Society and Politics*, 233–249.

125. Warriner, *Land and Poverty in the Middle East*, 57.

126. Hope Simpson, *Palestine, Report on Immigration, Land Settlement and Development*, 64.

127. Ibid., 68–69.

128. Ibid., 70.

129. Ibid., 141.

130. Ibid., 136.

131. See *Palestine, Statement of Policy by His Majesty's Government in the United Kingdom*, presented by the Secretary of State for the Colonies, London, October 1930, 1–24; known as the Passfield white paper.

132. See Mattar, "Politics of Moderation and the General Islamic Congress," in *The Mufti of Jerusalem*, 50–64.

133. Ibid., 63.

134. Ibid., 64.

135. See the discussion in T. R. Swedenburg, *Memories of Revolt, the 1936–1939 Rebellion and the Palestinian National Past* (Minneapolis: University of Minnesota Press, 1995), 199.

136. See B. N. al-Hout, "The Palestinian Political Elite During the Mandate Period," *Journal of Palestine Studies* 9, 1 (Autumn 1979): 85–111.

137. M. Budeiri, *The Palestine Communist Party, 1919–1948* (London: Ithaca Press, 1979).

138. B. Kalkas, "The Revolt of 1936: A Chronicle of Events," in Abu-Lughod, *The Transformation of Palestine*, 241–242.

139. This section depends largely on Swedenburg, *Memories of Revolt*, 122–133.

140. Ibid., 221–223.

141. Ibid., 223.

142. Mattar, *The Mufti of Jerusalem*, 78.

143. Ibid., 83.

144. The Balfour Declaration and the mandate agreement were never submitted to Parliament. Abboushi, *The Unmaking of Palestine*, 177.

145. N. Bethell, *The Palestine Triangle: The Struggle Between the British, the Jews and the Arabs, 1935–48* (London: Andre Deutsch, 1979), 347.

146. This is not the place to analyze the factors responsible for British behavior at this point. See W. Khalidi, *From Haven to Conquest: Readings in Zionism and the Palestine Problem Until 1948* (Beirut: Institute for Palestine Studies, 1971); and W. Khalidi, *Before Their Diaspora: A Photographic History of the Palestinians, 1876–1948* (Washington, DC: Institute for Palestine Studies, 1984). See also Hurewitz, *The Struggle for Palestine*; and Khouri, *The Arab-Israeli Dilemma*.

147. Khalidi, *Before Their Diaspora*, 305.

148. A. Shlaim, *Collusion Across the Jordan: King Abdullah, the Zionist Movement, and the Partition of Palestine* (New York: Columbia University Press, 1988).

149. See Khalidi on the numbers and types of arms confiscated from the Palestinians between 1936 and 1945; *From Haven to Conquest*, 845.

FOUR

After al-Nakbah: The Palestinian Diaspora, 1948–1993

Al-Nakbah meant the destruction of Palestinian society and patrimony and Palestinians' dispossession, dispersal, and destitution. This was largely the result of Zionist policy and tactics of expulsion in order to secure as much as possible of the land of Palestine for a Jewish state without indigenous Arab Palestinians. Of the total land of Palestine, the Israelis captured over 76 percent; the UN partition plan allotted them 55 percent. Map 4.1 shows Israel's 1948 cease-fire "borders," officially recognized as Israel by most governments, before further conquest and expansion during the 1967 Arab-Israeli war. From an estimated total population of 900,000 Palestinians in the areas occupied by Israel in 1947–1948, 750,000 to 800,000 became refugees.[1] In a matter of a few weeks in the spring of 1948, Palestine, a complex, developing, and differentiated society, was abruptly and haphazardly segmented, most of its people dispossessed and their lives completely disrupted.

The people of Palestine became divided into three widely dispersed and numerically unequal segments. First, 100,000 to 180,000 Palestinians remained in their homes and lands in what became Israel. Second, around 500,000 people remained behind Arab military lines in east central Palestine and the Gaza Strip. Third, more than 750,000 of the total 1948 Palestinian population of 1.4 million became refugees in east central Palestine (later known as the West Bank), the Gaza Strip, and neighboring Arab countries.[2] Table 4.1 provides numerical estimates of the Palestinian refugees and their destinations from varied sources.

While the largest area of Palestine became Israel, two other parts, east central Palestine (annexed in 1950 as the West Bank of the kingdom of Jor-

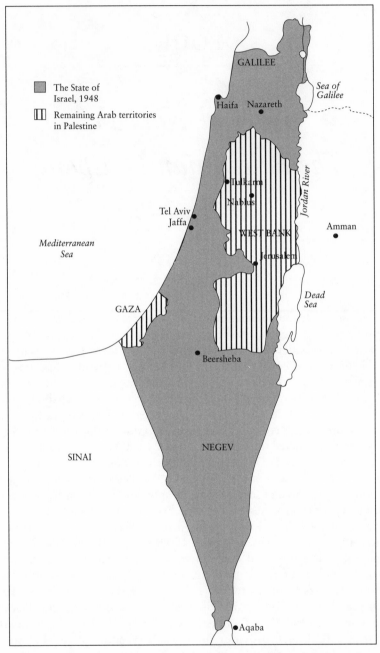

MAP 4.1   Israel and the West Bank and Gaza Strip, 1949 Armistice Frontiers
SOURCE: Adapted from Simha Flapan, *The Birth of Israel: Myths and Realities* (New York: Pantheon Books, 1987), 51.

TABLE 4.1 Estimates of Palestinian Refugees and Their Destinations, 1948–1949

Destination	British Government	U.S. Estimates	United Nations	Private Israeli Estimates	Israeli Government	Palestinian Sources
Gaza	210,000	208,000	280,000	200,000	–	201,173
West Bank	320,000	–	190,000	200,000	–	363,689
Jordan, Syria, Lebanon, etc.	280,000	667,000	256,000	250,000	–	284,324
Total	810,000 (Feb. 1949)	875,000 (1953)	726,000 (Sept. 1949) 957,000 (May 1950)	650,000 (end 1949) 600,000–760,000 (1948–1950)	520,000 (1948) 590,000 (1952)	850,276 (Nov. 1952) 770,100–780,000 (end 1948) 714,150–744,150 (mid-1948)

SOURCE: *Facts and Figures About Palestinians* (Washington, DC: Center for Policy Analysis on Palestine, 1992), 13.

dan) and the Gaza Strip, came under control of the Jordanian and Egyptian military authorities, respectively. Although the Arab Higher Committee, the national Palestinian political organization, was finally allowed by the Arab League to declare a government in Gaza, *Hukoumat 'Umoum Filastin* (the All-Palestine Government), in effect it was a symbolic and futile act. Both segments of Jewish- and Arab-occupied Palestine passed from under the political control of the Palestinian people. Palestine as a unitary state was no more. It lived on only in the imaginings, struggles, and plans of the Palestinian people.

Unable to return to their homeland after the cessation of hostilities, Palestinian refugees forged livelihoods in the areas and countries where initially they took refuge. Over the next two generations, however, voluntary Palestinian migrations took them in large numbers to the oil-exporting states of the Arabian peninsula, Europe, and the Americas. The flow of Palestinian dispersal between 1948 and 1995 with a projection for 2000 is provided in Table 4.2. Shortly after al-Nakbah nearly 80 percent of the Palestinian population lived in dismembered historic Palestine (Israel, the West Bank, and Gaza Strip), but by 1991 only a little over 40 percent remained there.[3] The majority composes the diaspora.

Although stateless (except for those in Jordan), everywhere in their diaspora the Palestinians built vibrant communities—at times under inhospitable conditions—that preserved their identity, social and cultural life, and political aspirations. In this chapter we analyze the structure and dynamics of these diaspora communities.

The well-documented political history of the region since al-Nakbah is framed largely by the Arab-Israeli state-to-state conflict in the context of the cold war. The social history of the Palestinians since 1948 and their struggle to regain their political right of self-determination have been portrayed by Western and Israeli scholars and media principally as a sideshow to the "larger" and "more significant" Arab-Israeli conflict, itself viewed as proxy Soviet-U.S. confrontations in the region. The Arab-Israeli wars of 1956, 1967, 1973 (the Suez War, the Six-Day War, and the Yom Kippur War, as these wars were called in Israel and the West), and the innumerable attacks, counterattacks, skirmishes, invasions, and short wars that often involved the superpowers diplomatically and otherwise captured the attention of most Western and many Middle Eastern journalists and scholars and confirmed the conflict's principal focus as that between states. Nonetheless, the civil wars in Jordan (1970–1971) and Lebanon (1975–1982) forced the Palestine question to the fore. The 1978 and the more massive 1982 Israeli invasions of Lebanon, both in reality Israeli-Palestinian wars on Lebanese territory, and the 1987 Palestinian intifada more directly reconfirmed the question of Palestine as the underlying cause of the Arab-Israeli conflict and reasserted the fundamental centrality of the

Palestinian-Zionist struggle over Palestine. Western politicians and experts alike also view the signing of an Israeli-PLO agreement in 1993 as the key that opens all other Arab doors in the current Middle East "peace process."

In short, Middle Eastern conflicts or peace processes and their international extensions have been invariably intertwined with the Palestine question and almost as often directly with the Palestinian national liberation movement, internal Palestinian politics, and the Palestinian people. In this chapter, then, we specifically analyze the causes, magnitude, distribution, and destination of the forced exodus of the Palestinian refugees. We also examine the demography, structure, transformation, and dynamics of Palestinian diaspora communities in the context of change in the host countries and the transformation of the Middle East region. And finally, we appraise the metamorphosis of these communities from aggregations of refugee populations into a national political community. We save a discussion of the significant role of the PLO in that change; in the development of economic and social service institutions among the diaspora Palestinians; and in the evolution of Palestinian political identity, ideology, and strategy for the following chapter.

Palestinian Refugees: The Dynamics of Dispossession

One profound consequence of al-Nakbah of 1948 and the Arab-Israeli war of 1967 was the displacement of more than half of the Palestinian population. In this multilayered quandary, commonly called the "refugee problem," there are numerous issues that need to be addressed. First of all, momentarily putting aside the major issue of responsibility, the presence and growing numbers of Palestinian refugees are poignant reminders of the Palestinians' loss of their homeland, historic Palestine. It is basically for this reason that the refugees have resisted any proposed settlement to their precarious situation short of return. The bulk of the 1948 Palestinians fled their homes, villages, and land primarily because of mortal fear created by systematic terror campaigns conducted by the Israeli state forces. Even as they took flight, however, there was never a question of return: It was always a matter of when and how, not whether they would return. As time went on and the tragedies accumulated, the mystique of "the return" became even stronger. In many a Palestinian home in the diaspora, families display olive wood carvings or framed needlework pictures with the words "*Innana raji'oun*" or "*Innana 'ai'doun*" (We shall return).

The irony deeply embedded in the refugee question is that as the Palestinians were expelled or fled in 1948, they were quickly replaced by hundreds of thousands of European and Oriental (Arab) Jews, displaced persons, and immigrants. Movable and immovable Palestinian property—homes, businesses, factories, orchards, and fields filled with produce—

TABLE 4.2 Summary of the Flow of Palestinian Dispersal Since 1948, with a Projection of the Likely Distribution by 2000

Country or Region of Residence	1948	1952	1961	1967 (prewar)	1967 (postwar)	1970	1975	1980	1985
				Percentages of Total in Region					
Total Population	100	100	100	100	100	100	100	100	100
Palestinians in Palestine	100	76	65	63	50	46	45	43	41
Israel		11	11	12	15	15	16	16	16
West Bank		47	37	34	22	20	19	17	16
Gaza		18	17	18	13	11	11	10	9
Palestinians Outside of Palestine	0	24	35	37	50	54	55	57	59
Lebanon	0	7	8	8	8	8	8	8	8
East Bank of Jordan	0	9	17	18	27	30	28	25	23
Syria	0	5	5	5	5	5	5	5	5
Outside Core	0	5	(4.5)	(6)	(10)	(11)	(13)	(19)	(23)
Kuwait	–	(2)	2	3	4	5	6	6.3	6.5
Gulf states	–	–	2.5	1	3	0.6	1	1.5	2.0
Saudi Arabia	–	–		2		1.3	2.5	4.5	5.1
Libya	–	–				0.3	0.3	0.5	0.5
Iraq	–	–				0.8	0.9	0.9	0.9
Egypt	–	–			1	1.0	1	1	1
Rest of the world	–	–			2	2	2	4	7

	1990/1991	1995	2000
Total Population	5,780,422	6,692,153	7,760,608
Palestinians in Palestine			
Israel	12.6	12.0	11.8
West Bank	18.6	18.3	17.8
Gaza	10.8	10.9	10.8
Palestinians Outside Palestine			
Lebanon	5.7	5.9	6.0
East Bank of Jordan	31.6	32.4	33.5
Syria	5.2	5.3	5.3
Outside Core			
Rest of the Arab World	7.7	7.7	7.7
Rest of the World	7.8	7.5	7.1

SOURCES: For 1948–1980 figures, J. Abu-Lughod, "Demographic Characteristics of Palestinian Population: Relevance for Planning Palestine Open University," *Palestine Open University: Feasibility Study*, part 2 (Paris: UNESCO, 1980) 39; for 1985–2000 figures, *Facts and Figures About the Palestinians* (Washington, DC: Center for Policy Analysis on Palestine, 1992), 4–5.

throughout the urban and rural areas was seized and the ownership was transferred to Jewish occupants by the newly formed Israeli state. Close to 400 villages and towns that the Israeli authorities could not or would not populate with immigrant Jews were plundered and razed.[4] Among the Palestinians who remained in what became Israel, village "populations were ejected forcibly in order to make room for Jewish settlements . . . a form of compulsory *internal* migration."[5] Official committees, formed by the Haganah before and the Knesset (Israeli parliament) after the declaration of Israel, handled the "absorption" (e.g., appropriation) of Palestinian property under the guise of "custodianship." Given that the Jews owned only 10 percent of the land within the gerrymandered borders allotted to them in the 1947 United Nation partition plan and composed only 55 percent of the total population there, the dispossession and transfer of the Palestinians became crucial to the realization of an exclusively Jewish Israel. So was preventing their return and, alternatively, denying their claims for compensation and reparations.

Causes of the Flight

The long-standing controversy over the flight/expulsion of the Palestinians revolves around a set of fundamental questions: Was the exodus deliberate, intended, forced, anticipated, planned? Or was it devoid of volition, a result of mass panic, uncontrolled crowd behavior? Contained in both Israeli and Palestinian accounts of the precipitant events are the elements of intention and panic alike, though each side places the burden of responsibility on the other. Many have attempted to reconstruct the critical events during the months of December 1947 through July 1949, in film and scholarly endeavors, using interviews and primary documents such as memories of leaders, newspapers, military reports, and so on. As expected, because the victor's version usually becomes hegemonic, the Israeli account of the events, causes, and consequences prevails in the media, popular films, novels, and textbooks in the West and, what is more important, in policies dealing directly with the refugee problem.[6]

This account has become an integral component of what Benedict Anderson would call Israel's "imagined community," the ideological manifestation and connective medium of a modern nation-state. In a word, it is the basis of Israeli nationality.[7] Essential to Israel's national definition are several recurrent themes in what it labels its "war of independence," the 1948 Palestinian Arab-Israeli war. These include, first, that the Palestinians and the wider Arab peoples and armies represented a potentially overwhelming military threat to the much smaller but better-trained and -armed Jewish forces. Second, Israel's role in creating the refugee problem was an unintended, albeit desirable, outcome of a series of life-or-death battles. Third, the burden of the refugees rests with the Arab armies and leaders who called for a mass exodus of the civilian population in order to clear the battlefields. Finally, continued open belligerence and hostility toward Israel blocked an immediate peaceful solution to the refugee problem, which was to permanently settle Palestinians among their fellow Arabs.

In contrast to the Israeli version of history, in the Palestinian view of the events there are only one or two heroes but many survivors, a few glorious battles and much tragedy and hardship. To Palestinians and sympathizers, the birth of Israel was their Nakbah, their catastrophe. In a sense, al-Nakbah put an abrupt halt to the Palestinian "imagined community," or the prospects of modern nation-statehood, because that implies territorial grounding and economic and cultural cohesion. Instead, they became a fractured people, scattered in diaspora in several neighboring and more distant Arab states and throughout the world. In the Palestinians' own recollection of the events of 1948—that is, in their histories and collective memories—the picture that surfaces is antithetical to that of the Israelis in one major respect. Palestinians have long believed that the Zionist project, since its early conception, was built on the eradication of Palestine and with it the Palestinian people. Moreover, once the Zionist project gained momentum in the wake of World War II (after being released from Great Britain as a declining hegemon and embraced by the United States as the emergent superpower), the next step was to carry out by force its vision of the creation of Israel on Palestinian land. Hence the ethical and material burden of the refugees was and continues to be Israel's responsibility; cast in legalistic terms, Israel's responsibility is codified by United Nations Resolution 194 (see Appendix 6), which spells out the Palestinian right of return and/or compensation, and in international law.

More recent Israeli scholarship, however, takes issue with both accounts and finds a middle ground between the polemical arguments hurled by the main partisans.[8] This revisionist history, based largely on recently declassified Israeli state documents, debunks the more tenacious myths surrounding 1948 and presents a more credible and complex chain of events. For example, Benny Morris closely examined an archival report entitled "The Emigration of Arabs of Palestine in the Period 1/12/1947–1/6/1948," which assesses the causes of the Palestinian exodus.[9] Culled from Israel's intelligence agency archives, the report provides valuable insight into how the Israeli state initially perceived its objective role in "the various factors which directly bore upon the movement of population and to indicate the destination of the exodus."[10] As interesting and useful to present-day analysis, it surveys the situation with regard to class, regional, and urban-rural differences in Palestinian society.

The report dismisses purely economic and political factors—such as the "lack of employment, food or any other economic hardship."[11] It further rejects as the prime and general motives for the exodus British withdrawal and the early flight of Palestinian leadership from the urban centers, factors the "old" and official Israeli historiography typically emphasize. Rather, it quite bluntly admits that "without doubt, hostile [Haganah and Israeli military] operations were the main cause of the movement of population."[12] Morris summarizes the eleven, often connected, factors as arrayed "in order of importance" by the intelligence service:

1. Direct, hostile Jewish operations against Arab settlements.
2. The effect of our [Haganah and Israeli military] hostile operations on nearby Arab settlements . . . (. . . especially the fall of large neighboring centres).
3. Operations of the [Jewish] dissidents [the Irgun Z'vai Leumi and Lohamei Herut Yisrael].
4. Orders and decrees by Arab institutions and gangs [irregulars].
5. Jewish whispering operations [psychological warfare], aimed at frightening away Arab inhabitants.
6. Ultimative expulsion orders [by Jewish forces].
7. Fear of Jewish [retaliation following] major Arab attack on Jews.
8. The appearance of gangs [irregular Arab forces] and non-local fighters in the vicinity of a village.
9. Fear of Arab invasion and its consequences [mainly near the borders].
10. Isolated Arab villages in purely Jewish areas.
11. Various local factors and general fear of the future.[13]

The unknown author(s) of this report, who, Morris speculates, combined field reports from military commanders during the first truce (June 11–July 9, 1948), added a statistical dimension in the text: Allowing for a 10–15 percent margin of error, the Israeli intelligence service placed the explanatory weight of the exodus upon the actions of the Haganah and Israeli military. The first three factors in the list above accounted for 70 percent of the total: factors 1 and 2 a full 55 percent and factor 3 (e.g., attacks by the Irgun) 15 percent, especially in the Jaffa–Tel Aviv area, in the northern coastal region, and around Jerusalem (the "action at Deir Yassin" is mentioned "as a 'decisive accelerating factor' of the exodus").[14] Factors 5, 6, and 7 made up 5 percent of the total and were considered "a final motivation and propellent, [rather] than a decisive factor." In other words, the "whispering operations" (also described in the report as "friendly advice" given to Arabs by Jews) and the "ultimative expulsion orders" had effect after military operations. "Orders to evacuate by Arab forces," also identified as an indirect factor, explained only 5 percent. Factors 8, 9, and 10 are appraised at a mere 2 percent of the total cause of the Palestinian exodus.

This piece of evidence, Morris maintains, confirms that neither side of the conflict is fully responsible for the exodus. The report assesses the causes and offers, according to Morris, "more than a hint of 'advice' as how to precipitate further Palestinian flight by indirect methods, without having recourse to direct politically and morally embarrassing expulsion orders."[15] Nowhere does the report declare that the causes or outcomes were deliberate or intended by the Haganah and Israeli military forces. Conversely, the report accords minimal responsibility to the Palestinians' leaders, both the Arab Higher Committee and the neighboring Arab governments, for the evacuation of the population. Although the intelligence agency monitored all transmissions closely, there was no mention of (nor had there been) calls for a blanket evacuation over the Arab radio stations or in the press. Actually, the opposite occurred: Arab leaders urged the Palestinian population, but especially the men of military age, to stay put.[16]

Morris asks, "What then is the significance of the IDF [Israeli Defense Forces] Intelligence Service report in understanding the Palestinian exodus of 1948?" Quite correctly he answers that "it thoroughly undermines the traditional official Israeli 'explanation' of a mass flight ordered or 'invited' by the Arab leadership for political-strategic reasons."[17] Given this deduction, warranted from the data, perhaps a bolder question to put to this new evidence might be, How significantly different are the report's conclusions from the official Palestinian explanation? To a certain extent, Morris addresses that query by reiterating his thesis: "Jewish military operations indeed accounted for 70 percent of the Arab exodus; but the depopulation of the villages in most cases was an incidental, if favorably regarded, side-effect of these operations, not their aim"; the exodus, he says, was "born of war, not by design."[18]

Norman Finkelstein provides a compelling critique of what he considers Morris's apologetics.[19] The terms "incidental" and "side-effect" are Morris's, not the Israeli intelligence agency's, Finkelstein points out; a "tone of satisfaction with the exodus does indeed pervade the report," which offers advice on how to hasten the exodus. In one respect the report could be interpreted as answering the "genuine ignorance or concern" of David Ben-Gurion, the Zionist leader and future prime minister of Israel, and others on the question of why Palestinians "fled"; alternatively, it could be seen as a how-to manual on causing flight or an evaluation of what tactics yield such results in the battlefield. Further evidence makes the latter appear more plausible. As discussed in the previous chapter, Plan Dalet, a thirteen-step, systematic campaign of terror and military operations to capture, control, and expel Palestinians from the territory allotted to the Jewish and Arab states in the 1947 partition plan, is one such example.[20] Reports from other sources confirm Jewish Zionist culpability. Sir John Bagot Glubb, the British commander of the Arab Legion, the Transjordanian army that fought in the 1948 war, disclosed in his autobiography that he asked a Jewish official of the Palestine Mandate government "whether the new Jewish state would have many internal troubles in view of the fact that the Arab

inhabitants of the Jewish state would be equal in number to the Jews."
Glubb reported that the official replied, "Oh no! That will be fixed. A few
calculated massacres will soon get rid of them."[21]

Through extensive and intensive interviews in refugee camps in southern
Lebanon, Rosemary Sayigh was able to reconstruct the processes of expulsion and dispersal of this group of peasants. Based on the recollections of
the 1948 refugees who went to Lebanon, these recorded stories and oral
histories could probably be generalized beyond this particular population.
She found the primary causes of the flight "so obvious only deliberate mys-
tification could have obscured them . . . : direct military attack on the villages; terrorism; lack of leadership; lack of arms; in short, chaos and
fear."[22] A secondary but still significant motive was the fear, generated by
personal experience and rumor, of rape and other atrocities Israeli soldiers
perpetrated against defenseless Palestinian civilians. As a man of peasant
origins intimated to Sayigh:

> My village, Sa'sa, didn't leave because of a battle. There was fighting around,
> there were air-raids and bombardments. But the reason we left was the news of
> the massacre of Safsaf, where fifty young men were killed. There were other
> massacres—Jish, Deir Yasseen—and there were stories of attacks on women's
> honour. Our villagers were especially concerned to protect their women, and
> because of this fear, many of the northern villages evacuated even before the
> war reached them.[23]

Crimes against *al-'ard* (the honor of the women of the family) tore at the
sturdy fabric of village life, woven as it was by kinship ties, familial obligations, and communal duties. The conquering Israeli troops were not bound
to such tradition, nor did they respect its sanctity. As Israeli agriculture
minister Aharon Cizling stated at a July 21, 1948, cabinet meeting, "It has
been said that there were cases of rape in Ramle. I can forgive acts of rape
but I won't forgive other deeds which appear to me graver."[24] The threat
against or actual violation of family honor, an integral component of the
Palestinians' culture and community, and the slim possibility of retaliation
in order to redeem al-'ard brought home the necessity of flight, at least temporarily, in order to protect the traditional way of life.

The reasons for the flight of approximately 400,000 Palestinians during
the June 1967 War (small numbers of whom the Israeli government eventually allowed to return) are not as politically controversial as those of the
1948 exodus, but they are similar. Dissatisfied with media reports that
tended to lump all refugees into a faceless mass, Peter Dodd and Halim
Barakat conducted a thorough study of the causes and socioeconomic characteristics of the refugees in a representative camp in Jordan proper shortly
after the conclusion of the 1967 war.[25] Of ninety-eight families interviewed,

TABLE 4.3 Reasons for Leaving Home, as Reported by the Refugees, 1967 War

Reason for Leaving Home	Number of Families
Fear	
Of airplanes	57
Of dishonor (al-'ard)	30
Threats to members of the family	22
Psychological pressures of Israeli occupation	8
Destruction of villages; destruction of homes; eviction	19
Economic pressures; sources of income being cut off	10
Total	167

NOTE: This table is based on the Zeezya sample of 100 families. Numbers show the number of families who gave the reasons listed for their departure from home. The total number of causes exceeds 100 because many families mentioned more than one cause.

SOURCE: P. Dodd and H. Barakat, *River Without Bridges: A Study of the Exodus of the 1967 Palestinian Arab Refugees* (Beirut: Institute for Palestine Studies, 1969), 47.

sixty-one were "first-time" refugees and thirty-seven had fled from refugee camps established after 1948 (they are referred to as "old" refugees). Although the bulk of the sample was "new" refugees who had no actual contact with Israelis (85 percent) nor experienced death or injury of a community member (71 percent),[26] the major direct cause of their flight was fear of impending death, destruction, and dishonor. Table 4.3 shows the reasons as reported by the 1967 war refugees.

In the folklore of the Palestinians in diaspora, the exodus of 1967 from the West Bank and Gaza was far less extensive than that of 1948 Palestine because they had learned an important lesson: While the protection of al-'ard (family honor) may have come before the protection of al-ard (the land) in 1948, priorities were reversed in 1967—al-ard came before al-'ard. Thus, unlike in 1948, most Palestinians in the 1967 war stayed put on their land in the West Bank and Gaza. Yet the events of 1948 and 1967 left an indelible imprint on the collective memory of Palestinians. They were experiences that still echo and create debate and division within the varied Palestinian communities.

The Expulsion:
Magnitude, Patterns, and Destinations

The expulsion of Palestinians in 1948 occurred with little warning or preparation. Usually, whole villages, towns, and urban centers were quickly evacuated or expelled as the Haganah and Israeli forces approached or attacked an area. Map 4.2 shows the distribution and destinations of the 750,000 dispossessed Palestinians. Although the causes of their flight varied by region, social class, and time period, several (forced) flight patterns can be discerned from statistical data as well as subsequent qualitative investigations. Overall, these patterns share a common characteristic: The bulk of the 1948 refugees resisted crossing the borders of Palestine. The majority of Palestinians who lived within the territory of what is now Israel left their homes as danger seemed imminent, as the fighting caught them defenseless, or as they were expelled. Most first found refuge in a nearby village where they may have had kin, on the outskirts of an urban center, or even in an unpopulated area (a field, forest, or mountainous area).

As Morris notes, there are more than a few recorded incidents of Palestinians' returning to their villages to collect their possessions, harvest their crops, and regain occupancy of their homes when direct hostilities ceased. In all but a few cases, notably Abu-Gosh and Beit Naqquba in the Jerusalem area and Al-Fureidis and Khirbet Jisr al-Zarka south of Haifa, returning Palestinians were expelled once again by direct order of Israel's leader, Ben-Gurion. Contrary to the image of masses of Palestinians steadily streaming across the nearest border, then, most refugees made multiple internal migrations before reaching an end point. Furthermore, that end point, for the majority of Palestinians, became east central Palestine (the West Bank) or the Gaza Strip. And those who crossed into Arab countries such as Lebanon tended to remain at first near the border of Palestine, wait for the repatriation they believed was imminent, and resist transfer to other areas.[27] As time went on and material resources were exhausted, refugees accepted transfer to camps in the interior of the host country.

In the chaos and panic of the exodus, most people confronted a common dilemma. Communities became disaggregated into family units, which became the primary decisionmaking bodies in both the 1948 and 1967 wars. Stripped of effective leadership and feeling a general distrust in existing authority, heads of nuclear and extended families assumed the responsibility of protecting their young, old, and women as well as their land, possessions, and country. Many men of military age were faced with the decision of fulfilling their civil *or* family duty. As Dodd and Barakat point out in their study of 1967 refugees, "such cross-pressures are rare in village society." Often the conflict would be resolved, as Sayigh found, by sending the women and children ahead to a safer area. However, "In the panic ... it was common for families to become separated and children to get lost."[28] Accordingly, the first activity of many Palestinian refugees in the diaspora was to locate and bring together their family members, find shelter, and acquire some sustenance. Some also attempted to gather together other relatives and covillagers, as did the founder of the Shatila refugee camp near Beirut, where the 1982 massacre occurred under the eyes of the Israeli army.[29]

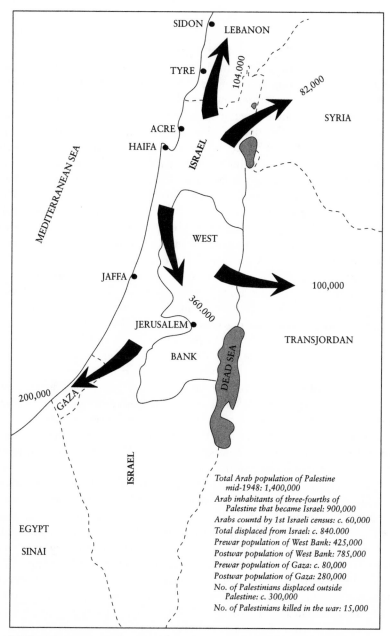

Total Arab population of Palestine
mid-1948: 1,400,000
Arab inhabitants of three-fourths of
Palestine that became Israel: 900,000
Arabs countd by 1st Israeli census: c. 60,000
Total displaced from Israel: c. 840.000
Prewar population of West Bank: 425,000
Postwar population of West Bank: 785,000
Prewar population of Gaza: c. 80,000
Postwar population of Gaza: 280,000
No. of Palestinians displaced outside
Palestine: c. 300,000
No. of Palestinians killed in the war: 15,000

MAP 4.2 Magnitude, Distribution, and Destination of Palestinian Refugees, 1948

SOURCE: R. Sayigh, *Palestinians: From Peasants to Revolutionaries* (London: Zed Press, 1979), 65.

Palestinian Population:
Demographic and Geographic Transition

Both forced expulsion and voluntary migration have had an important consequence on the demographics of the Palestinian people. There are no exact figures for the size, structure, and distribution of the population. The last census of the Palestinians was conducted during the British Mandate in 1931. Scattered sample surveys taken since then, each with its own sampling frame, biases, and concerns, form an uneven data base for making statistical statements about this fragmented and mobile population. Moreover, until the 1960s, all Arab countries lacked an adequate demographic base or a sufficiently comprehensive civil registration system.[30] Janet Abu-Lughod, who has compiled one of the most authoritative demographic studies on the Palestinians after al-Nakbah, recognizes that "it is virtually impossible to determine exactly how many persons of Palestinian birth or ancestry exist today."[31] What further complicates matters is that in different Palestinian diaspora communities the rate of intermarriage with non-Palestinians varies considerably. For example, intermarriage rates among Palestinians in Israel and those residing in camps are extremely low, whereas among those residing (outside the camps) in Lebanon, Jordan, Kuwait (before 1991), Europe, and the Americas are much higher.

As we noted previously, in 1995 only around 40 percent of the total population of Palestinians continued to live in historic Palestine (Israel, the West Bank, and Gaza Strip). The factors that impelled this demographic transformation between 1948 and 1995 were both economic and political. To start with, the greater economic investment favoring the East Bank encouraged many Palestinians from the West Bank to emigrate there throughout the 1950s and 1960s. Others, because of West Bank and Gaza Strip economic stagnation, migrated to the oil-exporting states of the Arabian peninsula and Libya, which were in desperate need of unskilled, skilled, and educated labor forces. Others emigrated to Lebanon, which also experienced an economic boom in part linked to the early oil bonanza of the 1960s.[32] As a result of this wave of voluntary migration, the percentage of Palestinians living inside historic Palestine dropped from roughly 80 percent after al-Nakbah in 1948 to 63 percent just before the June 1967 War.

The 1967 war also had a profound impact on Palestinian population movements. Israel's conquest of the rest of Palestine led, as we noted already, to a second major exodus, estimated at around 400,000 Palestinians.[33] Out of a total Palestinian population of approximately 2.65 million in 1967 the ratio of the Palestinians residing inside historic Palestine dropped sharply, from 63 to 50 percent after the war. Specifically, the West Bank population decreased by 12 percent as a result of the war (from a total of 34 percent of all Palestinians June 1, 1967, to 22 percent in December

1967), while the Gaza population declined by 5 percent (from 18 to 13 percent). Simultaneously, the ratio of Palestinians in the East Bank of Jordan jumped substantially from 466,000 (17.5 percent of all Palestinians) to 730,600 (27 percent).[34]

After their second displacement, in the June 1967 War, migrations to the oil-exporting states of the Arabian peninsula picked up momentum, especially in the oil boom period of the 1970s and early 1980s. Additionally, Palestinian migrations from (rather than to) Lebanon increased further during the civil war (1975 onward) and jumped greatly as a result of the Israeli invasion of 1982. Palestinian emigration to Europe and the Americas, too, increased substantially during the 1980s. It is estimated that in 1995 about 200,000 Palestinians resided in the United States and Canada and a similar number in the rest of the Western Hemisphere. The percentage of Palestinians outside historic Palestine *and* the neighboring Arab countries rose from 6 percent of all Palestinians before the June 1967 War to 23 percent (1.13 million out of 4.9 million) by 1985.[35] Both the ratio and absolute number increased further by 1991 but experienced a precipitous decline when Kuwait expelled between 300,000 and 350,000 Palestinians in the wake of the 1991 Gulf War (against Iraq's occupation of Kuwait). Most expellees returned to Jordan and Israel allowed a small number (possibly 30,000) to return to the occupied territories. Once the oldest, largest, and most vigorous Palestinian community in the Arabian peninsula, the Palestinians in Kuwait numbered fewer than 50,000 in the mid-1990s.

The diaspora Palestinians and those under occupation have remarkably high fertility and low mortality rates and thus a high rate of population increase. Already high during the mandate period,[36] the birthrate continued to rise, in large part because of better health conditions. However, the dispersed Palestinian society after al-Nakbah became occupationally differentiated, urbanized, educated, and socially mobile, factors typically associated with declining fertility rates. As a result, among the middle and upper social classes the rate of population increase declined. But the rate of increase among the Palestinians in Israel, those under occupation in Gaza and in most refugee camps—the proletarianized classes—continued to rise and peaked at 4 percent per annum, canceling out the decline among the bourgeois Palestinians.[37] Thus the overall rate of Palestinian population increase has been phenomenally high, more than doubling the size of the population every generation since 1948. In the twenty-first century, however, Palestinian population growth will probably slow down; indications of declining fertility are already evident.

The high rate of population increase among Palestinians also means a young population, the second key feature of the Palestinian population. Generally, Palestinians below the age of eighteen years have rarely represented less than 50 percent of the total population.[38] Indeed in the camps such as those of Lebanon, Jordan, and the West Bank and in Palestinian communities in Kuwait and Saudi Arabia the ratio of those below fifteen years reached much above the 50 percent level during the 1970s and 1980s. In the mid-1990s that ratio was estimated to be close to 60 percent in Gaza, especially in the camps. The range of median ages of between fifteen and eighteen years in various communities of Palestinians is dramatic if compared to the current median age of thirty-two years in an aging population like that of the United States.

Such a young population creates immense social, economic, and political implications. For example, the ratio of those of productive age is low compared to most Western countries: In Lebanon the Palestinian labor force was 17 percent of the population in 1951 but increased steadily to 30 percent by 1976.[39] And providing education and jobs for them is always an important consideration for whichever authority is in control of their lives. Further, the young Palestinian population has always provided a large supply of youthful activists who carried out the task of political and military mobilization. Also significant, labor migrations to the Arabian peninsula and the West often involved young men and thus created skewed population structures in both the home and work communities. In short, the characteristics of the Palestinian population, including especially the high ratios of population increase, will add to the dilemmas of resolving the Palestine problem. Overall, the Palestinian population has increased from roughly 1.4 million people in 1948 to an estimated 6.8 million in 1995 (see Table 4.4).[40] At current rates the Palestinian population will number an estimated 7.8 million by the year 2000.[41]

Communities in Diaspora

Palestinians in the diaspora were transformed from a nation largely of farmers and traditional rural residents, most of whom were illiterate, into dispersed communities that became highly proletarianized, urbanized, and literate. Palestinian women also changed, adding public, professional, and political roles to their more traditional ones. The small pre-Nakbah middle class and commercial, banking, industrial, and construction-based entrepreneurial bourgeoisie expanded and flourished significantly in the diaspora. Many of them achieved high economic, social, and, occasionally, political statuses. Many also achieved renown as academics, physicians and surgeons, scientists, mathematicians, engineers, businesspeople, journalists, writers, and politicians not only in the Arab world but also in Europe and North America.[42]

From the onset of al-Nakbah, there were two kinds of refugees. The middle- and upper-class Palestinians, many of whom left the areas of armed conflict and potential war zones just before the Zionist onslaught, took

TABLE 4.4 Global Distribution of Estimated and Projected Numbers of the Palestinian People

	1986	1990/1991	1995	2000
Jordan	1,398,050	1,824,179	2,170,101	2,596,986
West Bank/East Jerusalem	951,520	1,075,531	1,227,545	1,383,415
Gaza	545,100	622,016	726,832	837,699
Israel	608,200	730,000	800,755	919,453
Lebanon	271,434	331,757	392,315	463,067
Syria	242,474	301,744	357,881	410,599
Remaining Arab states	582,894	445,195	516,724	599,389
Rest of world	280,846	450,000	500,000	550,000
Total	4,880,518	5,780,422	6,692,153	7,760,608

SOURCES: *Facts and Figures About the Palestinians* (Washington, DC: Center for Policy Analysis on Palestine, 1992), 4.

refuge, as some did earlier in the 1936 revolt, in nearby Arab cities such as Amman, Beirut, Cairo, and Damascus. They rented apartments on a short-term basis with the hope of returning to their homeland after the conclusion of the hostilities. The second and by far the largest group of refugees was the mass of poor and peasant Palestinians, who were destitute and desperate. They became the refugee camp dwellers.

Refugee Camps and the role of UNRWA

The United Nations qualified "a needy person, who as a result of the war in Palestine, has lost his home and his means of livelihood" as a refugee. Later the definition was expanded to include "direct descendants." In September 1949, 726,000 Palestinians were classified as refugees (see Table 4.1 above). Initially, the Arab host countries helped the Palestinians, but their meager resources were quickly overwhelmed. Also in 1949 the United Nations passed General Assembly Resolution 194 (see Appendix 6) affirming the Palestinian refugees' right to repatriation and/or compensation and urged Israel to accept the return of the refugees. Israel refused. It stonewalled despite international, including some U.S., pressure to allow the return or compensation of the refugees. Nearly two years after al-Nakbah, the United Nations Relief and Works Agency (UNRWA) assumed relief operations (provision of tents, food staples, and health care) in Gaza, the West Bank, Transjordan, Lebanon, and Syria where Palestinians had clustered. Although UNRWA was conceived as a temporary agency, by 1955, as the refugee problem became more intractable, UNRWA reoriented its services toward integrating Palestinians into their surroundings. Education, housing, training, and employment within the camps were offered as a means toward that end. By 1992 UNRWA had become one of the largest international agencies, employing close to 19,000 people who served more than 2.7 million camp refugees (including those of 1967). Commensurately, its budget expanded "from $33.6 million a year . . . in 1950 to over $254.5 million in 1991."[43]

A large number of refugee camps were established by mutual agreement of the host country and the United Nations. In Lebanon, for example, fifteen such camps were originally erected, but several (including a large one east of Beirut, Tal al-Za'atar) were overrun in savage fighting by right-wing Lebanese militias and destroyed during the 1975–1976 civil war. As Table 4.5 shows, in the mid-1990s there were twelve camps in Lebanon, ten each in Syria and Jordan, nineteen in the West Bank, and eight in the Gaza Strip. In 1993 UNRWA listed 2.73 million officially registered refugees. Over nearly five decades, as their economic well-being improved, Palestinians sought residence outside the camps in the host countries or elsewhere. Accordingly, after two generations, as Table 4.5 indicates, camp dwellers constituted 52.2 percent of all registered refugees in Lebanon, 29.1 percent in Syria, 22.8 percent in Jordan, 26.3 percent in the West Bank, and 55.0 percent in the Gaza Strip.

The sites of camps were determined by the host country in accordance with internal economic and political considerations. In Lebanon the bulk of the refugees were herded into rural camps in the south and north of the country and in the eastern Beqa'a valley, which provided Lebanese landlords with cheap agricultural labor. Yet Shatila camp, near the city of Beirut, was founded spontaneously, as few other camps, through the effort of a former Palestinian rebel leader who was seeking immediate, temporary shelter for his family and kin. Shatila, like other small suburban camps and settlements in Lebanon, Jordan, and elsewhere, grew fast in subsequent years as it attracted people from rural camps who sought jobs in the booming construction industry of Arab capital cities. Migration from rural to urban camps was extensive during the urban boom years and was further increased by the presence of the PLO, first in Amman (1968–1970) and later in Beirut (1970–1982). The host governmental authorities ignored the urban-oriented movement of camp refugees, especially as the urban construction labor market demanded a vast pool of cheap labor.

At first the International Red Cross and then the UNRWA provided the refugees with tents and supplied them with trucked-in water, some food staples, and medical service. The first UNRWA installations in Shatila "were the clinic, the school and two lines of public latrines," although the "Beirut Water Company was not allowed to supply Shateela residents; instead there were four public water tanks filled periodically by UNRWA lorries."[44] Prevented from building more permanent housing, Palestinians in

Lebanon over the years erected dwellings (*barrakiyat*) of corrugated iron, tin, wood, and other materials. Not until 1969, with the emergence of Harakat al-Muqawama al-Filastiniyya (the Palestinian Resistance Movement, PRM)—as the national liberation movement in general and its leadership, the newly radicalized PLO, were called—did the camp dwellers begin to build concrete and cinder block housing, pipe in running water, and install some sewerage and electricity. In part this happened because the PRM took control of most camps (principally in Lebanon, Syria, and earlier in Jordan, but not in the West Bank and the Gaza Strip, which were under Israeli occupation) and in part because the new generation of skilled Palestinians built such amenities for themselves.

Thus in a little over one generation, refugee camps developed from precarious, wind-swept tent cities with hardly any services into highly congested minicities or shantytowns of concrete, asphalt, and some infrastructure. Table 4.5 shows that although running water eventually was piped into most residences in the camps, in 1992 only 56 percent of all shelters were sewered in Lebanon, 85 percent in Syria, 45 percent in Jordan, 31 percent in the West Bank, and 27 percent in Gaza. Otherwise, the camps had open sewers. Of course by then the population congestion was immense, the land area of camps strictly circumscribed by the respective Arab and Israeli authorities. The physical infrastructure, the social and medical services, and the quality of life became totally inadequate, perhaps miserable in the majority of the camps—worst among those under Israeli control.

Differential Social and Economic Integration

Table 4.4 provides figures on the size and geographic distribution of the Palestinian population in 1995, while Table 4.6 shows the occupational distribution of Palestinian males in selected countries and regions in selected years. There is a wide range in the size of the different communities, as there is in the pattern of occupational distribution, an important index of the character of economic integration into Arab host countries (and Israel). The social structure and political conditions of life of Palestinian communities in the diaspora countries is varied. Determinants of a host government's attitude and manner of treatment include the relative and absolute size of the Palestinian community, the degree of its economic integration or marginality (itself in part contingent upon size) in the host country's economy, and the degree of its political organization and influence (whether through formal political enfranchisement or not).[45]

In short, if the Palestinian community is organized and perceived by the host elite or government as a political and economic threat, then the host state will attempt to circumscribe or suppress outright the Palestinian community. This has been the case in Jordan (where the East Bank refugee and

TABLE 4.5 UNRWA General Information Concerning Refugees

	Lebanon	Syria	Jordan	Gaza	West Bank	Total
Demographic characteristics						
Country area (sq km)	10,452	185,180	91,860	360	5,500	293,352
Country population (CP)	3,400,000	14,618,390	4,139,458	963,000	1,571,575	24,692,426
Registered refugees (RR)	352,668	347,391	1,358,706	716,930	532,438	3,308,133
RR growth (%) (1995–1996)	1.9	3	5.5	4.9	2.9	4.3
RR as % of CP	10.4	2.4	32.8	74.4	33.9	13.4
Existing camps	12	10	10	8	19	59
RR in camps (RRCs)	192,052	101,027	258,204	395,987	148,105	1,095,375
Education/training						
Schools	74	110	198	155	100	637
Pupils (1995–1996) enrollment	36,498	62,046	148,004	129,494	45,812	421,854
Female pupils (%)	50.3	48.4	49.1	49.4	55.5	49.6
Vocational & technical training centers	1	1	2	1	3	8
Vocational & technical training places	608	800	1,224	732	1,260	4,624
Educational sciences faculty training places	N.A.	N.A.	855	N.A.	N.A.	1,455
In-service teacher trainees	98	108	175	164	106	651
University scholarships awarded	77	240	246	231	149	943
Total education posts	1,538	2,063	4,965	4,133	2,093	14,863
Infrastructure/services (as of 1993)						
Health center/units & dental clinics	40	29	36	25	49	179
Indoor water supply in camps (%)	89	75	92	100	98	92
Sewered shelters in camps (%)	56	85	45	27	31	47
Unemployment % (estimate)	40	10	20	30–40	30–40	28
Total 1993 budget ($ thousands)	31,540	36,537	61,183	63,896	47,846	297,185

SOURCE: United Nations Relief and Works Agency, *Annual Report* (New York: UNRWA, 1993 and 1996).

TABLE 4.6 Occupational Distribution of Palestinian Males in Selected Countries and Regions (in percentages)

Country or Region of Residence	Professional, Technical	Administrative Manager	Clerical	Sales and Commerce	Industrial, Transport, Utilities	Services (personal)	Agriculture, fishing, mining
Saudi Arabia	51.5	2.9	6.0	3.2	28.9	3.3	4.3
Jordanians	63.0	3.1	6.1	3.1	20.1	1.9	2.1
Palestinians	36.9	2.6	5.7	3.3	39.3	5.0	7.1
Kuwait	20.8	1.3	17.8	8.6	41.1	8.4	2.1
Jordan East Bank	9.7		7.0	11.8	45.4	11.2	14.5
Syria	10.8	0.7	8.2	8.9	57.0	6.6	7.9
Israel (1972 census)	6.6	3.9		8.2	51.4	10.0	19.9
Israel (1976 census)	6.2	0.4	3.9	7.3	57.3	9.7	15.2
West Bank	6.2	0.9	3.0	12.5	50.1	7.8	19.5
Gaza	5.1	0.6	3.1	11.9	47.4	8.7	23.2
Lebanon camps		3.7	1.4	15.3	46.1	8.9	24.7

SOURCE: J. Abu-Lughod, "Demographic Characteristics of the Palestinian Population: Relevance for Planning Palestine Open University," *Palestine Open University Feasibility Study*, part 3 (Paris: UNESCO, 1980), 61. © UNESCO 1980. Reproduced by permission of UNESCO.

migrant Palestinians constitute 55 percent of the host country's population
after the return of 300,000 from Kuwait), Lebanon (10–12 percent), and
Kuwait (37 percent until the Gulf War), but not in Egypt (0.01 percent),
Syria (2.4 percent), and Saudi Arabia (2.5–3.0 percent). Government authorities in Jordan and Kuwait moved against the Palestinians; in Lebanon
the government disintegrated during the civil war and anti-Palestinian
right-wing (Christian) and Shi'a militias attacked the Palestinian camps and
zones in the country. The examples of the two extremes of the relative size
of the Palestinian communities in relation to differing treatment in the host
countries—Jordan and Egypt—tell all.

The different Palestinian communities in the diaspora have had diverse
and unique social, economic, and political histories since 1948 and therefore have developed distinctive occupational and social structures. As is
clear from Table 4.6, the refugee communities in the occupied West Bank
and Gaza Strip and the indigenous Palestinian community in Israel were
completely proletarianized (lumpenproletarianized in Gaza) by Israel and
turned into cheap sources of unskilled labor power. So were most of the
Palestinian camp dwellers of Lebanon and Jordan (less so in Syria). Those
of the Arabian peninsula were socially more diverse. As a result, the communities have shown differing levels of political and economic involvement
and contributions in support of the Palestinian national liberation movement. For example, the PLO was anchored in Jordan during its early period, 1968–1970, and the Palestinians of Jordan were its principal social
base. After its expulsion from Jordan, the PLO's social and economic base
shifted to the Palestinians of Lebanon; this lasted from 1970 until the exodus from Beirut in 1982. Recruits for its political cadres and fighters nevertheless came from all the far-flung communities, including the Palestinians
of Israel (the so-called Israeli Arabs). The most prominent of the Palestinians from Israel is the celebrated Palestinian poet laureate Mahmoud Darwish, who emerged as the voice of the movement and the interpreter of its
struggles. Certain communities, like those of the Arabian peninsula, especially Saudi Arabia and Kuwait (before the 1991 Iraqi invasion), contributed financially more than others. As the diaspora communities have
become more differentiated from each other and experienced divergent social histories and political legacies, the future integration of Palestinian society becomes more problematic.[46]

The Camp Dwellers. The pattern of proletarianization and indeed
lumpenproletarianization is especially manifest among camp dwellers, as
shown in Table 4.6. The Shatila camp (with 75,000 residents in the early
1980s) near Beirut, the 'Ayn al-Hilweh camp (100,000 in the mid-1990s)
near Sidon, Lebanon, and the Baqa'a camp (about 65,000) on the outskirts
of Amman, Jordan, are tremendously overcrowded minicities whose labor

force has been engaged in unskilled and skilled labor, tertiary occupations, low-level clerical work, and part-time or temporary work in the nearby urban center and surrounding agricultural areas. To a much lesser extent than men, women, too, sought paid work, although mostly inside the camp.

A study by Samir Ayyoub of the class structure of the Palestinians in Lebanon found that 76.4 percent of the grandfathers of the sample respondents were self-employed (68 percent in agriculture, 2 percent in industry, and 22 percent in services) in Palestine, while only 21 percent of the grandchildren were so employed in Lebanon (17 percent in agriculture, 9 percent in industry, and 74 percent in services) in 1978.[47] The same study shows that only 15.6 percent of the grandfathers were employed in *wage* labor in Palestine, as were 39.6 percent of the parents and 63.3 percent of the respondents in the sample. Put differently, the source of income of 76.1 percent of the sample derived from wage labor, a high degree of proletarianization in one generation. In the 1950s in Shatila camp, unskilled workers earned the equivalent of 65 cents per day, grossly insufficient wages for the survival of their families. In general, in terms of income level and source of income, the class structure of the Palestinians in Lebanon in 1978 was 62.9 percent working class, 27.5 percent middle class, 7.8 percent upper middle class, and 1.8 percent bourgeois.[48]

By the 1960s camp dwellers had developed into specialists in the building trades: plumbers, tilers, plasterers, electricians, and so on.[49] What allowed many to escape the camp was what the Palestinians themselves call the "education revolution," which in one generation turned many of the children of proletarianized Palestinians refugees into professionals. Many of those who remained destitute were the unlucky ones who for a variety of reasons could neither take advantage of the educational and skill revolution nor emigrate. In Lebanon (and to a lesser extent in the other host countries) the reasons lay in part in the severe limits that the host government placed on official work permits. Urban camps have been centers of manual workers. Nonetheless, Shatila and other urban camps have often served as way stations for upgrading skills and emigrating to the Arabian peninsula oil-exporting economies and to the West. With the onset of the civil war in Lebanon and the Israeli invasion of the country in 1982, the assaults on (and destruction of some) refugee camps added another large group of displaced camp dwellers, *muhajjarin*, who sought shelter in the more secure camps and settlements.

Camps are small, complex cities. They have their own marketplaces, shops, and service providers, and UNRWA employs people in the schools, health clinics, and sanitary and welfare institutions.[50] Camps have a retail and service economy of their own. But as shown in Table 4.5 above, the necessary infrastructure of water, sewer, housing, electricity, and roads remains woefully inadequate in every Palestinian refugee camp in the Arab host countries and the autonomous areas of the West Bank and the Gaza Strip.

In general, camp life has been congested, unhealthy, desperate, violent, and brutish. Camp dwellers sought solace in tradition. Thus the dramatic transformation in the occupational structure of the majority of the Palestinians after al-Nakbah—from largely peasants to proletarians—did not initially produce any meaningful change in social relations, values, or culture. Based on ties of kinship, locality (villages or city quarters), patronage, and patrimonial political factions, traditional Palestinian social structure was reconstituted in the newly formed refugee camps.[51] Both the UNRWA and the active ingathering of kin by leaders such as the one who established Shatila helped reproduce this structure. Early on, then, the traditional patterns of kinship obligations and, to a lesser extent, patronage served the traumatized refugees well. Over the years, however, both began to undergo change as their functions in the context of dispersal, landlessness, wage labor, and increased social differentiation undermined their ability to serve the people's needs. In their stead, beginning in the late 1960s, factions of the PLO and their modern, secular organizing practices provided both social services and social safety nets for the camp dwellers. Yet village customs that were expressive and symbolic of the traditional values and culture[52] and therefore of identity did remain relatively strong within the camps. Nonetheless, considerable variation in camp structures existed as a result of the degree and character of control exercised by the Arab host countries or Israel.

Initially as well, the physical uprooting and social restructuring did not seem to have caused a change in political consciousness. Some of the kinship- (hamula-) based political structures and fragments of the political organization of the Arab Higher Committee and its titular leader, al-Hajj Amin al-Husseini, survived in Lebanon (less so elsewhere) and exerted some influence within refugee ranks. This naturally helped reinforce the reproduction in the diaspora of traditional rural values, customs, and social relations.

As more modern sociopolitical organizations (student unions, workers unions, and women's organizations) began to be reconstituted or emerge with a modern, secular pan-Arabist ideology, however, they modified those traditional social relations and values. Thus with the change in the regional political climate (the rise of Arab nationalism), the emergence of the PLO in 1964, and the surfacing of the PRM in 1968, social change, political consciousness, and activism significantly increased in the camps. One generation after al-Nakbah, an indigenous, more modern leadership emerged and attempted to establish among the dispersed communities and fractured society quasi-state institutions as a framework for the restoration of Palestinian political rights, repatriation, self-determination, and nationhood. We discuss this revolutionary transformation of the Palestinian people and the birth of the PLO in the next chapter.

Religion, typically a conservative social force, was embedded in the traditional popular culture of the camps, but it became irrelevant to the emergent secular nationalist discourse. New secular nationalist symbols proliferated, as did literature, songs, and gatherings: rallies, celebrations, funerals of martyrs. The tempo of daily life accelerated. Traditional social structures, including family and values, also began to change. Sayigh points out that the patriarchal, compound household gave way to looser, adjacent nuclear units.[53] Parents became less authoritarian. Even family solidarity and loyalty was modified by the activist political factions. While in some instances whole families were members or supporters of a specific political faction, in other instances fathers and sons or siblings differed in their factional political loyalties. Perhaps most significant, camp dwellers "became accustomed to women taking a more prominent political, economic, and social role,"[54] and as a result conjugal relations changed as well, particularly among the new generation of revolutionary male and female comrades. Despite the imperative for and ideology of change, women's status and participation in the resistance movement posed a serious dilemma.[55]

The secular, nationalist discourse and organization remained dominant until the 1980s, when the influence of religion among the camp dwellers and the poor Palestinian masses resurfaced in a politicized, radicalized, activist, even militant form, especially in the Gaza Strip. Many factors contributed to this phenomenon in Palestinian politics. Not least was the rise of political Islam throughout the Middle East. Most important in the Gaza Strip, however, were the unrelenting pressure of Israel's occupying army, the severe degradation of the people's economic well-being, and the ineffectiveness or failure of the secular PLO and PRM to end the occupation and relieve the misery.[56] While political Islam has not yet developed significantly in the diaspora Palestinian camps in the Arab host countries, it has nonetheless become an important factor in Palestinian, regional, and international political calculations. Its influence on the people is contradictory: It is politically radical, militant, and activist yet socially conservative and regressive, especially in relation to women's status and role in public life. However, it has also provided economic relief and social services for the needy and destitute.

The Middle Class. A minority of the non-camp-dwellers in Lebanon, a small and strongly Christian fraction of the Palestinians there, became highly educated, Westernized, and rapidly integrated into the expanding service economy of the country and the region.[57] Larger Palestinian middle and upper classes also evolved in Jordan on the East and West Banks, both because of the size of the community and because of the underdeveloped Transjordanian counterparts. Because they were new citizens of Jordan,[58] economic life in the private, public, and governmental sectors was open to them. Some even became prime ministers, cabinet members, ambassadors, and heads of major governmental agencies in the 1950s and early 1960s before tension, a power struggle, and conflict between the PLO and the Jordanian monarchy and between the two communities (Transjordanian and Palestinian) developed in the late 1960s. In Jordan, Lebanon, Kuwait (before 1991), Saudi Arabia, and elsewhere, an entrepreneurial, professional, and commercial Palestinian bourgeoisie emerged and became quite distinguished and socially disconnected from its compatriot proletarian camp dwellers.

The Palestinian middle and bourgeois classes in Lebanon, Jordan, and the Arabian peninsula played pivotal roles in the economic development of those countries. The Palestinian bourgeoisie was prominent in building the Lebanese, Jordanian, and peninsular banking institutions (e.g., Intra Bank, Arab Bank, etc.); airlines (Middle East Airlines and Trans Mediterranean Airways); design, auditing, marketing, consulting, construction, and other technical firms; the hotel and tourist industry; and other service industries. The Palestinian middle and upper classes in both countries expanded and flourished all the more during the regionwide oil boom of the 1970s and early 1980s. In the oil-exporting states of the Arabian peninsula, the Palestinian professional elite contributed considerably as well to the planning, design, and construction of the physical infrastructure (from sewers to hospitals and from roads to airports); the creation of the social and economic infrastructure (schools, universities, hospitals, factories, businesses, and banks); and the development of the public sector, the governmental bureaucracy, the diplomatic corps, and the economy in general. This role was most pronounced in Kuwait. A 1975 survey conducted in Kuwait by the United Nations Economic and Social Commission for West Asia (ESCWA) found that Palestinians "constituted 28 percent of all engineers, 34 percent of surveyors and draftsmen, 37 percent of all doctors and pharmacists, 25 percent of the nursing staff, 38 percent of all economists and accountants, [and] 30 percent of the teaching staff."[59]

As shown in Table 4.6, the Palestinian community in Saudi Arabia was also highly skilled: Over 50 percent of the labor force of the Palestinians (and Jordanians, many if not most of whom are Palestinians with Jordanian citizenship) occupied high technical, professional, and managerial positions. Here, as in Lebanon and Jordan, the rapid economic development of the oil-exporting countries afforded the Palestinians an opportunity for socioeconomic mobility. A new and larger class of nouveaux riches emerged and became even more removed from the diaspora camp dwellers and the proletarianized masses in the occupied territories of the West Bank and the Gaza Strip. Yet for a time, most remained close to and supportive of the PLO and its leadership.

Social Mobility and Political Influence: Expansion and Contraction. The expansion and increased influence of the Palestinian middle class and bourgeoisie, as we have pointed out, occurred especially in the context of the oil-based economic boom that raised sharply the growth rates of individual Arab economies and the income levels and standards of living of most people in the Arab east. The new Palestinian multimillionaires, however, internationalized their investments, interests, and residences by the early 1980s.[60] This dispersed elite developed as the most important philanthropic force (organizing itself in 1982 in the [Palestine] Welfare Association based in Geneva) and as a pivotal player in the politics of the Palestinian national liberation movement, especially within the PLO.

Making the most of the opportunity for acquiring individual fortunes and political influence, Palestinians were able to ride the tide of pan-Arab nationalism (whose ideology included the liberation of Palestine as a central tenet) during the 1950s, 1960s, and in particular the oil decade of the 1970s and early 1980s. Even when they were uncomfortable with it, regimes such as the Saudi Arabian monarchy nevertheless supported pan-Arabism, perhaps even favored Arab nationalists and Palestinians in some governmental and diplomatic positions. Although disenfranchised politically (except formally in Jordan), Palestinians nonetheless were a political factor in the support and spread of liberationist pan-Arab ideologies and movements (e.g., Nasserism, the Ba'ath Party, the Movement of Arab Nationalists, and others) and specifically the Palestinian resistance movement throughout the region. These political movements strongly supported the cause of Palestine and the Palestinians under the leadership of the PLO. In short, the popular pan-Arabist sentiment had opened many regional doors for the Palestinians.

By the early 1980s, however, this pan-Arabist tide ebbed for a number of reasons, including repeated political and military defeats and the rise of individual state nationalism, as each local state consolidated its power and ideology and privileged its citizens over other Arabs. Worst yet for the Palestinians, the successive defeats of its guerrilla factions at the hands of both other Arabs and Israel, especially the forced exit of the PLO from Beirut in 1982, coupled with charges and practices of corruption and malfeasance by its political cadres, reduced the luster and élan of the Palestine cause and the credibility of its leadership. With the general and severe downturn in oil revenue in the second half of the 1980s, which led to the decline in the regionwide Arab oil economy, and the economic well-being of the eastern Arab peoples, pan-Arab nationalist politics also gave way to the more immediate, persistent bread-and-butter or social class issues and to the cultural threats from the West as perceived by activist Islamists. Thus the growth and influence of the Palestinian elite in the Arab world in general peaked by the early to mid-1980s then waned. This decline began in

Lebanon as early as 1966 with the collapse of the Palestinian-owned and influential Intra Bank (the Lebanese government refusing to step in and stem the erosion of liquidity), in Jordan in 1970 in the wake of "Black September" (the high point of the civil war there), and in Kuwait and the Arabian peninsula states even prior to the 1991 Gulf War.

The economic downturn in the latter countries was a consequence of the coincidence of two factors: First, oil-exporting countries, as we noted above, experienced a sharp drop in oil-based revenues; second, oil states began to employ their own newly trained citizens, who progressively replaced the Palestinians and other Arabs in governmental and public agencies. As private and public economic, financial, commercial, technical and political advisers, consultants, and planners, Palestinians not only lost out to citizens of the oil states but also to competition from other Arabs and increasingly from individual entrepreneurs, firms, and agencies from other parts of the world (especially the United States). The 1980s thus witnessed not only the waning of Palestinian influence in the Arabian oil-exporting states but also the beginnings of a reverse Palestinian migration (back to Jordan, the West Bank and Gaza, and Lebanon) and dispersal (to Western Europe and the Americas) from the oil economies of the Arabian peninsula.

In the post–Gulf War period, as economic stagnation in the oil-exporting states and economic decline and structural crisis in the nonoil states of the region have become critical, socioeconomic issues dominate over political issues.[61] These issues and the commensurate ideological concerns over Western cultural penetration into the Arab Islamic region have been championed vigorously by a resurgent, vigorous, and militant movement, political Islam. And although more recently political Islam has come to advocate the Palestine cause more vocally, the ebb of secular pan-Arab nationalism also brought about the ebb of Palestinian political and economic influence in and commensurate support from the Arab world. The expansion and contraction of possibilities for social mobility and Palestinian elite influence in the Arab Mashreq parallels the fortunes of the camp dwellers and the PLO. The coup de grace in the demise of official and informal Palestinian influence both in the oil-exporting Arabian peninsula states and elsewhere took place in 1991 during the Gulf War. The position of PLO leader Yasser 'Arafat on the Gulf War had angered the oil monarchs, who stopped the previously generous aid to the organization and expelled and circumscribed many of the activists. Worst yet, around 350,000 Palestinians who had long been resident in the Gulf and the Arabian peninsula were forced to flee or were expelled from Iraq, Kuwait, Saudi Arabia, and other Gulf countries during and after the 1991 Gulf War. Most expellees returned to Jordan, a few to the West Bank and Gaza Strip, and some middle- and upper-middle-class families emigrated to the West.

Palestinians as Minorities in Arab Host Countries

In nearly all the Arab host countries, as we noted earlier, exilic Palestinians live in refugee camps or city districts and neighborhoods that are often overwhelmingly Palestinian. For example, the Palestinians in Lebanon were divided evenly between camp dwellers and those living on their own in urban residences.[62] While destitute refugees found shelter in UNRWA camps, the better off and socially mobile lived in relatively segregated ethnic communities in certain urban quarters.[63] Successive waves of migration brought kin, clanspeople, and covillagers to the same locations. As a result, the social relations, employment opportunities, and political involvements of Palestinians in Arab host countries have been principally with other Palestinians. According to a 1978 study, during the presence of the PLO in the country 70 percent of the Palestinian workers in Lebanon were employed by Palestinian employers.[64]

In general, the middle and upper classes, both Christian and Muslim, tended to assimilate economically and socially more readily—although less so politically—into the host countries than the depeasantized or proletarianized camp dwellers. Since 1968, the year the Palestinian resistance movement first galvanized the camps, this distinction widened, especially in the Palestinian communities of Jordan and Lebanon. As we have discussed, the level of Palestinian consciousness and identity varied by social class position. However, after the emergence of the PRM and the radicalized PLO in 1968, the level of support increased among all social classes and the tension with host governments and elites reached across the class structure. Some segments of the Palestinian middle and upper classes also suffered employment and social discrimination, ostracism, and containment.

Their relatively segregated existence enabled the exiled Palestinian communities to reproduce much of their prediaspora social and cultural traits: distinctive Arabic dialects, to a certain degree dress, social customs, and folklore. It also enabled them to memorialize their shared loss of country, property, and livelihood and reinforced their collective consciousness. "In their daily lives, Palestinians are constantly reminded of their identity, both by their own community and by the non-Palestinian authorities under whose jurisdiction they must live."[65] Thus, despite the potential for assimilation and acculturation within the Arab economies (uneven though it has been from country to country), their experience of social segregation in and political repression by the Arab host states strengthened their social and cultural identity as well as their solidarity and political consciousness. This is best expressed by a passage from Fawaz Turki's passionate and powerful book, *The Disinherited: Journal of a Palestinian Exile*:

> If I was not a Palestinian when I left Haifa as a child, I am one now. Living in Beirut as a stateless person for most of my growing up years, many of them in

a refugee camp, I did not feel I was living among my "Arab brothers." I did not feel I was an Arab, a Lebanese, or as some wretchedly pious writer claimed, a "southern Syrian." I was a Palestinian. And that meant I was an outsider, an alien, a refugee, a burden. To be that, for us, for my generation, meant to look inward, to draw closer, to be part of a minority that had its own way of doing and seeing and feeling and reacting.[66]

Exile, the traumatic experience of being expelled from one's homeland or of being born stateless, without rights, or with a stigmatized identity, is common to almost all Palestinians. For the majority, insecure, second-class status among and repression by their fellow Arabs has reinforced their self-consciousness. Of course, the Palestinian identity of those in the West Bank and the Gaza Strip who have been under occupation by Israel has also evolved. They have found a strong bond in their aspirations and struggles to redeem their homeland. The situation of the diaspora communities and individual refugees encouraged them to seek change through political means, at first in the pan-Arabist movements and later through the PRM and the PLO.

Palestinian diaspora communities may thus be usefully conceptualized as minority groups in the Arab host countries.[67] Minorities are defined by the society of which they are a part. They are collectivities viewed and treated as different by the majority in that society and by its established institutions. The Palestinians are culturally, linguistically, religiously, and racially similar to the Arabs of the host countries. Yet they have been defined as different and treated accordingly because of their legal and political status: They have been circumscribed socially, economically, and politically. But the Palestinians also have viewed themselves as different; they have rejected *tawtin*—mass naturalization and settlement—and sought freedom of economic and political action within their own (especially camp) communities. They also sought support from the people and institutions of the host countries for a liberation struggle that always had political and security implications for the host states themselves. "In general, then, Palestinians in the diaspora [sought] separate rights as a means and not as an end."[68]

A key factor in the lives of Palestinians in diaspora communities has been their uncertain legal status. Different states have granted them different rights. Although Jordan granted most Palestinians citizenship and the right to work within its new expanded borders after 1948, the other Palestinian diaspora communities had no legal identity and thus no psychological, social, economic, or political security. In Lebanon, for example, Palestinians were treated as foreigners in relation to the right-to-work laws and were subject to quotas in private companies and agencies; work in the public sector and enrollment in the state university were closed to them. In 1951 Lebanon's labor minister "attempted to illegalize all employment of Palestinians."[69] When the number of Palestinians was estimated at 225,000 in 1969, only 1 percent held official work permits.[70] Although labor shortages in Kuwait opened the job market for them, their schooling was separate from that of the native Kuwaitis.[71] In Syria, however, all institutions, including the governmental bureaucracies, the public sector, the universities, and the military, were open to Palestinians, who were allowed fully to participate in private and public life without full citizenship. However, their political and guerrilla organizations and the freedom of military action were tightly controlled.

In the Arabian peninsula, all the oil-exporting states treated Palestinians as foreign guest workers allowed to live there only if officially employed or married to a native. And although many were born there to Palestinian parents, they had no rights to citizenship, residence, or work upon achieving adulthood, as the parents had no rights to retirement in the country: After thirty to forty years of life and work in oil-exporting states, most Palestinians have been forced to leave to retire elsewhere. Like all foreigners, they have been legally prohibited from owning productive or profitable property such as businesses, land, or factories, except as minority holders. They have also been prohibited from participating in political life, although through agreements with the PLO, they could participate in organized celebrations, fund-raising, and the like in support of the Palestinian political movement. Nowhere have the Palestinians been allowed to participate in the host country's public life except in Jordan, where this privilege has been limited and controlled.

Nonetheless, as we noted above, Palestinians were always a political presence or factor by virtue of their participation in and support from the pan-Arabist movements and ideology of the time. But the pan-Arab nationalist movements and ideologies were themselves perceived as threats to most established regimes. In short, nearly everywhere the Palestinians have lived in the diaspora they have been viewed with suspicion and distrust and treated as less than full members of the societies—even where they have full citizenship, as in Jordan (and, for that matter, Israel)—by the authorities who have jurisdiction over them. Such exclusion and distrust has reinforced their unique identity, bonded them together, and politicized their existence. The dispossessed and stateless Palestinians have had powerful incentives to struggle for the restoration of their political right of self-determination and statehood, thus magnifying the dilemma of their exilic existence.

Power Struggles and Violence:
Palestinians Versus Arab Host States

Majority-minority intergroup relations are fundamentally power relationships. Interpersonal and intergroup relations are typically constrained by the policy the more powerful majority adopts toward the minority. Official majority group policy is upheld by governmental and other formal institutions. But it may also include unofficial and unarticulated attitudes that nevertheless have significant consequences. Even if a particular majority group policy is dominant, other policies and actions may be pursued by other segments of the majority community. Similarly, the minority group response varies. Majority-minority relations, then, produce a complex dialectic that over the years develops a pattern of confrontation or accommodation between the two communities but that may become disrupted by internal and external economic or political developments.

These principles have governed the experience of the Palestinians in Arab host countries. While majority policy varied in Arab host countries, common to all of them has been rhetorical support for the Palestinian cause and simultaneous denial of freedom of action (especially political and military) to pursue that cause. The principal reason for this paradox was not only the oft-stated fear of military retaliation by Israel but also the perceived challenge to the established regime and elites. It is this contradiction that explains the experience of violence in some of the diaspora communities.

Violence, Transience, and Vulnerability.   Political organizing to pursue the cause of national liberation not only challenged Israel but also threatened the host regimes where the Palestinians were a sizable minority, where they were economically significant, and especially where they were organized and allied politically with regime opposition (before the rise of political Islam, typically pan-Arabist movements or parties). Thus the Palestinians in Arab host countries have been problematic minorities insofar as they have resisted subordination to and restrictions by the majorities through domestic and regional pan-Arab nationalist allies. In two instances, in Jordan and Lebanon, this dialectic led to armed conflict and civil war between the organized and politicized Palestinian diaspora communities and the Arab host. The communities in these two countries became intensively involved in the Palestinian national liberation movement that blossomed after the 1967 Arab-Israeli war.

At different but extended times in Jordan, Lebanon, Kuwait, and elsewhere and in the West Bank and Gaza where the Palestinians resisted Israeli occupation forces (see Chapter 6), violence was an integral part of their lives ever since the mandate period. Edward Said expressed this phenomenon best:

> The one thing none of us can forget is that violence has been an extraordinarily important aspect of our lives. Whether it has been the violence of our uprooting and the destruction of our society in 1948, the violence visited on us by our enemies, the violence we have visited on others, or, most horribly, the violence we have wreaked upon each other—these dimensions of the Palestin-

ian experience have brought us a good deal of attention, and have exacerbated our self-awareness as a community set apart from others.[72]

The extent and persistence of violence in the lives of the Palestinians over at least the last half century has been as awesome, shattering, and traumatic for the Palestinian people as it is incomprehensible for others. It began with the violence of the uprooting and continues in the daily violence and humiliation by the police, intelligence and security apparatuses, and military forces in the Arab host countries, in Israel proper, and in the occupied territories.

As will be clear in Chapter 6 on the occupation and the intifada, violence since Israel's occupation of the West Bank and Gaza Strip has been extraordinarily severe, commonplace, and extensive. Between December 1987 and 1993, over 1,283 Palestinians were killed in the West Bank and the Gaza Strip, an estimated 130,472 sustained injuries requiring hospitalization, 2,533 of their homes were demolished or sealed, 481 were deported, and 22,088 have been administratively detained (never brought before a court of law), many of them beaten and tortured. Occupation authorities have confiscated 116,918 acres and uprooted 184,257 trees ("for security reasons"). One of the most egregious acts by Israel has been collective punishments of all sorts, especially the twenty-four-hour curfews: 14,997 such curfews have been imposed on population centers of 10,000 or more. This has been in addition to the (almost) constant curfew imposed on the entire West Bank and Gaza Strip from January 16 to February 28, 1991.[73] Such violence has not abated since the 1993 Oslo Accords, as we discuss in Chapter 7. Indeed, as we show in the Epilogue, the most draconian curfews occurred after the accords were signed.

In the Arab host countries, violence against the Palestinians has peaked and ebbed continuously, most recently in Kuwait. In Jordan it culminated during September 1970, labeled "Black September" by the Palestinians because of the high death toll they suffered, when King Hussein of Jordan ordered his regular troops to launch an all-out assault on the refugee camps to suppress the guerrillas of the PRM in and around Amman.[74] Innocent thousands were killed as the Jordanian army, supported with heavy armor, reconquered and occupied the Palestinian camps that were in guerrilla hands. In Lebanon the extent of violence against the Palestinians took a horrendous toll over a long period. From the humiliating rule of the police, the security agents, and the Deuxième Bureau (the Lebanese army intelligence unit) in the 1950s and 1960s, the Palestinians sustained horrific assaults and casualties during Lebanon's civil war (1975–1982), the two Israeli invasions, the massacres in Sabra-Shatila and Tal al-Za'atar camps by right-wing Christian Maronite militias (the area around the former camp was under Israeli control), and several bloody and devastating sieges by

Shi'a militias (with Syrian support) in 1985–1986 (after the exit of the PLO from Beirut). During the civil war, the Palestinians and their Lebanese allies also fought against the Syrian army (in 1975–1976), which intervened in Lebanon on the side of the rightist Lebanese militias.

From 1970 onward in Lebanon, the Palestinians and their Lebanese allies also suffered constant and immensely costly attacks, bombings, shelling, incursions, and assassinations at the hands of Israel. According to Tabitha Petran, between 1968 and 1975, the start of the Lebanese civil war, Israel perpetrated 6,200 acts of aggression against Lebanon,[75] ostensibly in retaliation for Palestinian attacks. This unrelenting and escalating Israeli warfare on the Palestinians and their Lebanese allies peaked in two major Israeli invasions (1978 and 1982) of the country, which caused tens of thousands of deaths, a much greater number of wounded, and tremendous physical and economic destruction. The deaths, maiming, destruction, social hardships, and psychological trauma inflicted on both the Palestinians and Lebanese are immeasurable. After the departure from Beirut of the PLO bureaucracy, regular PLA troops, and the factional guerrillas in 1982, the Palestinian population there succumbed to severe political repression and commensurate economic degradation from a rightist Lebanese government. Although the PLO leadership received U.S. government assurances for protection of the remaining Palestinian civilians, none was provided. In turn, 'Arafat, the Palestinian leadership, and the PLO abandoned them as well. For example, the safety net payments to the families of those killed in the fighting (Palestinians martyrs) were terminated, many if not most social service institutions lost their funding, and in general the Palestinians of Lebanon lost all their previous political protection. Conditions have not changed much since the decline of the Lebanese rightists and the ascendance to power of a centrist government. In the mid-1990s, the UNRWA reported that the condition of Palestinians in Lebanon is desperate.[76]

The large (400,000 strong) and long-standing (94 percent of the "returnees" in a sample survey had lived there more than fifteen years)[77] Palestinian community in Kuwait was suddenly attacked and most of it expelled in 1991 in the context of the invasion of Kuwait by Iraq. Collectively accused of collaborating with the Iraqi occupiers, the Palestinians were savaged by Kuwaiti vigilantes, militias, and the regular army upon its return to the country behind the allied forces of liberation. A large number of Palestinians were stripped of their private property and valuables; many killed, maimed, or tortured; and most expelled from Kuwait—a form of ethnic cleansing. The economic disaster that befell the Palestinian community of Kuwait is incalculable, not only because it thrived there (reportedly 30 percent of Kuwait's private business was Palestinian owned or controlled) but also because a large group of others in both Jordan and the occupied territories were dependent on the financial remittances from that community (estimated at peak oil-boom years between $1.0 and $1.5 billion per year). Anti-Palestinian hysteria that led to the collective accusation, punishment, and pogroms is only the current manifestation of a phenomena that originated with the Zionists, especially during the 1947–1948 wars in Palestine. Attitudes and actions not unlike those expressed and perpetrated by the Kuwaitis were practiced by certain East Jordanians and right-wing Lebanese militias during the civil conflicts in these Arab host countries in the 1970s.

Finally, and perhaps most tragic, is the violence Palestinians perpetrated against one another. Conflicts over strategy and policy led to schisms, armed conflict, and assassinations within the ranks of the PRM and the PLO. Certain defectors, such as Abu Nidal and his group, became notorious terrorists who assassinated Palestinian diplomats because of their political views. Worst of all inter-Palestinian violence, however, was the small-scale Palestinian civil war in 1983 in and around the Nahr al-Bared refugee camp in north Lebanon. Anti-'Arafat dissidents (with the aid of the Syrian army) and loyalists of the PLO chairman's faction shelled each other, in the process killing many of their own civilian people caught in the crossfire.

The recent expulsion or flight of Palestinians from Kuwait points to another feature of the precarious Palestinian existence since al-Nakbah: transience and impermanence. Transience and associated social and psychological insecurity were noted above with respect to the 1967 refugees, many of whom were displaced for a second or third time in their lives. Not only were Palestinians forced across state borders, as from Palestine (1948, 1967), the occupied territories (1967–1993), Jordan (1970–1971), Lebanon (1975–present), and Kuwait (1990–1991), but they were also often forced to move inside a given country. In many instances in Lebanon (but also in Jordan as a consequence of the 1967 war and Black September and in Syria as a result of the 1973 Arab-Israeli war), the displaced Palestinians, the muhajjarin of the civil war, have had to move several times within twenty years, as a result losing not only kinspeople and friends but also homes, possessions, and jobs. This militarily, politically, and economically forced transience has been the lot of a large number (and percentage) of the Palestinian population. Even the relatively secure and assimilated Palestinian middle class in Lebanon was forced (as were much of the Lebanese middle and upper classes) to emigrate (flee) from the country to Europe and North America during and after the Israeli invasion of 1982.

This uncertain and vulnerable existence, characterized by all too frequent dislocation, has long generated tremendous psychological anxiety, insecurity, and constant angst among diaspora Palestinians. Stateless, without a legal identity or a passport with which to travel, and without a territorial homeland, one Palestinian worker, expelled from Kuwait and refused entry back into Lebanon, was forced to fly back and forth between the airports of

the two countries nearly twelve times—he was labeled "the Flying Palestinian" by the journalists who covered his saga—before his case was finally resolved. In another incident, the remains of Palestinians were not allowed to
be buried in certain countries and had to be flown elsewhere. In 1995, when
the government of Libya expelled a large number of Palestinians, neither the
Arab host countries from which these refugees had originally emigrated nor
Israel, which continues to control the autonomous Palestinian areas (nominally under the Palestinian Authority, or PA, of 'Arafat), allowed them to
enter their territories. Thus they were stuck for weeks in legal and physical
limbo in tents on the Libyan-Egyptian border and on ferryboats in the harbors of Cyprus before Syria accepted those on the ferryboats on humanitar-
ian grounds and Libya consented to the return of others from the border. In
early 1997 some still remained in the border area.

The Oslo and Cairo Accords between the PLO and Israel have allowed the
return to the autonomous areas of the West Bank and Gaza Strip of some
Palestinians who had been deported from the occupied territories and others
who entered for the first time in their young lives as members of the
PLO/Palestinian Authority police force and bureaucratic personnel—the nucleus of the Palestinian Authority that took control of the Israeli-evacuated
areas. While the Palestinian Authority is not a state and the right of return is
still subject to Israeli approval, the direction of Palestinian dispersal has been
reversed for the first time since 1948. It is a symbolic step that may give hope
to the millions of dispossessed and dispersed Palestinians. However, whether
this will be a beginning for a more extensive process of repatriation remains
to be seen. For those who returned, a measure of psychological security may
have been achieved, but for the millions still in exile and hundreds of thousands in legal limbo, statelessness and insecurity continue to be their lot.

After the destruction of their society and their exodus into the diaspora,
Palestinians lost hope in the possibilities of repatriation and restitution.
They became pessimistic about their future. With the rise of the Palestinian
resistance movement and the radical PLO, however, they acquired new optimism. Repeated defeats, tragedies, and suffering have in fact turned them
into simultaneous pessimists and optimists. This paradoxical psychological
state was sardonically and satirically captured by Emile Habiby, an "Israeli
Arab," in his ingenious, Kafkaesque novel *The Secret Life of Saeed, the Illfated-Pessoptimist: A Palestinian Who Became a Citizen of Israel*.[78] (The
term "pessoptimist" is a translation of the Arabic neologism *al-mutasha'il*,
which combines the words for "pessimist," *mutasha'im*, and "optimist,"
mutafa'il.) The protagonist is a Palestinian Arab who one day wakes up to
discover that his society has disappeared and that he is a stranger in his
own country. Both the writer and the fictional character experienced the
paradox of surviving Palestine's destruction and its overnight transformation into an alien Israel; the story's setting is thus not the diaspora.

Nonetheless, the pessoptimist manifests the psychological makeup of all Palestinians, including those of the diaspora.

To further comprehend the Palestinian plight and psychological paradox, we must identify their experiential impact on the individual. Diaspora Palestinians since 1948 have had no identity or a state to provide them legitimacy or shield them effectively from harm or difficulty. Except for those in Jordan, they carry identity cards issued by host governments that identify them as refugees. These identity cards or laissez-passer travel documents nevertheless typically deny them legitimate legal standing or recognition. They see it as intensely ironic that they who are without legal identity have to prove their "identity" at every turn. Stopped at borders and denied entry, reentry, or residence, they nonetheless try to make an acceptable, "official," stable, and secure place for themselves in an international order that gives them no legitimacy. This dilemma is expressed poignantly and tragically in the novella *Men in the Sun* by Ghassan Kanafani,[79] a novelist and artist who was assassinated by Israelis in Beirut in 1972. *Men in the Sun* is a story of three Palestinian refugees impelled by exile and unemployment to seek illegal entry from southern Iraq into Kuwait in pursuit of a job. They are to be smuggled into Kuwait inside a tanker truck. As the truck driver converses with the border guards in the oppressive heat of the desert sun, the three men suffocate to death, forgotten by everyone. This novella captures diaspora Palestinian life, which has often been tenuous, transient, discontinuous, uncentered, scattered, and marked, as Edward Said writes, by "the artificial and imposed arrangements of interrupted or confined space, by the dislocations and unsynchronized rhythms of disturbed time."[80] As Said also notes, for Palestinians no straight path leads from home to school to maturity to job to stability and security. All passages in personal life are accidental, all progress is tenuous, all residence is exile, and every ordinary action requires extraordinary effort and resourcefulness. It is a heavy psychological toll, which has generated among exile Palestinians both ritualistic and innovative coping mechanisms.

Two Cases: Palestinians in Jordan and Lebanon

To better depict the lives, sentiments, aspirations, and political and military actions of Palestinians in the diaspora, we end this section by reviewing the communal political history of Palestinians in two Arab host countries, Jordan (briefly) and Lebanon (in greater detail). The Palestinian communities in Jordan and Lebanon are appropriate examples because the former, always a large and important community, gave early support to the PRM/PLO, and the latter became the movement's anchor during its pivotal and influential years and its greatest political independence. (Although the Palestinian community in East Jordan is the largest diaspora community, it has not been as directly nor as intimately involved in the struggles of the PRM/PLO since the PLO and all its factions were expelled from Jordan in 1970 in a brutal civil war.)

Shortly after the 1949 armistice agreement between Transjordan and Israel, King Abdullah annexed east central Palestine and created the kingdom of Jordan. Jordan thus granted citizenship to all Palestinians under its jurisdiction, the only Arab country to do so. But only a fraction was politically enfranchised, as the right to vote was tied to landownership. Palestinians emerged as the numerical majority (roughly 60–70 percent of the population including the West Bank before the 1967 war and about 55 percent without the West Bank after that) of the new country. When the PRM first surfaced in 1968, a power struggle quickly ensued between the Jordanian regime of King Hussein and the PRM guerrillas and the PLO anchored in the camps in and around Amman and in the Jordanian hills facing Israel. Spectacularly popular throughout the Arab world for resisting Israel after the devastating Arab defeat in six days in the June 1967 war, Hussein's regime could not at first move against the Palestinian guerrillas.

However, by 1970 the regime succeeded in orchestrating an antiguerrilla propaganda campaign and unleashed against them a savage military attack in September (Black September), which drove them out of the camps and the city of Amman at a horrendous cost in lives of innocent camp civilians, estimated in the tens of thousands. In 1971 the mountain-based Palestinian guerrillas were driven out of the western hills of Jordan; they took refuge in southwestern Lebanon. After their departure, the Palestinian camps and other population concentrations in Jordan lived under a police state until the 1990s, when Jordan instituted some political liberalization and some democratic reforms.

Palestinian communal history in Lebanon is divided into three broad eras: 1948–1969, including the rule of the Deuxième Bureau; 1969–1982, "the days of the revolution" (as a respondent in Sayigh's study termed them) and of civil war; and 1982 to the present, the era of camp sieges, political suppression, and economic degradation.[81] While the liberal economic and political conditions of Lebanon allowed a small Palestinian middle class (professionals, small business people, etc.) and bourgeoisie (wealthy entrepreneurs and investors) to flourish until the start of the civil war—many, especially Palestinian Christians, were encouraged by the Lebanese government to purchase Lebanese citizenship—the majority did not fare as well. And indeed while these conditions also allowed the PLO to prosper, the camp dwellers bore the brunt of civil conflict, Israeli attacks and invasions, and economic exploitation.

The Palestinian camps were controlled through the first decade after al-Nakbah by the Lebanese police and security agents, the cooperative remnants of the Arab Higher Committee of al-Hajj Amin al-Husseini, and the

UNRWA. But the first modern civil war in Lebanon in 1958, a harbinger of the more savage and longer civil conflict of 1975–1982, introduced far more repressive and direct state control of the camps through the army's Deuxième Bureau. The camp Palestinians were bullied and cowed by agents of the Deuxième Bureau; they were exploited economically and forced to pay bribes and other gratuities for any legal or informal business transactions.

The rule of the Deuxième Bureau ended in 1969 when the surging PRM, with the considerable support of the leftist, progressive, and pan-Arabist parties of Lebanon (a coalition that called itself the Lebanese National Movement, or LNM), gained control of the camps and the right to conduct guerrilla warfare against Israel from Lebanese territory. Describing the joy of the "liberation of the camp," a resident said: "After they put up the Palestinian flag, people felt as if they liberated Nablus."[82] The power struggle and military confrontation between the PRM and the Lebanese army was resolved in favor of the PRM in an agreement—the Cairo agreement—arbitrated by the still popular President Gamal 'Abdul-Nasser of Egypt.

This agreement and the rising strength of the PRM ushered in the second era for the Palestinians in Lebanon. From 1969 until the exit of the PLO and its forces in 1982, the camps were under Palestinian jurisdiction as quasi-liberated zones of the new "Palestinian revolution." During this period the PRM, formally in control of the PLO, developed its civil, economic, political, administrative, and military institutions. A veritable Palestinian economy evolved with the PLO not only because of expanding employment in its variegated bureaucracies but also because of the development of its factories (producing clothing, furniture, leather goods, ironwork, some arms, and handicrafts), printing and publishing, filmmaking, and other industries. The sharp impulse for economic development occurred during the early part of the Lebanese civil war, as Palestinian muhajjarin poured out of the industrial enclaves of Christian Maronite–controlled east Beirut and into the west Beirut areas under the control of the PLO and the LNM. This triggered the rapid expansion not only of the PLO's productive enterprises but also social service and social welfare institutions, all in an effort to provide jobs for unemployed muhajjarin and camp residents. Individual camp dwellers addressed their economic dilemmas by holding down two jobs and having more members of the family (especially women) take jobs, albeit low-paying ones. Sayigh reports that by 1982, 65 percent of the camp Palestinians were employed by Palestinian employers.[83] One important consequence of this effort "was that, instead of emigrating to oil-producing countries, more highly educated Palestinian workers now stayed in Lebanon to work with the 'Revolution' in *sha'abi* (popular, low-income) areas."[84]

The PLO consolidated and strengthened its governing structures—a cabinet (the Executive Committee), a parliament in exile (the Palestine National Council, PNC), and an army (the Palestine Liberation Army)—all the outwardly formal institutions of a government-in-exile. And with the disintegration of the Lebanese government between 1975 and 1982, the PLO with its LNM allies exercised de facto sovereignty over large segments of Lebanese territory and emerged as a state-within-a-state until it was driven out by Israel.

The PLO accomplished its institutional development in a short period in Lebanon despite a large number of enemies: Internal and external (regional and international) states and other actors were arrayed against it. Of course it also had allies within Lebanon and in the region. Lebanon became the battleground of domestic, regional, and international (superpower) proxy wars. Practically every Arab state or political movement, Israel, Iran, many European states, the United States, and the Soviet Union intervened in Lebanon diplomatically, politically, militarily, financially, and through in-kind grants and many other services (training, intelligence, etc.). More bewildering, such interventions often favored one subfaction or another of the opposing coalitions (right-wing Christians vs. the LNM and the PRM/PLO) and complicated enormously the course of conflict and the prospects of resolution of the civil war. Often interventions were linked to regional political upheavals or wars that altered regional balances of power and also had global repercussions. These include, for example, the October 1973 Arab-Israeli war (the Yom Kippur War), the 1978 Israeli-Egyptian Camp David Accords, the Iranian revolution, and the sharp rise in the price of oil. What began as a civil war triggered by internal Lebanese contradictions—a rigid sectarian political structure superimposed on and resisting change in a society that had experienced radical social, economic, and political transformation—and aggravated only in part by the Palestinian presence in the country quickly became embroiled in regional and international politics.[85]

Israel's invasion of Lebanon in June 1982, the three-month siege of Beirut, the massacre of hundreds of Palestinians in Shatila camp, and the U.S.-brokered exit of the PLO from the city signaled the end of the "days of the revolution" in Lebanon and the start of the current phase. Both the U.S. and Lebanese governments promised to guarantee the safety of Palestinians left behind in the country. Neither government honored its commitment; nor could the powerless and distant (in Tunis) PLO provide much protection to the largely disarmed Palestinian community in Lebanon. Palestinians in and outside the camps came under intense political, military, and economic pressure.

Lebanese Shi'a militias waged a savage war against the Palestinian camps south and southwest of Beirut. The Shi'a territory of south Lebanon had long been neglected by the central government and had been a zone of warfare between the Palestinian guerrillas and Israel since 1968. By the late 1970s, Shi'a villagers had enough of war and dislocations. They had also had enough of the arrogant, at times oppressive and corrupt behavior of Palestinian guerrillas in the south. Shi'a migrations to Beirut, in part to escape the conflict, accelerated through the decade. It led them to the southern and southeastern suburbs of the city, where they first joined and cooperated with the Palestinians (in several camps). Shortly after the civil war erupted, the alliance began to fray as communal sociopolitical (and after the Iranian revolution, intimations of religious Shi'i-Sunni conflict) and economic competition and power struggles between the various militias (Amal and Hizbullah against the PRM/PLO) developed.[86]

Amal-Palestinian conflict peaked between 1985 and 1987 in what was known as the war of the camps, the Amal militia's assaults on the camps. There were many reasons for this war, but the Amal leadership took advantage of Syrian support, the unconfirmed rumors of (and general Lebanese hostility to) 'Arafat's efforts to return to Lebanon, and the Lebanese consensus on the need to disarm the camps. The brutal and destructive war of the camps[87] ended in a stalemate but sealed the demise of the Palestinian presence in Lebanon. Even before the sieges, the Lebanese army had occupied the camps and patrolled them, but the Palestinians became *mustabaheen* (an Arabic term indicating a group that is unprotected and vulnerable to repression and killings) for the piecemeal pogroms[88] they suffered when Amal struck. After the sieges the Syrian army in Lebanon came to control the camps.

Israel's invasion had devastated the already limping Lebanese economy, spurring emigration of both the Palestinian and Lebanese middle classes. Without resources and legitimate travel documents, camp dwellers were trapped and bore the brunt again of hostile and alienated Lebanese. The civil war in Lebanon took its toll on the PRM/PLO-LNM alliance as well. The LNM lost its own solidarity and coherence, and some factions become alienated from the Palestinians. Worst of all, large segments of the previously supportive Lebanese Shi'a community, long outside the formal LNM alliance, were increasingly becoming anti-Palestinian by the time of the Shi'ite Iranian revolution of 1979. Facing the enmity of Israel, the newly installed rightist Lebanese government, the right-wing Christian coalition, and the rapidly politicizing and mobilizing Shi'a community, the Palestinians in Lebanon lost altogether their long-established popular Lebanese base of support. Once party to the de facto sovereign PLO power over large sections of Lebanon during the civil war, the remaining Palestinians were reduced to a dazed, defeated, and unprotected minority in besieged camps.

Finally, as Sayigh writes, the Palestinians in Lebanon after 1982 had become an "endangered species." In the wake of the Oslo Accords, Lebanese politicians and government officials spoke out in strong terms against the tawtin (naturalization and settlement) of Palestinians in Lebanon. The destiny of the Palestinian community in that country now depends to a large extent on the agreements that will issue from the "final status" negotiations between Israel and the Palestinian Authority/PLO on the occupied territories, borders, settlements, Jerusalem, and the Palestinian refugees.

Conclusion

Beginning in 1948 the Palestinians lost their homeland and became dispossessed, dispersed, and destitute. The majority were herded into refugee camps, becoming dependent on the UNRWA dole, or into urban neighborhoods of the major cities in the Arab host countries. There they were suppressed politically and exploited economically. Within only ten years after al-Nakbah, they began a long struggle for economic well-being, social and psychological security, affirmation of identity, and restoration of political rights of self-determination and independent statehood. The Palestinian refugees have risen phoenixlike from the ashes of the destruction of their society to preserve their identity, flourish economically and socially, and build a political movement of national liberation. The year 1993 was a turning point in their history because their political representative, the PLO under 'Arafat, signed with Israel, the state that dispossessed and dispersed them, the Oslo Accords, arguably the key political event for the Palestinians since 1948. Stunning and significant as that event is in Palestinian political and social history, the signatories to that accord agreed to postpone consideration of the status of the refugees for three years. The structural dilemmas of the Palestinian diaspora communities is thus unchanged, the Palestinians perhaps far more vulnerable and anxiety ridden. Arab host states (especially Lebanon) and Israel have expressed opposition to any tawtin, repatriation, or compensation. The destiny of a large segment of the nearly 4.0 million diaspora Palestinians, then, remains uncertain, insecure, and in legal limbo.

Notes

1. J. L. Abu-Lughod, "The Demographic Transformation of Palestine: Relevance for Planning Palestine Open University," in *Palestine Open University Feasibility Study*, part 2 (Paris: UNESCO, 1980), 160–161.

2. Ibid., 6.

3. Ibid., 16–46.

4. W. Khalidi, ed., *All That Remains: The Palestinian Villages Occupied and Depopulated by Israel in 1948* (Washington, DC: Institute for Palestine Studies, 1992); see also W. Khalidi, *Before Their Diaspora: A Photographic History of the Palestinians, 1876–1948* (Washington, DC: Institute for Palestine Studies, 1984).

5. G. Kossaifi, "Demographic Characteristics of the Arab Palestinian People," in K. Nakhleh and E. Zureik, eds., *The Sociology of the Palestinians* (London: Croom Helm, 1980), 21. Emphasis added.

6. For example, after Israel occupied the West Bank and Gaza Strip in 1967, the military administration objected to the historical content of several textbooks used in UNESCO/UNRWA schools. Subsequently, after debate and discussion, the textbooks were replaced or revised in all UNRWA schools. "This had the actual effect of permitting Israel to interfere with the curriculum not only of the Palestinians under occupation, but also all students in Jordan, Lebanon and Syria"; I. Abu-Lughod, "Educating a Community in Exile: The Palestinian Experience," *Journal of Palestine Studies* 2, 3 (Spring 1973): 95.

7. B. Anderson, *Imagined Communities: Reflections on the Origin and Spread of Nationalism* (New York: Verso, 1991).

8. See S. Flapan, *The Birth of Israel: Myths and Realities* (New York: Pantheon Books, 1987).

9. B. Morris, *1948 and After* (New York: Oxford University Press, 1990), 69–88. See also M. Palumbo, *The Palestinian Catastrophe: The 1948 Expulsion of a People from Their Homeland* (London: Quartet Books, 1987); and N. Nazzal, *The Palestinian Exodus from Galilee* (Beirut: Institute for Palestine Studies, 1978).

10. As cited in Morris, *1948 and After*, 71.

11. Ibid., 73.

12. Ibid., 74.

13. Ibid.

14. Ibid., 75–76.

15. Ibid., 71.

16. E. Childers, "The Other Exodus," *Spectator,* 12 May 1961.

17. Morris, *1948 and After*, 86. This conclusion, as well as the general approach of the "new" history, has triggered much debate, scathing critiques, and personal attacks. See S. Teveth, "Charging Israel with Original Sin," *Commentary* 88, 3 (September 1989): 24–33, and S. Teveth, "The Palestine Arab Refugee Problem and Its Origins," *Middle Eastern Studies* 26, 2 (April 1990): 214–249. Further, see the rejoinder by A. Shlaim, "The Founding of Israel," in *Commentary* 89 (February 1990): 2.

18. Morris, *1948 and After*, 87.

19. N. G. Finkelstein, *Image and Reality of the Israel-Palestine Conflict* (London: Verso, 1995), ch. 3, "Born of War, Not by Design," 51–87.

20. Relying on Zionist sources, W. Khalidi reconstructed this particularly successful effort to rid the young state of Israel of Palestinians and enlarge its territorial base before the British withdrew its forces. "Plan Dalet: The Zionist Masterplan for the Conquest of Palestine, 1948," *Middle East Forum* 37, 4 (November 1961): 22–28. See also Palumbo, *The Palestinian Catastrophe*, ch. 2, "Plan Dalet," 34–46.

21. J. B. Glubb, *A Soldier with the Arabs* (London: Hodder & Stoughton, 1957), 81. See also the report of A. Yitzhaqi in *Yediot Aharonot,* 14 April 1972. Reproduced in *Journal of Palestine Studies* 1, 4 (Summer 1972): 142–146.

22. R. Sayigh, *Palestinians: From Peasants to Revolutionaries* (London: Zed, 1979), 64.

23. Ibid., 92.

24. Quotation cited by Palumbo, *The Palestinian Catastrophe*, 133.

25. Methodological considerations are given ample attention by the researchers in chapters 3 and 4. P. Dodd and H. Barakat, *River Without Bridges: A Study of the*

Exodus of the 1967 Palestinian Arab Refugees (Beirut: Institute for Palestine Studies, 1969): 8–20, 21–37.

26. Ibid., 44.

27. R. Sayigh, *Too Many Enemies: The Palestinian Experience in Lebanon* (London: Zed, 1994), 36.

28. Sayigh, *Palestinians: From Peasants to Revolutionaries*, 84.

29. Sayigh, *Too Many Enemies*, 35–36.

30. United Nations ECWA, *Statistical Abstract of the Study on the Economic and Social Situation and Potential of the Palestinian Arab People in the Region of Western Asia* (New York: United Nations, 1983), 2–3.

31. J. Abu-Lughod, "A Rift in Their Souls: The Palestinians in Exile," in P. F. Krogh and M. C. McDavid, eds., *Palestinians Under Occupation: Prospects for the Future* (Washington, DC: Center for Contemporary Arab Studies, Georgetown University, 1989), 33.

32. S. M. Ayyoub, *The Class Structure of Palestinians in Lebanon* (in Arabic) (Beirut: Beirut Arab University, 1978), 173–174.

33. J. Abu-Lughod, "Demographic Characteristics of the Palestinian Population: Relevance for Planning Palestine Open University," in *Palestine Open University Feasibility Study*, part 2 (Paris: UNESCO, 1980), table 5, 23.

34. Ibid.

35. Ibid., table 8, 39.

36. Ibid., 6.

37. A. L. Adlakha, K. G. Kinsella, and Marwan Khawaja estimate that Gaza's natural growth rate in 1995 was 4.6 percent; "Demography of the Palestinian Population with Special Emphasis on the Occupied Territories," *Population Bulletin of ESCWA* 43 (1995): 11, table 3.

38. The estimates in Abu-Lughod's "Demographic Characteristics of the Palestinian Population" are carefully argued and internally consistent and differ substantially from those of the U.S. government and the UNRWA cited in D. Peretz, *Palestinians, Refugees and the Middle East Peace Process* (Washington, DC: United States Institute of Peace Press, 1993). We believe Abu-Lughod's estimates are more correct. See, however, a recent U.S. government study cited in note 37 above.

39. Ayyoub, *The Class Structure of Palestinians in Lebanon*, 240.

40. Ibid., table 2, 15. See also Adlakha et al., "Demography of the Palestinian Population," 5–27. This study by the International Division of the U.S. Census Bureau estimates total Palestinian population in Middle Eastern countries in 1995 at only 6.45 million. However, it excludes Palestinians outside the Middle East, a number that would easily bring the total number to 6.8 million. See also G. F. Kossaifi, *The Palestinian Refugees and the Right of Return* (Washington, DC: Center for Policy Analysis on Palestine, 1996).

41. *Facts and Figures About the Palestinians* (Washington, DC: Center for Policy Analysis on Palestine, 1993), 4.

42. See J. K. Cooley, *Green March, Black September: The Story of the Palestinian Arabs* (London: Frank Cass, 1973); see also J. Wallach and J. Wallach, *The New Palestinians: The Emerging Generation of Leaders* (Rocklin, CA: Prima Publishers, 1992).

43. Peretz, *Palestinians, Refugees and the Middle East Peace Process*, 6. In the 1995 United Nations General Assembly session, the United States attempted to

eliminate the UNRWA on the grounds that it was no longer necessary given the signing of the PLO-Israel Declaration of Principles. The move was defeated.

44. Sayigh, *Too Many Enemies*, 39.

45. L. A. Brand, *Palestinians in the Arab World* (New York: Columbia University Press, 1988), 18–19.

46. Abu-Lughod, "Demographic Characteristics of the Palestinian Population," 58.

47. Ayyoub, *The Class Structure of Palestinians in Lebanon*, 253.

48. Ibid., 263–265.

49. Sayigh, *Too Many Enemies*, 42.

50. Peretz, *Palestinians, Refugees and the Middle East Peace Process*, 24.

51. Sayigh, *Too Many Enemies*, 59–64.

52. Ibid.

53. Ibid., 105–108.

54. Ibid., 108.

55. See especially J. Peteet, *Gender in Crisis: Women and the Palestinian Resistance Movement* (New York: Columbia University Press, 1991).

56. See Z. Abu-Amr, *Islamic Fundamentalism in the West Bank and Gaza* (Bloomington: Indiana University Press, 1994).

57. Ayyoub, *The Class Structure of Palestinians in Lebanon*, 231.

58. Transjordan was renamed the kingdom of Jordan in the early 1950s when it annexed east central Palestine and labeled it the West Bank, in contrast to Transjordan proper, which was then called the East Bank.

59. Cited in Peretz, *Palestinians, Refugees and the Middle East Peace Process*, 22.

60. The biggest shareholder and owner of the largest private Arab bank (also one of the larger banks in the world) is a Palestinian, as are the shareholders and managers of the largest and most successful Arab (now international) construction companies.

61. S. K. Farsoun, "Oil, State and Social Structure in the Middle East," *Arab Studies Quarterly* 10, 2 (Spring 1988): 156–175.

62. E. Khouri, *Palestinian Statistics* (Beirut: PLO Research Center, 1979), 62.

63. See S. Khalaf and P. Kongstad, *Hamra of Beirut: A Case of Rapid Urbanization* (Leiden: E. J. Brill, 1973).

64. Ayyoub, *The Class Structure of Palestinians in Lebanon*, 251.

65. Peretz, *Palestinians, Refugees and the Middle East Peace Process*, 28.

66. F. Turki, *The Disinherited: Journal of a Palestinian Exile* (New York: Monthly Review Press, 1972), 8.

67. This part is taken largely from N. H. Aruri and S. Farsoun, "Palestinian Communities and Arab Host Countries," in Nakhleh and Zureik, *The Sociology of the Palestinians*, 112–146. See also L. A. Brand, "Palestinians in Syria: The Politics of Integration," *Middle East Journal* 42, 4 (Autumn 1988): 621–637.

68. Brand, *Palestinians in the Arab World*, 11.

69. Sayigh, *Too Many Enemies*, 23.

70. S. Hijjawi, "The Palestinians in Lebanon" (in Arabic) *Journal of the Center for Palestinian Studies* (Baghdad) 22 (May-June 1977): 44.

71. See S. Ghabra, *The Palestinians in Kuwait: The Family and Politics of Survival* (Boulder, CO: Westview Press, 1987).

72. E. W. Said, with photographs by J. Mohr, *After the Last Sky* (London: Faber and Faber, 1986), 5.

73. Tally kept by the Palestine Human Rights Information Center, Jerusalem/ Washington, *Washington Report on Middle East Affairs* 13, 1 (June 1994): 19. See also a report on the situation during the first year of the intifada by Al-Haq, *Punishing a Nation: Israeli Human Rights Violations During the Palestinian Uprising, December 1987–December 1988* (Boston: South End Press, 1989).

74. "Black September" later became the name of a secret Palestinian organization that attacked the Israeli athletes at the Olympic Games in Munich in 1972.

75. T. Petran, *The Struggle Over Lebanon* (New York: Monthly Review Press, 1987), 142.

76. *Report of the Commissioner-General of the UNRWA in the Near East, 1 July 1992–30 June 1993* (New York: United Nations, 1994).

77. Y. J. El-Uteibi and M. Amous, "Jordanian Returnees Profile" (Returnees Compensation Center, the Hashemite Charity Organization, Geneva, photocopy), 20.

78. E. Habiby, *The Secret Life of Saeed, the Illfated-Pessoptimist: A Palestinian Who Became a Citizen of Israel*, translated by S. K. Jayyussi and T. Le Gassick (New York: Vantage, 1982).

79. G. Kanafani, *Men in the Sun*, translated by H. Kilpatrick (Washington, DC: Three Continents Press, 1991).

80. Said, *After the Last Sky*, 20.

81. See Sayigh, *Too Many Enemies*; see also R. Brynen, *Sanctuary and Survival: The PLO in Lebanon* (Boulder, CO: Westview Press, 1990), and H. Cobban, *The Palestinian Liberation Organization: People, Power and Politics* (Cambridge: Cambridge University Press, 1984).

82. Sayigh, *Too Many Enemies*, 91.

83. Ibid., 109.

84. Ibid.

85. See S. K. Farsoun and W. Carroll, "The Civil War in Lebanon: Sect, Class and Imperialism," *Monthly Review* 28, 2 (June 1976): 12–37; see also S. K. Farsoun and R. B. Wingerter, "The Palestinians in Lebanon," *SAIS Review* 3 (Winter 1981/82): 93–106; W. Khalidi, *Conflict and Violence in Lebanon* (Cambridge: Harvard University Press, 1979). See also J. Randal, *Going All the Way: Christian War Lords, Israeli Adventurers, and the War in Lebanon* (New York: Viking Press, 1983).

86. See A. R. Norton, *Amal and the Shi'a: Struggle for the Soul of Lebanon* (Austin: University of Texas Press, 1987). See also A. AbuKhalil, "Shi'ites and Palestinians: Underlying Causes of the Amal-Palestinian Conflict," in E. Hagopian, ed., *Amal and the Palestinians: Understanding the Battle of the Camps* (Belmont, MA: Association of Arab-American University Graduates, 1985); and A. AbuKhalil, "The Palestinian-Shi'ite War in Lebanon," *Third World Affairs* (1988): 77–89.

87. On the sieges, see Sayigh, *Too Many Enemies*, ch. 9–11.

88. Ibid., 201.

FIVE

The Rise and Fall of the Palestinian National Liberation Movement, 1948–1993

Palestine and the Palestinians have had a long and eventful history. At the crossroads of the Old World and of three continents, Palestine was often the destination of conquerors and the center of conflict, for it is as well a Holy Land for three major monotheistic religions: Judaism, Christianity, and Islam. As a result, Palestine's social and political history was characterized by abrupt and wrenching change, a tendency that continues to confound its people in a more intensive manner in the second half of the twentieth century. Palestine was Arabized and Islamized beginning with the seventh century but experienced severely disruptive European interventions at three important periods of its history: the Crusades in the early medieval period, imperialism in the nineteenth century, and Zionism in the twentieth century. Regional and domestic resistance to the medieval Europeans never ceased. After nearly two centuries of rule by feudal European Christian kings, Palestine was restored to its Islamic and Arab heritage by the victory of Saladin over the Crusaders in Hittin in northern Palestine in 1187. And despite the four centuries (1517–1917) of Ottoman Turkish dominion over the country, it remained Arab and, of course, Islamic in its culture, but with a unique and important Christian Arab presence.

Nineteenth-century European imperialism, however, was a different sort of conquest. It was indirect, economic in essence, and profoundly transformative of the economic, social, political, and ideological-cultural structures of both the country and the region beyond. Although de-Arabization and de-Islamization were never a threat, Western imperialism launched the Arab Mashreq, including Palestine, into an economic process of capitalist underdevelopment and dependency. As part of that process, the Arab Mashreq was economically and politically balkanized. Each fragment became increasingly subject to European influence, if not control. World War I and the great Arab revolt against the Ottoman Turkish overlords promised to end this slide. But instead of a new era of independence, socioeconomic advancement, and modernization in a united Arab kingdom, as the leaders of the revolt expected and hoped for, the Arab Mashreq was jurisdictionally fragmented and succumbed to direct British and French colonialism.

Britain and France created and assumed control of the balkanized Arab Mashreq, the states of Syria, Lebanon, Palestine, Transjordan, and Iraq, using a variety of political and jurisdictional structures under the auspices of the League of Nations. As we have seen earlier, Palestine was unique among all the other new states in the region in that it became not merely a mandate of Britain but also a promised "homeland" for European Jews. During the mandate period (1917–1948), the powerful mix of forces unleashed on Palestine—British imperialism, Jewish settler-colonialism, uneven capitalist development, and modernization—wrought profound and dramatic change in Palestinian society and overwhelmed the Palestinian people.

The League of Nations decision (at the insistence of imperial Britain) to create in Palestine a homeland for the European Jews—aggressively pursued by the Zionists and diligently implemented by Britain as the mandatory power—led to the immigration, settlement, and empowerment of European Jews in the country. Political and armed resistance to British colonialism peaked in a failed Palestinian revolt between 1936 and 1939. As we have also seen in earlier chapters, European Jewish immigration into the country never ceased, and the Jewish immigrant-settlers amounted to one-third of the population within only one generation between the 1920s and 1948. The Palestinian-Zionist conflict over Palestine climaxed in the post-WWII period and led in 1947 and 1948 to military confrontations that resulted in the destruction of Palestinian society, the dismemberment of its patrimony, and the dispossession and dispersal of most of its people. Unlike the neighboring Arab countries—Syria, Lebanon, Transjordan, Iraq, and Egypt—that achieved political independence after WWII, Palestine was de-Arabized and de-Islamized. In 1948 it became a Jewish state (Israel) that controlled most of the territory of the country but that contained a minority of 12 percent Palestinian Arabs.

Those Palestinians who remained in what became the state of Israel survived not only as alienated strangers in their own country but also as a suppressed and exploited second-class minority. Those who were indigenous to or fled as refugees to Palestinian territory that was behind Arab military lines were incorporated into Jordan (as the West Bank) or were administered by Egypt (the Gaza Strip). All others became refugees in the newly independent Arab states. Thus from a single, dynamic society that was in the throes of rapid social and economic transformation, struggling for independence from British colonialism, and resisting Zionist settlement and immigration, Palestine's people were in 1948 scattered into separate and disconnected communities residing in historic Palestine and in neighboring Arab countries.

A generation later, the rest of Palestine, the West Bank, and the Gaza Strip, came under Israeli military occupation in the wake of the 1967 Arab-Israeli war. All of historic Palestine succumbed to Israeli control by 1967. Although Israel's occupation of the West Bank and Gaza Strip changed many things for those Palestinians under its control, it did not change the fact of Palestinian division into increasingly dissimilar and differentiated communities. Since 1948 the Palestinian communities experienced eventful, diverse, and unique histories: wrenching and bloody civil wars in Jordan and Lebanon and severe suppression in the aftermath, mass expulsion from Kuwait, oppressive and expropriative occupation in the West Bank and the Gaza Strip, greater and more widespread dispersal, and even (in the context of the oil boom) a certain economic success for some.

Despite the repeated traumas, losses, setbacks, dispossession, and dispersals and despite the social, political, and ideological differences among the dispersed communities, the Palestinians in the diaspora nevertheless forged a national liberation movement (under the umbrella of a single organization, the PLO) that mobilized and politically united the communities, internationalized their cause, and gained them strong support and legitimacy—except, of course, from Israel and the United States. Perhaps most dramatically, however, Palestinians in the West Bank and the Gaza Strip launched an uprising, the intifada, against Israel's occupation, gained even greater international sympathy, and made more urgent their cause. How the Palestinians forged their national liberation movement in the context of dispersal and occupation, how the PLO was born, how and why this movement and the PLO became transformed, and how the intifada affected their cause, modified their goals, and revised their strategy are the subjects of this chapter.

Palestinian National Liberation and the PLO

In the immediate wake of their dispossession and expulsion from Palestine in 1948, the Palestinian refugees were so traumatized and consumed with mere physical survival (most became wards of the international community, the United Nations) that they were politically paralyzed. The shattered remnants of the All-Palestine Government, successor to the Arab Higher Committee of the pre-Nakbah era, were unable to resist annexation of east central Palestine as the West Bank of Jordan, rescue the Gaza Strip from the

Egyptian administration, or provide political leadership, organization, or direction to the dispersed and destitute refugee communities outside the borders of Palestine.[1] Indeed, as we have seen in the previous chapter, these diaspora communities were politically suppressed, as were the Palestinians who remained in the areas incorporated into Israel. However, this paralysis did not last long; by 1957 it gave way to new political activism anchored in a new and younger generation of Palestinians and in new ideologies. One current of the new activism was formal, bureaucratic, organized by Arab nationalist states through the Arab League, and led from above by a Palestinian professional elite. The other was varied, spontaneous, underground, populist, and emerged independently and almost simultaneously in most locations of the diaspora Palestinian population concentrations.

Renewed Palestinian Activism in the Arab Political Context

The 1950s was a period of feverish political activism throughout the Arab Mashreq. Political parties or movements ranged ideologically from Communist parties on the left to conservative movements such as al-Ikhwan al-Muslimin (the Muslim Brotherhood) on the right. The dominant and ascendant current, however, was secular pan-Arab nationalism. Parties and movements such as the Ba'ath Party, the Movement of Arab Nationalists (MAN, also called the Arab Nationalist Movement, or ANM), and the Nasserists (after the populist pan-Arab appeals of Egyptian president 'Abdul-Nasser) were active and competitive throughout all Mashreq Arab countries.[2] They vied with one another for influence in the Arab world and in support of Arab independence from European control, unity, and especially the cause of Palestine. Pan-Arab parties not only called for the liberation (decolonization) of all Arab countries, including Palestine, from Western and Israeli political domination but also for Arab-controlled autarkic economic development and independent social and cultural transformation.

The newly formed Arab state borders have been porous to social and political movements (or parties) and ideologies that are pan-Arabist (and more recently pan-Islamist) in agenda. All pan-Arab political groups actively recruited Palestinians among their ranks. Indeed MAN was founded and organized by Palestinian students led by George Habash at the American University of Beirut in Lebanon.[3] Habash also founded the successor organization, the Popular Front for the Liberation of Palestine (PFLP). Through pan-Arab political movements, Palestinians thus found a window of opportunity for political expression and activism despite the repression of some of the insecure and suspicious Arab regimes. In responding to such pan-Arabist appeals, especially those of the Nasserists and Ba'athists, which were politically in opposition to established Western-dependent, conservative or liberal regimes (as in Jordan, Lebanon, Iraq, and even Syria at the time), Palestinians more readily earned the enmity of the Arab regimes under which they lived and who earlier had intervened on their behalf and lost the 1948 war with Israel.

Palestinians were swept up by the tide of pan-Arab nationalism in the 1950s and thus became politically active despite the lack of independent Palestinian organizations. This pan-Arabist tide crested as a result of the 1956 Suez War (the second Arab-Israeli war), in which Israel, in collusion with Britain and France, invaded the Sinai Desert and the Suez Canal zone of Egypt through the Gaza Strip. Not only was that war a catalyst for the rapid transformation of the political order of many Mashreq Arab states away from the influence of the conservative or liberal Western-dependent regimes to that of the radical nationalist and internationally nonaligned ones, but it was also a strong impetus for Palestinian activism. Besides Egypt, which in 1952 experienced a coup d'état by pan-Arabist army officers led by Colonel Gamal 'Abdul-Nasser, Syria and Iraq also succumbed to such nationalist military regimes (eventually, in those instances, stabilized under respective wings of the Ba'ath Party). Although they did not give way to pan-Arabist regimes, Jordan and Lebanon nevertheless came under tremendous indigenous and regional nationalist pressure that forced the two states to align their domestic and foreign policies with those of the Arab nationalists;[4] many of the emergent oil-exporting states of the Arabian peninsula did the same.

For the Palestinians, the new collective experience of defending themselves against Israel in Gaza in 1956 so soon after the 1948 Nakbah was an early stimulus for the reemergence of independent Palestinian political-military activism. Popular resistance erupted in the Gaza Strip against Israel's conquest and occupation of the territory during the Suez War. It was aided by the training some Palestinians had received at the hands of the Egyptian army in the Gaza Strip between 1948 and 1956.[5] Israel was forced to withdraw from Sinai and the Gaza Strip under strong (especially U.S.) international pressure. Soon after, Palestinians in the Gaza Strip and elsewhere began independent, clandestine campaigns of political organizing and military training. It was an underground political movement kept secret not only from Israel but also from the by then authoritarian and repressive nationalist regimes of Egypt, Syria, and the conservative Arab monarchies, especially Jordan. Public knowledge of the existence of one of the underground movements was betrayed only by its publication, *Filastinuna* (Our Palestine), whose "language was angry, bitter, making up in impetuous uncouth vigour for what it lacked in sophistication. Its first aim—as its name indicated—was simply to 'call to life' the Palestinians, to restore their common identity and purpose."[6] *Filastinuna* denounced the Arab states for their

> hysterical or anaesthetizing broadcasts and rousing speeches, the contents of which we all know in advance. ... The Arabs have [bound] the Palestinians' mouths, tied their hands, deprived them of their freedom of action in what is left of their country, resisted the idea of their regroupment, turned them into a

theatrical claque which applauds this and reviles that. . . . We cannot just sob and wail . . . we cannot just recite our woes and reiterate our complaints. We must gird ourselves—we alone—to solve our problems in our own way.[7]

The founders, organizers, and leaders of this movement were Gaza Strip university student activists studying in Egypt who surfaced after the Arab defeat in 1967 as the leaders of Fateh.[8] The name "Fateh"—the inverse Arabic acronym for Harakat al-Tahrir al-Watani al-Filastini (the Palestine National Liberation Movement)—also has echoes in historic Arab-Islamic symbolism. Arab-Islamic historians refer to the conquest, or the opening, Islamization, and Arabization of the Middle East, as the fateh of the regions of al-Sham (or Syria), al-Iraq, and Misr (or Egypt). Fateh was led by a collective leadership of a few close comrades, including especially Salah Khalaf, whose nom de guerre was Abu Iyad; Khalil al-Wazir, or Abu Jihad; Farouk al-Qaddoumi, or Abu Lutuf; Khalid al-Hassan, or Abu Said; and Yasser 'Arafat, or Abu Ammar, who emerged as the spokesman (and leader) of Fateh and, in 1969, chairman of the PLO.[9]

What distinguished Fateh from the start was that its ideology went against the grain of the pan-Arabism of the times. The group believed that the cause of Palestine would be advanced and won only by Palestinians, not by the Arab states, reversing the conventional discourse of pan-Arabism. Fateh emerged and remained the largest, most populist, and most influential of the new political and guerrilla organizations (to be identified and analyzed below) to be established among the diaspora Palestinians and that together defined Palestinian politics and the character of the struggle for the liberation of Palestine since 1968.

Origins of the PLO and the PRM

The sociopolitical ground for the emergence of a new, militant, and radical movement among the Palestinians had been laid, as we noted above, during the 1950s and the 1960s. In a study on the Palestinians in the Arab world, Laurie Brand notes that "in the absence of a government to defend them, Palestinians throughout the diaspora . . . began to reassemble the pieces of their shattered political, economic, and social structures. . . . The institutions they revived or reconstructed—women's, teachers', students', and workers' organizations as well as charitable societies—were the natural heirs of pre-1948 institutions."[10]

While the activities of the women's, workers', and teachers' unions and the charitable organizations in different diaspora communities were important in reaffirming Palestinian identity, developing political consciousness, creating representative institutions, establishing welfare institutions,[11] and restarting the process of building a (diaspora-wide) movement of national solidarity and mobilization, the student organizations gave this effort political content, direction, and method. As a group they constituted the first purely Palestinian diaspora organizations to call for an independent Palestine, mandatory conscription of Palestinians, and freedom of political action. The Palestinian student movement, independently in Egypt and Lebanon, created organizational structures that allowed the students to pursue clandestine political and military activism after their student days.[12] Others in the Gaza Strip, after Israel's withdrawal, established a legislative council there and set up the Palestine Arab National Union (PANU) as a framework for above-ground Palestinian political organizing. The Gaza-based efforts had the blessing and patronage of the nationalist Egyptian government of 'Abdul-Nasser.

Almost simultaneously, from his Beirut exile al-Hajj Amin al-Husseini was pressuring the League of Arabs to form an independent Palestinian state. The league, which had increasingly come under the influence of the Arab nationalist regimes, decided to reconstitute the political organization (create a *kiyan*, an entity) of the dispersed Palestinians and give them a political voice. An early decision was to establish a Palestinian army, the Palestine Liberation Army (PLA), units of which would be under the commands of the various Arab states' armies. However, in 1964, during the first ever Arab summit, urgently called to discuss and counter Israel's plan to divert the waters of the Jordan River, the Palestinian Arab League diplomat Ahmad al-Shuqayri was authorized (over the objection of King Hussein of Jordan, who had already annexed east central Palestine) to convene a new Palestine National Council (a legislative congress). The appointed council met in Jerusalem in 1964 and founded the PLO as its executive arm.

This Shuqayri-led PLO attempted to organize the diaspora Palestinians on a regional, not corporate, basis, opening offices in many Arab cities where they were concentrated. However, the bureaucratic and appointive character of the PLO and the PLA commanding officers was elitist, organized from the top, and did not succeed in inspiring or mobilizing the Palestinian people. Recognized as a full member of the League of Arab States, the PLO and the PLA—a tiny formal standing army—were in effect created by the Arab League as organizational mechanisms for Palestinians to express their identity and political aspirations. From the beginning, however, there was no agreement as to the nature and goals of the proposed PLO either among the Arab leaders or between those leaders and the grassroots Palestinian activists. Jordan, for example, which had annexed the West Bank and the majority of whose population is ethnically Palestinian, was unhappy with a separate and independent organization representing all Palestinians. But in the view of many of the Arab leaders the organization was a means not only to pursue and influence the cause of Palestine but also to *control* Palestinian political and military activity on their borders, especially as they feared Israel's aggressive retaliation against them. Ironically, it was for those very reasons and because of their disappointment in the Arab states' inaction on the Palestine question that the new underground activists were at the time opposed to the elitist, bureaucratic PLO of the Arab League.

Two separate political efforts were then evident among the Palestinians by the 1960s: the first was by the PLO—above ground, elitist, toeing the line of Arab states (especially Egypt), and legitimized by the Arab League; the second was by Fateh and other groups—underground, secretive, populist, activist, and radical. They competed against each other and to a lesser extent against the notables of the West Bank and Gaza Strip for the support of the Palestinian people. Early on in that period, several Palestinian unions and other sociopolitical organizations formally declared their support for the PLO. Thus despite the absence of support from the underground political movement, the PLO was gaining legitimacy in the eyes of many Palestinians. And thus the modern occupational or sectoral organizations that had been growing in size and scope—the General Union of Palestinian Students (GUPS), the General Union of Palestinian Workers (GUPW), the General Union of Palestinian Women (GUPWom), the General Union of Palestinian Teachers (GUPT), and the health service organization called the Palestine Red Crescent Society (PRCS)—became important loci of political competition between the two movements. The radical underground current that came to be collectively called Harakat al-Muqawama al-Filastiniyya (the Palestinian Resistance Movement), or simply al-Muqawama (the Resistance), and its guerrillas, the *feda'iyyin* (self-sacrificers), were independent of the PLO and anchored among the people and the dispersed but interconnected Palestinian civil institutions then emerging.

The ideology and strategy of the clandestine Palestinian groups were significantly influenced by the revolutions in Algeria, Cuba, and China and the Vietnam War and the general radicalization of Third World peoples in the 1950s and 1960s. The PRM viewed these as revolutions and national liberation movements that had succeeded through guerrilla tactics and people's war in the face of overwhelming military power. Hence the populist Palestinian organizations came to see armed struggle as the key to redeeming the lost homeland.

Unlike the Arab nationalist states, they believed that the liberation of Palestine would take place not in a conventional war against Israel but through a long drawn out struggle of guerrilla warfare and people's war. Fateh specified four stages of guerrilla warfare: hit-and-run operations, limited confrontations, temporary occupation of liberated zones, and, finally, permanent occupation of liberated areas. For this strategy to succeed, as it did in Vietnam, the guerrillas needed secure bases in an "Arab North Vietnam" and "Arab Hanoi" to support them (this latter aspect was not formally conceptualized until later). Fateh accordingly launched its first feda'iyyin guerrilla attack against Israel on January 1, 1965, a date the PLO under 'Arafat now regularly celebrates as the start of the contemporary "Palestinian revolution," as the PRM also came to call itself and as it also became popularly known in the Arab media. The guerrilla attacks on Israel may have contributed to the tensions that led to the 1967 Arab-Israeli war. For example, in 1966 Israel launched an attack on the village of Al-Sammu' in the West Bank, ostensibly in retaliation for such operations. Another important political and guerrilla group, the Popular Front for the Liberation of Palestine (PFLP), also began both guerrilla warfare and underground political organizing in order to prepare the people for a long-term struggle and to gain pan-Arab support.[13]

While most organizations agreed on the form of struggle, they disagreed on the role of the Arab states in that struggle and Palestinian relations with those states. The growth of Arab nationalism in the two decades after WWII led some Palestinian activists to theorize that common Arab action, that is, Arab unity, was the road to the liberation of Palestine. This was the view not only of the PFLP but of many other organizations that were influenced by one or another variation of pan-Arab ideology (Nasserist, Syrian Ba'athist, or Iraqi Ba'athist). In contrast, as we noted above, Fateh leaders adopted the inverse view: They were convinced that the liberation of Palestine was the road to Arab unity.[14] Fateh believed Arab armies should defend their borders against Israel and support and protect the Palestinian guerrillas returning from military operations inside Israel—creating Fateh's equivalent of an "Arab North Vietnam." The PFLP and other more radical groups, however, believed this was not possible unless Arab revolutionary regimes gave the Palestinian guerrillas genuine, active backing. Thus the PFLP called for revolution in the entire Arab world as context and prelude to the liberation of Palestine. In a study of Palestinian nationalism, William Quandt notes that the "PFLP and the PDFLP [were], in some ways, the most realistic in their views relative to the current limitations on the use of force. Their belief that Arab society must be radically transformed before it will be able to make use of advanced technology and weaponry against Israel is certainly easy to accept after the 1967 war."[15] But as Quandt also points out, this strategy threatens established Arab regimes.

These conflicting views not only derived from but also contributed to the fundamental contradiction that marked the entire history of relations between the militant and populist Palestinian guerrilla movement and the Arab states, that is, the contradiction between the *raison d'état* and the logic of popular revolutionary movements. Both sides of the Palestinian liberation movement (the pan-Arabists and the Palestine-first theoreticians) believed that they could not win against Israel without the support of the Arab states, and yet the movement's autonomous growth and development always led to disputes with the host countries over either sovereignty or foreign policy.[16] In Jordan and Lebanon, it was the former; with Egypt, Syria, and Iraq it was the latter. These contradictions also generated different policies and practices by the Palestinian organizations toward the respective Arab regimes. For example, in the gathering conflict between the Palestinian guerrillas and the Jordanian regime the radical pan-Arabist groups called for elimination of the regime in order to create in Amman an "Arab Hanoi," while Fateh advocated coexistence and mutual noninterference in internal affairs but support for the guerrillas. In the end, neither practice was viable and the Palestinian guerrillas were savaged by the regular Jordanian armed forces during Black September 1970. With regard to Egypt and Syria, the PRM opposed their policy of accepting in 1970 the plan of U.S. Secretary of State William Rogers for a negotiated settlement based on UN Security Council Resolution 242: the land-for-peace formula. Peace with and recognition of Israel on the basis of this UN resolution by these leading Arab states would have undermined Palestinian rights and the PRM's ideological consensus and political-military momentum. In short, Palestinians feared that they would be sold out by the Arab states. In any case, the emergent Palestinian guerrillas were saved by Israel, which rejected and thus killed the Rogers initiative.

Although united in their overall goal, then, Palestinian politics and activity in the diaspora was diverse, complex, dynamic, and often contradictory. Differences among the political organizations and guerrilla groups were significant and would have major consequences for the objectives and conduct of the struggle. Accordingly, a central concern and goal of the leaders of the PRM was always (except when 'Arafat unilaterally signed the Oslo Accords) political consensus and unity among the different groups. Both were also important in securing wide support not only among the Palestinian people but also among the Arab countries. Finally, consensus and unity were also central in the political debates that over the years moved and transformed the ideology, strategy, and political and diplomatic initiatives of the PRM and the PLO (which it controlled after 1969). Nevertheless, all efforts at genuine organizational unity among the groups at various times failed because of a number of complex internal and external factors, and the PLO remained the umbrella organization for the groups until the Oslo process, as we see in Chapters 7 and 8, tore it apart.

A Turning Point:
The 1967 War and the Rise of the PRM

The official PLO and organizations of the PRM were separate, unconnected, and competing movements for a brief period between 1964 and 1968. The 1967 Arab-Israeli war, however, changed that and the course of history in the

Middle East. In six short days, the nationalist Arab republics of Egypt, Syria, and Iraq (all of which had promised the Arab peoples political independence, socioeconomic transformation, jobs, education, economic well-being, and the liberation of Palestine), in alliance with monarchic Jordan, were defeated by Israel. The war changed the balance of power not only between Israel and the surrounding Arab states but also among the latter, especially the nationalist republics and the conservative oil-exporting monarchies of the Arabian peninsula. For the Palestinians, it also tipped the balance of power to the feda'iyyin organizations of the PRM against the discredited elitist establishment of the PLO, which was associated with the defeated Arab states. It also tipped the balance against the scattered notables who remained in the West Bank and Gaza Strip and who, under the Jordanian monarchy, competed to represent or speak for some of the Palestinians (they lost all the more power after 1967, once they were under Israeli occupation).

The Arab world was reeling from the defeat. A sense of doom and paralysis had set in, especially in the defeated countries. This created a regional political vacuum and gave the feda'iyyin guerrilla groups the opportunity to forge ahead autonomously. In short, they became, perhaps for the first time in recent history, independent actors in the Palestinian, Arab, and Middle Eastern arenas. Their revolutionary ideology was popular and was spreading widely within the diaspora Palestinian communities and the Arab world. But the conservative Arab monarchies, especially those of the Arabian peninsula who feared the "Arab revolution" as much as Israel, also emerged from under the shadow of the nationalist republics. Thus two opposing political tendencies appeared simultaneously in the Arab Mashreq: a revolutionary one led by the Palestinians and a conservative, accommodationist other led by Saudi Arabia and a defeated and chastened Arab nationalist Egypt of 'Abdul-Nasser.

Most significantly for Palestine and the Palestinians, Israel conquered and occupied the remaining Arab areas of Palestine—the West Bank (including the Old City and East Jerusalem) and the Gaza Strip. It also occupied the Golan Heights of Syria and all of the Sinai peninsula up to the eastern bank of the Suez Canal of Egypt. Israel's conquests thus brought the rest of the territory of Palestine and all the Palestinians resident in historic Palestine under its rule. After the pivotal 1948 Palestine catastrophe, the 1967 war redefined and restructured the politics of the Middle East.

In the wake of the 1967 defeat, the discredited and militarily devastated nationalist Arab states were unable to mount any kind of resistance to the Israeli occupation. Only the Palestinian feda'iyyin had the temerity and will to launch guerrilla attacks against the overwhelming Israeli occupation forces. In 1967 the Palestinian feda'iyyin attempted to establish underground cells and bases in the occupied West Bank in an effort to start guerrilla attacks from within the occupied territories.

It seemed that the classical pattern of Revolutionary War from within could now be applied, and that Fath's great hour had come. People and weapons were hastily smuggled to the West Bank. Yasser 'Arafat himself came to lead the organization of his network. Some groups began to be active. However, almost all their cells were detected by the Israeli authorities and their members were put in prison. In a matter of weeks the whole network collapsed. New attempts to set up an organizational network followed towards the end of the year, and these too were thwarted.[17]

But in the occupied Gaza Strip, despite declining intensity, the Palestinian resistance to Israel's occupation was significant until at least 1971–1972. It was largely eliminated only after Israel resorted to severe military repression and draconian security measures. Contrary to the successful resistance in Gaza, failure to mount resistance from within the West Bank was probably largely due to the lack of political and military preparation and organization on the part of the feda'iyyin. The differences in the traditions of the two Palestinian areas reflected the different policies of nationalist Egypt in the Gaza Strip and monarchic Jordan in the West Bank. In both cases, however, the Algerian model of revolution from within failed.

Failure in the West Bank forced the retreat of the feda'iyyin militants to secure bases principally across the Jordan River and allowed attacks on Israeli occupation troops and installations from those bases in Jordan. "'Incidents' on the border between Jordan and Israel rose from 97 in 1967 (after June) to 916 in 1968, 2,432 in 1969, 1,887 (up to August) in 1970 [because of Black September and the civil war in Jordan]. They then fell to 45 in 1971."[18] In March 1968 Israel launched a punitive invasion into the East Bank of Jordan whose objective was the small village and refugee camp of Al-Karameh, a base for the Palestinian guerrillas. Instead of fading and withdrawing in the onslaught of a powerful force, as guerrilla tactics prescribe, the Palestinian feda'iyyin, principally those of Fateh, stood their ground and fought a desperate but heroic battle against the superior Israeli force.[19] In so doing they inspired the regular Jordanian forces, deployed in the neighboring hills, who then joined the battle and together with the feda'iyyin bloodied the Israelis and forced them to retreat behind their cease-fire lines in the occupied West Bank.

While the 1967 Arab-Israeli war was a turning point in the contemporary political history of the Arab-Israeli conflict, the inspiring battle of Al-Karameh was the pivotal counterpoint that allowed the radical, revolutionary guerrilla organizations to move aboveground, take off politically, and redefine the nature and tactics of the Palestinian-Israeli conflict. Tens of thousands of Palestinian and Arab volunteers joined the ranks of the feda'iyyin in the next few months.[20] The new ideology of national liberation—people's war and guerrilla tactics—spread like wildfire in the Arab Mashreq, and the Arab-Israeli conflict came to be refocused increasingly as the Palestinian-Israeli struggle.[21]

The battle of Al-Karameh had several meanings for both Palestinians and Arabs. In Arabic the noun *al-karameh* means dignity, and the battle was seen as the beginning of the restoration of Arab dignity after the humiliating defeat of the Six-Day War. Further, it was fought by Palestinians who had been distrusted and hounded previously by the defeated states who had promised to liberate Palestine for them. Perhaps more significant, the revolutionary ideology of the feda'iyyin, an amalgam of Third World–style ideas of social, economic, and political-military revolution—and thus radical societal transformation—became a popular and widespread political discourse throughout the eastern Arab world. That is why the PRM and the guerrilla groups called themselves and became known as the Palestinian revolution, the spearhead of a new Arab revolution.[22] The popularity of the feda'iyyin guerrillas and their organizations was reflected not only in the Arab media but also in the support and praise they received from ordinary people, intellectuals, political leaders, and states. For example, unable to contain their rapidly rising influence in his own kingdom in the wake of the 1967 defeat, King Hussein of Jordan declared in 1969 that "we are all feda'iyyin."

One of the major consequences of the rise and popularity of the feda'iyyin was radicalization of the PLO. PLO chairman al-Shuqayri resigned his position and in 1968 was replaced on an acting basis by Yahya Hammouda. In the same PNC meeting of that year, representatives of the feda'iyyin guerrillas forced the amendment of the 1964 PLO charter in accordance with their new revolutionary views. Also in the 1968 PNC meeting the feda'iyyin formally gained control of the PLO and with it inherited the formal legitimacy from the Arab League. An internal debate on whether the PLO should be one group among many existing ones or the representative for all was resolved in favor of the latter.[23] The radical militant groups of feda'iyyin thus turned the PLO into the revolutionary umbrella organization under the influence and leadership of Fateh and Fateh's leader, 'Arafat.[24] But despite this organizational unity, each of the constituent political groups retained a broad measure of autonomy from the PLO, their independent actions, rhetoric, ideology, and internal quarrels often giving the impression of chaos and lack of discipline. In any case, from then on the political history of the Mashreq, the Palestine question, the Arab-Israeli conflict, the cold war in the region, and the "peace process" of the 1990s cannot be understood without consideration of the role and actions of the revolutionary PLO of the feda'iyyin, its long-term political transformation, deradicalization, and eventual demise.

The Arrival—and Departure— of the Revolutionary Moment

The feda'iyyin and their radical Arab allies' call for mobilizing, training, and arming the Arab peoples in all Arab countries for a people's war against Israel fell on the deaf ears of the fearful defeated rulers, including the charismatic and popular 'Abdul-Nasser of Egypt. The revolutionary moment had arrived in the Arab east, but it was to pass quickly. No general and popular mobilization was instituted by any Arab leader or regime. Instead, all the political leaders of the radical nationalist republics and the conservative monarchies closed ranks and pledged to support one another under the ideology of Arab solidarity while simultaneously paying much lip service to the Palestinian movement. The Egyptian regime of 'Abdul-Nasser agreed to an accommodation with the conservative oil-exporting monarchies of the Arabian peninsula (ending thus the Arab cold war[25]), launched an attrition war against the Israeli army entrenched on the east bank of the Suez Canal, but also consented in 1970 to the special mission of mediation by Gunnar Jarring, envoy of the United Nations, for a political solution to the conflict between Israel and the Arab states on the basis of UN Security Council Resolution 242, which specified land for peace. In these actions 'Abdul-Nasser of Egypt in effect abandoned the liberation of Palestine as a goal and tenet of Arab nationalist ideology—and thus the cause of the Palestinians—and sought instead only "elimination of the consequences of the (1967 Israeli) aggression," a slogan that meant the restoration of the territorial status quo ante in return for an Arab-Israeli peace. The Palestinian people, feda'iyyin, and the new leaders of the PLO felt betrayed.[26]

In Jordan, where the Palestinian feda'iyyin were based and where their influence was growing by leaps and bounds, a power struggle between them and the regime of King Hussein quickly erupted despite his rhetorical statements of support. In need of a supportive regime and safe haven, all factions of the feda'iyyin regarded Amman as the potential "Arab Hanoi." In the populist revolutionary climate of the times, the Palestinian feda'iyyin felt relatively secure (or were perhaps fatally arrogant) as the proverbial fish in the ocean (to use Mao Zedong's metaphor) of Palestinian communities, especially in the refugee camps. Indeed the exaggerated rhetorical support of nearly all political leaders and Arab governments and the unprecedented popular political and financial support they had among all the Arab peoples may have lulled the feda'iyyin and masked an Arab state policy of retrenchment and accommodation (with one another; with the West, especially the United States; and indirectly with Israel) by all the discredited regimes. Thus while declaring his support, King Hussein was maneuvering to contain if not suppress the feda'iyyin. The leftist feda'iyyin organizations, especially the PFLP and the Democratic Front for the Liberation of Palestine (DFLP), were suspicious and clashed with Hussein's army a number of times in the years right after the 1967 war. Unlike the reluctant Fateh leadership, they pushed for a confrontation with King Hussein's regime and expected (as did Fateh) his army (which had not only a large number of Palestinians but also some who were in important positions) to crack and join them. However, between

1968 and 1970 Hussein successfully prepared the army and the local political climate for a showdown with the increasingly arrogant and provocative feda'iyyin. His regime stoked the communal and ethnic rivalry between Palestinians and Transjordanians (especially between the feda'iyyin and his army, which was composed largely of Transjordanian bedouins) and played up, in a traditional and religiously conservative society, the threat of the feda'iyyin's secular social revolutionary (Marxist and Maoist) ideology in order to mobilize strong opposition to them.

As we noted earlier, in September 1970 King Hussein launched a vicious assault on the feda'iyyin bases in the urban Palestinian refugee camps in and around the capital of Amman. The feda'iyyin were trapped in a month-long, static defensive war, unsuited for the hit-and-run tactics of the guerrillas or their light arms. As the Jordanian army suffered minimal Palestinian desertions in the course of the fighting, the result was a bloody and costly defeat for the guerrillas at the hands of the more professional and heavily armed Jordanian units. The Arab world watched in horror and helplessness the high Palestinian civilian toll and the demise of their new heroes. The halfhearted intervention of the radical nationalist Ba'ath regime of Syria in support of the feda'iyyin came to naught (because of internal disagreement over policy and fear of Israeli intervention, the PLA units and the Syrian tank column that entered Jordan to help the feda'iyyin were denied air support by General Hafez al-Asad, the Syrian air force commander and minister of defense). And despite their radical pan-Arabist ideology, the troops of Ba'athist Iraq, who had been stationed in Jordan since the 1967 war, also watched the unfolding bloody drama without intervening.

During the civil war, Israel, with the blessing of the United States, was poised with both rhetoric and armed forces to intervene on behalf of King Hussein should the Syrian tanks succeed in tipping the balance in favor of the Palestinian feda'iyyin. The fighting during that month of Black September in Amman ended only because of the active mediation of 'Abdul-Nasser. But the defeat of the feda'iyyin in Jordan (and the untimely death of 'Abdul-Nasser later that same year) was the end of the revolutionary moment in the Arab world. Although the feda'iyyin and their revolutionary program went on for another twelve years in Lebanon, there they were effectively contained in small area of a small country and were soon (in 1975) embroiled in a civil war that was largely not of their own making.[27] Furthermore, because of the defeat in Jordan and local and regional changes, the feda'iyyin were forced to scale down sharply their revolutionary political program, although not their rhetoric. Nonetheless, while the revolutionary program was effectively abandoned, the goal of "liberating Palestine" by other (e.g., diplomatic) means was not. The revolutionary moment had passed, but popular momentum and determination propelled the PLO forward.[28]

The PLO of the Feda'iyyin:
Structure, Function, and Dynamics

Once the feda'iyyin had taken control of the PLO, the PLO's charter was changed during the fourth PNC meeting in 1968 to conform to the new Palestinian national political consensus and its revolutionary ideology: liberation of Palestine through a people's war (Articles 8–10). The PLO also became largely independent of direct control by any one Arab government. In the amended charter of the PLO of the feda'iyyin, this independence was affirmed in article 28: "The Palestinian Arab people insists upon the originality and independence of its national revolution and rejects every manner of [Arab] interference, guardianship and subordination." Similarly, in article 26, the revolutionary PLO assumed for itself the task of liberating Palestine: "The Palestine Liberation Organization, which represents the forces of the Palestinian revolution, is responsible for the movement of the Palestinian Arab people in its struggle to restore its homeland, liberate it, return to it and exercise the right of self-determination in it. This responsibility extends to all military, political and financial matters, and to all else that the Palestine issue requires in the Arab and international spheres."

As the original elitist and traditional leadership was removed, the PLO came to be anchored in the principal autonomous political and guerrilla organizations: Fateh under the leadership of 'Arafat, the PFLP under the leadership of Habash, the DFLP (a splinter of the PFLP) under the leadership of Nayef Hawatmeh, the PFLP–General Command (another split from the PFLP) under the leadership of Ahmad Jibril, other smaller organizations, and in 1987 the Palestine Communist Party (the Palestine People's Party, or PPP, after 1991) of the West Bank and the Gaza Strip. The only major political organization that has remained outside the framework of the PLO is the newest, Hamas (an acronym for Harakat al-Tahrir al-Islami, the Islamic Liberation Movement, and an Arabic word that means "zeal" or "enthusiasm"), which emerged in 1987 and is based primarily in the Gaza Strip, as is al-Jihad al-Islami (Islamic Jihad), a similar but smaller and more radical organization. As were the feda'iyyin of the 1950s and 1960s, Hamas and al-Jihad al-Islami have also been clandestine movements whose armed wings for the most part remain underground even after the establishment of the limited Palestinian Authority in the Gaza Strip and the West Bank in 1994–1995.

The pan-Arab popularity, prestige, and political-ideological influence of the feda'iyyin groups led several Arab nationalist parties and governments to create, fund, and support their own guerrilla organizations among the Palestinians. Thus the hoped-for Palestinian autonomy was quickly compromised as Arab governments extended their influence in the PLO through their client organizations. The largest and most important of these was the Sa'iqa (Vanguards of the Popular War of Liberation), which was created and materially supported by Syria's ruling Ba'ath Party and the Arab Liberation Front (ALF), which was founded and funded by Iraq's Ba'ath Party. Initially, there were several other smaller independent and semi-independent groups; these disappeared as the years progressed, while new minuscule factions emerged in the context of ideological splits, power struggles, and personality conflicts at different junctures, including the civil war in Lebanon and its aftermath. By 1975 all feda'iyyin groups, including those who were clients of some Arab states, were represented in the PLO Executive Committee. Together, the feda'iyyin organizations steered PLO functions, policy, strategy, and tactics into a more activist direction.

PLO Expansion and Development

The PLO under the feda'iyyin experienced two major spurts of expansion and development. The first was in the wake of the 1969 takeover, when the PLO's internal organization was rationalized and consolidated and new functions added; the second was during the civil war in Lebanon (1975–1982), when its social and economic functions were dramatically enlarged. (See the organizational chart of the PLO, Figure 5.1.)

Besides the PNC, the Palestinian legislature-in-exile, and the Executive Committee, the new leaders of the PLO established the Central Council (a consultative-legislative subgroup of the PNC), the Political Department (the agency for external relations), and the Military Department. The PLA was composed of four units—the Yarmouk Brigade, the Hittin Division (based in Syria), the 'Ain Jalut Forces (based in Egypt), and the Qadisiyyah Division, based in Iraq—all of which were named after historic victories that had preserved the Arab and Islamic character of Palestine and the region: The Yarmouk battle, on the border of Palestine, was a pivotal seventh-century victory of the Arab-Islamic forces over the Byzantine armies in the Near East that allowed the Islamization and Arabization of the fertile crescent. At Hittin in Palestine in the twelfth century, Saladin defeated the Crusader armies and re-Arabized and Islamized the region. 'Ain Jalut, also in Palestine, was the site of a battle in the thirteenth century in which the Mongol invaders were defeated by the rising Egyptian-based Mamluke dynasty. And the battle of Al-Qadisiyyah in Iraq in the seventh century completed the conquest of Iraq by the Arab-Islamic forces against the then non-Islamic Persians.

The new PLO also set up the Palestine National Fund (PNF); the Department of Education; the Red Crescent Society for health services; Departments of Information, Popular Mobilization, and the Occupied Homeland; a research center; a planning center; a social affairs institute; and the Samed (Economic) Institute (originally an organization for the support of the children of feda'iyyin martyrs who fell in battle or were killed by Israeli bombing).[29] In

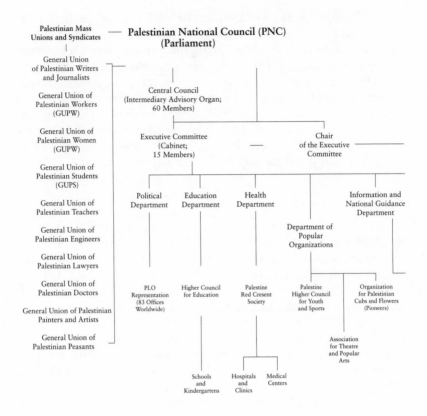

FIGURE 5.1 PLO Structure.
SOURCE: G. Halsell, "Yasser Arafat: The Man and His People," *Link* 15, 3 (July/August 1982): 8–9.

effect, the PLO grew into an organization that provided needed services, protection, and leadership directly for the diaspora Palestinians and indirectly for those under occupation and in a more veiled manner even for those others who had remained inside Israel, the so-called Israeli Arabs. By the mid-1970s, the PLO had developed the structure of a de facto government-in-exile. It and its constituent groups raised funds from a number of sources, including private contributions from Palestinians and sympathetic Arabs and Muslims, taxes on Palestinians employed in the Arabian peninsula (collected by those governments on behalf of the PLO), Arab governments, their own investments, and international sources. In its peak years before its exit from Beirut, the PLO budget reached several hundred million dollars a year.

In addition to mobilizing, serving, and protecting the Palestinian communities (of course differentially, depending on the access to the Palestinian

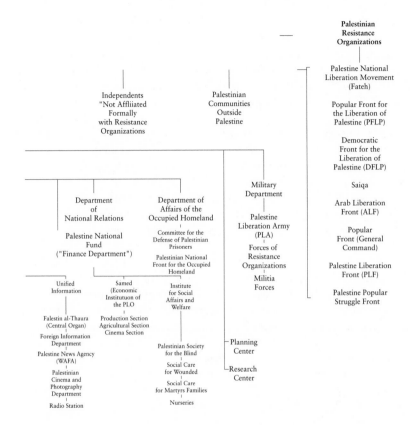

communities it had in the respective Arab host countries and the occupied territories), the PLO also made several important political achievements by the mid-1970s. During the 1973 Arab summit in Algiers, the Arab states recognized the PLO as the "sole representative of the Palestinians." Shortly afterward, a meeting between President Anwar Sadat of Egypt and King Hussein of Jordan produced a communiqué that stressed that the PLO was the representative of all Palestinians except those of Jordan. Again at the 1974 Arab summit in Rabat, however, the PLO was recognized, in spite of the objections of King Hussein (who still hoped to regain the West Bank and whose kingdom had a Palestinian majority even among the East Bank residents), as "the sole legitimate representative of the Palestinian people."

In a series of resolutions starting in 1969 (especially Resolution 2535), the United Nations General Assembly recognized and reaffirmed the "inalienable rights of the people of Palestine." By 1974 the General Assembly also recognized the PLO as the sole legitimate representative of the Palestinian people; invited 'Arafat to address the assembly; then voted Resolution 3236 (Appendix 7), the most comprehensive international affirmation of Palestinian rights of self-determination and national independence; and granted the PLO permanent observer status at the United Nations with rights of participation in most of its agencies. Recognition of Palestinian rights and PLO legitimacy had already been achieved in many important regional organizations: the Islamic Conference, the Nonaligned Countries, the Organization of African Unity, the Afro-Asian Peoples' Solidarity Organization, the Warsaw Pact members, the World Peace Council, and more than 100 individual states, most of them in the Third World and the Soviet bloc. Through these diplomatic achievements, the PLO internationalized the recognition of and support for Palestinian rights as never before.

The second period of expansion in the structure and function of the PLO was, as we noted in Chapter 4, during the civil war in Lebanon. The PLO was faced with a social crisis among its people, who had been displaced in that civil war, losing their homes and jobs and becoming destitute. It rose to the occasion, established nearly fifty different industrial and business enterprises, expanded its social services and training institutes, enlarged its own bureaucracy, and, including its military units, employed close to 70 percent of the Palestinian labor force in the country. These achievements gave the PLO structural solidity and strong legitimacy in the eyes of the Palestinian people and others.

The PLO: Ideology, Strategy, and Peace Plans

The politics of the diaspora Palestinians became anchored in and circumscribed by PLO's constituent groups after its takeover by the feda'iyyin. However, they and their organizations remained entangled in domestic and regional Arab politics both directly and indirectly. An analysis of that political history is important but would take us too far from our focus on the PLO in regard to the Palestinian diaspora communities. In discussing the policies and dynamics of the PLO, then, we simply note the impact of the major regional and international events and entanglements. There are a number of possible foci for analysis of Palestinian, specifically PLO, politics: internal to the communities and the PLO, PLO-Israeli conflict, PLO-Arab relations, and PLO-international relations.[30] Here we examine internal politics of the PLO and the Palestinian communities, which sheds light as well on the other facets of PLO politics. Although we might examine the internal dynamics of communal Palestinian and PLO politics by looking at the relationship between the PLO and the people, the relationship among the competing factions, and the methods of advancing the cause of Palestine, the most efficient analysis highlights the evolution of the ideology, political strategy, and peace plans of the PLO. Before we discuss these, however, we identify and analyze internal differences and divisions, which of course have an impact on Palestinian politics.

Internal Divisions

Ever since it came to be controlled by the feda'iyyin guerrilla organizations, the PLO has been dominated by Fateh and Fateh's strategy. One source of difference and division within the PLO was the ideology and practice of Fateh as distinct from those of the internal loyal "opposition," the ideologically leftist PFLP, and to a lesser extent the DFLP and the other less autonomous groups. Fateh was populist, nationalist, and actually opposed to formulating an ideological program of its own. Its only clear formulation other than the goal of liberating Palestine was the method by which it would be liberated: through revolutionary violence or a people's war of national liberation, including guerrilla tactics, a significant component of the overall political struggle against the Israeli enemy. This revolutionary armed struggle, Fateh believed, was also a method to mobilize the people. Fateh's simple program and ideology appealed to all Palestinian social classes, from proletarianized refugees to the high bourgeoisie. Thus Fateh's revolutionary rhetoric and strategy never achieved a fundamental or radical break with the Palestinian or Arab social or political past.

Fateh preached populist revolution to its Palestinian constituency but stability, support, and nonintervention in the deradicalized and conservative Arab regional environment. It effected no social or economic revolution among its refugee constituency, although it did provide extensive social services. Its leadership was pragmatic and retained strong and mutually supportive relations with both the deradicalized nationalist Arab states and the conservative, oil-exporting monarchies of the Arabian peninsula.[31] The oil-exporting regimes therefore gave both Fateh and the PLO generous financial support until the 1991 Gulf War. Despite occasional internal splits, factors such as the extensive financial resources, its populist and traditional nationalist appeal, and perhaps its simple program and loose organization helped Fateh become and stay the most popular and important political organization in the diaspora communities and in the West Bank and Gaza Strip territories under occupation. In contrast, the radical rhetoric, ideology, and practices of the leftist organizations, especially the PFLP and the DFLP, isolated them from broad financial support and kept them small in number, although not in influence.

Most crucial, these factors also allowed Fateh to transform its goal and strategy: from the liberation of *all* of Palestine through armed struggle to an independent state in the West Bank and Gaza Strip through diplomacy. This transformation occurred in stages during the previous two decades, in internal debates within the feda'iyyin guerrilla movement, in response to regional and international political developments, and over the strenuous objections of the leftist hard-liners and some pan-Arab parties and regimes. The loyal opposition to Fateh until the 1993 signing of the Oslo and Cairo Accords (a serious break occurred thereafter) was made up of the PFLP, DFLP, and other lesser organizations (different ones at different times) that have been dependent on various Arab governments, the Palestine People's Party, and Fateh's own left wing. Of course the newer and more radical Hamas and al-Jihad al-Islami, as we stated earlier, are outside the umbrella of the PLO and seem unalterably opposed to the PLO and the Oslo Accords.

Deriving from a strong pan-Arab nationalist background, the PFLP transformed itself into a Marxist-Leninist party in the late 1960s: militant and revolutionary in its social and economic agendas. It came closest to the Third World activist ideology of the Latin American revolutionary Che Guevara. It viewed as enemies of the Palestinian people and its goal of liberating Palestine not only Israel (and internationally organized Zionism) and imperialism (represented after World War II by the United States) but also the reactionary Arabs (especially the conservative oil-exporting regimes and the other Arab comprador bourgeoisies): the tripartite and objectively allied forces of Zionism, imperialism, and Arab reaction. It defined the enemies and friends of the Palestinian revolution in terms of class. Thus for the liberation of Palestine to succeed, revolution must take place among dispossessed Palestinians and in the Arab world among the disadvantaged classes of peasants, workers, and the petty bourgeoisie. The PFLP insisted on the need to revolutionize not only the Palestinian people and society but also the rest of the Arab world and even saw itself as part of the worldwide revolutionary forces. It thus rejected all "defeatist peace proposals" and sought alliances with revolutionary or progressive political groups in the Arab world, the Third World, and Western Europe.

Because the PFLP differed substantially from mainline, centrist Fateh in ideological formulations, it therefore also differed with it in strategy and ultimate goals. It agreed with Fateh on the necessity of armed struggle, guerrilla tactics, and a people's war against Israel but differed on revolutionary violence against reactionary Arab, imperialist and external (worldwide) Israeli targets, and the use of selective terror. The PFLP preached and practiced such an ideology until 1972.[32] After that it shifted increasingly away from such external or international activity and fell in line with the other organizations; indeed from 1975 onward they all became consumed by the civil war in Lebanon and in 1982 by the Israeli invasion of the country. With the 1982 exit and dispersal of the feda'iyyin from Beirut, the opportunities for guerrilla warfare (much less a people's war) against Israel virtually disappeared.

For the PFLP, liberated Palestine was to be not only secular and democratic but also a socialist country. In the context of the Arab world, the PFLP tended to work politically at the grassroots level and to build bridges with the opposition parties or movements, whereas Fateh (and the PLO it controlled) increasingly stressed working with the governments and formal institutions of the respective countries. In short, the PFLP and its cadres emerged as the hard-liners in the politics of the diaspora Palestinians, while Fateh and its leadership can be portrayed as, at best, flexible and pragmatic and, at worst, too accommodating to superior power and soft on principle. From the point of view of the PFLP, Fateh has since the early 1970s given up on the revolutionizing of the Palestinian and Arab political environment necessary for the long-term struggle, become contented and bureaucratized, tired of armed struggle, come under the influence of the Palestinian bourgeoisie and its Arab allies, developed a stake in the Arab state system (the status quo), and begun to seek a diplomatic solution from a weak and disadvantaged position. Nonetheless, in the sixteenth session of the PNC in 1983, the PFLP, along with other hard-liners and "rejectionists," joined Fateh's majority in accepting the Fez Arab summit peace plan, proposed by King Fahd of Saudi Arabia. The Fez plan was a response to the "peace proposals" offered by U.S. president Reagan at the end of the 1982 Lebanon invasion, proposals that denied Palestinian self-determination and sought to reimpose Jordanian dominion over the occupied territories. The Fez plan instead called for the establishment of an independent Palestinian state in the West Bank (including East Jerusalem) and the Gaza Strip in return for peace with Israel in accordance with UN Security Council Resolution 242. Both the United States and Israel ignored the Fez plan, and the Palestinian/Arab-Israeli impasse persisted. The PLO centrists became more frustrated.

We can summarize the Fateh-PFLP differences as ones over goals (until 1983, liberation of all of Palestine vs. an independent state in the West Bank and the Gaza Strip), strategy (armed struggle, sociopolitical revolution, and diplomacy vs. diplomacy) and tactics (until 1972, the use of external operations vs. those only inside Israel). In general, it was a difference over the nature of the Palestinian national liberation movement itself: Was it a revolution or merely an independence movement? For the PFLP, it was the former; for Fateh, the latter. And what of the nature of liberated Palestine—would it be a socialist Arab state with a Jewish minority, as the PFLP imagined it, or an independent ordinary Arab state in the West Bank and the Gaza Strip, as Fateh planned it? The PFLP is much smaller and has had far less resources than Fateh, but it nevertheless always commanded a strong minority following and a stronger overall political influence. Because many Arab and Palestinian intellectuals, current and former activists and sympathizers in the Arab nationalist movements (especially MAN), and journalists supported it, the PFLP developed greater influence than its size would suggest. In one sense, the PFLP and its leader, Habash, have been "the conscience" of the Palestinian national liberation movement. This difference in both approach and principle between the PFLP and mainstream Fateh is clear in the opposing stands the two organizations took regarding a number of issues over the years, the most significant of these being policy differences over the Oslo Accords and derivative accords. The PFLP denounced the accords and the defeatist leadership of the PLO and in 1996 formally withdrew from the 'Arafat-controlled PLO.

The second important group in the Palestinian political divide is the DFLP. Having split from the PFLP in 1969, the Democratic Front has since been both an opponent of and collaborator with mainstream Fateh and its leadership. Although it, too, rejected "defeatist peace proposals," it was more willing to support the strategy of diplomacy. It differed from the PFLP in that its ideology was more orthodox Marxist and much more attuned to Soviet policy during the cold war. The subtle theoretical differences over the nature of Arab society and the roles of social classes that exist between the ideologies of two fronts need not detain us here; in general, the DFLP has been more similar to than different from the PFLP. Its singular contribution is a theoretical reconceptualization of the Palestine question and its formulation of a solution: Liberated Palestine, it says, cannot be Arab, Muslim, or Jewish but must be nonsectarian, a "secular democratic state" where Muslims, Jews, and Christians are equal citizens. For a while during the 1970s, this was the political platform and preferred position of the Palestine national liberation movement and many of its cadres and intellectuals. As we see in the next section, this notion was not voted officially into any PNC resolution. Events and strategic realignments in the Middle East moved fast throughout the 1970s and 1980s and favored a new concept—the "two-state solution" (Israeli and Palestinian states side by side in historic Palestine), which became and continues to be the formal Palestinian position for solving the Palestine conflict. In regard to the Oslo Accords, the DFLP underwent a serious split in which a tiny faction, led by its second in command, Yasser 'Abed-Rabbo, called itself Fida and joined the 'Arafat faction within the PLO in supporting those accords. The majority, under the leadership of the DFLP founder, remained opposed.

The left wing of Fateh, a minority coalition of several political tendencies, played a critical role in maintaining the mainline of the organization and the loyal opposition (PFLP, DFLP, and others) unified during serious policy rifts. However, beginning with differences in policy in the Lebanon war in 1976, leaders of the leftist faction within Fateh drifted away from the mainline and in 1983, after the disastrous siege of Beirut by Israel and the exit of the PLO from the city, organized an internal rebellion that led to a small-scale Palestinian civil war. Although the rebellion was supported by Syria, it failed. The Fateh rebels emerged as a small, separate faction bitterly opposed to 'Arafat and mainline Fateh and have kept themselves as well outside the framework of the PLO. They charged 'Arafat and his supporters with deviation from, even treason to, Fateh's, the PLO's, and the Palestinian revolution's principles. They, too, expressed vehement rhetorical opposition to the Oslo Accords.

Although the 1983 internal Fateh rebellion failed, it had serious consequences, not the least of which was that it left 'Arafat little or no internal opposition to 'Arafat's policy and leadership. This became all the more true as his top two lieutenants (Khalil al-Wazir and Salah Khalaf), who also managed Fateh's most important agencies (the military and the intelligence), were assassinated in the late 1980s, the first by the Israeli intelligence service and the second by the renegade organization of Abu Nidal. Along with other important internal factors (sole financial control) and external factors (diplomatic recognition), this left 'Arafat the undisputed singular leader of both Fateh and the PLO. In that context 'Arafat consolidated his hold and became dictatorial and autocratic. He tended to ignore the institutional (consultative, legislative, and executive) institutions of the PLO and to make unilateral decisions with a group of dependent allies and clients. It was in the context of this situation that 'Arafat and three other secret collaborators agreed to the Oslo Accords.

The Palestine People's Party (formerly the Palestine Communist Party, founded in the West Bank during the Jordanian era, 1951–1967) became increasingly active and important during Israel's occupation and the eruption of the intifada. It developed a significant following, especially in the West Bank. Its political platform was far more moderate than the hard-line PFLP, reflecting the traditional Soviet position on Palestine-Israel, and thus was closer to the transformed centrist Fateh, which sought a diplomatic resolution to the Palestine question. Some of its leaders were deported by Israel from the occupied territories and one, Suleiman al-Najjab, officially joined the Executive Committee of the PLO as representative of the party in 1988. The PPP was central in organizing the unified underground leadership of the intifada. Albeit a strong supporter of 'Arafat, the "peace process" in general, the Madrid conference, and the Washington negotiations, it broke with 'Arafat over the Oslo and Cairo Accords. Since the establishment of the Palestinian Authority, the leadership of the PPP has disagreed among itself, and the party has lost popularity and influence. Nonetheless, its skilled and activist cadres continue to fill important leadership positions in the social service and cultural organizations that were so important in mobilizing people during the intifada. Some are now central to the "third alternative," a movement in opposition to both the "capitulationist" 'Arafat faction and the militant and socially conservative Hamas and Islamic Jihad. This initiative is being organized as the nationalist (insistent on Palestinian national rights and therefore highly dissatisfied with the

Oslo Accords and subsequent agreements), democratic, and socially progressive political force. Since the establishment of the Palestinian Authority in the autonomous areas of the West Bank and the Gaza Strip, the PPP has fragmented into disparate factions. Besides the faction active in the "third alternative," another has joined the new cabinet of 'Arafat in the Palestinian Authority.

The rest of the guerrilla organizations are too small and too numerous to discuss in detail. Suffice it to say that many of them have been clients of one or another Arab regime and thus have complicated internal Palestinian politics and the resolution of political dilemmas or policy debates and often tied the hands of the PLO leadership, which could not afford to alienate its Arab state patrons. The largest and most important of those has been the Sa'iqa, a guerrilla organization dependent on and tied to the ruling Ba'ath Party in Syria. It had a significant presence and was an important player within the PLO until the civil war in Lebanon. Then it was caught in the conflict between the Syrian army and the Palestinian and Lebanese allies when Syria entered Lebanon in 1976 on the side of the right-wing (Christian) militias. After that, Sa'iqa declined rapidly, except among the Palestinians in the camps in Syria. In short, apart from the small organizations that were clients of important Arab regimes, the organizations that determined internal Palestinian political dynamics and policy remained Fateh, the PFLP, the DFLP, and the PPP.

Given the sharp differences in both ideology and method among the principal organizations and as often among those who were clients of Arab regimes, the PLO and the Palestine national liberation movement in general were saddled with problems of unity and cohesion, finding shared goals and common strategy. The differences among the constituent organizations of the PLO over short- and long-term goals, tactics, and direction called into question the legitimacy of the PLO leadership and its ability to act. This dilemma has become more complex with the rise of Hamas and al-Jihad al-Islami in the Gaza Strip and the West Bank, as their ideology and tactics are considerably at odds with those of the secular, Fateh-controlled PLO.

Islamic activism in defense of Palestine and Palestinian rights goes, as we have noted earlier, back to the 1920s but was most significant in the leadership of the great Palestinian revolt of 1936–1939. The origins of Hamas are in the Palestinian branch of the movement of al-Ikhwan al-Muslimin, the Muslim Brotherhood, founded in Egypt in 1928. While secular Arab and Palestinian nationalism eclipsed the Islamic political groups, they never disappeared. Indeed in Palestine and the Arab world they reemerged stronger than ever in the wake of the Arab defeat in the 1967 Arab-Israeli war. In the occupied territories, the Ikhwan's rise to political influence was aided by numerous external and internal factors, including financial support from the oil-exporting Arab states, the social services they offered to the wretched people of the Gaza Strip, the ideological example and support of the Islamic revolution in Iran, the rise of militant Islamic resistance to Israel in southern Lebanon (especially Hizbullah), the general ascendance of political Islam in the Arab world (e.g., in the Sudan, Egypt, Algeria, and elsewhere), and, in retrospect, even Israel. Israel directly and indirectly aided the Islamic movement in a misguided effort to weaken the strong, popular, and secular PLO groups in the occupied territories. The Islamic political movement in the West Bank and Gaza and among the diaspora Palestinians was weak prior to the intifada. As its followers did not engage the Israelis in armed struggle before the intifada, they did not suffer the same repression the secular groups belonging to the PLO did. As *New York Times* correspondent David Shipler reported: "The Israeli military governor of the Gaza Strip, Brigadier General Yitzhaq Segev, once told me how he had financed the Islamic movement as a counterweight to the PLO and the Communists."[33]

Islamic political ideology sees all of Palestine as holy Muslim land (indeed waqf land) that must be liberated, an Islamic society and state to be established there. Muslim strategy for its liberation was always *jihad* (armed struggle), but this was not practiced until after the intifada broke out. We do not need here to review and analyze the explanations and justification for such inaction before the intifada nor the history of conflict between the Islamic movement and the constituent organizations of the PLO. During the intifada the Islamic movement adopted more activist, militant, and violent tactics against the Israeli occupation army. Immediately upon the outbreak of the intifada in 1987, the clerical leadership of the Islamic movement in Gaza organized Hamas to pursue the intifada and actively resist Israel. Hamas declared its goal of the liberation of all of Palestine and its strategy of armed struggle at a time when mainstream Fateh and other constituent members of the PLO had abandoned this ideology and strategy. It has refused to join the PLO except on its own terms as the majority party and has challenged the Palestinian Authority of the autonomous areas. It rejected the Israel-PLO Declaration of Principles and derivative accords, and its suicidal operations and those of al-Jihad al-Islami since the signing of the declaration have complicated Palestinian-Israeli negotiations and have reinforced Israeli insistence on security issues, affecting the 1996 Israeli elections. Hamas and the Islamic political movement are engaged not only in resisting the Israeli occupation but also in a power struggle with the PLO and the Palestinian Authority in both the autonomous and occupied territories.

Nevertheless, it should be clear that since the demise of the feda'iyyin's revolutionary program, the exit of the PLO from Beirut, and the eruption of the intifada, there has been within the PLO a political consensus on pursuing, through diplomatic means, a two-state solution to the Palestine problem. While Fateh, under 'Arafat's leadership, was able to bring about the change in Palestinian ideology, aspirations, and strategy through resolu-

tions in the PNC—the legal and legitimizing institution for debate and decision of the PLO—it committed the PLO to the Oslo Accords without such
action. Post hoc ratification by the rump Central Council is seen by most
even within Fateh as illegitimate. Since the Oslo, Cairo, and the Oslo II Accords of 1993–1995, Fateh has entered its most significant internal political
crisis, which threatens to splinter it, the PLO, and the Palestinian national
liberation movement (as we show in Chapter 7). Fateh's integrity, destiny,
and dominance over the PLO and Palestinian Authority depends on the future course of events in the autonomous areas in the Gaza Strip and the
West Bank and on the results of the second stage or the "final status" negotiations of the PLO-Israeli "peace process."

Political consensus sustained the legitimacy and relative coherence of the
PLO despite its exile to Tunis and financial decline during the 1980s. This
consensus also allowed the weakened PLO, a year after the start of the intifada, to pursue aggressive diplomatic initiatives that opened the door to
dialogue with the United States but only partially broke the Palestinian-
Israeli impasse. However, the consensus began to fray over the terms of the
1991 Madrid conference and was finally torn apart by 'Arafat's acceptance
of the Oslo, Cairo, and Oslo II Accords. 'Arafat, according to the opposition, had gone much too far (that is, conceded much too much) beyond the
formal Palestinian consensus codified in the PNC resolutions.

The key element in Palestinian political unity in the context of communal
and institutional dispersal has long been agreement on goals and aspirations. But just as important for the PLO was that decisions were based on
the consensus of all the major factions. While consensus over ultimate goals
was relatively easy to achieve and may have given the organization coherence and solidity, it often created paralysis in decisionmaking and in the interpretation and implementation of those decisions. When consensus was
not reached, especially on pivotal issues of diplomacy (e.g., over whether to
accept a diplomatic route or the terms of a certain peace initiative advanced
by others), the organization was politically immobilized. 'Arafat had no authority to act but often did so unilaterally. And unilateral action by 'Arafat,
although the elected chairman of the PLO, often deepened the internal conflict and the political dilemma of the organization in the eyes of both regional and international powers. These problems were compounded by the
debilitating practices—newly discovered and expounded upon by the intellectual and journalistic circles of the Arab world and the West—of political
deviation, nepotism, corruption, and autocracy on the part of 'Arafat and
the Fateh leadership of the PLO. Perhaps more significant, such divisiveness
caused a commensurate breakdown in the functioning of PLO institutions,
which at frequent and crucial times not only paralyzed the PLO and allowed 'Arafat to act with impunity but also hurt the cause of Palestine and
its people. The PLO's paralysis has, for example, allowed 'Arafat to estab-

lish the Palestinian Authority in the West Bank and Gaza Strip and to merge it with the PLO bureaucracy without any formal or official consideration, forethought, or planning.

The PLO, which has always represented the whole Palestinian people, has become, in the immediate wake of the Oslo agreement, indistinguishable from the Palestinian administration of the autonomous territories. It has been deliberately marginalized by 'Arafat and has effectively lost its national, all-Palestinian representative function and its policymaking authority. Little if any formal or informal activity takes place within the agencies and institutions of the PLO. It has left the diaspora communities—the largest segment of the total Palestinian population—without the needed social and economic services, disenfranchised politically and bereft of any organizational recourse to pursue their neglected rights. They have no voice in their own destiny—a feat accomplished not by their enemies but by their own erstwhile leader. Palestinians in the diaspora in the post-Oslo era are thus alienated from their presumed leadership and currently immobilized. And yet little except grumbling, passive anger, and cynicism has surfaced to challenge or pressure 'Arafat and his inner circle.

Evolution of Ideology and Strategy

As we noted in the previous chapter, the traumatized and dispossessed Palestinians after the 1948 Nakbah spontaneously articulated a simple hope of return: "*Innana 'Ai'doun*" or "*Innana Raji'oun*," slogans that developed into a whole mystique of redemption of their homes and homeland.[34] As the years passed and the prospect of returning to their homes and properties in Palestine faded, new conceptualizations emerged. This simple wish to return home was increasingly coupled with more militant views, as represented by the names of the clandestine guerrilla groups that preceded the feda'iyyin organizations: Abtal al-'Awdah (Heroes of the Return) and Shabab al-Tha'r (Vengeance Youth).

With the emergence of the feda'iyyin groups, the slogans and strategies for the liberation of Palestine were more formally discussed and formulated. In the regional and the international (especially Third World) context of decolonization and nationalism, the feda'iyyin guerrilla groups developed a basic consensus on the idea that Israel, a European settler colonial project in the era of decolonization, was anachronistic. Thus it was the right of the dispossessed Palestinian people to liberate their homeland from the colonial settlers, to return to their homes, and to rebuild their independent Arab country, itself an inseparable part of the larger Arab umma.

This early political consensus that was enshrined in the national charter of the PLO (1968) only peripherally addressed the status of the Israeli Jews: Those who had resided in the country prior "to the Zionist invasion" were welcome to stay and live as Palestinians (article 6); by implication all others were not. And as the charter stated, "The partition of Palestine in 1947 and the creation of Israel are both null and void . . . [as is the] Balfour Declaration" (articles 19 and 20). In general, the substance of the charter affirmed the Arabness of Palestine and the right of its dispossessed people to struggle for its liberation. In any case, the radical political consensus of the high revolutionary moment (1968–1970) was not to last long, as first the 1970 Black September attack on the guerrillas then the October 1973 Arab-Israeli war and the diplomatic offensive of President Sadat of Egypt changed dramatically the political climate in the region. In the atmosphere of the Soviet-U.S. détente of the time, the more orthodox Marxist DFLP's proposal for a "secular democratic" state in Palestine for all its people— Muslim, Jewish, and Christian—eventually emerged as the PLO's new consensus and was offered as the peace plan of the Palestinian militants.

The roots of this formulation went back to the radical revolutionary era. Although the 1968 charter articulated a hard-line position on "Jewish settlers"' in Palestine (the Israelis), Fateh became involved in internal discussions whose conceptions were at variance with the charter's language. For example, in its own third congress in 1968, a few months after the national charter was ratified, Fateh after much internal debate expressed a new vision of the future Palestine as "a democratic, progressive, non-sectarian state in which Jews, Christians and Muslims would live together in peace and enjoy the same rights."[35] The grounds for this political formulation was prepared by another internal debate on the nature of the differences between Judaism and Zionism. In late 1967 a Fateh leader, most likely 'Arafat, declared: "We are not the enemies of Judaism as a religion nor are we enemies of the Jewish race. Our battle is with the colonialist, imperialist, Zionist entity which occupied our homeland."[36] Indeed Fateh's first official press release in January 1968 specified that its military operations were not against the Jewish people with whom the Arabs had lived in harmony for so many centuries but against international Zionism.[37] During the second Solidarity Conference with the Arab Peoples held in Cairo in late January 1969, a Fateh statement that appeared in a French publication, the *Tribune Socialiste,* declared:

> There is a large Jewish population in Palestine and it has grown considerably in the last twenty years. We recognize that it has the right to live there and that it is part of the Palestinian people. We reject the formula that the Jews must be driven into the sea. If we are fighting a Jewish state of a racial kind, which had driven Arabs out of their lands, it is not so as to replace it with an Arab state which would in turn drive out the Jews. What we want to create in the historical borders of Palestine is a multiracial democratic state . . . a state without any hegemony in which everyone, Jew, Christian or Muslim, will enjoy full civic rights.[38]

This view of a future secular democratic state in Palestine where the Palestinian natives (Muslim and Christian) and the foreign Jewish settlers would live together in harmony and democracy as the solution for the Palestine problem coexisted with the vision of the PLO charter, which stressed an Arab Palestine but in effect superseded the latter. Contributing to this revised view were the theoretical innovations of the DFLP on the issue. In the sixth PNC meeting in 1969, the DFLP position paper rejected all chauvinistic solutions (e.g., driving the Israeli Jews into the sea) and called for a popular democratic solution to the Palestinian and Israeli problems by "setting up . . . a popular democratic Palestinian state for Arabs and Jews alike in which there would be no discrimination and no room for class or *national* [ethnic] subjugation and in which the right of both Arabs and Jews to perpetuate and develop their indigenous cultures would be respected."[39]

What is important about this proposal is that it went beyond the vague concept of coexistence and acknowledged the presence of two nationalities (ethnic groups), or nations, in the country. Such recognition of two different nations in one country meant, from their Marxist-Leninist perspective, the recognition of the right of each to self-determination and therefore to separation or independence. This implicitly meant the recognition of the state of Israel. Needless to say, this and the earlier Fateh formulation generated much debate and much opposition, especially from the radical pan-Arabist groups but also from within Fateh's own ranks. The idea was adopted by the sixth PNC in slightly modified form: The revolutionary struggle would continue until victory and the construction of a democratic state. A secular democratic state in Palestine was declared as the PLO position for a just solution to the Palestinian-Israeli conundrum. Palestinian activists considered this a moral, revolutionary proposal by the victims of the conflict to resolve politically and peaceably the Palestinian-Israeli problem. Israel and its Western supporters, however, cynically dismissed or ignored it. Nevertheless, the goal of establishing in Palestine a secular democratic state for all the people of Palestine, and not exclusive to any one religious group or sect, also prepared the ground for a second and later debate on the two-state solution.

In the rapidly changing context of the Middle East of the 1970s—including Egypt's go-it-alone policy in search of peace with Israel and the rise of oil revenues and of Arab financial and diplomatic power—the prospects for diplomatic initiatives in the area increased. However, instead of the PLO's emerging at the center of the international diplomatic search for a political solution, the United States refloated the idea that Jordan was representative of the Palestinian people, and this only a year after the Arab League voted the PLO Palestinians' "sole legitimate representative." The twelfth PNC meeting in 1974 rejected both the idea of Jordanian representation and UN Security Council Resolution 242, which did not refer to Palestine or the Palestinians except as part of the "refugees" of the 1967 war.

Under the combined external pressure of the Soviet Union and the Arab states and internal pressure of Fateh and the DFLP, the PLO reformulated its ideology and developed a new policy goal: Instead of a secular democratic state in a unified Palestine, it proposed a two-state solution to the Israel-Palestine dilemma. Israel and a Palestinian state would exist side by side in historic Palestine. This concept, however, was not formally voted on by the PNC. The compromise language that passed as a resolution in the PNC, with the support of the PFLP, was the idea of establishing a "national authority" on any part of Palestine liberated from occupation. Just as significant, the PLO redefined the nature and terrain of struggle. In the thirteenth PNC meeting in Cairo in 1977, "negotiations" for a resolution of the conflict were accepted as a "form of struggle" (a formulation that led the dissenting PFLP to suspend its membership in the PLO Executive Committee).

For the PFLP, the DFLP, and other radicals, the projected "national authority" would be a revolutionary one, in control of liberated zones in Palestine, which would be bases for carrying on the armed struggle. However, for Fateh, and therefore the PLO, it meant simply a Palestinian authority (as a basis for an eventual state) on any part of Palestine liberated from or relinquished by Israel, an authority that would coexist with Israel. Although dramatically different, the two interpretations nonetheless coexisted within the movement, paved the way for acceptance of the Arab League's peace plan in 1983, and did not cause any serious or paralytic divisiveness within the PLO until the Oslo Accords. Of course, as we argue in Chapter 7, limited autonomy over civilian matters in the Gaza Strip and the West Bank population centers as prescribed by the Declaration of Principles and subsequent agreements is a far cry from the "national authority" envisioned either by mainline Fateh or the radical PFLP. It is neither a liberated nor a sovereign zone.

The PLO and the rest of the world were stunned by Egyptian president Sadat's visit to Jerusalem and Egypt's acceptance of the Camp David Accords in 1978 and Egypt's signing of a bilateral peace treaty with Israel in 1979—developments agreed to by Israel and Egypt under the auspices of the United States and thrust in the disbelieving faces of the Palestinians and all other Arabs. As a face-saving mechanism for these accords, the Egyptian-Israeli agreement provided—without any consultation with the PLO—for a regime of Palestinian autonomy (over the people but not the land) in the West Bank and the Gaza Strip for five years. In the fourteenth PNC meeting in 1979, the PLO formally rejected this autonomy provision and the Israel-Egypt peace treaty itself; the rest of the Arab world did likewise. The Arab League expelled Egypt, moved its headquarters from Cairo to Tunis, and ostracized the Egyptian government politically and financially.

Because of the bilateral peace treaty between Israel and Egypt, the eastern Arab world lost the most powerful armed forces and the principal military deterrent against Israel. The regional balance of power thus suddenly shifted significantly in favor of Israel over all the Arab states of the Fertile Crescent and the PLO, which led Israel, under the right-wing Likud coalition government, into military adventurism. The most important and dramatic example was the 1982 invasion of Lebanon, during which Israel expelled the PLO from Beirut and altered the strategic Palestinian-Israeli situation considerably, an event that set the PLO on a course of rapid decline. The newly expressed PLO goal of establishing a "national authority" in liberated Palestine came increasingly to be interpreted as a two-state solution by diplomats, the media, and much of the Palestinian leadership. Accordingly, with the active support of the PLO, the 1983 Arab summit in Fez developed a peace plan in which it clearly specified the establishment of an independent Palestinian state in the West Bank and the Gaza Strip as a condition for Middle East peace; confirmed the right of all states, including the proposed Palestinian state, to live in peace and security; but only indirectly recognized the state of Israel. The PNC ratified this plan that year in its sixteenth meeting. This PNC meeting, unlike earlier ones, did not reject outright the Reagan proposal (made in the wake of the end of the Israeli siege of Beirut and the exit of the PLO from the city), to which the Fez plan was a response. It noted diplomatically both the positive aspects and the shortcomings of the Reagan plan.

The sixteenth PNC meeting was thus a landmark session. The decisions had moved the Palestinian national liberation movement and the PLO, officially and formally now, from its former revolutionary or radical political agenda (liberation of all of Palestine and thus the dismantling of the Israeli state) to a more diplomatically acceptable formulation and a strategically more realizable goal (coexistence of a Palestinian state with Israel in historic Palestine). Such a formulation was regarded internationally as necessary for a political or peaceful solution of the Palestine problem. In short, the sixteenth PNC session resolutions formally confirmed the significant shift from the PLO ideology of national liberation of all of Palestine to a goal of establishing an independent Palestinian state in the West Bank and the Gaza Strip. The Palestinian national liberation movement was officially deradicalized and transformed into an independence movement.

Contrary to numerous reports in the Western and Israeli media and scholarship, the Arab states (since the 1967 UN Security Council Resolution 242) and the PLO (indirectly since 1974 and directly and officially since 1983) accepted the "existence" of the state of Israel and since 1983 have sought a peaceful solution to the Arab-Israeli conflict. As Naseer Aruri, Noam Chomsky, and Cheryl Rubenberg have shown, it was in fact Israel and the United States that never accepted Palestinian national rights or the varied peace plans offered and pursued by the Arab states and the PLO over the years.[40] Chomsky and Aruri have compellingly argued that Israel and the United States were the "rejectionists" of a just peace in the area.[41]

The pivotal sixteenth PNC session came after the 1982 PLO exodus from Beirut but before the breakout of the Palestinian civil war—the leftist Fateh rebellion, backed by Syria, against 'Arafat's centrist faction. Thus the seventeenth PNC session held in Amman in 1984, after the successful rapprochement between the PLO and King Hussein of Jordan, was a rump session principally of 'Arafat loyalists that merely reaffirmed his power over both the core of Fateh and the PLO. But it divided the PLO, as the session was boycotted not only by the Fateh rebels but also by the long-established opposition—the PFLP, the DFLP, and others. No PNC meeting was held until April 1987 in Algiers. After much hard negotiation between the Fateh centrists and the opposition, aided by the mediation of Algeria, national Palestinian unity was restored and the eighteenth PNC meeting was held. This brought back to the PLO fold the PFLP, DFLP, and others but not the Fateh rebels, who stayed out of the PLO and attempted to organize from their base in Damascus an oppositional coalition with other dissidents. Their viability and credibility would not have been high except for the support of Syria.

In retrospect, it seems that all the internal disagreements and divisiveness among the constituent parties or groups of the PLO between the pivotal 1983 meeting of the PNC and the 1987 meeting were of little significance and reflected, after the exit from Beirut, a movement that had lost its consensus and an organization that had lost its bearings. This was in part because it was forced out of its long-term and highly autonomous base in Lebanon, which was near its homeland and where it could always exercise a military option. It also lost the momentum of the earlier (1974–1982) initiatives of the previously influential Arab diplomacy. The price of oil had plummeted from a high of $42 per barrel on the spot market in 1982 to $8 in 1986. International Arab (financial and diplomatic) power waned rapidly.

During the second half of the 1980s, the oil-exporting states were in serious economic retrenchment. The regionwide oil-based Arab economy was in a deep recession that affected not only Arab states' finances but also those of the PLO. Most directly relevant to the oil monarchies was the long (1980–1987) Iraq-Iran war, which threatened their security and drained their decreasing financial resources. In addition to being in economic trouble, the Arab world was in political disarray by the end of the 1980s. Egypt was ostracized, Iraq (and the oil monarchies) was consumed by its war with Iran, Lebanon was still paralyzed by the civil war and occupation, and Syria was at odds with the PLO of 'Arafat (and in strategic alliance with Iran against the rest of the Arab states). The PLO was isolated, and the Palestine question fell sharply among the political priorities of the Arab world.

The best indication of this decline in significance is the set of resolutions adopted by the 1987 Arab summit in Amman, scarcely 40 miles from the occupied West Bank. The lead item of the resolutions, and therefore the prime concern of the assembled Arab rulers, was the threat of the revolutionary Islamic Iran. The Palestine question was addressed in a pro forma and perfunctory manner at the end of the resolutions, and at the meeting 'Arafat was treated as something less than a head of state. This event had a profound impact on the Palestinians, especially those under occupation. In this Arab climate of economic retreat, political retrenchment and insecurity, and gathering social discontent, the long-standing premier Arab cause of Palestine and the diminished, dispersed, and distant (from Palestine) PLO were distinctly of far less import to the Arab states and rulers. It appeared thus that the cause of Palestine and the fortunes of the PLO were rapidly on the eclipse when suddenly, in December 1987, shortly after the Arab summit and the eighteenth meeting of the PNC, a dramatic uprising, an intifada, broke out among the Palestinians of the occupied territories.

The Political Impact of the Intifada

The Western media that covered the intifada, especially the confrontations between stone-throwing Palestinian youths and the heavily armed Israeli occupation soldiers, captured on film images that were far different from those long held of the Arab-Israeli or Palestinian-Israeli conflicts. The old myth of Israel's David facing the Arab Goliath was shattered and actually reversed: Israel now appeared before all the world as the vicious Goliath beating up on the Palestinian David. Thus the remarkable and sustained intifada had significant political consequences. Its simple ideological message exposed once and for all the brutal character of Israel's occupation and the Palestinian wish for an end to that occupation. As important, the intifada and its spokespeople tirelessly reaffirmed the oneness of the Palestinian people (under occupation and in the diaspora) and the legitimate leadership of the PLO.

The intifada unexpectedly and considerably reenergized the Palestinian national movement and brought back the Palestine question and the PLO to the diplomatic center stage not only in the region but also internationally. Surprisingly, this was the case despite (perhaps because of) the unfolding of other stunning international and regional political developments. The collapse of communism and the end of the Iraq-Iran war were important events that, with the intifada, triggered ideological and political changes within the PLO and advanced its diplomacy. In 1988, a little less than a year after the intifada made its dramatic political impact and jogged the PLO out of its impasse, the PNC held what may be considered another landmark meeting, perhaps the most significant since its founding and its capture by the feda'iyyin guerrilla organizations. It recognized UN Security Council Resolutions 242 and 338 (see Appendix 8), which set the conditions for a Middle East political settlement (the land-for-peace formula), proclaiming the state of Palestine with the occupied territories as its patrimony and East Jerusalem (including the Old City) as its capital (see Appendix 9). It also authorized the Executive Committee and its chairman, 'Arafat, to pursue diplomatic initiatives. At a meeting in Stockholm, the PLO and a U.S. Jewish delegation issued a joint statement (see Appendix 10) in which the PLO:

1. Agreed to enter into peace negotiations at an international conference under the auspices of the UN. . . .
2. Established the independent state of Palestine and accepted the existence of Israel as a state in the region;
3. Declared its rejection and condemnation of terrorism in all its forms, including state terrorism;
4. Called for a solution to the Palestinian refugee problem in accordance with international law and practices and relevant UN resolutions (including right of return or compensation).

In light of these developments, the United Nations invited 'Arafat to address the General Assembly. When the U.S. government denied him a visa to enter New York, the General Assembly moved its meeting to Geneva, where 'Arafat offered what he called the Palestinian peace initiative (see Appendix 11). In his speech to the General Assembly, 'Arafat expressed the desire of the PLO to participate in an international peace conference under the auspices of the United Nations in which the PLO would seek a comprehensive settlement among the parties concerned in the Arab-Israel conflict on the basis of UN Security Resolutions 242 and 338, and he asked that "actions be undertaken to place . . . occupied Palestinian land under temporary United Nations supervision, and that international forces be deployed there to protect . . . [the Palestinian] people and, at the same time, to supervise the withdrawal of the Israeli forces from [the] country."[43] Both the United States and Israel boycotted the United Nations session in Geneva, even as more than 100 states formally recognized the state of Palestine.[44] Israeli prime minister Yitzhak Shamir described the Palestinian peace proposal as a "monumental act of deception," while the U.S. government insisted on clarification of what it interpreted as ambiguous language. The United States specifically demanded that 'Arafat "renounce" violence and terrorism, not merely "denounce" those kinds of acts on both sides of the conflict. 'Arafat complied with U.S. demands, as he, along with many others in the PNC, believed that only the United States could mount any kind of pressure on Israel to accept the offer. The day after the Geneva event, President Reagan announced at a White House press conference that the United States would open a dialogue with the PLO. The U.S. ambassador to Tunisia, Robert Pelletreau, was appointed to initiate the direct talks, the United States carefully avoiding the involvement of high-level State Department officials.

Finally, after a quarter of a century of struggle, the PLO, with the reluctant acquiescence of the United States, was able to enter both directly and indirectly into the deliberations of international diplomacy in the forums and venues concerned with the question of Palestine. Although Israel ignored its official recognition by the PLO and objected to the U.S.-PLO dialogue, the PNC actions and 'Arafat's follow-up statements were nevertheless crucial first steps in the process of breaking the critical impasse that had long prevented, in the words of Western diplomats and media, Arab acceptance of Israel—although the Arab states and the PLO had in fact long sought a political solution to the conflict. Mutual Arab-Israeli recognition and normalization were now possible.

But it was not until the defeat of radical Arab nationalism (the Iraqi version) and the restructured strategic balance in the region in the wake of the 1991 Gulf War that a revived U.S.-led "peace process" started in earnest. The Gulf War and the collapse of the Soviet Union allowed the United States to emerge as the sole hegemonic power in the Middle East region. Stung by charges of a double standard regarding its position on the occupation of Kuwait by Iraq and that of the West Bank and the Gaza Strip by Israel, the United States moved quickly to restart its Middle East "peace process." The United States officially ignored the PLO as it focused on bringing to the negotiating table only representatives of the Palestinians of the occupied West Bank and Gaza Strip and the government of Israel. Israeli-, U.S.- (and indirectly) PLO-approved Palestinian leaders from the West Bank and Gaza Strip who were not officials of the PLO were chosen. However, as these Palestinian leaders insisted that they openly consulted with and were led by the PLO, a diplomatic charade was conducted in which both Israel and the United States pretended that the PLO was not involved.

This was the diplomatic background to the Madrid peace conference of November 1991, which Israel; the surrounding Arab states of Syria and Lebanon and a joint Jordanian-Palestinian delegation from the West Bank and Gaza Strip; and the two sponsors, the United States and Russia, attended. The conference was the opening session of multilateral and bilateral peace negotiations between Israel and its Arab neighbors. Twelve bilateral sessions over two years were held in Washington and came to no agreement. It was this new impasse that in part led to the secret back-room negotiations between Israel and the PLO that led to the 1993 Oslo Accords.

Conclusion

It should be clear that the PLO has come a long way and its accomplishments are many. Not the least were preserving Palestinian identity; providing services to stateless, dispersed, dispossessed, and suppressed communities; developing representative institutions for its constituency; reaffirming its national political rights; and internationalizing the Palestine cause. Through the PLO, the Palestinians made such achievements in spite of tremendous physical, communication, and financial difficulties; diplomatic obstacles; and savage warfare against them not only by Israel but also by fellow Arabs.

The PLO went through three phases in its ideological, strategical, and organizational evolution before it signed the Oslo Accords in 1993. The first, between 1964 and 1968, was a start-up period during which the PLO was a creation of the Arab states, more of an organization to control Palestinian activism than it was to give Palestinians a political voice. The second, from 1968 to 1982, was a time of social and political revolution during which it established and developed all its civil and service institutions, gave specificity and coherence to the Palestinian political cause, made most of its important political achievements and ideological transformation, and placed the Palestinians and the Palestine question on the international political agenda. This phase ended in military defeat in 1982 in the Israeli siege of Beirut and the PLO exodus from the city. This second phase was also the high mark of diaspora Palestinian political, economic, and social development, an era during which the PLO failed to liberate any part of Palestine. The third phase began in 1982 and ended in 1993 with the signing of the Oslo Accords. Eventful though this period was—especially because of the outbreak of the intifada, the collapse of communism and the Soviet Union, and the 1991 Gulf War—the PLO not only failed to advance the cause of Palestine and the Palestinians but also blundered into making serious concessions of principle (e.g., recognition of the state of Israel without a reciprocal Israeli recognition of the right of the Palestinian people for self-determination and an independent state of their own) and degenerated into an isolated and decrepit bureaucracy rendered ineffective by mismanagement, autocracy, corruption, nepotism, declining funds, and political bankruptcy.

The varied diaspora communities of the Palestinian people were during this period set adrift, and nearly all their PLO-funded institutions were in disarray or became inoperative. Economic and social disaster befell the large Palestinian community in Kuwait, which was expelled from the country because of 'Arafat's policy in the 1990–1991 Gulf crisis. After the Gulf War, the PLO sank even further into financial bankruptcy and political irrelevance. Despite its earlier concessions, it thus was largely ignored in the new U.S.-initiated "peace process." Had it not been for the unwavering support for and recognition of the PLO as the political representative of *all* the Palestinians (under occupation and in the diaspora) by the West Bank and Gaza Strip Palestinians and their leaders and the emergence of a militant Islamic resistance movement, Hamas, the PLO may have vanished into oblivion.

To be sure, in the context of the intifada, an uprising not of its own making, the PLO under 'Arafat revised formally and officially Palestinian ideology, goals, and strategy and its position became internationally more acceptable diplomatically. But instead of taking advantage of the locally, regionally, and internationally changed political climate to bring about a just and honorable resolution to the Palestine conflict—an independent Palestinian state in the West Bank and Gaza Strip, mutual recognition of and by Israel, and sustaining the rights of the refugees—as it declared, the 'Arafat-controlled PLO stumbled into the Oslo Accords.

It has become clear to most Palestinians that the 'Arafat PLO regime sought to maintain itself in the diplomatic game and to retain international legitimacy by ignoring the rights of their own constituency and offering un-principled concessions to the enemy, first to the U.S. government in order to engage with it in a mere dialogue (without receiving formal diplomatic recognition), then to Israel by accepting Israel's dictates on who the Pales-tinian negotiating team should be in order to be an indirect participant in the Madrid peace conference and the fruitless twelve rounds of the Wash-ington Arab-Israeli peace negotiations. And finally and in a move disas-trous for the Palestinian people, as we see in Chapter 7, it accepted the Oslo Accords for limited autonomy in the Gaza Strip and the West Bank cities, areas that nevertheless have remained under overall Israeli control and sov-ereignty, and for an uncertain future for the occupied territories and the central issues of the conflict (the refugees, Jerusalem, borders, sovereignty, and settlements), which are to be determined in the "final status" negotia-tions by 1999.

The PLO's signal achievement in the Oslo Accords was its recognition by Israel as representative of the Palestinian people. But the concessions of principle the PLO made in those agreements not only indicate its demise as an organized transnational framework for serving and expressing the rights of the Palestinian people but have also raised serious questions about the potential for the restoration of the Palestinians' historic rights, the recon-struction of an independent Palestinian society, and indeed the very exis-tence of the Palestinian people's collective identity.

Notes

1. Al-Hajj Amin al-Husseini, the leader of the All-Palestine Government, was in exile in Lebanon and Iraq.

2. On Arab nationalism, see G. Antonius, *The Arab Awakening: The Story of the Arab National Movement*, 3rd ed. (London: H. Hamilton, 1955); S. G. Haim, ed., *Arab Nationalism: An Anthology* (Berkeley: University of California Press, 1964); and H. Sharabi, *Governments and Politics of the Middle East in the Twentieth Cen-tury* (Princeton: Van Nostrand, 1962).

3. W. Kazziha, *Revolutionary Transformation in the Arab World: Habash and His Comrades from Nationalism to Marxism* (London: Charles Knight, 1975).

4. N. H. Aruri, *Jordan: A Study in Political Development, 1921–1965* (The Hague: Nijhoff, 1972); see also N. H. Aruri and S. Farsoun, "Palestinians in Arab Host Countries," in K. Nakhleh and E. Zureik, eds., *The Sociology of the Palestini-*

ans (London: Croom Helm, 1980); and F. Qubain, *Crisis in Lebanon* (Washington, DC: Middle East Institute, 1961).

5. D. Hirst, *The Gun and the Olive Branch* (London: Futura, 1977); see also, W. B. Quandt, "Political and Military Dimensions of Contemporary Palestinian Nationalism," part 2 in W. B. Quandt, F. Jabber, and A. M. Lesch, *The Politics of Palestinian Nationalism* (Berkeley: University of California Press, 1973), 55–56.

6. Hirst, *The Gun and the Olive Branch*, 197.

7. Ibid., 272.

8. "Fateh" is often transliterated into English as "Fatah" or "Al-Fatah," both of which are inaccurate. Occasionally it is also transliterated as "Fath," a rendition of classical Arabic.

9. H. Cobban, *The Palestinian Liberation Organization: People, Power and Politics* (Cambridge: Cambridge University Press, 1984), ch. 2: "The Phoenix Hatches (1948–67)," 21–35.

10. L. A. Brand, *Palestinians in the Arab World* (New York: Columbia University Press, 1988), 3–4.

11. Ibid., 39.

12. Cobban, *The Palestinian Liberation Organization*, 21–35.

13. There was an important difference between the two radical groupings. Fateh followed the Cuban model of the "foco theory," by which a guerrilla group triggers a revolution through direct armed attacks. PFLP theorized, in accordance with the Soviet and Chinese models, the importance of political organizing before and during the initiation of armed struggle. As we see later in this chapter, Fateh's popularity took off precisely because of its armed activism.

14. See Abu Iyad, with Eric Rouleau, *My Home, My Land* (New York: Times Books, 1981), 20–23. See also Khaled al-Hassan, one of the senior Fateh leaders, as quoted by Cobban, *The Palestinian Liberation Organization*, 24; and Quandt, "Political and Military Dimensions of Contemporary Palestinian Nationalism," 51, 55–58.

15. Ibid., 117.

16. See F. Jabber, "The Palestinian Resistance and Inter-Arab Politics," part 3 in Quandt et al., *The Politics of Palestinian Nationalism*, 157–216. For a more critical perspective, see R. D. McLaurin, "The PLO and the Arab Fertile Crescent," in A. R. Norton and M. H. Greenberg, eds., *The International Relations of the Palestine Liberation Organization* (Carbondale: Southern Illinois University Press, 1989), 12–58.

17. Y. Harkabi, *Fedayeen Action and Arab Strategy* (London: Institute for Strategic Studies, 1968), 27; see also Cobban, *The Palestinian Liberation Organization*, 36–38, 178–179.

18. A. Gresh, *The PLO: The Struggle Within* (London: Zed, 1985), 14.

19. J. K. Cooley, *Green March, Black September: The Story of the Palestinian Arabs* (London: Frank Cass, 1973); see also Hirst, *The Gun and the Olive Branch*, and Cobban, *The Palestinian Liberation Organization*, especially ch. 3, "The Joy of Flying (1967–73)," 36–39.

20. M. Hudson, "The Palestinian Arab Resistance Movement: Its Significance in the Middle East Crisis," *Middle East Journal* 23, 3 (Summer 1969): 300ff.

21. Hirst, *The Gun and the Olive Branch*; Quandt et al., *The Politics of Palestinian Nationalism*; Cobban, *The Palestinian Liberation Organization*.

22. This political discourse was opposed throughout the Arab world by a conservative and fundamentalist Islamic political discourse that also surfaced and was financially supported by the oil-exporting regimes of the Arabian peninsula, especially Saudi Arabia.

23. Gresh, *The PLO: The Struggle Within*, 11.

24. See Cobban, *The Palestinian Liberation Organization*, 42ff; and Hirst, *The Gun and the Olive Branch*.

25. M. H. Kerr, *The Arab Cold War* (New York: Oxford University Press, 1971).

26. See F. Jabber, "The Arab Regimes and the Palestinian Revolution," *Journal of Palestine Studies* 2, 2 (Winter 1973): 79–101; see also W. Kazziha, *Palestine in the Arab Dilemma* (New York: Barnes and Noble, 1979).

27. See S. K. Farsoun and W. Carroll, "The Civil War in Lebanon: Sect, Class, and Imperialism," *Monthly Review* 28, 2 (June 1976): 12–37. See also S. Farsoun and R. Wingerter, "The Palestinians in Lebanon," *SAIS Review* (Winter 1981/82): 93–106.

28. There are a number of books on the history and politics of the PLO. These include R. N. El-Rayyes and D. Nahhas, *Guerrillas for Palestine: A Study of the Palestinian Commando Organizations* (Beirut: An-Nahar Press, 1974); R. Brynen, *Sanctuary and Survival: The PLO in Lebanon* (Boulder, CO: Westview Press, 1990); R. Khalidi, *Under Siege: PLO Decision-making in the 1982 War* (New York: Columbia University Press, 1986). See also J. R. Nassar, *The Palestine Liberation Organization* (New York: Praeger, 1991); and B. Rubin, *Revolution Until Victory? The Politics and History of the PLO* (Cambridge: Harvard University Press, 1994); already cited are Cobban, *The Palestinian Liberation Organization,* and others.

29. C. Rubenberg, *The Palestine Liberation Organization: Its Institutional Infrastructure* (Belmont, MA: Institute for Arab Studies, 1983). See also Nassar, *The Palestine Liberation Organization*; and Brand, *Palestinians in the Arab World.*

30. See Cobban, *The Palestinian Liberation Organization*; Norton and Greenberg, *The International Relations of the Palestine Liberation Organization;* see also I. S. Lustick, ed., *From Wars Toward Peace in the Arab-Israeli Conflict 1969–1993* (New York: Garland, 1994); and I. S. Lustick, ed., *The Conflict with Israel in Arab Politics and Society* (New York: Garland, 1994).

31. Cobban, *The Palestinian Liberation Organization*, and Quandt et al., *The Politics of Palestinian Nationalism.*

32. Because of its front organization, Black September, Fateh has also been charged with international terror, most notably in the 1972 killings of Jordanian prime minister Wasfi al-Tal in Cairo and the Israeli Olympic athletes in Munich.

33. D. Shipler, *Arab and Jew: Wounded Spirits in a Promised Land* (New York: Penguin, 1987), 177.

34. Hirst, *The Gun and the Olive Branch*, 266.

35. Cited in Gresh, *The PLO: The Struggle Within*, 32.

36. Ibid., 30.

37. Ibid., 31.

38. Ibid., 33.

39. Ibid., 40.

40. N. Chomsky, *The Fateful Triangle: The United States, Israel and the Palestinians* (Boston: South End Press, 1983); see also his extensive writings on the same

subject in numerous issues of *Zeta* magazine during the 1980s and 1990s. See also N. Chomsky, *Deterring Democracy* (New York: Vintage, 1992) and *World Orders: Old and New* (New York: Columbia University Press, 1994); and especially N. Aruri, *The Obstruction of Peace: The U.S., Israel and the Palestinians* (Boston: Common Courage Press, 1995).

41. See Chomsky, *Deterring Democracy,* and Aruri, *The Obstruction of Peace.*

42. See Appendix 10.

43. See Appendix 11.

44. In mid-January 1989 the president of the United Nations Security Council accepted the PLO's request for the right to speak directly to the council as "Palestine" (on the same basis as all UN member nations).

SIX

Palestinian Resistance to Israeli Occupation: The Intifada

Throughout Palestine's long history, international, regional, and local events have been linked: Trade, invasion, and pilgrimage routes often put this territory and its people at the center of international attention. Modern Palestinian history in particular stands out against the backdrop of world events. Forced into exile by the catastrophic wars of 1948 and 1967, Palestinians were dispersed in exile throughout the globe or suspended in political limbo on the land they had inhabited for centuries.[1] In the mid-1990s, about 40 percent of the estimated 6.8 million Palestinians resided in historic Palestine; the rest were scattered throughout the Arab world, with significant numbers in Jordan, Syria, and Lebanon, the Arabian peninsula, and abroad.[2] From their precarious positions since 1948, Palestinians have engaged in various forms of resistance at critical historical periods and in everyday life.

After 1967, Palestinians in the West Bank and Gaza Strip directly confronted the Israeli occupation with demonstrations, tax revolts, merchant and labor strikes, displays of the Palestinian flag or national colors, and clashes with soldiers. To proclaim oneself a Palestinian who belonged in Palestine was considered a security offense—punishable with a prison sentence under Israeli military law—against the illegitimate occupation and against the state of Israel itself. Opposition led to repression but did not silence their call for self-determination and statehood. The prickly cactus bush called the *sabr* became a national symbol because it dots Palestine, marking the areas of destroyed villages. In Palestinian folklore it is known as a symbol of patience and perseverance. Like the enduring cactus, the

Palestinians remained steadfast (*samedoun* or *samedin*) in their struggle despite great pressures threatening to separate and destroy the people's relationship with their land and cultural heritage.

Toward the end of the 1980s, twenty years after Israel captured the West Bank from Jordanian rule and the Gaza Strip from Egyptian control, Palestinians combined *sumoud* (perseverance) with a more demonstrative form of resistance, intifada (uprising). The often-recounted incident that sparked the intifada on December 8, 1987, was sadly common in daily life under occupation. On a narrow and congested road in Gaza, weary Palestinian men waited to cross a military checkpoint, the only entrance into the territory, after a day of low-paid work in Israel. Unexpectedly, a military tank swerved into a line of cars: Four men died upon impact and seven sustained serious injuries. A rumor that the crash was deliberate, in retaliation for the death of the relative of an Israeli soldier, quickly spread throughout the densely populated towns and refugee camps. According to official reports, brake failure caused the crash. To Palestinians the rumor was more credible. More than 6,000 people from all over Gaza joined the people of the Jabalya refugee camp, where three of the four killed had lived, to bury their dead. The funeral erupted into a massive spontaneous demonstration that continued the next day. The Israeli military, as usual, used live ammunition, beatings, arrests, and tear gas to try to disperse the angry protesters. In the clash scores were injured, and twenty-year-old Hatem al-Sisi became the first martyr of the intifada against the brutal Israeli occupation.

Although the media failed to report the incident, through well-established grassroots channels of communication, the news was disseminated and demonstrations fanned into the West Bank, Jerusalem, and among Arabs inside Israel. On December 10 another youth was killed by the Israeli occupation forces at Balata refugee camp, nearby Nablus. Again, people poured into the streets to protest, and this in turn prompted a violent response from the military. Few initially suspected that the increasingly organized demonstrations would last beyond a few days or weeks. Men, women, and children armed with the most readily available materials—stones, slingshots, burning debris, and makeshift barricades—were facing one of the most advanced military forces in the world, one accustomed to dealing with more limited demonstrations.[3] The defense minister of Israel, Yitzhak Rabin, refused to cut short his trip in the United States. When he did return, he pledged that "the disturbances in the territories will not occur again. . . . Even if we are forced to use massive force, under no circumstances will we allow last week's events to repeat themselves."[4]

Since its dramatic eruption, the intifada has never been crushed. It has, however, gone through three stages coinciding with pivotal regional events, the last of which effectively ended it. The initial phase, December 1987 until the 1991 Gulf War, was marked by a forceful unification and recognition of the Palestinian people's right to self-determination. Palestinians asserted not only their *right to exist* but also their *right to resist* Israel, with resounding international support. In the second phase, after the Gulf War until the 1993 Oslo Accords, the intifada waned because of relentless Israeli repression and political and economic isolation of the Palestinians by the regional hegemonic states in the Gulf. The Arab-Israeli peace process, sponsored and initiated by the United States, first in the Madrid conference and subsequently in bilateral negotiations in Washington, shifted the focus and force from the grassroots, from which the intifada sprung, to the higher-level leadership. In its current phase, which began after the Oslo Accords were announced and signed in September 1993, the intifada has largely ended but threatens to reemerge, possibly against the new hard-line Likud Israeli government elected in 1996. A significant proportion of Palestinians are engaging in protest against the occupation *and* the leadership of the PLO. This chapter analyzes the political, economic, and social contours of the first two phases, leaving the third to be discussed in the following chapter.

The intifada, however, cannot be understood as an isolated event frozen in particular time periods. In order to comprehend its underlying significance, we must view it as a dynamic part of the Palestinian struggle, as an alternative means with a singular goal: freedom from occupation and independent statehood—which the Israelis have historically tried to deny rhetorically and obstruct concretely. It is this obstructionist denial of Palestinian rights to the land that over time has dialectically formed the Palestinian resistance effort. The roots of the intifada can be traced to the formation of Israel as an exclusionary Jewish state on the land of Palestine. The conflict has become more complex because of the presence of intransigent Jewish settlers near populated Palestinian areas; acute underdevelopment and de-development[5] of nearly all productive sectors and social institutions; a large, young population, born under occupation, coming of age for employment; and so forth. The core of the problem, however, is that this contested space is intricately tied to the idea and realization of self-determination, cultural integrity, and personal dignity for 6.8 million Palestinians.[6] For Palestinians, Palestine means their humanity. And the intifada was a means to reclaim their humanity.

Israel, as it is presently formed and conceived by early Zionists, necessarily attempts to negate the rights of an entire people in order to justify its own existence and maintain its security. United Nations General Assembly Resolutions 194, passed no less than twenty-eight times since 1948, calls upon Israel to repatriate or compensate hundreds of thousands of Palestinians into the exclusive Jewish state (see Appendix 6). Israel ignored each of these calls and the legal basis on which they are founded. Moreover, out of this logic, it continued to pursue a strategy of dislocating Palestinians from their land, physically and illegally. We have already discussed the near annihilation and dispersal of Palestinians from inside the 1948 armistice lines (the so-called green line). With regard to the 1967 occupied territories of the West Bank and the Gaza Strip, Edward Said comments on this process: "There was a proliferation of over a thousand laws and regulations designed not only to enforce the subaltern, rightless position of Palestinians under Israeli jurisdiction, but also to rub their noses in the mud, to humiliate and remind them of how they were doomed to less-than-human-status."[7] Their legitimate struggle against complete dispossession and alienation from Palestine was distorted by labeling the Palestinians terrorists, Jordanians, refugees—anything other than Palestinians. Their basic human rights were systematically denied by all but a minority of Israelis. Most important because it is a key cause of the intifada, nearly all sectors of Palestinian society—the bourgeoisie and laborers, Muslims and Christians, men and women, the landless and landed, even the children—were burdened by the occupation.

A Palestinian—no matter where, how old, or how bold—was a political-ideological threat to the state of Israel. In this sense, the Palestinian-Israeli relationship cannot be described as a protracted war between two equipped armies. Nor can it be considered an ethnic conflict, as for the Kurds in Turkey and Iraq or among the sects in Lebanon. Rather, the relationship stems from and is a living remnant of the colonialist and racist European era of the eighteenth and nineteenth centuries. It is a national liberation struggle with classical features entangled in dynamic local, regional, and international power relations. Since 1948, Palestinians were left in a sociopolitical limbo, "deprived of nationality, of citizenship in a body-politic, and of the protective arm of a state in the international community."[8] It is ironic that Palestinians were rendered stateless just as the modern nation-state model of governance emerged throughout the once colonized continents of Asia, Africa, and Latin America.

From its relative vantage position, in its colonialist effort, Israel used tactics and pursued strategies of the classical era: economic exploitation, mass expulsion from the land, extensive incarceration of resisters, killing. These strategies and tactics were applied in a more vicious manner in the occupied territories after 1967. The Palestinians countered these pressures and survived in their diaspora with armed resistance, material sacrifice, and in some cases assimilation and integration into other cultures. Fragmentation and dislocation spawned duplicit, parallel organizations. Grassroots formations responded to their particular and general conditions under occupation. These in turn provided the basis of survival for its individual members and the Palestinian cause as a whole. Ironically, the Israeli strategies did their part not by dividing the Palestinians but by bringing them together in a landless state, using an illegitimate legal structure enforced by a heavy military presence. These tactics and the response to them made the Palestinians *seem* disjoined but in fact forced the range of their political, social, and economic movements closer together.

In each instance the Israelis tried to suppress the Palestinians, "to rub their noses in the mud;" even the young were bitterly reminded of their lost land, villages, orchards, and rights. The intifada surprised all the major actors because organizers became increasingly entrenched below the surface of everyday indignities and disempowerment, where the collective idea of what was and what could affirm an individual's humanity. Palestinians emerged throwing stones from the ground beneath them, from the land they firmly believed they had to liberate in order to liberate themselves. The process of shaking off the oppressive apparatus of Israeli military rule and asserting a unified Palestinian identity in the larger Arab context became what is internationally known as the intifada.

Thwarted Expectations: New Problems and New Solutions (1967–1979)

The Israeli military occupation, on June 6, 1967, of the West Bank and Gaza Strip signaled the beginning of the end of pan-Arabism and put the burden of struggle for the national liberation of Palestine onto the Palestinians themselves. This was made evident as the Israeli army moved across the 1949 armistice lines and began to restructure the legal, social, and economic conditions in a manner tantamount to annexation. On June 27, 1967, the Israeli Knesset added to the existing Jordanian and Egyptian rules of law the Law and Administrative Ordinance, which enabled "the Government to extend Israeli law, jurisdiction and public administration over the entire area of Eretz Israel" (former mandatory Palestine).[9] All Palestinians were issued a *hawiyya*, an identity card, registered with the military, written in Arabic and Hebrew, that became a mechanism of collective and individual state control and surveillance. Gaza and the West Bank were kept separate by different systems of local civil administrations but unified under the authority of the minister of defense. At the same time, the newly conquered territories were to become economically integrated yet subservient to Israel.

On June 28, 1967, the Knesset widened the borders of West Jerusalem to illegally incorporate the Palestinian capital in the east, including the Old City, with more than 100,000 Arab residents. It declared Jerusalem the nonnegotiable "eternal" capital of Israel, seized 1,000 acres of privately owned Palestinian property by 1968 and another 3,500 acres by 1970, and began building and populating a belt of settlements around Jerusalem with Jewish citizens.[10] The annexation of Jerusalem has been one of the few belligerent acts unilaterally and repeatedly condemned by the United Nations General Assembly *and* Security Council, the latter of which is dominated by the United States, which protected Israel from international condemnation through its veto on dozens of occasions. On July 4, 1971, the General Assembly unanimously passed Resolution 2253 (ES-V), urging Israel to "rescind all measures taken [and] to desist forthwith, from taking any action which would alter the status of Jerusalem." On September 25, 1971, the UN Security Council also passed a resolution deploring Israel's actions on Jerusalem, labeled them totally invalid, and called on Israel to rescind all its actions and measures to change the status of the city (Appendix 13). Israel blatantly ignored international pressure.

Israel left the status of the West Bank and Gaza Strip open to direct negotiations with Arab states: Jordan, which had interest in at least a partial recovery of its West Bank, Egypt regarding the Gaza Strip, and Syria with respect to the militarily strategic and fertile Golan Heights. At the same time, however, there were calls for de facto annexation of the territories by a new movement within the Knesset, the Greater Land of Israel, led by prominent military and political figures who later formed the Likud Party coalition in 1969. Minister Menachem Begin, supported by the minister of defense, General Moshe Dayan, argued for the creation of strategic Jewish settlements. These created "facts on the ground" (similar to the Zionist infiltration of mandatory Palestine) were intended to rule out the possibility of returning the land to Arab control.[11] At this point, Palestinian sovereignty was not a consideration. That summer the first Jewish settlements were installed in the West Bank, the Gaza Strip, Egypt's Sinai peninsula, and Syria's Golan Heights.

The document that became the key legal referent for control of the occupied territories, Resolution 242, was passed by the United Nations Security Council on November 22, 1967 (see Appendix 1 for the text). Resolution 242, based on the principles of recognition of states' "territorial integrity," "the inadmissibility of acquisition of territory by force," and *"withdrawal of Israel from territories occupied in the recent conflict,"* is commonly called the "land-for-peace formula." To Israel's advantage, the language of the last phrase is ambiguous. Purposely omitted was the definite article "the" from the resolution, as originally intended by the United States and the Soviet Union in their July 1967 draft. The omission of this single word reinforced Israel's position that these borders were indefinite and therefore open to political interpretation and negotiation. The only mention of the Palestinians is in reference to "a just solution to the refugee problem"—an echo of the 1917 Balfour Declaration, which urged the early Zionists not to "prejudice the civil and religious rights of the non-Jewish communities in Palestine," who then composed over 90 percent of the population. Moreover, the reference to refugees in this context meant all Arab refugees, including Egyptian and Syrian.

Following the 1967 war, Israel's military enveloped an estimated 1.3 million Palestinians, created over 400,000 new refugees, and added at least

20,000 to the camps. Their rights, as civilian inhabitants in territories acquired by war, are defined by numerous international treaties, conventions, and charters. The most essential of these are The Hague regulation of 1907 and the fourth Geneva convention "Relative to the Protection of Civilian Persons in Times of War" of 1949. Each is founded on a broad conception of human rights under which Palestinians would be regarded as "protected persons," safeguarded against the "forcible transfer" of the population. Article 3 of the fourth Geneva convention asserts that "the following acts shall be prohibited at any time and in any place whatsoever with respect to [protected] persons: a) violence to life and person, in particular murder of all kinds, mutilation, cruel treatment and torture. . . . [Furthermore] wilfully causing great suffering or serious injury to body or health" of protected persons.[12]

Israel contests these conventions, even as a signatory of the charter and member of the United Nations, arguing that the Arab parties rejected the 1948 partition plan that would have granted independent statehood to Palestinians in 32 percent of British Mandate Palestine. As this argument goes, Jordan and Egypt did not constitute a "legitimate sovereign" in the occupied territories and therefore applicable international conventions did not apply. Israel overruled them with Military Order 144, which effectively barred international human rights observers from the territories (except by special Israeli high court permission). Naseer Aruri notes the irony that "this occupation is uniquely distinguished by the claim that it does not constitute an occupation,"[13] a claim repeatedly contradicted by Israel's preconditions to negotiate with Arab states (and later the PLO) only on the basis of UN Resolutions 242 and 338.

Regarding the conduct of the occupier in relation to administrating the conquered territories, regulation 43 of The Hague convention forbids the occupier to significantly alter existing legislation of the occupied territory, unless it is "absolutely impossible" to abide by the established law. According to Meron Benvenisti, Israel has repeatedly violated this principle:

> During the years the military government has been in existence [1967–1986], more than 1,500 orders and amendments have been issued, divided by subject as follows: agriculture—29; banks—14, business—66; commerce—48; currency—55; education—26; censorship and freedom of expression—14; health—20; institutions (including Israeli institutions and municipalities)—173; insurance—16; judiciary—197; land—97, legislation—24; public order—239; security—304; taxes—85; traffic—96; a total of 1,503 legislative acts (including repeals).[14]

These laws are drawn from four independent legal traditions: Ottoman, especially in regard to land appropriation and taxation; British Mandate defense emergency regulations (passed in 1945), invoked primarily to justify curfews, censorship, and house demolitions; Jordanian and Egyptian civil laws, which regulate criminal and landlord-tenant disputes; and Israeli civil law, under the jurisdiction of the military courts, which is often derived from state security considerations. All combine to create a "complex web of legal traditions" of which only part is effectively enforced, legitimate, or even clear to Palestinians, who in turn tend to practice customary law ('*urf*) in order to settle civil disputes outside of the official civil or religious courts.[15] This tangle of laws applied in the military court system Israel erected in the occupied territories had the politicolegal function of maintaining control over the Palestinians living under occupation.[16]

Inside the Prison of Occupation: Emergence of New Palestinian Leadership

The impact of this heavy legal apparatus on Palestinian society dramatically rearranged both the broad contours of the economic class structure and the inner character of the traditional political hierarchies. The hegemony of traditional rural landed notables and interlocked urban elites, who presided over the Arab Higher Committee and who had become Jordanian clients or loyalists, was challenged by an emergent class of modern professionals and intellectuals (lawyers, medical doctors, professors, students, poets, and artists). These leaders directed their political concerns toward organizing smaller merchants, manufactures, clerks, and teachers as well as the uprooted peasantry, made refugees and wage laborers. Aruri summarizes the various interests of the reformed alliances that tied socioeconomic conflicts to the national question:

> landowners, traditionally a pillar of the *status quo*, because their land has been steadily confiscated; businessmen because they have to endure the highest taxes ever levied in Palestine and operated in a market totally controlled by Israel; professionals because they are subjected to regulations intended to create despair and encourage emigration. And women, who together with relatives are herded to jail or subjected to exorbitant fines.[17]

Charitable societies, often affiliated with the religious groups, also contributed to local resistance efforts. In total, these nascent groupings over time became institutionalized and closely tied to the PLO. During the 1980s they formed both a political challenge and substitute to the Israeli military state apparatus.

Their aim, as Joost Hiltermann argues, was to "outadminister" instead of "outfight" the occupier by establishing a parallel hierarchy within the territories and hence undercut its ability effectively to rule the population. In Gramscian[18] terms, Palestinians engaged in a "war of position" by attempting to surround the dominant state apparatus through the establishment of counterinstitutions and transformation of existing institutions within civil society toward an alternative ideological and material base articulated by political activists. The state apparatus was to be won in the final moment, in the "war of maneuver," and would be occupied by a new hegemonic bloc, with its vectors of authority and control firmly extended in the transformed social formation. Antonio Gramsci sought to explicate "the entire complex of practical and theoretical activities with which the ruling class not only justifies and maintains its dominance, but manages to win the active consent of those over whom its rules."[19] The explanatory brilliance of Gramsci's concept is that revolutionary change is not an automatic outcome of economic exploitation; it must accompany a crisis in the belief system surrounding the state developed by the ruling class to serve its own end.[20]

The applicability of Gramsci's concept of hegemony, even in its abstracted form, to the Palestinian case is limited in two major respects. First, Israel, as an occupier, especially after Likud rose to power in the late 1970s, relied most on coercive military power in order to secure its hegemony. What few concessions it offered to Palestinians were circumscribed not only by the pursuit of profit but also by the ethnic-nationalist dimension to favor all strata of Jewish labor. Second, Israel had to contend with a fragmented Palestinian community with exogenous leadership (the PLO) that acted as a counterweight to Israeli leadership inside the territories. Although Israel threatened the use of force against the people over which it maintained an occupation, it could never consensually co-opt or legitimize its presence to the Palestinians. Ideologically and materially, Israel was only able to ascertain compliance from a few Palestinian collaborators (including those who administered the Village Leagues, an Israeli creation) willing to undermine the larger Palestinian cause in exchange for personal protection and privilege.[21]

The *process* of developing alternative civil institutions under occupation, however, closely resembles what Gramsci described as the "war of position."[22] Israel's ideological and material strength took the form of military infallibility—or its power, on the one hand, to resist international pressure to relinquish the occupied territories and, on the other hand, to assert its rule over the Palestinians so forcefully. Its alignment with the United States, a global hegemon, explains Israel's regional military dominance throughout the cold war and after the collapse of the Soviet Union. Moreover, Israel at some points in its history tried to gain the ideological consent for its existence from certain sectors of the Palestinian society by offering municipal "autonomy," a far cry from the explicit goal of statehood. Failing these attempts, Israel resorted to its draconian power of coercion.

Although many smaller organizations emerged during the early period of the occupation, a semiclandestine umbrella group, the Palestine National Front (PNF, established August 15, 1973) took a leading role in counter-hegemonic resistance efforts. The leaders of the PNF represented various student, labor union, and women's organizations from a wide political spectrum—communist to nationalist—under the banner of "an inseparable part of the Palestinian national movement represented in the Palestine Liberation Organization."[23] Through nonviolent strategies of civil disobedience, it played a leading role in organizing protests against Israeli land confiscation, deportation of political leaders, and the treatment of political prisoners.[24] One of its most successful efforts was the Palestinian boycott of municipal elections in Jerusalem that threatened to legitimize Israeli annexation.

The necessity for an ideological and tactical turn toward diplomacy became painfully obvious as Israel mounted its military forces against Palestinians inside the occupied territories and in Lebanon. As we discussed in the previous chapter, two significant episodes weakened the PLO: the civil war in Lebanon (1975–1982) and the Israeli invasion of Lebanon (1982). Both assaults were designed to preempt a formation of a Palestinian state-in-exile and resulted in the massacre of tens of thousands of Palestinians, most of them civilians residing in refugee camps. According to Said, in Lebanon "Over 20,000 Palestinians and Lebanese Muslims were killed by Israeli troops in the summer of 1982 alone." The figure for the rest of the protracted war could easily be much higher. Said further estimates that there has been "a ratio of 100 Palestinians killed for every Israeli killed."[25]

Outside of the occupied territories throughout the early 1970s, a series of events made a primarily political rather than military strategy feasible to Palestinian leadership. The PLO, at the June 12, 1974, Palestine National Council meeting, replaced the vision of a secular democratic state in all of Palestine with the goal of an "independent Palestinian state" in any part of Palestine liberated from occupation. Implicit in this revision was the recognition of Israel, as required by Resolution 242. This move was affirmed later that year at the seventh Arab summit meeting in Rabat, Morocco, on October 28, where Arab leaders recognized "the right of the Palestinian people to establish an independent national authority under the command of the Palestinian Liberation Organization, the sole legitimate representative of the Palestinian people, in any Palestinian territory that is liberated." One month later PLO chairman 'Arafat addressed the international community at the United Nations, in New York, with this plan. The United Nations General Assembly Resolution 3236 (Appendix 7) reaffirmed "the inalienable rights of the Palestinian people in Palestine" to self-determination and national independence and granted the PLO observer status.

These moves invigorated the local activists in the West Bank and Gaza Strip and prompted widespread demonstrations of solidarity throughout the occupied territories that even spilled over into Palestinian areas inside Israel. The Israeli military arrested over 200 Palestinians and deported five leaders, among them Hanna Nasir, the president of Bir Zeit University (the largest and most important educational institution in the West Bank).[26] In 1976 Prime Minister Rabin initiated municipal elections in the West Bank,

and for the first time Palestinian women voted. Rabin expected a nationalist boycott, as in earlier Jerusalem elections, which would then "democrati-
cally" install Israeli collaborators. His strategy backfired, and openly pro-
PLO PNF candidates swept eighteen of the twenty-four councils by an
overwhelming majority.[27] Most of the other seats were won by conservative, traditional leaders who were independents or loyal to the Jordanian
monarchy, not Israeli collaborators.

The victory of the PNF was dampened the next year by the Likud's rise to
power in the Israeli parliamentary elections of 1977. In October 1978 the
PNF (strongly influenced by homegrown communist activists) was somewhat opposed by more conservative Fateh leaders and declared illegal by Israel. But by then it had reorganized and expanded under the more mainstream, Fateh-dominated National Guidance Committee (NGC). NGC's
first major challenge was to counter plans to grant Palestinians autonomy
but not statehood, embodied in the 1978 Camp David Accords signed as the
Israeli-Egyptian peace treaty by Begin and Sadat and witnessed by President
Jimmy Carter of the United States. Palestinians from the entire political
spectrum (Islamists, nationalists, and communists) resoundingly rejected the
plan on the basis that it "condemned the West Bank and Gaza to a permanent exile, with less real authority than a [South African] Bantustan."[28] The
Palestinian activist Fayez Sayegh warned that it was "as seductive and destructive as a siren call."[29] On the day the treaty was signed (September 17),
the entire West Bank and Gaza Strip were put under strict curfew; widespread demonstrations in protest ensued nevertheless.

The NGC proposed the establishment of an independent state of Palestine that would coexist alongside Israel, a more decisive step toward conciliation with Israel than the PLO's official position. As Salim Tamari points
out, "this fact is extremely important: the formation of the National Guidance Committee—militant, pro-PLO and popular, and at the same time
willing to make territorial compromises with the state of Israel, with the
aim of co-existence between the Israeli state and a future Palestinian state—
[became] the subject of the most ferocious attack by the Likud [govern-
ment]."[30] Israelis, especially those from the Likud Party, believed the NGC
posed a real threat to its own plans to colonize the occupied territories into
"Greater Israel." Accordingly, the Israeli occupation army carried out mass
arrests of grassroots activists and organizers, deported two elected mayors,
and banned the NGC.[31]

Beginning in 1978, the main party of the PLO, Fateh, and Jordan,
formed a "joint committee" in coordination with the people of the West
Bank and the Gaza Strip. A "steadfastness fund" channeled up to
$100–150 million annually to the occupied territories from various donor
Arab states in the form of direct money transfers, medical supplies, educational hardware, communication technology, and qualified personnel. Its

expressed aim was to organize and build civil institutions at the grassroots level. The national Palestinian movement in the occupied territories was divided into two ideological camps: a leftist grouping composed of the PFLP, DFLP, the Palestine Communist Party (PCP), and progressives from within Fateh against the conservative and dominant elements of Fateh and the Muslim Brothers. The tension between them expressed itself most importantly over the expenditure of the steadfastness fund. "The conservative forces tend[ed] to organize resistance along the lines of traditional institutions, such as municipal councils, professional unions, women's organizations, notables. The left . . . trie[d] either to build new organizations or to radicalize the rank and file of existing organizations."[32] Although these conflicts were not debilitating to the resistance movement—it may be argued that they led to greater politicization and mobilization of the Palestinians under occupation—they did have two major effects. The first was the increasing political influence of the Palestinians of the occupied territories (known as those of al-dakhel) and those in the diaspora (those of al-kharej). The second was the emergence of tension between the inside and outside wings of the national movement. With the intifada, this division becomes all the more important.

Economic Subordination of the Occupied Territories: Policies and Practices

On the economic front, in the post-1967 war period, Israel's previously staggering economy boomed because of an enormous influx of financial and military transfers, mainly from the United States. The aid was invested primarily in three sectors: industry, tourism, and the military. This upward structural shift reoriented Jewish labor toward higher-paid technical service sectors and created a demand for low-skilled and cheap labor, especially in construction and agriculture, which was filled by Palestinians from the newly conquered territories.[33] The Israeli Central Bureau of Statistics recorded a steady increase of Palestinian daily labor migration into Israel from 1968 (especially after 1970) until the intifada, in terms of absolute numbers and percent of population. These figures exclude undocumented labor, which is estimated to be as high as 50 percent in the construction sector and roughly 45 percent of the total Palestinian work force in Israel (estimated numbers vary by year and season).[34]

Part of the explanation for the high rates of undocumented labor is that Palestinian employment opportunities are strictly regulated by several mechanisms tied to economic and political considerations of the Israeli state. Palestinians must apply for a work permit, gained only after obtaining security clearance from the Israeli occupation forces, and present proof of potential employment by an Israeli. These permits must be renewed periodically for a fee and are limited to employment in what Israel deems "nonstrategic" sectors.[35] Very often, Israeli employers prefer to hire illegal workers in order to avoid paying benefits to Israelis who have trade union protection.

Although data are sparse, several studies show that after 1970, Palestinian women increasingly entered the nondomestic work force as migrant laborers into Israel and in the occupied territories. They represent at least 5–10 percent of the total work force. Most of them are unmarried or widowed women drawn into the formal labor sectors in order to supplement their families' incomes, not to achieve independent status (although that can become an unintended outcome). On the whole, Palestinians, with no real effective recourse to prevent or take action against exploitation, constitute a "reserve army of labor in the Israeli economy."[36] Moreover, women make up the "most exploited segment . . . an 'invisible' proletariat."[37]

The possibility of gaining membership and benefits in the Histadrut, Israel's largest trade union federation, is slim for Palestinians, primarily because of a historical preference to protect and privilege Jewish labor. According to Hiltermann, "The Histadrut has not acted to protect West Bank and Gaza workers from exploitation by the Israeli government. From its establishment in 1920, the Histadrut has systematically favored Jewish over Arab labor, while attempting to co-opt Arab labor without, however, fully integrating it."[38] Moreover, not only are Palestinians limited to lower-wage job sectors, but they are also discriminated against in terms of benefits and wages for comparable positions relative to Jewish Israeli workers.[39]

Efforts to organize workers into Palestinian labor unions have consistently been labeled subversive, "terrorist" activity by the military authorities. Gaza has a short history of trade unionism under occupation; "the military authorities outlawed all trade-union activities, and no labor organizing took place until 1979 when the ban was lifted, but even then little unionist activity occurred until 1986-1987."[40] In the West Bank, however, even before the ban was lifted, communist organizers initially resumed activities in the major urban centers and reestablished links with Jordan's unions. Before 1967 thirteen out of the twenty-four unions were located in Jerusalem. Palestinian unions were particularly targeted as points of contention in the "reunification of the city under Israeli rule."[41] Efforts were made to co-opt workers into the Histadrut, against which the PNF successfully organized. Consequently, after a stringent crackdown in 1969, the center shifted to Nablus.

As Israel continued to try to break up Palestinian unions, they became informal and hidden. Restrictions on printing and distributing union material, public meetings, recruiting and registering new members, and establishing new unions—as well as other nationalist organizations—compelled activists to circumvent the authorities in order to reach the masses. They accomplished this directly and indirectly by two means: encouraging democratic participation within the union structure, which enlarged the pool of potential leaders, who are often targeted by the military for town or house arrest, deportation, and imprisonment; and organizing unions by trade, geographic location, and political affiliation. Although decentralization and dispersion weakened the numerical strength of a particular group, they allowed for tighter coordination and for members to more easily elude the authorities. Unions transcended such difficulties by networking not in the usual manner, within trades, but through political blocs between regions. In a constrained environment, unions primarily provided their members social rather than economic protection and service. They were particularly successful in administering health care services and medicine at minimum cost to members and their families. Unions also tried to provide legal aid and counsel, education, and recreational facilities.

Voluntary work committees (the first founded in 1972) and student federations (in the secondary and higher educational levels) organized projects that fused nationalistic ideology with localized social activity. Guided by a small core of leaders, as few as twenty or as many as thousands of participants would join together in a particular location and engage in tree planting, harvesting, road building, or cleanup efforts in villages or refugee camps. It is estimated that shortly after the intifada broke out there were "more than 400 local organizations, institutions, associations and committees operating in virtually all Palestinian towns and villages and refugee camps."[42]

The Islamic movement, embodied in the Muslim Brotherhood, initially focused less on resisting the Israeli occupation and more on countering secular tendencies prevailing throughout the West Bank and the Gaza Strip.[43] Consequently, given "the Brotherhood's emphasis on the Islamic restructuring of society and religious education . . . [t]he emerging Palestinian nationalist movement had far greater appeal."[44] Because the group's central ideology was not jihad, or active opposition to the Israelis, before a total Islamization of Palestinian society, the Israelis allowed (even encouraged) it to proliferate. The Muslim Brotherhood established libraries, religious and nursery schools, and sports and social clubs with funding from Muslims worldwide, but particularly in the Gulf states. It distributed *zakat* (alms to the poor, one of the five pillars of Islam) to thousands in the Gaza Strip and West Bank. Nearly 10 percent of all real estate in the Gaza Strip is waqf land, which is protected from state taxation. Between 1967 and 1987, "the number of mosques in the West Bank rose from 400 to 750, in the Gaza Strip from 200 to 600."[45] These became sites for the Muslim Brotherhood to do political work and recruit with little interference from the Israelis.

During the 1970s, especially after the 1979 Iranian revolution, an important division within the Muslim Brotherhood occurred. Two 1948 refugees from Gaza, Fathi al-Shiqaqi and 'Abd al-'Aziz 'Adud, formed Islamic Jihad, which retained an emphasis on the formation of an Islamic state but by more militant means. Ideologically, Islamic Jihad inverted the relationship between "the centrality of the Palestine issue and proper timing for liberating the country" advocated by the Muslim Brotherhood.[46] In other words, Islamic Jihad believed that Islamization of Palestinians comes in the process and after the liberation of Palestine, not before. Once again, Islamic Jihad did not gain wide political support, nor did it manage to sway many of the Muslim Brothers, whose popularity rested in the organization's ability to distribute social services through its institutions. Nearly every person in every sector of society, then, could find some outlet to vent political and social frustration through nonviolent and often productive means toward a common end. The formation of these alternative organizations provided a buffer between the intrusive encroachments of the Israeli military, economic, and political systems into the increasingly more vulnerable Palestinian society of the West Bank and Gaza Strip.

Settler Colonialism: Land, Water, and Labor

Under the right-wing Likud Party government, which controlled the Israeli parliament from 1977 to 1992, Israel aggressively pursued one objective: to gain control of the occupied land and its resources without formally incorporating the Palestinian people into Israel as citizens of its parliamentary democracy. This goal had three strategic prongs, supported more or less by both the Israeli political Right and Left: (1) to extend Israel's control of the territories by establishing Jewish settlements with security and administrative links only to Israel (officially sanctioned in the Israeli Knesset on March 6, 1980); (2) to restrict, control, even de-develop the Palestinian economy and proletarianize its labor; (3) to suppress resistance movements by coercive methods, such as extended incarceration or deportation of leaders, censorship of the Palestinian press, and collective punishment. Together, all three tactics were intended to force Palestinian migration or submission by narrowing the opportunities for political, economic, and social independence, creating a relationship of controlled dependency.

To a large extent, the Likud government was successful in its effort, as reflected in part by the increase in numbers and expenditures for settler activity. "Between 1978 and 1987, the average growth was 5,960 Jewish settlers a year, as against 770 during the years of the Labour rule. Under Labour, $750 million of public money were invested, compared with $1.67 billion spent by the Likud."[47] In terms of absolute numbers, in 1976 there were 3,176 Jewish settlers in the West Bank, but by 1986 the number climbed to 60,500 amid the Palestinian population of 938,000 (including 125,000 in East Jerusalem).[48] The majority of settlers were enticed by the generous state subsidies attached to the development projects.[49] A slim but vocal minority, aligned politically with rightist coalitions, were ideologically driven to settle in the occupied territories. These groups, such as Gush Emunin and Kach (named after its slain leader, Meir Kahane, an ultraorthodox militant emigrant from Brooklyn, New York), posed a mortal menace to the Palestinians living in close proximity.

On the eve of the intifada in 1987, 120 Jewish settlements of various sizes and durability peppered the West Bank. For example, Ma'ale Adumim, located on a large strip of land between Jerusalem and Jericho, could be likened to Tel Aviv in terms of quality of construction, whereas settlements deeper in the West Bank tended to be constructed of flimsy, prefabricated housing materials. The majority of all settlements were populated with fewer than fifty families.[50] In most cases, once a settlement was established, large tracts of land surrounding the compound were closed off to Palestinians as a security measure. Accounting for state/public, private, and security purposes, by 1992 approximately 55 percent of the total land area of the West Bank and 30 percent of the Gaza Strip had been appropriated by the Israeli government.[51]

Israel's state apparatus—through administration and expansion of settlements, which gave added justification for increasing its military presence—rapidly encroached upon increasingly slimmer areas of possible indigenous Palestinian economic and political development. In blatant disregard of international conventions, Israel burdened the Palestinians of the West Bank and Gaza Strip with a significant part of the expense of building the occupation, including the expanding settlement and land and water appropriation activity. It did so through heavy direct and indirect taxation and by turning the Palestinians into a captive tariff-free export market,[52] as well as a cheap and captive labor source: "The military government's revenue from only two sources, income tax and net indirect taxes on local production, equaled 12 percent of the Occupied Territories' GNP. These two sources alone covered all of its budget expenses. As a result, budget revenues from all other sources were transferred to the Israeli government treasury, for a net gain of $150 million for 1984."[53]

Although prohibited under the fourth Geneva convention, large transfers of revenue from the occupied territories to Israel became a permanent feature of the occupation. There was a deliberate attempt to stifle and curtail Palestinian development in order to bolster the Israeli economy. This strategy was bluntly summed up by Defense Minister Rabin in 1984: "There will be no development initiated by the Israeli government, and no permits will be given for expanding [Palestinian] industry and agriculture which may compete with the state of Israel."[54]

Already in 1984, Israeli products accounted for 90 percent of all imports into the West Bank and Gaza Strip, or 11 percent of all Israeli exports.[55] Most of the exports to the Palestinian economy were substandard manufactured consumer goods. As Sheila Ryan states, the Palestinian market became "a convenient dumping ground for shoddy Israeli industrial products which could not compete with the local manufactures of the industrialized countries of Europe and North America."[56] Israel imported 73 percent of the total commodity exports from Palestinians, with the value of industrial goods roughly six times greater than agricultural products.[57] This high figure, however, was not to the benefit of Palestinians because most of these products were "re-exported Israeli goods . . . originally imported by subcontractors in unfinished form. These are finally sold in the Israeli market or exported elsewhere."[58]

At first these tactics had an uneven impact on the Palestinian class structure. This dependency relationship hit hardest the 844,000 Palestinians in the twenty-seven refugee camps who often had no other source of employment except in Israel. This problem was most acute in the Gaza Strip. Its population density is nearly ten times that of the West Bank, and refugees from 1948 Palestine compose more than 66 percent of the total population compared with 40 percent in the West Bank.[59] Of the total Palestinian labor force, approximately 51,300 (31 percent) from the West Bank and 53,900 (46.1 percent) from Gaza worked in Israel, mostly in low-paid industrial and construction sectors without social benefits or job security.[60] Table 6.1 summarizes the distribution of the West Bank and Gaza Strip labor force by sector in the occupied territories and Israel in 1986. Not shown in the table are Palestinians from the occupied territories employed in Israel in professional, technical, or clerical occupations because the percentage is negligible, around 2 percent.[61] This pattern is repeated within the West Bank and Gaza Strip, where the top-level governing powers are held by Israelis. The Civil Administration (CA), which is under the military area commanders, is responsible for all economic matters regarding Palestinian life. A 1993 World Bank mission reports that "currently the CA has about 22,000 employees, of which approximately 95 percent are Palestinians. Most policy-making and senior administrative positions in the CA are, however, staffed by Israelis."[62]

The service sector dominates the Palestinian economy. It makes up about 85 percent of gross domestic product (GDP) and employs 47.3 percent of the work force.[63] Merchants, professionals, educators, wageworkers, and so forth were over time greatly disadvantaged by Israeli policies and consequently the occupied territories fell below the average level of Arab regional development. Public infrastructure such as roads, telephones, electricity, and hospitals, which facilitates the distribution of goods and services, are underdeveloped in the cities, villages, and camps alike. Table 6.2 provides a comparison of selected indicators in the occupied territories, the Middle East, North Africa, and Jordan. Particularly burdensome for merchants and manufacturers was the imposition of the value-added tax (VAT) in 1976. The costs associated with inadequate facilities result in higher prices, lower per capita income, and inferior products.

Palestinian agricultural products were undersold by Israeli farmers because they were not permitted to purchase advanced machinery or were

TABLE 6.1 Distribution of Palestinians in the Labor Force, 1986
(numbers in thousands)

	West Bank		Gaza Strip		Total West Bank and Gaza Strip	
	Number	Percent	Number	Percent	Number	Percent
Israel	51.3	30.7	43.4	46.1	94.7	36.6
Agriculture	5.5	10.7	9.4	21.6	14.9	15.7
Industry	9.1	17.7	7.4	17.1	16.5	17.4
Construction	26.0	50.7	19.4	44.7	45.4	48.0
Services	10.7	20.9	7.7	16.6	17.9	18.9
West Bank and						
Gaza	117.5	69.3	50.8	53.9	116.5	63.4
Agriculture	33.0	28.3	8.5	16.8	41.5	24.9
Industry	18.2	15.7	9.0	17.8	27.2	16.4
Construction	14.7	12.7	4.2	8.3	18.9	11.4
Services	49.8	43.1	29.0	57.1	78.8	47.3
Total of both	167.0	100.0	94.2	100.0	216.2	100.7
Agriculture	38.5	23.1	18.0	19.4	56.5	27.7
Industry	27.2	16.3	16.5	17.5	43.7	16.7
Construction	40.8	24.4	23.5	25.0	64.3	24.6
Services	60.5	36.2	36.2	38.4	96.7	37.0

SOURCE: M. Benvenisti, *1987 Report: Demographic, Economic, Legal, Social, and Political Developments in the West Bank* (Boulder, CO: Westview Press, 1987), 19.

outright prohibited from growing and selling certain crops. For example, it is illegal to pick thyme, a popular spice used in preparing traditional Arabic dishes, because it competes with the kibbutzim's monopoly on the product. A more potent example is the Gaza Strip's citrus production, which before 1967 employed 25 percent of the total work force, took up 20 percent of the land area, and was sold for $150 a ton on the Western European market.[64] Joan Mandell traced the decline of this sector from 1967 to the mid-1980s. First in 1968 Israel banned independent Palestinian export to European markets but continued to allow export to the Arab world in order to circumvent the Arab boycott of Israeli goods. In 1983 an "exit permit" to Jordan cost roughly $150, while the average price per ton of fruit dropped to $60. "Fifteen to 20 percent of Gaza's citrus trees were felled in 1983 as a result of restricted markets, rising fuel and fertilizer costs and water restriction."[65] Nevertheless, the initiation of widespread use of mechanical irrigation systems, fertilizers, as well as other technical devices increased total crop output per dunum over the course of Israeli occupation of the West Bank and Gaza Strip. Accompanying these changes, however, were the processes of arable land expropriation and proletarianization of the rural

TABLE 6.2 Comparison of Selected Indicators Occupied Territories, Middle East and North Africa, and Jordan, 1991

	Occupied Territories	Middle East and North Africa[a]	Jordan
GNP per capita (US$)	1,715	1,940	1,050
GDP per (US$)	1,275	–	1,130
Gross enrollment ratios			
Primary (school age pop.)	102	97	94
Secondary (% school age pop.)	80	60	65
Pupil-teacher ratio (primary school)	30	26	17
Repeaters: primary (% total enrollment)	7[b]	11	5
Illiteracy (% of population age 15+)	40	45	20
Persons per physician	847	1,668	767
Persons per hospital bed	658	653	516
Age dependency ratio[c]	1.08	0.87	0.92
Total fertility rate (births per woman)	7.3	5.3	5.3
Infant mortality (per 1,000 live births)	42	60	29
Life expectancy (years)	66	64	69
Households with safe drinking water (%)	90	83	96
Urban water supply (liters per capita)	60	–	137
Households with electricity (%)	85	–	98
Electricity consumption (kwh/capita)	680	–	1,130
Telephone subscribers (per 1,000 pop.)	22	–	67

[a]Includes eighteen countries extending from Algeria to Iran.
[b]Data for UNRWA schools only.
[c]Defined as the ratio of dependent population (under fifteen and over sixty-four) to the working-age population (fifteen–sixty-four).
SOURCE: World Bank, *Developing the Occupied Territories: An Investment in Peace*, vol. 1: *Overview* (Washington, DC: World Bank, 1993).

and refugee labor force, which both reduced the percentage of the total population and the percentage of gross national product (GNP) of Palestinians in agriculture.

Water, shared unequally by Israelis and Palestinians, was capped at pre-1967 levels. Restrictions included access to surface water sources and wells. In the Gaza Strip, the imbalance was most severe: 750,000 Palestinians consumed on average 30 percent of the water, while the rest was allotted to 4,000 Israeli settlers. Gaza's water, used by Palestinians for agriculture and drinking, was contaminated by raw sewage that flowed through open sewers in the camps and by high saline levels from the inflow of seawater. The contaminated water was neither tested nor monitored regularly and treated only with chlorine.[66] The settlers sink deeper wells into freshwater sources, also contributing to lower water tables in Palestinian wells. In the words of

Sharif Elmusa, "On the whole, Israel, when it comes to the water sources of the area, acts like a great sponge."[67]

While the Israeli assault on the entire Palestinian economic infrastructure and resources has been heavy, Sara Roy argues that the Gaza Strip has undergone a process of "de-development."[68] This concept, adapted from the wider literature on dependency and modernization theories, is defined as the total *regression* of political institutions, social structures, and economic infrastructures necessary to facilitate economic growth and independence. Moreover, this process is not spontaneous or due to internal constraints within a society. Rather, as in the case of the Gaza Strip, de-development is intentionally "shaped and advanced by a range of policies, themselves a reflection of the ideological imperatives of the Zionist movement" that seeks to dispossess Palestinians from their land. In Roy's analysis, the Gaza Strip constitutes a separate social, cultural, economic, and political entity from the West Bank. It is distinguished by a culture torn apart by the inescapable violence of everyday life, virtually complete economic dependence on Israel, and a chaotic political system based on competing political groups with incompatible ideologies and aims.

Such conditions were fostered by the Israeli military authorities in the enclosed, narrow, and densely populated strip. Industrial de-development offers a prime illustration of the effect of Israeli policies as well as the deep divide between the Gaza Strip and West Bank. In 1987 total industrial revenue amounted to $7 million, or $961 per worker, compared with $1,650 per worker in the West Bank. The relative contribution of branches to revenue has remained largely unchanged since 1967, indicating little flexibility, vertical integration, or growth. These factors are also evident in low productivity rates and the character of industrial revenue.[69]

De-development keeps necessary infrastructural supports for economic sectors such as industry, agriculture, and private business from performing essential functions. For example, in 1981 Israel allowed one branch of the Bank of Palestine to open in the Gaza Strip, mainly to cash checks from earnings in Israel. As Roy notes, "One of the bank's greatest handicaps has been its inability to issue letters of credit. Thus, although it has been the only bank in an area of over 800,000 people, it has not been able to support local enterprises."[70] Productive sectors are forced to turn toward commercial banks outside of the occupied territories, international donor agencies, moneychangers, or family and friends. None of these sources effectively strengthens the domestic savings or investment potential of the Gaza Strip, making any investment a high-risk venture and in turn undermining self-reliance.

The Palestinian economy, vulnerable to external shocks, was squeezed even tighter by the international recessionary period of the 1980s. Regional and local growth due to the sharp rise in oil prices prior to that period shriveled when oil revenues and the subsequent demand for expatriate workers in the Gulf fell dramatically. During the oil boom, between 1973 and 1982, the emigration rate of mostly skilled young men averaged seventeen per 1,000. After 1985 the Bank of Israel officially reported that the emigration rate fell to three per 1,000. This decline meant a serious drop in standard of living afforded by the extra revenue generated by work in Gulf: "Remittances into Jordan, much of which were destined for the Occupied Territories, dropped from $1.5 billion in 1982 to $887 million in 1988."[71] The externally available revenue and ladder of employment opportunity made life under occupation more viable; Palestinians could create alternative institutions to supplement the meager social services provided by the Israeli occupation authorities.

As the income from employment in the Gulf states and in the local economy narrowed, Palestinian youth in particular perceived and experienced the structural constraints of the occupation. Their individual and collective futures looked bleak. Families, villages, towns, and cities turned inward to meet the daily needs of their members in the areas of food production, health services, and job training. Local developmental projects organized (for the most part) separately by the four main PLO parties gave the participants a feeling of personal self-worth infused with national aspirations. Most significant, a sense of community, interdependence, and cooperation emerged during the period of structural economic crisis in the mid-1980s.

The (Almost) Forgotten People

Within the occupied territories, sentiments of solidarity were cemented by a perception of isolation from internal pressures and external political forces. In 1985 Israeli defense minister Rabin of the National Unity Government formed in 1984 announced Iron Fist II. This program stepped up the presence and power of the military in the West Bank and Gaza Strip. It was designed to crush, once and for all, Palestinian resistance. Within one month a dozen political leaders were deported without formal trials, sixty-two activists were placed under administrative detention, and the military killed five people. Documented reports of human rights violations, including collective punishment, arrests, and killings, rose dramatically from 1984 onward.[72] Israeli repression reached more people and in turn raised the collective stakes against the occupation. But the unintended consequence of Iron Fist II was to toughen the Palestinians' resolve against the occupation and drive political organization further underground.

The larger regional and international political contexts also contributed to the sense of isolation and stagnation—even abandonment—of the Palestinian struggle. The PLO was becoming an ineffective player on the Arab and international scene. The Israeli government objected to and the Reagan administration in the United States rejected the 1985 Hussein-'Arafat initiative, which offered land for peace (based on UN Resolution 242), and a Jordanian-Palestinian confederation. Also in 1985 Israel bombed the PLO's headquarters in Tunis, killing more than seventy officials. One year later Jordan's government ordered the closure of all twenty-five PLO offices in Amman and deported its top leader, Khalil al-Wazir.[73]

The Palestinian leadership became increasingly marginalized in the wider political arena. The sense of stagnation, however, was offset by an important restructuring of the PLO from within the organization. After nearly five years of divisive fragmentation, the four principal constituents of the PLO regrouped at a PNC meeting in Algiers in April 1987. United, for the first time ever, in strategy and action were the popularly supported Palestinian Communist Party, the Popular Front for the Liberation of Palestine, the Democratic Front for the Liberation of Palestine, and Fateh.

In the occupied territories, the factions that once competed for popular support among the general population began to coordinate their efforts and resources. Ann Mosely Lesch describes firsthand the impact of these changes:

> The effect of the rapprochement among the key groups was already evident by June 1987. When I visited the West Bank that month, I found that the social unionist organizations sponsored by the different movements were beginning to work together and that a common sense of purpose was beginning to emerge. The organizational basis for the intifada was, in fact, being established. Moreover, the Islamic movement began to participate alongside the nationalist groups, for the first time. . . . They construed the primary enemy as Israel, not their fellow Palestinians.[74]

These reinvigorated, determined activists found promise in grassroots models of resistance. They were particularly inspired by the effective strategies practiced by the Shi'a resistance and other organizations of southern Lebanon against the Israeli occupation (1983–1985). The key to their success was collective mobilization, which could sustain and promote individual sacrifice for the collective good in the face of a common threat. A sort of moral determination combined with mass resistance on the part of the Shi'a against the Israeli occupation hurt the occupiers and created deep political divisions in Israeli society. With the political will lost, Israel's military was compelled to withdraw from most of Lebanon—to the so-called security zone along the northern Israeli border.

Daring operations perpetrated by lone militants also intrigued the Palestinians. For example, on November 25, 1987, a single Palestinian guerrilla from southern Lebanon soared into an Israeli military compound in the Galilee on a hang glider. He entered by foot, and before he was overwhelmed he killed six troops. This event captured the attention of the international media and became an embarrassment to the Israeli army, once presumed to be an infallible military force in the region. The experience in Lebanon and individual actions such as this one both exposed and created cracks in the Israeli military hegemony.

The event that finally crystallized the realization that the Palestinian struggle had lost its prominence for Arab leadership occurred at the November 1987 Arab summit in Amman. While Israeli soldiers were beating up Palestinian schoolgirls in the West Bank nearby, those who attended the summit declared that the Arab enemy was Iran, 1,000 miles to the east. As we noted above, in the communiqué of the summit the Palestine question was, contrary to custom, relegated to the end, almost as an afterthought. Furthermore, Jordan proposed that Arab states normalize relations with Egypt (ostracized since it signed the Camp David Accords and a peace treaty with Israel) in order to throw strategic weight on the side of Iraq in the Iraq-Iran war and to isolate Syria and Libya, supporters of Iran. In January of that year, for the first time since the 1979 signing of the Egyptian-Israeli peace treaty, Egypt attended the conference of the Islamic Organization (a league of Islamic states) in Kuwait. To Palestinians, these moves toward regional reconciliation with Egypt were sobering. In retrospect, they signified the end to Palestinian hopes for settling the conflict within the larger Arab-Islamic context. The strategy of self-reliance and the ideology of unification finally replaced dependence on the diplomacy of Arab leadership and the hoped-for reasonableness of the United States and Israel.

Surprise: The Intifada Erupts

The initial outbreak of the intifada—mass demonstrations, confrontations with soldiers, labor and merchant strikes—occurred unexpectedly before the PLO, the Israeli public, the Israeli army, and the world that watched. The harsh response of the occupation forces and the daring displayed by the Palestinians are often explained by the lack of readiness of the military. It was, however, the strength of the masses mobilized for direct confrontation with their occupiers that overwhelmed the Israeli military, at least initially. The brutal actions of the Israeli army—the beatings, teargassing, house demolitions, and point-blank shooting of lethal rubber bullets and live ammunition—were not uncommon and, as discussed above, had been on the rise over the prior years. Table 6.3 provides data on Israeli human rights violations of the Palestinian people under occupation from 1987 to 1994, one year after the Oslo Accords were signed.

What distinguished the intifada from past resistance efforts was not the increasingly draconian Israeli measures but the level of inclusion of nearly all sectors of Palestinian society and that the media captured the horrifying images of their everyday life and the heroic struggle of an unarmed popula-

TABLE 6.3 Human Rights Violations, December 1987 to June 1994

	Dec. 1987	1988	1989	1990	1991	1992	1993	1994[a]	Total
Killings									
Shot	22	285	301	143	94	112	157	111	1,225
Teargassed	6	22	14	10	2	1	2	0	94
Beaten	0	33	19	9	3	4	5	0	73
Total	28	334	334	162	99	117	164	111	1,392
Victims									
Children under 16	8	83	112	38	30	27	46	18	362
Females over 16	2	12	8	7	2	2	2	5	40
Males over 16	18	282	214	117	67	88	116	85	987
Killings/deaths still under investigation	–	9	13	9	19	54	58	30	192
Injuries[b]	180	46,000	34,000	22,350	18,082	4,516	5,278	381	130,787
Expulsions	8	32	26	–	8	415	–	–	489
Additional detentions	157	5,000	3,500	4,100	2,393	1,750	1,251	60	18,211
Curfew days[c]	60	3,091	3,192	5,704	896	953	2,880	712	17,488
Trees destroyed	18,000	25,000	52,698	10,000	34,000	19,898	22,801	3,091	185,489
Land confiscated (in dunums)	–	10,000	75,000	277,335	80,549	14,669	49,466	720	457,834
Military demolition									
Security	1	112	163	142	75	12	4	–	510
Military operation	–	–	–	–	–	–	101	6	107
House sealing	–	24	126	126	67	35	24	–	382
Additional demolition unlicensed	17	423	347	102	277	160	111	15	1,402

[a]Data for January–June 1994. Includes major human rights violations in the autonomous areas of the Gaza Strip and Jericho under the Palestinian Authority and in the rest of the West Bank.

[b]Refers to Palestinians who sought medical treatment for injuries by Israeli security forces, including bullet, beating, and teargas-related injuries.

[c]Total days for all areas in the West Bank and Gaza Strip.

SOURCE: Palestine Human Rights Information Center, *Human Rights Update*, vol. II, no. 6 (June 1994) 1.

tion against a vicious army. In the beginning the intifada dramatically re-arranged what seemed to be an immutable power relationship built over the twenty years of occupation. The major structural pillars of coercion and domination nearly toppled, and the Palestinians turned what had been lia-bilities into assets. This is not to say that the Israelis suddenly became pas-sive or even victims of the stones thrown by Palestinians. If the strength of the sides in the intifada were measured by the level of violence each inflicted, then the Israelis would certainly be considered the victors. Defense Minister Rabin deployed more than 10,000 troops in the Gaza area—three times as many as used to occupy the strip in 1967 and ten times as many as those who patrolled it before the uprising. In the West Bank, according to United Nations reports, the number of soldiers grew from 700 to 8,000 in response to the intifada.[75] In the first three months of the intifada, with license from their commanding officers, troops killed more than 100 Palestinian demon-strators and bystanders, wounded hundreds, and placed thousands under military detention (imprisonment for up to six months without trial, subject to indefinite renewal).[76] Supplementing the army, vigilante settlers roamed throughout Palestinian areas, taunting and harassing the locals. On many occasions settlers opened fire, killing or wounding Palestinians in retaliation for a stone-throwing incident or less. Over time the Israeli military imple-mented sophisticated "antiriot devices": night-vision equipment, television cameras in strategic locations, shielded jeeps, and stone-hurling machines.[77]

Palestinians could have been overwhelmed by Israeli military, but they mobilized efforts on the economic, political, and social fronts. Within one month, Al-Qiyada al-Wataniyya al-Muwahhada li-l-Intifada (the Unified National Leadership of the Uprising, or UNLU), created by the five major political groups represented in the PLO, captured the spontaneous momen-tum of the people and began to channel it into coordinated action through the already established popular committees and the institutionalized chari-table, professional, and volunteer organizations (the latter of which were declared illegal by Israel on August 18, 1988). An accurate profile of indi-vidual members cannot be ascertained, for like the *shabab* (young men), masked with *kaffiyya*s (traditional Arab checkered headdresses) who con-fronted the army, the UNLU leadership's effective strategy was for members to remain elusive, mobile, and interchangeable.[78]

Parallel to the UNLU, and in coordination with it, the leaders of the mainstream Muslim Brotherhood organized a militant wing to join the up-rising, drawing members from the younger Muslim Brothers and those in the Islamic Jihad. Based in Gaza, Hamas made its presence known in its first leaflet issued in January 1988. Hamas put forth its ideology, aim, and strategy in its charter on August 18, 1988. The main thrust of the text is guided by an ideology that attempts to "cleanse" Palestinian society of both secular and Zionist influences "toward raising the banner of Allah on every inch of Palestine."[79]

Article 27 of the charter states Hamas's position regarding the PLO in relation to the wider struggle (see Appendix 13 for the text of this key article). In this passage Hamas calls the PLO "the father, brother, relative or friend" of the Islamic resistance movement because, as it asserts, "Our nation is one, plight is one, destiny is one, and our enemy is the same." It clearly establishes the point that the Islamists and the PLO share the same side of the battlefield, but they will not "be its soldiers" unless "the Palestine Liberation Organization adopts Islam as its system of life." Short of that, "the position of the Islamic Resistance Movement toward the Palestine Liberation Organization is the position of a son toward his father, and a brother toward his brother, and the relative toward his relative" but not his friend.[80] Hamas thus explicitly rejected direct confrontation with the PLO but implicitly positioned itself as an alternative, even a rival, to its leadership and social programs.

Women also began to articulate and demonstrate a wider role in the struggle than they had before the intifada. But as Islah Jad argues, "Women's role in the popular committees became an extension of what it traditionally had been in the society: teaching and rendering services" across the political spectrum.[81] There was, however, a rural-urban divide, such that urban women's political activity and productive work were imbued with a greater progressive social content, whereas rural women's roles were more constricted by the traditional division of labor (albeit one with a nationalist flavor). During the intifada, women carved out a significant and fresh presence in the public space. They were on the front lines, in direct confrontation with soldiers (nearly all of whom were men, even though Israeli women as well are required to serve in the military). Yet the "woman question" became subsumed by the "nationalist question" in the sexually segregated mosques, cafés, and prisons where political strategizing was done.[82]

Because participation was so high and from such a wide cross-section of the population, the Israeli army targeted nearly everyone who participated in the intifada as a possible leader. Space in existing prison facilities became inadequate to hold as many as 9,000–10,000 Palestinians in detention at a given time.[83] For mass arrests, involving all of the males in a village or camp who were fourteen to sixty years old and were suspected of "terrorism," the Israeli army turned local schools into impromptu detention and interrogation centers. For more lengthy detention, the army hastily built tent camps that were "often the scene of brutal treatment of detainees."[84] The most notorious of these were Ansar II and III in the Gaza area and the Naqab (Negev) Desert.

The prisons were so overcrowded and the courts so overloaded with cases that the system broke down. Families and official agencies, such as the International Committee of the Red Cross (ICRC), were entitled to know the whereabouts and health of prisoners but often did not. Military Orders 29 (in the West Bank) and 410 (in the Gaza Strip) revoked the right of legal counsel unless it was deemed necessary by the prison commander.[85] The effects of the inhumane treatment of prisoners went beyond the individual immediately involved; whole families and villages feared for the prisoner, who most likely would be subjected to "some form of physical ill-treatment or torture" during interrogation by the Israeli secret service, Shin Bet.[86] Like the schools that the Israeli army turned into jails, it is said that the prisoners turned jails into schools of the intifada. Inside the overcrowded detention centers, prisoners banned together to exchange information about the events of the intifada, maintain their familial and political connections with the outside, and strategize for the future.

The intifada was triggered in the camps, but it soon spread to the main urban centers and the 500 villages (many of them, especially in the north, isolated and remote). It was virtually impossible for the Israeli military to subdue all areas continuously or isolate key individuals effectively. Instead, it dealt out collective punishment in order to quell resistance area by area.[87] As mentioned in Chapter 5, Al-Haq documented the increase in curfews, which are in clear violation of several articles of both the fourth Geneva convention and The Hague regulations:[88]

> In the period between 9 December 1987 and 9 December 1988, the military government in the Occupied Territories imposed a minimum of 1,600 curfews on various locations in the West Bank and Gaza Strip. Of these, an estimated minimum of 400 were prolonged curfews which were in force 24 hours a day and lasted from 3 to 40 days. . . . The scope of the measure has meant that almost every one of the estimated 1.7 million Palestinian residents of these regions has been forcibly confined to their home on at least one occasion during the past year. . . . The effect has been not only a complete disruption of daily life and near-catastrophic economic losses, but widespread hunger and medical emergency. . . . With few exceptions, on any given day at least 25,000 Palestinians have been involuntarily confined to their homes, and this figure has reached into the hundreds of thousands with persistent regularity.[89]

Palestinians realized that the collective struggle required individual sacrifices. More and more people became directly involved with the intifada. Continuing the struggle, once it began, became a priority and necessity for survival, escalating the fight and advancing the cause.

Economic Resistance

The UNLU's first *bayan* (communiqué), issued one month after the intifada began, extolled the Palestinian people's struggle as a whole. A more important aspect of the bayan was that it horizontally linked vertically positioned class actors to the wider struggle, reconciling the immediate and long-term interests and sacrifices of each class against Israel as the greater economic and political enemy:

In the name of God, the merciful, the compassionate . . .

All Sectors of our heroic people in every location should abide by the calls for a general and comprehensive strike. . . .

Brother workers, your abidance by the strike by not going to work and to plants is real support for the glorious uprising, a sanctioning of the pure blood of our martyrs, a support for the call to liberate our prisoners, and an act that will keep our brother deportees in their homeland.

Brother businessmen and grocers, you must fully abide by the call for a comprehensive strike. . . . We will do our best to protect the interests of our honest businessmen against measures the Zionist occupation force may resort to using against you. We warn against the consequences of becoming involved with some of the occupation authorities' henchmen who will seek to make you open your businesses. We promise to punish such traitor businessmen in the not too distant future. Let us proceed united to forge victory.

Brother owners of taxi companies . . . we pin our hopes on you to support and make the comprehensive strike a success. . . .

Brother doctors and pharmacists, you must be on emergency status to offer assistance to those of kinfolk who are ill. . . .

Let us proceed united and loudly chant: Down with occupation; long live Palestine as a free and Arab country.[90]

Compliance with the directives was enforced by the immediate and widespread legitimacy of the UNLU. The Israeli army tried to issue false *bayanat,* but these could be easily identified because the demands were unfeasible or divisive. Few wished to ignore the calls of the leaders and began to "shape their daily lives around the announcements."[91] Moreover, according to Salim Tamari, the individuals associated with the village leagues, once the cradle of collaborators and a bastion of Israeli hegemony, "publicly recanted their former roles," and many who were employed by the civil administration as tax collectors joined a mass resignation in the summer of 1988.[92]

With the economic sector mobilized, the UNLU pressed for a Palestinian withdrawal from the Israeli economy. First and most effective was a general boycott of Israeli products that were either unessential consumer goods (such as beer, cigarettes, and clothing) or had a Palestinian-made equivalent (such as soap, soft drinks, eggs, meat, and candy). Second, the strikes against Israeli employers, with an emphasis on construction in settlements, were observed by an estimated 40–60 percent of the migrant work force.[93] Third was a general tax revolt against direct taxation and licensing, accompanied by mass resignation of tax collectors. The most celebrated was that of the town of Beit Sahur.[94] By the end of 1988, the sum cost of the intifada in terms of loss of revenue from the territories, the increase in military spending, property damage, and the slowdown of tourism was estimated to be around $2–3 billion, equivalent to 4.5–5 percent of the Israeli GNP.[95]

But the initial impact of the intifada was overall more devastating to the Palestinian economy than to the Israeli economy. Strikes, curfews, and the high rate of imprisonment and wounding of wage earners meant a steep decline in real wages for entire families and villages. Where the military might have failed to suppress the uprising, the Israeli army began meting out economic punishment by sector—an extension of pre-intifada practices. In the West Bank cities, phone lines, electricity, and fuel supplies were often cut. Everywhere, from the start, merchants' shops were forced open during strike hours or welded shut if they disobeyed the order. Another crude and widespread tactic Israel used against merchants was to wantonly destroy foodstuff and equipment: "In many cases in the West Bank documented by al-Haq, soldiers entered shops and spoiled the goods, mixing bleach with flour, trampling on bread, smashing eggs, breaking a refrigerator full of meat and upturning stalls."[96]

Prolonged curfews particularly disrupted agricultural production in the villages. Entire crops were lost because farmers were unable to spray, irrigate, or harvest their fields. When the Israeli military lifted the curfew or siege, collective efforts were made to do the necessary work to save the crops, but often the effort was too late. Additional constraints were placed on village farmers to prevent them from processing and exporting their produce. Military Order 1252, "Order Concerning the Transportation of Goods (Judea and Samaria) 1988," effectively prohibited the export of olive oil products to Jordan and Israel. There were prohibitions on other products, such as quarry stone, sage, eggs, antiques, medicine, and gasoline, but none was as devastating to the local economy as the ban on olive oil, which represents approximately 14.5 percent of total agricultural production and roughly 5 percent (but as high as 12 percent in good years) of total West Bank GNP.[97] Obtaining a license to export permitted products and operate processing machines was contingent upon payment of taxes and fines.[98] And not just the individual applying for a permit or license but the applicant's entire family had to have a clear record.

Another economic coercive tactic used by the Israeli army to corner the participants of the intifada and undermine general support in Gaza was the reissuing of the hawiyya. Operation Plastic Card, launched on June 6, 1988, required all Gazans who worked in Israel to obtain a new, brightly colored identity card. In order to qualify to purchase this card (which cost about $10), the applicants had to have clear records and had to have paid any taxes that they or their relatives owed. The UNLU immediately called for a boycott, and local activists attempted to confiscate and destroy as many of what the Israeli military called "honesty cards" as possible. Nevertheless, by the fall of that year the army managed to win this battle and isolate some of the core activists.[99]

International Response

One main feature that set the intifada apart from previous resistance efforts was the international material and ideological support. Demonstration of solidarity, involving thousands of protestors, erupted throughout the world, in West Germany, Italy, Canada, the United States, the Netherlands, and Japan. According to Lamis Andoni, "Between December 1987 and August 1988 the security and police departments dealt with 117 demonstrations of anywhere between 100 and 2,500 people organized in Jordan in support of the intifada."[100] All Arab regimes, regardless of their reservations about the PLO or fears that the intifada could become a model of insurrection against their own states, were compelled to pledge moral and financial support to ensure the continuation of the Palestinian uprising.[101] It is partly for these reasons that the intifada continued well beyond its predicted demise.

Shortly after the intifada began, Jordan pledged to continue to pay the salaries of teachers and civil servants regardless of strikes, curfews, or resignations. The government also offered pensions to families of those who were disabled or killed in the intifada. As a symbolic gesture, "Iraq began paying pensions to the families of those killed in the intifada equivalent to the pensions given to the families of its own soldiers killed in the [Iran-Iraq] Gulf war."[102] At an emergency Arab summit meeting in Algiers six months after the intifada began, PLO chairman 'Arafat played an active role in securing money, medicine, and foodstuffs for the people of the West Bank and Gaza Strip. Unofficial sources reported that the Gulf states of Saudi Arabia, Kuwait, Qatar, and the United Arab Emirates together pledged $118 million for the first year of the uprising.[103] The summit also reaffirmed its annual $150 million payment to the PLO and extended the annual $100 million contribution to the PLO-Jordanian joint committee beyond the ten-year period established at the 1978 Baghdad summit.[104]

In the United States, the world's greatest ideological and financial ally of Israel, the images of Israeli brutality stirred a general outcry from the public. Until then it had for the most part been ignorant of the Palestinians' condition under occupation, and it was shocked at the unprecedented intensity and severity of the conflict. Israel's image was marred by the repeated acts of brutality reported in the newspapers. Throughout the major cities of the United States, Israel's Ministry of Tourism had launched a promotion during the religious holiday season. Billboards featured a panoramic view of the Old City of Jerusalem; under it a caption read, "Jerusalem, Just a Stone's Throw Away from Tel Aviv." The campaign was quickly retracted. The Israeli state was forced to play the defensive in public relations.

Opinion polls tapping into the U.S. public's attitudes toward the Israel-Palestinian conflict showed a general decline in the support usually accorded to the Israelis. A 1988 Gallop survey, confirmed by numerous others, found that about 30 percent of Americans "view Israel less favorably" than prior to the intifada. Surveys also revealed a sharp difference between public opinion and U.S. government policies. Another Gallup survey of

February 26–March 7, 1988, asked respondents, "As you may know, the United States does not currently deal directly with the PLO. So do you favor or oppose direct talks between the U.S. and the PLO as a way to help resolve the conflict over Gaza and the West Bank?" Despite the use of such direct language in the question, 53 percent answered favorably and only 26 supported official U.S. policies.[105]

The best example of the unconditional support the U.S. government typically grants Israel is the high level of financial aid—reported as well over $3 billion annually. According to Martha Wenger's investigation, however,

> This does not count some $2.5 billion in private US funds which go to Israel each year: an estimated $1 billion in short- and long-term loans from US commercial banks; some $500 million worth of Israel bonds sold by US firms . . . ; and about $1 billion in donations from private citizens.
>
> Adding these amounts brings the total to $6.2 billion ($6,200,000,000) a year, or $1,377 per Israeli.[106]

A substantial majority, 70 percent, of Americans became weary of the official funding of Israeli policies. Once again, Gallup surveys found that 41 percent thought that U.S. aid to Israel should be decreased, and 19 percent believed that it should be stopped completely. Moreover, 22 percent indicated that their negative opinion was influenced by Israel's handling of the intifada.[107]

Israelis' public opinion was almost opposite to that of Americans. Surveys showed 69 percent of Israelis favored taking a "tougher stand" in quelling (what was then labeled as) "the disturbances," 23 percent believed the level of response was appropriate, while only 7 percent thought it should be softened.[108] These attitudes were reflected in the Knesset, where even before the intifada, calls for a "transfer" solution (an Israeli code word for the expulsion of the Palestinian population from the occupied territories) to the conflict over the West Bank and Gaza Strip were made by right-of-center political figures. Deputy Defense Minister Michael Dekel of the Likud Party openly endorsed the policies advocated by the Kach Party, which was banned by the Israeli Supreme Court for its racist platform in 1986.[109] In a speech to Israeli settlers on April 1, 1988, Prime Minister Shamir compared Palestinians to "grasshoppers" who could be crushed. To further this point, the minister of industry and trade and former defense minister, Ariel Sharon, moved with his family into the Muslim quarter of Jerusalem's Old City.[110]

Consequences of the Intifada

Within this politically charged context, the intifada in less than a year not only upset the power relations locally inside Israel and externally tied to the occupation but began to reorder them. On July 31, 1988, in a historic tele-vised speech, King Hussein reversed four decades of Hashemite policy re-garding Jordan's administrative responsibility for the West Bank and its claim to represent the Palestinians of the territories as a legitimate substi-tute to the PLO.[111] The king severed these links without consulting the PLO beforehand. Andoni speculates that he hoped to catch the PLO off guard in order to demonstrate the organization's inability to "handle the re-sponsibility it had always sought."[112] The Jordanian government immedi-ately followed through on its new position: The next day it began to dis-entangle itself by revoking the Jordanian citizenship of West Bank Palestinians (reducing it to two-year travel documents) and stopping salaries of most of the 24,000 government employees (except those of the Department of Awqaf, the religious endowments).[113]

Four months later, as we noted in the previous chapter, the PNC held its nineteenth session in Algiers (November 12–15, 1988) in order to con-cretize its new position in view of these rapid and profound political changes. This historic session brought forth the Declaration of Independ-ence of Palestine (text in Appendix 9) with Jerusalem as its capital. No less significant was 'Arafat's address to the forty-third session of the United Nations General Assembly, in Geneva on December 13, 1988,[114] where he formally and unequivocally recognized Israel's right to exist, denounced terrorism, and accepted territorial concessions. His speech reiterated the main points of the resolution passed at the PNC session.[115]

Palestinians inside the occupied territories celebrated their "national in-dependence day" with demonstrations in widespread support of the PNC statement. The resolutions, however, drove a deeper wedge between Hamas and the UNLU. The Islamists issued an appeal to the PNC in Algeria that restated their position: "We condemn all the attitudes calling for ending the *jihad* and struggle, and for establishing peace with the murderers, and the attitudes which call for acceptance of the Jewish entity on any part of our land."[116] Nonetheless, the majority of Palestinians perceived that opening dialogue between the United States and their sole and legitimate representa-tives as indeed "an achievement of the intifada" (UNLU bayan 31). It was a welcome political victory, as Palestinians were being hurt badly by the eco-nomic struggle against Israeli occupation.

The political optimism among all Palestinians that the intifada would produce a political solution—a negotiated settlement with Israel—to end the occupation, with the United States as the mediator, never materialized. Supported by the United States, Israel remained intransigent, offering its own version of a peace agreement, that of Palestinian autonomy over civil-ian affairs, and not the land or resources. Such a proposal resembled the provisions of the Camp David Accords and did not include the PLO or an independent Palestinian state in the end. U.S. and Israeli obstructionism to any peace except on their own terms (demeaning to Palestinians through the denial of Palestinian national rights) undermined the Palestinian diplomatic initiative.[117] The Israeli-U.S. counterproposal outraged the Palestinians under occupation and in the diaspora, all of whom overwhelmingly rejected it, as did the PLO. Thus the parties reached another deadlock.

Conclusion

The intifada is a historical culmination of all previous efforts by the Palestinian people to resist dispossession and suppression of national identity. It constituted the fourth major national effort in defense of the Palestinian homeland against Zionism's and Israel's efforts to dispossess them completely and Judaize the country in the twentieth century. The first was the 1936–1939 revolt against the authorities of the British Mandate, the second was the 1947–1948 armed resistance to the partitioning of Palestine, and the third was the founding of the revolutionary PLO between 1964 and 1968. Unlike these previous endeavors, the intifada was strongly unified. It joined together the young and the old, men and women, urban dwellers and villagers, Muslims and Christians, the poor and the rich, and all political currents to form a genuine grassroots movement, representing the latest climactic expression of the collective Palestinian will.[118] It erupted twenty years after the start of the occupation and forty years after the United Nations vote to partition Palestine.

The intifada did not occur in a sociopolitical vacuum but was the culmination of a process of resistance that took different forms in response to Israeli actions. Israel practiced four major processes of subjugation in its effort to turn the occupied territories into an internal colony and Judaize the areas. As we detailed above, these were political repression, economic exploitation, institutional destruction, and ideological and cultural suppression, combined with the establishment of privileged Israeli settlements on the occupied Palestinian land. These processes had sown the seeds of destruction of Israel's own policy. They generated discontent, blocked "legitimate" means for redressing grievances, denied Palestinian identity, and triggered innovative strategies of resistance by the Palestinian people. The critical mechanism the Palestinian people developed against centralized hegemonic Israeli control were "popular sovereignties," self-reliant local committees, a blend of traditional and modern structures of sociopolitical organization, social service institutions, communication, and mobilization that provided popular, decentralized empowerment.

The intifada won international sympathy and support, but the PLO leadership, without credible international reach, failed to transform that sympathy into international solidarity for the Palestinian people and their cause. The intifada was not a mere political event; such a view locks it into a narrow calculation of immediate losses and gains. Instead, it should be seen as a totalizing force rejecting the normalization of the occupation. The brilliant success of the intifada against Israeli repression, it is clear, galvanized not only the people under occupation but also reenergized the diaspora communities and healed the divisions within the PLO. Despite the new diplomatic initiative, including some major concessions by the PLO, the intifada was never able to overcome the obstructionism of Israel and the United States. Therefore the political impasse of the Palestinian-Israeli conflict remained. Palestinians sacrificed too much, and perhaps had too great expectations, to accept a solution that fell short of restitution and independent statehood. Indeed as the intifada began to wane in 1990, Fateh and the PLO were floundering and suffering serious shock: the assassinations of two of their top three leaders (Khalil al-Wazir in 1988 and Salah Khalaf in 1990).

In 1990 Iraq's invasion of Kuwait and in 1991 the U.S.-led allied Gulf War against Baghdad introduced a dramatic and strategically transformative dimension into the Middle East. The war quickly redirected attention away from the ongoing intifada and realigned the regional balance of political power to the disadvantage of the Palestinians. Although the Gulf crisis overshadowed the intifada and the Palestine question and reduced significantly Arab support for them, it nevertheless gave the PLO leadership, under 'Arafat and his loyalists, a new window of opportunity to move the Palestinian issue once again onto the international political agenda. However, the ill-considered actions of Chairman 'Arafat—in actuality siding with Saddam Hussein of Iraq but rhetorically claiming otherwise[119]—isolated and delegitimized the PLO and with it the Palestinian cause not only in the international arena but also among a large number of Arab governments and peoples, especially the wealthy oil-exporting states and the politically influential ones such as Egypt and Syria. Thus in the context of Israeli-U.S. obstructionism to a just peace in the Middle East, 'Arafat's incompetent and inept actions squandered the achievements of the intifada and set the stage for the precipitous decline of the PLO in the 1990s, making room for the start of both the inconclusive "peace process" initiated by the U.S. government and the secret negotiations with Israel that led to the Oslo Accords in 1993. These accords, signed by the PLO and Israel under U.S. auspices, are a political earthquake in both the regional and the Palestinian contexts. Their terms and consequences, as we argue in the next chapter, will determine the destiny of Palestine and the Palestinians.

Notes

1. J. L. Abu-Lughod identifies five categories of Palestinians and systematically discusses them in "Palestinians: Exiles at Home and Abroad," *Current Sociology* 36 (Summer 1988): 61–69.

2. *Facts and Figures About the Palestinians* (Washington, DC: Center for Policy Analysis on Palestine, 1993).

3. For example, an Israeli kibbutz, Beth-Alfa, supplied water cannons to the apartheid state of South Africa until 1987. This point raises the issue of why live ammunition and lethal rubber bullets were used against the Palestinians protesters. J. Hunter, "Israel and South Africa: Sidestepping Sanctions," *Middle East International,* February 20, 1988, 16.

4. J. Kifner, "Israel Vows to Stress Riot Training," *New York Times,* December 30, 1987, A6.

5. S. Roy, *The Gaza Strip: The Political Economy of De-development* (Washington, DC: Institute for Palestine Studies, 1995).

6. This figure is an approximation based on demographic projections from census data collected by the British Mandate in 1931, 1967 Israeli census data, and more recent sample surveys. See Abu-Lughod, "Palestinians: Exiles at Home and Abroad," 69.

7. E. W. Said, "Intifada and Independence," in Z. Lockman and J. Beinin, eds., *Intifada: The Palestinian Uprising Against Israeli Occupation* (Boston: South End Press, 1989), 7.

8. S. N. Anabtawi, "The U.N., the Palestine Refugees and the Palestinian Revolution," in N. Aruri, ed., *Palestinian Resistance to the Israeli Occupation* (Wilmette, IL: Medina University Press, 1970), 51.

9. D. Peretz, *Intifada: The Palestinian Uprising* (Boulder, CO: Westview Press, 1990), 4.

10. See M. T. Dumper, "Jerusalem's Infrastructure: Is Annexation Irreversible?" *Journal of Palestine Studies* 22, 3 (Spring 1993): 78–95. Dumper puts the questions of demography and politics aside in this article and instead focuses on the issues of integrated water, electricity, and sewage systems of East and West Jerusalem. Admitting the political difficulty of dividing Jerusalem, he finds "no overwhelming functional and technical obstacles to prevent" reversed annexation (93).

11. For a detailed summary of this debate, see C. D. Smith, *Palestine and the Arab-Israeli Conflict* (New York: St. Martin's Press, 1988), 208–211.

12. For a further discussion, see N. Aruri, ed., *Occupation: Israel over Palestine,* 2nd ed. (Belmont, MA: Association of Arab-American University Graduates, 1989); and W. T. Mallison and S. V. Mallison, *The Palestine Problem in International Law and World Order* (New York: Longman, 1986); see also M. Benvenisti with Z. Abu-Zayed and D. Rubinstein, *The West Bank Handbook: A Political Lexicon* (Boulder, CO: Westview Press, 1986).

13. Aruri, *Occupation,* 8.

14. Benvenisti, *The West Bank Handbook,* 196.

15. A. K. Wing, "Legitimacy and Coercion: Legal Traditions and Legal Rules During the Intifada," *Middle East Policy* 2, 2 (1993): 87–103.

16. A brilliant study of the structure and application of the Israeli military law and court system in the occupied territories is L. Hajjar, "Authority, Resistance and the Law: A Study of the Israeli Military Courts in the Occupied Territories," Ph.D. dissertation, American University, 1995.

17. Aruri, *Occupation,* 19.

18. A. Gramsci, *Selections from Prison Notebooks* (New York: International Publishers, 1971).

19. Ibid., 244.

20. M. Carnoy, *The State and Political Theory* (Princeton: Princeton University Press, 1984), 79.

21. S. Tamari, "Israel's Search for a Native Pillar: The Village Leagues," in Aruri, *Occupation*, 603–618.

22. S. K. Farsoun and J. M. Landis, "Structures of Resistance and the 'War of Position': A Case Study of the Palestinian Uprising," *Arab Studies Quarterly* 11, 4 (Fall 1989): 59–86.

23. J. R. Hiltermann quoting Arabi Awad, one of the founders of the PNF who was deported along with seven other leaders shortly after its establishment in December 1973; *Behind the Intifada: Labor and Women's Movements in the Occupied Territories* (Princeton, NJ: Princeton University Press, 1991), 44.

24. See S. R. Dajani, *Eyes Without Country: Searching for a Palestinian Strategy of Liberation* (Philadelphia: Temple University Press, 1994).

25. Said, "Intifada and Independence," 11.

26. N. H. Aruri, "Dialectics of Dispossession," in Aruri, *Occupation*, 22.

27. L. Hajjar, M. Rabbani, and J. Beinin, "Palestine and the Arab-Israeli Conflict for Beginners," in Lockman and Beinin, *Intifada*, 109.

28. Aruri, "Dialectics of Dispossession," 26.

29. Ibid., vi.

30. S. Tamari, "The Palestinian Demand for Independence Cannot Be Postponed Indefinitely," *MERIP Reports* 100–101 (October-December 1981): 34.

31. Hiltermann, *Behind the Intifada*, 48.

32. Tamari, "The Palestinian Demand," 30. Cited in Hiltermann, *Behind the Intifada*, 48.

33. Hiltermann, *Behind the Intifada*, 17–18.

34. M. K. Shadid, "Israeli Policy Toward Economic Development in the West Bank and Gaza," in G. T. Abed, ed., *The Palestinian Economy: Studies in Development Under Prolonged Occupation* (London: Routledge, 1988), 127.

35. Hiltermann, *Behind the Intifada*, 21.

36. Ibid., 25.

37. Ibid., 30.

38. Ibid., 23.

39. This observation is derived from an extensive study on Palestinian-Israeli income and employment differentials. The fifth major finding was that "not only have noncitizen Arabs been segregated to lower-status occupations, but their income has been considerably lower than that paid to other [Israeli] incumbents in these occupations." M. Semyonov and N. L. Epstein, *Hewers of Wood and Drawers of Water: Noncitizen Arabs in the Israeli Labor Market*, report number 13 (New York: Cornell International Industrial and Labor Relations, 1987), 115.

40. Hiltermann, *Behind the Intifada*, 61.

41. Ibid., 62.

42. Abed, *The Palestinian Economy*, 6.

43. The discussion of the Palestinian Islamic movement is based on Z. Abu-Amr, "Hamas: A Historical and Political Background," *Journal of Palestine Studies* 22, 4 (Summer 1993): 5–19.

44. Ibid., 7.

45. Ibid., 8.

46. Ibid., 9.

47. Ibid., 48.

48. M. Benvenisti, *1987 Report: Demographic, Economic, Legal, Social, and Political Developments in the West Bank* (Boulder, CO: Westview Press, 1987), 55.

49. According to Benvenisti, industrial enterprises and facilities for tourism "established across the green line receive a grant of 30 percent and loans at a real interest rate of 0.5 percent, or if dollar linked at 6 percent. These enterprises are also entitled to a grant for land development, structures and equipment, and a 5 percent rebate on financial charges." For housing, "the aid consists of a mortgage (11.5 percent) unlinked to the cost of living index, a linked but interest free loan (65.5 percent) and a linked loan bearing 6 percent interest (11.5 percent). Moreover, the price of an apartment is also subsidized in that the cost of the land is only 5 percent its actual value, and the infrastructure is provided to the settlement free of charge. Thus one can purchase an apartment only 30–45 minutes from Jerusalem for a cash payment of $2,000"; *The West Bank Handbook*, 111.

50. A. Dehter, "How Expensive Are West Bank Settlements?" *The West Bank Data Project* (Jerusalem: Jerusalem Post, 1987), iii.

51. S. Tamari, professor of sociology at Bir Zeit University in the West Bank, makes this important point about the confiscation of Palestinian land: "There is an extra-territorial definition of public land in Israel so that it belongs to the Jews in totality and not to the Israel Jews in the State of Israel. Israeli citizens who are non-Jews have no access to this land, but Jews who are not Israeli do have access"; "What the Uprising Means," in Lockman and Beinin, *Intifada*, 130.

52. M. Benvenisti makes the point that "this 'export' is possible because Israeli manufactured goods enjoy massive protection, estimated at 60% of the value of the products on the international market"; *1986 Report: Demographic, Economic, Legal, Social, and Political Developments in the West Bank* (Boulder, CO: Westview Press, 1986), 7.

53. United Nations Conference on Trade and Development, "The Palestinian Financial Sector Under Israeli Occupation," UNCTAD/ST/SEU/3 (Geneva, July 8, 1987), 101.

54. Ibid., 25.

55. In 1983 total Israeli exports to the West Bank and the Gaza Strip amounted to $680.5 million, while Israel exported to the United States $1,329.2 million, about twice as much. Y. A. Sayigh, "Dispossession and Pauperization: The Palestinian Economy Under Occupation," in Abed, *The Palestinian Economy*, 260. By 1986 total Israeli exports to the Palestinians grew to $780 million; Tamari, "What the Uprising Means," 129.

56. S. Ryan, "The West Bank and Gaza: Political Consequences of the Intifada," *Middle East Report* 74 (January 1979): 3.

57. Sayigh, "Dispossession and Pauperization," 261.

58. Ibid.

59. Economic Intelligence Unit, *Israel/The Occupied Territories, 19931994* (London: Economic Intelligence Unit, 1994), 43.

60. Figures are for 1984 as reported in the *Statistical Abstract of Israel 1984,* no. 35 (Jerusalem: Central Bureau of Statistics, 1984), tables XXVII/19 and XXVII/20: 762 and 763. This may be an underestimate because of the unaccounted, undocumented, and illegal employment.

61. World Bank, *Developing the Occupied Territories: An Investment in Peace,* vol. 1 (Washington, DC: World Bank, 1993), 5.

62. Ibid., viii.

63. Compare the dominance of the service sector to others: agriculture accounts for roughly 30 percent of GDP, industry about 8 percent, and construction approximately 12 percent. Ibid., viii.

64. J. Mandell, "Gaza: Israel's Soweto," *Middle East Report* 136/137 (October-December 1985): 12.

65. Ibid.

66. United Nations Conference on Trade and Development, "Prospects for Sustained Development of the Palestinian Economy in the West Bank and Gaza Strip," UNCTAD/DSD/SEU/2 (Geneva September 27, 1993), 29.

67. S. S. Elmusa, *The Water Issue and the Palestinian-Israeli Conflict* (Washington, DC: Center for Policy Analysis on Palestine, 1993), 7.

68. Roy, *The Gaza Strip.*

69. Ibid., 236.

70. Ibid., 272.

71. S. K. Farsoun and J. M. Landis, "The Sociology of an Uprising: The Roots of the Intifada," in J. R. Nassar and R. Heacock, eds., *Intifada: Palestine at the Crossroads* (New York: Praeger, 1990), 24.

72. The fullest and most reliable data source has been collected by Al-Haq, an international commission of jurists concerned with human rights violations against the Palestinians living in the occupied territories. Their data, published annually, are sworn testimony (not hearsay) by victims and eyewitnesses.

73. He was later assassinated at his home in Tunis on April 16, 1988, and buried in Damascus, Syria. The *Washington Post* (April 21, 1988) reported that the operation was planned by the Mossad (the Israeli secret intelligence service) after being approved by the Israeli cabinet.

74. A. M. Lesch, "The Palestinian Uprising—Causes and Consequences," UFSI report 1 (Washington, DC: Universities Field Staff International, 1988-1989), 4.

75. Further, "Annual reserve duty for men was increased from the normal 30 days to 62 days. (In contrast, at the height of the fighting in Lebanon, reserve duty extended for 45 days.)" Ibid., 9.

76. P. Johnson and L. O'Brien with J. R. Hiltermann, "The West Bank Rises Up," in Lockman and Beinin, *Intifada,* 29.

77. B. E. Trainor, "Israelis vs. Palestinians: Tactics Are Refined," *New York Times,* March 30, 1989, A9.

78. Based on a sample of 330 people under administrative detention, one study found that an average leader was between twenty-one and thirty years old and had completed at least seven to eleven years of schooling. This study was conducted by the Israel Bar Association and presented to the Knesset by member Dedi Zucker of the Citizen Rights Movement. Cited in Peretz, *Intifada,* 65.

79. "Charter of the Islamic Resistance Movement (Hamas) of Palestine," *Journal of Palestine Studies* 22, 4 (Summer 1993): 130–131.

80. Ibid..

81. I. Jad, "From Salons to the Popular Committees: Palestinian Women 1919–1989," in Nassar and Heacock, *Intifada,* 135.

82. Ibid.

83. Al-Haq, *Punishing a Nation: Israeli Human Rights Violations During the Palestinian Uprising, December 1987–December 1988* (Boston: South End Press, 1989), 346.

84. Ibid., 348.

85. Ibid., 338.

86. Ibid., 341.

87. Peretz, *Intifada*, 67.

88. Al-Haq, *Punishing a Nation*, 255.

89. Ibid., 254.

90. All references to the texts of communiqués are from Lockman and Beinin, *Intifada*, appendix II, 327–394.

91. This observation is from an eyewitness account of the intifada; Johnson, O'Brien, and Hiltermann, "The West Bank Rises Up," 30.

92. Tamari, "Israel's Search for a Native Pillar," 617. Communiqué 6 (February 2, 1988) explicitly called upon "the municipal and local committees and the committees in the camps which have been appointed by the Zionists occupation authorities to resign immediately" (p. 334).

93. This figure does not account for casual day laborers or illegal migrant workers.

94. See the study of the town of Beit Sahur by M. J. Nojeim, "Planting Olive Trees: Palestinian Non-Violent Resistance," Ph.D. dissertation, American University, 1993.

95. Figures are extrapolated from Peretz, *Intifada*, 77, 150.

96. Al-Haq, *Punishing a Nation*, 388.

97. Ibid., 406–407.

98. Ibid., 405.

99. Hiltermann, *Behind the Intifada*, 185.

100. L. Andoni, "Jordan," in R. Brynen, ed., *Echoes of the Intifada: Regional Repercussions of the Palestinian-Israeli Conflict* (Boulder, CO: Westview Press, 1991), 173.

101. L. Andoni, "Solid Arab Backing," *Middle East International,* February 6, 1988, 7.

102. M. Jansen, "The Funds Which Help the Intifada," *Middle East International,* June 24, 1988, 6.

103. Ibid.

104. Ibid.

105. For a thorough and interesting discussion, see F. Moughrabi, "The Intifada in American Public Opinion," in Nassar and Heacock, *Intifada*, 247.

106. M. Wenger, "The Money Tree: US Aid to Israel." *Middle East Report* 164–165 (May-August 1990): 12–13.

107. Moughrabi, "The Intifada in American Public Opinion," 248.

108. J. Kifner, "Arrests of Palestinians Approach 1,000," *New York Times,* December 26, 1987, A7.

109. Peretz, *Intifada*, 30.

110. "Home for Sharon Amid Arabs," *New York Times,* December 17, 1987, A14.

111. For a comprehensive and detailed overview of this historic transition in Jordanian-Palestinian relations as well as the intifada's impact on Jordanian politics, see Andoni, "Jordan."

112. Ibid., 170.

113. Ibid., 174.

114. 'Arafat was denied a visa to enter the United States in order to address the United Nations at its headquarters in New York on the grounds that he belonged to a "terrorist organization." On December 1, 1988, the United Nations General Assembly voted 151–2, with one abstention by Britain, to condemn the United States for violating a 1947 headquarter agreement that requires the United States not to obstruct persons with legitimate business at the United Nations.

115. Z. Abu-Amr, "The Politics of the Intifada," in M. C. Hudson, ed., *The Palestinians: New Directions* (Washington, DC: Center for Contemporary Arab Studies, Georgetown University, 1990), 5; omissions not in the original. For a full reproduction of the document produced at the November 1988 PNC meeting, see *Journal of Palestine Studies* 17, 2 (Winter 1989).

116. As cited by Abu-Amr, "The Politics of the Intifada," 9.

117. N. Aruri, *The Obstruction of Peace: The U.S., Israel and the Palestinians* (Monroe, ME: Common Courage Press, 1995); see also N. Chomsky, *World Orders: Old and New* (New York: Columbia University Press, 1994).

118. Farsoun and Landis, "Structures of Resistance," 60.

119. For a more complex interpretation of the behavior of the PLO in the Gulf crisis, see N. G. Finkelstein, *The Rise and Fall of Palestine* (Minneapolis: University of Minnesota Press, 1996), ch. 4 and the epilogue.

SEVEN

The PLO-Israel Accords
and the Future of Palestine
and the Palestinians

What is to become of Palestine and the Palestinians? The "peace process" on which the PLO and Palestinian leaders from the occupied territories embarked in 1991 in Madrid is a turning point in Palestinian history. After almost two years of frustrating and fruitless public negotiations between Israel and the Palestinian delegation from the occupied territories, top secret PLO-Israeli negotiations cultivated by the Norwegian government suddenly produced an accord. In late August 1993, Israel and the PLO announced agreement on a "set of principles" to resolve the 100-year conflict between the two peoples. Initialed in Oslo, the Declaration of Principles on Interim Self-Government Arrangements (called the Oslo Accords because it also included documents of mutual recognition between Israel and the PLO) was signed in September 1993 on the lawn of the White House.

How will the Declaration of Principles and the subsequent Cairo, Paris, and Oslo II Accords serve the cause of Palestine and the Palestinians? Specifically, will the accords lead to self-determination and an independent state for the Palestinian people? Or will the final outcome be the "technical resolution" of the Palestine question,[1] which in effect means the historic dissolution of the Palestinians as a people and the emergence of the diaspora communities as second-class minorities? Analysis of the accords and their implications for an independent future for Palestine and the Palestinians as a people is the subject of this chapter.

The Road to the Oslo Accords

The PLO's decline and isolation, the escalating cost of the intifada for Israel, and the United States' hegemony in the world (because of the end of the Soviet Union) and the Middle East (through the victory over Iraq) were the circumstances behind the Madrid peace conference and the Oslo Accords. What finally pushed the PLO toward the accords were the "bridging measures" proposed by the administration of U.S. president Bill Clinton, an attempt to resolve the impasse in the Washington peace talks (the negotiating formula following the Madrid conference). After ten rounds of futile Palestinian-Israeli negotiations, the Clinton administration in June 1993 prepared a proposal it labeled "Declaration of Principles," the first usage of the phrase before the Oslo Accords. The proposal contained three elements that were unprecedented even in U.S. diplomacy.

In effect the U.S. proposal reconceptualized the legal status of the West Bank and Gaza Strip as *disputed* rather than *occupied* territories; second, it made no reference to the long-standing formula (embodied in UN Security Council Resolutions 242 and 338) of exchanging land for peace in order to resolve the Arab-Israeli conflict and made no mention of Israeli military withdrawal from the territories; third, it proposed that matters relating to Palestinian sovereignty were outside the scope of the negotiations for the interim agreement. Accordingly, issues of land and water, Israeli settlements, and Jerusalem were deferred for a number of years. The proposal was significant as well in that it contained no mention of the rights of the 1948 and 1967 Palestinian refugees. In turn, because the issues of land and the nature of the authority over the land were to be dealt with separately and in the future, negotiations concerning the interim period would be limited to authority over the *people* and *not* the *territory*. Hence the Palestinians of the West Bank and Gaza Strip were reduced in this U.S. proposal to "inhabitants" in those territories with only some civil but no national political rights. Both the Palestinian negotiating delegation and the PLO leadership were shocked and alarmed by this new and sharply biased formulation, itself a substantial departure from the conventional and long-standing U.S. policy and from the guarantees (to the Palestinian delegation) of the Bush administration.[2] With a broker (the United States) who seemed more Israeli than the Israelis, the impasse became all the more inescapable, and the PLO, without informing the Washington Palestinian negotiating team, opted for direct secret negotiations with Israel, where the terms could not possibly be worse.

The Declaration of Principles thus ushered in the current phase of the Palestinian-Israeli struggle. It is a dramatic turning point in the contemporary (twentieth-century) history of the Middle East. It was the breakthrough, on Israeli terms, not only for the political settlement of the Palestinian-Israeli conflict but also of the Arab-Israeli confrontation. Because of its terms, however, what it ignored of Palestinian rights, and what it committed the PLO to do, the Oslo Accords plunged the Palestinian people and its political institutions into the most serious and profound moral, cultural, identity, and political crisis. Most Palestinians agreed with Edward Said that "it was a betrayal of our history and our people."[3] Palestinians everywhere—inside and outside the occupied territories—were divided over the legitimacy, meaning, and consequences of the Oslo Accords.

Will this declaration and its derivative agreements lead to an independent Palestinian state in the West Bank and Gaza Strip as 'Arafat, his faction within the PLO, and supporters (and even some Israelis and U.S. media[4]) claim? Or will it lead, as many critics (including some Israelis) believe, to continued domination of the territories by Israel, in a new form, but henceforth legitimized by the accords and the recognized, official Palestinian leadership? The central issues that divide the Palestinians currently are the declaration, the derivative agreements, the conduct of the 'Arafat regime, and the future. Complicating these questions have been the politics, economics, and dynamics of the implementation of the agreements (the Oslo, Cairo, Paris, and Oslo II Accords) and their consequences not just for the West Bank and the Gaza Strip (initially under the Labor and since late 1996 the Likud government of Israel) but also for *all* the people of Palestine during the interim phase and in the future.

The Oslo Declaration of Principles

After the 1991 Gulf War, it became clear to the United States, Israel, and the pro-Western Arab states that a new Middle East order would not be possible without resolution of the Palestine question. The imperial U.S. imperative for control of oil, markets, and strategic areas in the region dictated that.[5] For Israel, resolution of the Palestine problem would solve simultaneously both its domestic dilemma (the cost of the intifada) and its regional dilemma (by ending its political and economic isolation). Political settlement of the Palestinian question would also allow the Israeli economy to move in new and more favorable directions. As an Israeli analyst stated:

> For twenty years the occupied territories provided a partial substitute for the international market and a clandestine outlet to the Arab world. But the economic benefits of occupation—cheap and reliable labor supply and a captive market—were sharply reduced by the intifada. The costs of the occupation to the Israeli economy have come to overshadow its benefits. For these reasons, settling the conflict—meaning, in effect, decolonization of the occupied territories through accommodation with the PLO—became an economic necessity for Israel.[6]

And yet despite this strategic, political, and moral leverage and the internationally more sympathetic view of the Palestinians in the hands of the

PLO, 'Arafat, isolated and weakened as he and the PLO were, signed a controversial agreement that has jeopardized the destiny of the Palestinians as a people and their movement for independent national existence. The Oslo agreement was a surprise to everyone except the dozen or so Palestinian, Israeli, and Norwegian officials directly involved in the negotiations. Not even Israel's superpower mentor and ally, the United States, was aware of the negotiations or the content of the agreement. On the Palestinian side, reportedly only four, including 'Arafat, knew of the negotiations and of the content of the accords when they were initialed.

Notwithstanding Western official and media euphoria, the accords have met with a mixed reaction among both the Palestinian and Arab peoples and governments. Even PLO officials have been divided in their opinions. Political positions regarding the agreement and its consequences are highly polarized and have become hardened and more divisive over the years. The controversy over the original accords, the flawed course of their implementation, and political developments since the signing threaten, perhaps for the first time since 1948, to destroy the political unity of the Palestinian people.

Arguments in Support of the Declaration

Chairman 'Arafat and the faction of the PLO that is supportive of him claim that the Oslo Accords represent the best deal they could acquire under the unfortunate circumstances[7] (which of course were in large measure of their own making). They typically challenge their critics not with explanations but with a question that they consider to be the final and definitive comeback: "What is the alternative?" Further, they add that these "bad" Oslo Accords nevertheless will allow the Palestinians a toehold in their own homeland from which to carry on the struggle for self-determination, that it will put the Palestinians in a much better position to achieve statehood.[8] Finally, Arab proponents of the agreement say, any new reality is better than the old status quo.

For its part, Israel can claim that it achieved through this agreement all of its long-sought tactical and strategic goals. In a Knesset speech, Prime Minister Rabin boasted, for example, that the agreement "reflects the triumph of Zionism over all the Arabs." We will not review in detail the self-serving justifications 'Arafat and his faction make in support of the agreement. Nor will we examine Israel's reasons for backing the accords, or the claims presented disingenuously, in triumphalist and high-sounding moral terms by the U.S. government and media. Instead, we will give consideration only to those views of the more independent Palestinian and Arab observers and activists.

Among Palestinian intellectuals and activists, the best case for the declaration is made by Walid Khalidi, a Palestinian professor at Harvard University's Middle East Studies Center. In an address delivered to the annual meeting of the American-Arab Anti-Discrimination Committee in Washington, D.C., in 1995, Khalidi outlined the reasons for supporting not only 'Arafat but also the Declaration of Principles. After characterizing the declaration as "a Zionist composition in terminology, purpose and detail," Khalidi listed its accomplishments for the Palestinians: (1) recognition of the PLO by Israel; (2) recognition of the PLO by the United States; (3) establishment of the principle of Israeli withdrawal from occupied Palestinian land; (4) establishment of the principle of more than municipal elections—a central Palestinian authority emerging out of general elections that would have legislative powers and a strong police force; (5) establishment of the principle of a timetable for accomplishing the above; (6) establishment of the principle of the transfer of powers to the Palestinian authority; (7) establishment of the provision of funds by world powers.

A Palestinian participant in the multilateral part of the Madrid-inspired negotiations summarized this supportive sentiment as follows:

> Israel and the Palestinians have for the first time met, recognized each other, and formally and irrevocably . . . committed themselves to a commonly defined path of peace. . . . [The declaration allows] the first Palestinian entity on Palestinian soil run by the Palestinians themselves. Henceforth the question is not one of *whether* there will be a Palestinian entity, but of *what* is going to evolve out of Gaza/Jericho—its territorial extent, its political ethos, and its form of governance.[9]

In combination, according to Khalidi, these Israeli "concessions" create "new conditions and thus provide new opportunities provided we [Palestinians] know how to exploit them." Khalidi thus rejects opposing the declaration on the grounds that "bringing it down would bring about a [Palestinian] fratricidal bloodbath." Similarly, forcing 'Arafat out would play into Israel's already strong hands: "It would remove the symbol linking Palestinians inside Palestine with those in the diaspora. It would also initiate a [destructive] struggle for succession." Thus the only course of action now open to Palestinians is to support 'Arafat and the negotiated framework. "A sovereign Palestinian state in the 1967 frontiers with East Jerusalem as its capital," according to Khalidi, "is potentially realizable from the womb of Oslo." Khalidi does not elaborate on how to realize sovereignty, nor does he explain the contradiction in his assessment that such a "Zionist composition," as he calls the agreement, could lead to a sovereign Palestinian state, the idea of which is internationally supported except by "two states: Israel and the United States." But therein lies the dilemma.[10]

Khalidi and others do not provide any guidance as to how the balance of power between Israel and the Palestinians will or can be changed in order for the Palestinians to gain the sovereignty that Khalidi, too, poses as the central goal of their struggle. Actually, the balance of power since the signing of the agreement continues to shift more in favor of Israel. This is because the United States, other Western powers, and most Arab states and even the PLO itself have accepted the disabling constraints on the Palestinians spelled out in the agreement. Further, a process of normalization between Israel and a number of Arab states that started under the Labor government of Israel was stalled in the wake of Likud's election victory in 1996 and its intransigent rhetoric and actions.

Arguments Critical of the Declaration

Criticism by Palestinians, Arabs, and others of the various accords, 'Arafat's handling of Palestinian affairs, Israel's posture and actions, and the role of the United States and European governments are numerous. To begin with, the Declaration of Principles was signed by 'Arafat without public debate or approval and without official, legitimate PLO institutional consideration and ratification. By signing the agreement, 'Arafat squandered the efforts of a century of Palestinian struggle and sacrifice for national political rights—rights that have been repeatedly confirmed by international law and codified in numerous United Nations resolutions and by many other international forums.

In the White House signing ceremony in 1993, Prime Minister Rabin of Israel, as Said has observed, gave in effect the Palestinian speech, whereas:

> Arafat pronounced words that had all the flair of a rental agreement, words that made no mention of the extent of his people's suffering and loss. The Palestinians saw themselves characterized before the world as its now-repentant assailants—as if the thousands killed by Israel's bombing of refugee camps, hospitals, schools in Lebanon; its expulsion of eight hundred thousand people in 1948 (whose descendants now number about three million, many of them stateless refugees); the conquest of their land and property; its destruction of more than 400 Palestinian villages; the invasion of Lebanon; to say nothing of the ravages of twenty-six years of brutal military occupation—were reduced to the status of terrorism and violence to be renounced retrospectively or dropped from reference entirely. In return for exactly what?[11]

Basically, in return for recognition of the PLO (and Chairman 'Arafat himself) as representative of the Palestinians but not of the fundamental Palestinian rights.[12] By conceding or postponing so much, 'Arafat neither advanced the cause of the Palestinian people nor resolved the dilemma of its national liberation movement.

In the context of the post-Soviet and post–Gulf War era, 'Arafat did resolve the problem of his own diminished leadership and that of the financially strapped and sinking PLO. In effect, 'Arafat traded basic Palestinian rights to Israel in return for recognition of his own leadership and of the legitimate role of PLO, which his faction controls. As a result, 'Arafat, long vilified as an evil terrorist by the U.S. and Israeli media and politicians, was suddenly catapulted to center stage on the international scene, labeled by his former detractors as a "peacemaker," given extensive access to the media, and received enthusiastically at the White House and the U.S. Congress. Yet, as we noted above, only a few years earlier 'Arafat was denied entry into the United States when he was officially invited to address the United Nations General Assembly. Still, the euphoria orchestrated by the Clinton administration "only temporarily obscure[d] the truly astonishing proportions of the quite sudden Palestinian capitulation."[13]

What are those Palestinian rights that are threatened by the agreement? These include the internationally codified basic rights of self-determination and independent sovereign statehood, repatriation or compensation for both the 1948 and 1967 refugees, the restitution for the land and resources illegally confiscated in the West Bank and Gaza Strip, and reparations for the people of Palestine. If accorded these rights by Israel, then the issues of borders and (East) Jerusalem would no longer be matters for negotiation because the frontiers of Israel and the 1967 occupied territories are clear. What would remain to be negotiated would be the modalities of Israeli withdrawal, the restoration of Palestinian land, and the payments of compensations and reparations for resource and land confiscation (for 1948 Palestine and the long occupation of the West Bank and Gaza) by Israel; elimination of the illegal Israeli settlements; Israeli legal culpability for violations of individual human, civil, and property rights; and finally, establishment of security arrangements for both sides.

Instead of using international law and UN resolutions as the legal framework for negotiations, 'Arafat obviated the internationally codified Palestinian rights and turned them into mere negotiating positions. Indeed the Declaration of Principles is a document that is above the prevailing international legal conventions and is not based on any legal foundation. As Laura Drake notes: "The declaration of principles stands outside the bounds of international law and runs contrary to it, both in particular and as a whole, through its affirmation of the legitimacy of the most important facets of the occupation. At the same time it politically (not legally) superseded, indeed replaced, international law as the sole framework within which the Palestinian-Israeli conflict is being addressed."[14]

While the reference in the declaration to United Nations Security Council Resolutions 242 and 338 (the land-for-peace formula) is important, the document ignores many other UN resolutions. It disregards, for example, UN General Assembly Resolution 194, which confirms the collective right of return of Palestinian refugees to their homeland or compensation. The accord provides for the return of some individual refugees from the 1967 war, which it refers to as "displaced persons," but not for the 1948 refugees, who remain an item for the "final status" negotiations.[15] It should be clear, then, that the declaration excludes from its provisions the Palestinian refugees, nearly *two-thirds* (about 4.0 million) of all Palestinians who are outside the occupied territories.

All UN Security Council resolutions on Jerusalem are also ignored in the agreement.[16] The status of Jerusalem is placed on the agenda for future negotiations. Also elided are resolutions on illegal Israeli settlements in the occupied territories.[17] Transfer of population of the occupying power and settlement in conquered territories under occupation contravenes not only UN resolutions but also provisions of the fourth Geneva convention on war and occupation. By disregarding these internationally recognized violations and by consenting to the continuing presence of all Israeli settlements in the West Bank and Gaza Strip—presumably pending final negotiations—the PLO under 'Arafat validated and legitimized the illegal settlements and provided Israel with an illegal claim to the land. Indeed the derivative implementation agreement reached in Cairo on May 4, 1994 (the Cairo Accords), specifically excludes "settlements, settlers and settler-related resources (land and water) from any Palestinian jurisdiction, interference, or control."[18] With PLO acquiescence, then, the two Cairo Accords and the Oslo II agreement give Israel the ability to populate the region more heavily and expand the infrastructure of the settlements.

Accordingly, since the agreement was signed Israel has increased the number of settlers and confiscated more land not only for expanding settlements but also for building a network of superhighways interlinking the settlements with each other and with Israel proper while bypassing Palestinian towns.[19] These highways cut the West Bank in half along a north-south axis and further divide it along east-west axes into small quadrants or cantons connected only by existing antiquated roads and controlled by the Israeli army. These construction projects not only expropriate more Palestinian land (a loss estimated at 20 square kilometers, absorbing much actively tilled farmland) but build highways reserved strictly for Israeli use: "Its implementation will allow the [Israeli] army to control all the strategic sites and roads [after deployment]. . . . Vehicles of Palestinian residents will not be permitted to travel on the strategic routes."[20] Perhaps most extraordinary is that 'Arafat gave explicit consent to building these highways— roads on Palestinian land that Palestinians are not allowed to travel—in the implementation agreement (Oslo II) for the West Bank.

Much as disregarding international law and United Nations resolutions jeopardizes Palestinian rights, the grossest blunder committed by 'Arafat's PLO in the accords is its failure at the outset to extract from Israel an explicit recognition that the Palestinians are a people with the right to self-determination and that it is an *occupying power* in control of the Palestinian territories.

Such recognition would in turn mean that the accords would be nothing less than a declaration of principles governing the negotiations over the modalities, timing, and time frame for Israeli withdrawal from the occupied territories, the transfer of power to the PLO, the establishment of an independent sovereign Palestine, and the restitution of the rights of the refugees.

Until the Oslo Accords were signed, the international consensus supported the idea of a complete Israeli withdrawal from the occupied West Bank and Gaza Strip and the right of the Palestinians to establish an independent state in the evacuated areas. Article XXXI of the Oslo II Accords[21] states: "Neither party shall be deemed, by virtue of having entered into this agreement, to have renounced or waived any of its existing rights, claims, or positions." But as Norman Finkelstein argues, "Seemingly balanced, this provision actually signals a most crucial concession by the Palestinians. In effect, the PLO grants a legitimacy to Israel's pretense of possessing 'existing rights' in the West Bank and Gaza. . . . The broadly affirmed title of Palestinians to the occupied territories is now put on a par with the broadly denied title of Israel to them."[22] The PLO, then, consented to negotiate with Israel as a claimant to the land—as the Clinton administration had proposed earlier—rather than the occupier that it is.[23] In other words, after having recognized the existence of Israel and ceding to it the great majority of historic Palestine, the PLO accepted the idea that the remaining Palestinian land (the West Bank and Gaza Strip) is disputed territory, not occupied, and therefore negotiable. Related to that grand concession, the PLO failed to raise, much less include in the accords, an important provision: the question of Israeli compensation and *reparations* to the Palestinians. The Israelis not only destroyed Palestinian society and appropriated its lands, physical, economic, and private resources in 1948, but they also undermined the economies and appropriated the resources of the West Bank and Gaza Strip during twenty-nine years of occupation.

Another serious mistake 'Arafat and the PLO negotiators made is their failure to structure the negotiations and resultant agreements on the principle of equitable reciprocity. Remarkable as it may seem, the Oslo and derivative agreements do not provide for any reciprocity between the Palestinians and Israelis. Oslo II privileges Israelis in Palestinian areas and provides no reciprocity. The *Washington Post* noted:

> In no case, for example, will Palestinians have criminal jurisdiction over an Israeli citizen, and no Israeli may "be apprehended or placed in custody or prison by Palestinian authorities." There are no such limitations of Israeli power over Palestinians. Likewise, civil courts in the West Bank or Gaza may adjudicate disputes involving Israelis only with the consent of the Israeli party. Israelis will have guaranteed freedom of movement on every Palestinian road. Palestinian legislation deemed inconsistent with today's pact will be void. None of these provisions have a parallel on the other side.[24]

While Israel totally ignored the internationally codified rights of the Palestinians, including an independent state, the PLO recognized the legitimate (not merely de facto) existence of the state of Israel. 'Arafat was also forced to renounce PLO—not denounce mutual, reciprocal—violence and terrorism, and he promised to amend the PLO charter. In return, not one word in the accords obligates Israel to end its violence against the Palestinians in the occupied territories or its attacks on refugee camps in Lebanon and elsewhere or formally and officially to renounce its ambition to appropriate the land and resources of the West Bank and Gaza.

Although some Palestinian observers praised the linkage between interim and final status negotiations made in the Declaration of Principles, the agreement actually failed to specify the mechanism for progress from the interim to final status, nor did it outline, at a minimum, the final status outcome. It thus disenfranchised the Palestinian diaspora communities and intensified, at least for the five-year interim period, their legal and political limbo. For many of them, especially those in Lebanon and Libya, the situation has become even more precarious and dangerous as the agreement placed them in legal limbo in a hostile political environment.[25]

Last, the PLO leadership botched its negotiating strategy. The PLO consented to postpone "consideration" of the most pivotal and central issues—the refugees, Jerusalem, settlements, borders, sovereignty—until the so-called final status negotiations, three years after signing the first implementation agreement in 1994. Instead of achieving a single comprehensive agreement with Israel to be implemented in stages, it agreed to negotiate in stages and thus fragment further the implementation process. In the context of increasing Israeli strength and a commensurate decline in the Palestinian position, this strategy further disadvantaged the Palestinian people. In all agreements Israel has de facto veto power over issues of Palestinian sovereignty, internal affairs, and economics, whereas the Palestinian side has neither reciprocal rights, an equivalent veto, nor even the capacity to seek external binding arbitration.

Agreements on the Interim Period

The five-year limited autonomy provision embodied in the Declaration of Principles transferred specific and limited spheres (article VI.2 of the Oslo II Accord) to the Palestinian authority (education and culture, health, social welfare, direct taxation, and tourism). It permitted the establishment of a Palestinian police force and an elected council (the Palestinian Interim Self-Governing Authority, PISGA) whose size, powers, and responsibilities were negotiated in the third implementation agreement extending limited, autonomous self-rule to the West Bank in September 1995. Further, it allowed the creation of a group of specific economic authorities (electric, water, land, seaport, a monetary authority, and a Palestinian development bank). Israeli-Palestinian economic relations and structures of control are outlined in detail (article XI, annexes III and IV). In addition, some joint economic actions on a regional basis are set out in other protocols of economic cooperation (the Paris protocol, signed April 29, 1994, and the two Cairo Accords, signed May 4 and August 29, 1994).

The first of the Cairo Accords, formally called "Agreement on the Gaza Strip and Jericho Area," launched the five-year interim period. Israel withdrew from 62 percent of the Gaza Strip and from the small district of Jericho, a total area of only about 1 percent of historic Palestine (see Maps 7.1 and 7.2). But the agreement allows the Israeli army to move freely in the autonomous areas and to maintain therein military installations and zones. Thus while the Israeli military will presumably be "withdrawn" from Gaza and Jericho first, it will simply be redeployed in the rest of the West Bank "outside populated areas." "Ultimate internal" as well as "external" security and foreign relations are to remain with Israel. Further, the Cairo agreements provided Israel's military administration exclusive authority in "legislation, adjudication, policy execution, in addition to conferring responsibility for the exercise of these powers in conformity with the norms of international law."

In accordance with the Cairo I and II and Oslo II agreements, the entire corpus of Israeli military laws and orders remained in effect in the autonomous areas except for "such legislative, regulatory and other powers Israel may expressly grant." The PLO therefore accepted the legitimacy of a large number of military orders (subject to amendments by mutual agreement) used by Israel over the twenty-nine years of occupation not only to control the people but also to constrain its economic activity—conditions that, as we have shown in the previous chapter, exploited and de-developed the territories. In short, the Gaza Strip and the West Bank remained under the authority of the Israeli military occupation regime.

Palestinian attorney Mona Rishmawi points out that several important themes run through the agreements. These include Palestinian dependency rather than separation, shared Palestinian-Israeli sovereignty (over the West Bank and Gaza) rather than autonomy (much less independence), preferential treatment of Israelis in the territories, and Israeli impunity.[26] As Joel Singer, the Israeli legal architect of the accords, writes, the powers of the Palestinian Authority (PA; relabeled Palestinian National Authority, or PNA, by 'Arafat and the PLO) are limited to the specific spheres noted above, whereas all other matters not specifically delegated to it remain in the hands of the Israeli military government, which has not been dismantled.[27] Thus the jurisdictional, legislative, and executive powers of the Palestinian Authority and Legislative Council are subject to Israeli military laws and authority.

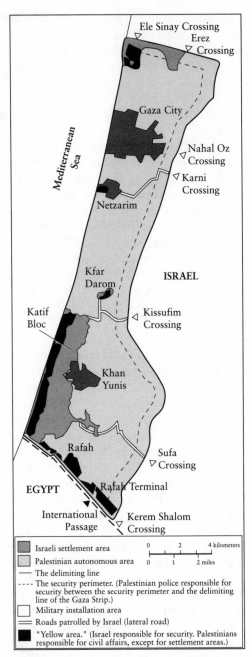

Ele Sinay Crossing
Erez
▽ Crossing

Gaza City

Mediterranean
Sea

▽ Nahal Oz
Crossing

▽ Karni
Crossing

Netzarim

Kfar
Darom

ISRAEL

Katif
Bloc

◁ Kissufim
Crossing

Khan
Yunis

Rafah

Sufa
▽ Crossing

EGYPT

Rafah Terminal

International
Passage

▽ Kerem Shalom
Crossing

■	Israeli settlement area
░	Palestinian autonomous area
—	The delimiting line
- - -	The security perimeter. (Palestinian police responsible for security between the security perimeter and the delimiting line of the Gaza Strip.)
□	Military installation area
═	Roads patrolled by Israel (lateral road)
▪	"Yellow area." (Israel responsible for security. Palestinians responsible for civil affairs, except for settlement areas.)

```
0        2        4 kilometers
0      1      2 miles
```

MAP 7.1   The Gaza Strip, After the Cairo Accords
SOURCE: *Settlements and Peace: The Problem of Jewish Colonization in Palestine*
(Washington, DC: Center for Policy Analysis on Palestine, 1995), 16.

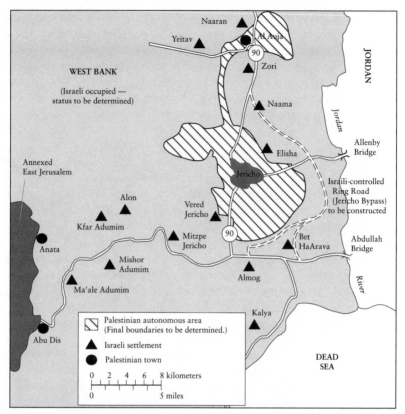

MAP 7.2   Jericho, West Bank, After the Cairo Accords
SOURCE: *Settlements and Peace: The Problem of Jewish Colonization in Palestine* (Washington, DC: Center for Policy Analysis on Palestine, 1995), 15.

It is remarkable that 'Arafat and the PLO consented to negotiate with Israel over purely internal Palestinian matters (the structure, size, powers, and responsibilities of the Palestinian Legislative Council and executive authority), thus allowing Israel at the very least to influence, if not control, internal Palestinian affairs. Israel and its military occupation government, not the Palestinian people, are then the legitimate source of the limited autonomy authority of the PA. The interim PA has no sovereignty over Palestinian territory—except over certain social and economic aspects of the Palestinian people's lives—and no basis to establish such independence in the future, as all its laws and activities are circumscribed and must be approved by Israel, pending "final status" negotiations. This lack of authority is ensured not only by the legal provisions and constraints noted above but also by the liaison, review, and other joint committees established by the Declaration of Principles to govern all the powers of the PA. These committees are supposed to manage through consensus all security, economic, and administrative issues and address differences in views between Israel and the PA. In effect, however, they provide Israel with veto power over all Palestinian decisions and any unapproved or undesirable (from its own point of view) Palestinian legislation or activity and are thus effective mechanisms for Israeli control of the PA and the territories.

The Oslo II Accords

The second-phase agreement, formally entitled the Israeli-Palestinian Interim Agreement on the West Bank and Gaza (labeled Oslo II by some and Taba by others), initialed on September 24, 1995, in Taba, Egypt, and signed in Washington, D.C., four days later, incorporated the Cairo and Paris agreements, superseded them, and reaffirmed the same themes and structures worked out between the two sides in the those earlier implementation agreements. The Oslo II agreement comprises over 400 pages setting forth the structure of future relations between Israel and the PLO and the Palestinians of the occupied territories, including security arrangements, legal matters, economic relations, elections and the structure and powers of the Palestinian governing body and Legislative Council (which supersedes the current PA), the transfer of powers of civil affairs, release of Palestinian prisoners, and Israeli-Palestinian cooperation.

Oslo II divides the West Bank into three zones. The first, or Area A—3 percent of the total area—is made up of the disconnected municipal areas of six Palestinian cities. Israeli troops there are to be redeployed over a period of not longer than six months to just beyond the near suburbs, or in a ring around the cities roughly 1 to 2 kilometers out, in stages from those in the north to the others in the south (except in the cities of Hebron, where the Israeli military will continue to be deployed over 25 percent of the heart of the city to "protect" the 400–450 Israeli settlers in the midst of about 150,000 Palestinians, and East Jerusalem). The second zone, or Area B— approximately 27 percent of the West Bank—covers the populated areas of about 450 villages and towns in the rural districts (where two-thirds of the West Bank Palestinians live). There the Israeli military and Palestinian police will "share" authority in joint patrols, the Palestinians overseeing civil affairs and maintaining public order inside the villages and the Israeli military having "overall security authority," including the right to intervene in those villages. The third, or Area C, incorporates existing and future Israeli military installations, settlements, and unpopulated (state land) areas—the rural land outside the towns, which makes up 70–73 percent of the land of the West Bank; this will remain under Israeli control. Israel was to redeploy from Area C (except from those Israeli military and other installations and settlements) over eighteen months in six-month intervals and yield only civil affairs to the new Palestinian Legislative Council. As of early 1997, it had not.

According to Rabin, Israel's prime minister at the time, the PA will gain full or shared "autonomous civil" control over 27 percent of the 5,600 square kilometers of the West Bank, including the 4 percent (200 square kilometers) of the major cities. It will gain control of public order and civilian affairs for 250,000 urban Palestinian residents, or 19 percent of the total population of the West Bank. The Legislative Council/Palestinian Authority will eventually acquire civil authority and responsibility for public order in Area B, which contains 69 percent of the Palestinian population; it will gain the same authority over Area C after eighteen months, although Israel retains the right to intervene militarily at its own discretion. Before the final publication of the text of the agreement, the principal Israeli negotiator, Foreign Minister Shimon Peres, was quoted by the Israeli press as having said: "The Deal kept the following in Israeli hands: 73% of the lands of the territories, 97% of security, and 80% of the water."[28]

In all, the PA gained limited civil autonomy over less than 4 percent of the area of historic Palestine. Israel redeployed from five of the major cities by January 1996. The newly elected right-wing Likud government of Binyamin Netanyahu at first stonewalled on implementing the redeployment agreement and, after the violent upheaval in September 1996 over the opening of the archaeological tunnel under Al-Haram al-Sharif, was intent on renegotiating the terms of withdrawal. After long-delayed and crisis-ridden negotiations, the Netanyahu government agreed to a redeployment of Israeli troops from Hebron, which was carried out on January 16, 1997. This action left the Israeli army in exclusive control of about 20 percent of the city (the heart of the old city and the whole eastern sector), where 400–450 Jewish settlers and more than 20,000 Palestinians reside. While the Palestinian officials defended the Hebron agreement, others criticized it not only for legitimizing the division of Hebron and the existing Israeli settlement at the city's core but also because "the gradual implementation of the interim agreements is accompanied by a gradual erosion of international resolutions that rendered legality and legitimacy to Palestinian national rights."[29]

The Netanyahu government failed to redeploy Israeli troops from Area B, as stipulated in Oslo II. But the Hebron agreement included a new accord on Israeli redeployment from Areas B and C. It established a revised timetable for the redeployment: "'twelve months from the implementation of the first phase of the future redeployments (the first week of March 1997) but no later than mid-1998.'"[30] The agreement did not, however, formally specify the location and extent of the territorial redeployment Israel was expected to initiate. In March 1997 Netanyahu's government offered to withdraw from 9 percent of the rural areas in Area B (amounting to only 2 percent of land not in Palestinian hands), but 'Arafat's PA rejected the proposal as insulting.

As in the Gaza Strip, the Israeli civil administration will be dissolved and the military administration will be "withdrawn" but will retain ultimate authority.[31] Chapter 3, article XVII, section 4.a of the Oslo II agreement specifically states that "Israel, through its military government, has the authority over areas that are not under the territorial jurisdiction of the Council, powers and responsibilities not transferred to the Council and Israelis." Thus "although no longer physically present, Israeli administration remains very much in evidence within the PA areas as well. Birth certificates, identity cards, driver licences, applications of various sorts, even Palestinian passports, must all be registered with and approved by the military government in order to attain official status."[32] The Israeli military forces will *not* leave the West Bank. Indeed, Israel will establish sixty-two *new* military bases there. It will retain control of entrances and exits to the cities and all the roads of the West Bank. Any Palestinian town or city can be sealed and village reentered at will by Israel.[33] All commercial traffic between the autonomy areas is controlled by Israel. "Thus, a truck carrying tomatoes from Gaza to the West Bank town of Nablus must stop at the border, unload onto an Israeli truck, then reload the produce onto a Palestinian truck upon entering Nablus."[34] Israeli settlers will travel on superhighways that will bypass Palestinian cities, towns, and villages and on all other roads, while Palestinians will be allowed to use only existing old roads and will have to stop frequently for security checks on all highways.

As Map 7.3 shows, Oslo II created a disconnected patchwork of zones of control and overlapping jurisdictions that violates the integrity not only of the West Bank but also the West Bank in relation to the Gaza Strip. And this violates article IV of the original Oslo Declaration of Principles, which declared the West Bank and Gaza Strip a "single territorial unit, whose integrity will be preserved during the interim period." However, this "textual claim that Oslo II preserves the 'integrity' of the West Bank and Gaza as a 'single territorial unit' . . . is mockingly belied by the map's yellow and brown blotches denoting relative degrees of Palestinian control awash in a sea of white denoting total Israeli sovereignty."[35] This patchwork of control is what some Palestinian commentators (including Hanan 'Ashrawi, the former spokeswoman of the Palestinian delegation to the Washington talks) called the "Swiss cheese" or "leopard spots" model of Israeli domination: The holes in the Swiss cheese or the spots on the leopard are the Palestinian-controlled areas, while the rest of the piece or body is dominated by Israel. As a result, Israeli action on the ground created "disabling discontinuity," as Said once called it, between the main Palestinian cities and subregions and thus undermined (if not completely eliminated) the foundation of a contiguous Palestinian patrimony.

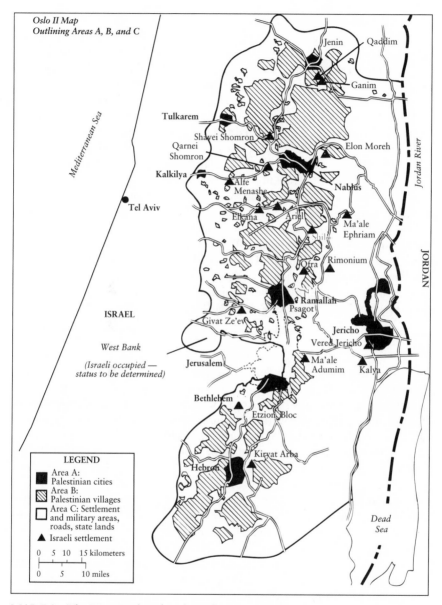

Oslo II Map
Outlining Areas A, B, and C

Mediterranean Sea

Jenin   Qaddim

Ganim

Tulkarem

Shavei Shomron

Qarnei
Shomron   Elon Moreh

Kalkilya

Alfe
Menashe   Nablus

Tel Aviv

Elkana   Ariel

Ma'ale
Ephriam

Shilo

Ofra   Rimonium

ISRAEL   Ramallah
                                   Psagot
Givat Ze'ev

Jericho
                              Vered Jericho
West Bank

(Israeli occupied —   Jerusalem   Ma'ale
status to be determined)   Adumim   Kalya

Bethlehem

Etzion Bloc

LEGEND
■ Area A:
  Palestinian cities
▨ Area B:
  Palestinian villages
□ Area C: Settlement
  and military areas,
  roads, state lands
▲ Israeli settlement

Kiryat Arba

Hebron

Jordan River

JORDAN

Dead
Sea

0 5 10 15 kilometers

0   5   10 miles

MAP 7.3   The West Bank, After the Oslo II Accords

SOURCE: *Report on Israeli Settlement in the Occupied Territories* 5, 6 (November 1995): 5.

Oslo II marked the final transformation of Israel's belligerent occupation over the Palestinian territories into legitimate rule with the official partnership of 'Arafat's PLO: "Oslo has allowed for the full rehabilitation of Israel. No longer condemned as an occupying power, Israel rather stands beyond reproach as a full-fledged peacemaker."[36] Israel achieved what it set out to do since at least the signing of the Camp David Accords with Egypt in 1978: It won limited functional civil autonomy for the Palestinians of the occupied territories and a legalized tight grip on the land, resources, economy, and security of the areas. How extremely limited geographically and politically this autonomy is became clear in the violent upheaval that followed the opening by Israel in September 1996 of an archaeological tunnel under the foundation of al-Haram al-Sharif in Jerusalem. Israel quickly imposed a tight blockade on Palestinian-inhabited and -controlled cities and on the jointly controlled towns and villages, banning movement between centers of Palestinian population. The blockade hardly eased after an emergency summit in Washington, D.C., called by President Clinton to address the bloody conflict. The incident demonstrated that Israel retains ultimate control over the lives of the Palestinians in the West Bank and Gaza Strip whenever it wishes to exercise its power.

The Legislative Council

The agreement provided for Palestinian elections for a Legislative Council to govern the West Bank and Gaza Strip and a separate but simultaneous ones to elect the head, or *ra'ees* (the Arabic term was used in the document in order to sidestep the controversy of calling the head of the authority "president," as the PLO wanted, or "chairman," as Israel demanded), of the executive authority after the completion of Israeli redeployment from the six Palestinian population centers. The council, according to the agreement, was to have eighty-two (a final figure of eighty-eight was accepted by Israel) representatives. Candidates for the council have to be approved by Israel; those "who commit or advocate racism" and "those who pursue the implementation of their aims by unlawful or non-democratic means" will be rejected.[37] A Palestinian living in Jerusalem cannot be a candidate unless he or she has a valid address in an area under the territorial jurisdiction of the PA.

The council is to have legislative powers over only the civil aspects of Palestinian life (forty designated areas) specifically authorized by Israel. Its legislative and executive powers are to be restricted to those areas and are subject to review and final approval by the Israeli authorities. Article XVIII, section 4.a states: "Legislation, including legislation which amends or abrogates existing laws or military orders, which exceeds the jurisdiction of the Council or which is otherwise inconsistent with the provisions of the [Declaration of Principles], this agreement, or of any other agreement that may be reached between the two sides during the interim period, shall have no effect and shall be void *ab initio*."

The council will have the right to establish courts, also as specified and authorized by Israel. But the Palestinian Authority may not conduct independent foreign relations (except in relation to economic aid agreements with donor countries and to cultural, scientific, and educational arrangements), control the Palestinian borders with Jordan or Egypt in addition to Israel, or control the air space or the electromagnetic spectrum for radio, television, and military communications (except for the bands authorized by Israel).[38] Israel is to retain control of natural resources in the West Bank and Gaza Strip, especially land and water, but it "promised" to increase the Palestinian share of West Bank water (the Palestinians' own water). The authority and powers of the Legislative Council and of the executive authority of the PA will remain in force until May 1999, when the final status agreement will presumably take effect. The Oslo II accord also provides for release of some categories of the thousands of Palestinian political prisoners still held in Israeli jails and concentration camps. Once again, as in the original Declaration of Principles, 'Arafat promised (in a separate letter to Rabin) to revoke from the PLO charter, the Palestinian national covenant, articles that question the legitimacy of Israel (referred to by the media as the articles calling for the destruction of Israel) and call for armed struggle to liberate Palestine; this would occur within two months of the inauguration of the elected Legislative Council.

Most important decisions affecting Palestinian life in the West Bank and Gaza Strip will be subject to a Joint Civil Affairs Coordination and Cooperation Committee, which, along with a large number of subcommittees, will operate by consensus and thus control Palestinian decisions.[39] Although this arrangement may seem fair, consensus gives Israel an effective veto power over all aspects of Palestinian life, including such important issues as water use, planning and zoning of land, custody of abandoned land, control of archaeological and religious sites, and the electric power grid.[40]

The Cairo and Oslo II Accords explicitly absolve Israel of any legal liability during its long (since 1967), brutal occupation of the Palestinian territories. Chapter 3, article XX, section 1.a of the Oslo II accord states:

> The transfer of power and responsibilities from the Israeli military government and its civil administration to the Council, as detailed in Annex III, includes all related rights, liabilities and obligations arising with regard to acts or omissions which occurred prior to such transfer. Israel will cease to bear any financial responsibility regarding such acts or omissions and the Council will bear all financial responsibility for these and for its own functioning.

Describing the terms of the provision that transferred the financial liability to the PLO/PA, Naseer Aruri notes: "These provisions are tantamount to a blanket amnesty granted to the perpetrator by the victim, even prior to a peace agreement and while the victim has no assurance that his legal subordination can be altered under this agreement."[41]

Economic Control

The best illustration of continuing Israeli control and subordination of the Palestinian territories of the West Bank and Gaza Strip is the economic provisions of the Declaration of Principles and the subsequent protocols and accords. These agreements cover trade, taxes, banking, labor, insurance, tourism, and so on, delineating the specific, limited spheres of autonomous Palestinian decisionmaking and the rules and conditions governing the future relationship between Israel and the autonomous Palestinian areas.[42] Specifically, the Paris protocols establish an Israeli-Palestinian customs union, demanded by Israel in order to sustain the level of its import tariffs, trade standards, import-licensing regulations, and protected industries. The varied accords keep open Palestinian markets to Israel but restrict (through quotas and other measures) Palestinian exports to Israel's market. In none of these protocols is there any equity or reciprocity in trade or economic relations between the two entities. Israel thus dictated the terms of all the agreements. In explaining the asymmetrical outcome, Israeli foreign minister Peres said, "In some ways we are negotiating with ourselves."[43]

Nonetheless, George Abed, a Palestinian economist and an official of the International Monetary Fund (IMF), is cautiously optimistic about the Paris Accords. Especially in three economic areas, the accords grant elements of sovereignty "more favorable to the Palestinians than one would have expected from a careful reading of the [Declaration of Principles]."[44] Abed identifies the following positive terms: endorsement of the principle of free trade between Israel and the territories, the PA's right to define its own tariff and import policy over a large number of commodities, and the right to establish its own monetary authority, including the powers to license and regulate banks and manage financial reserves.

Despite such a positive interpretation of the economic agreements, most observers note that through all the provisions, Israel had set both the framework and the constraints on the growth and development of the Palestinian economy for the duration of the interim period and in the future as well as Israeli-Palestinian-Arab economic relations beyond the interim period. The clear consequences of these circumscribing agreements is to keep the Palestinian economy "completely within Israel's economic orbit . . . in a tight economic embrace,"[45] subordinate and dependent, its market captive and open to Israeli goods and its labor cheap, unorganized, controlled, and exploitable by the more powerful and state-supported economy of Israel.

After having de-developed Gaza,[46] underdeveloped the West Bank, confiscated vast economic assets (especially land and water), and proletarianized the Palestinians during its long occupation,[47] Israel has gained, through these protocols structures of controls that would reproduce the predatory colonial economic relations with the Palestinian territories in both the interim period and beyond. The agreement reached on water use should suffice as an example. Although Israel granted the Palestinians a small increment in water to meet immediate domestic use, water allocation is governed by "existing quantities of utilization" (Oslo II Accord, annex III, appendix I, article 40). Average annual quantities give Israelis 80 percent and Palestinians 20 percent of their own West Bank water, a per capita allotment four times greater for the Israelis than for the Palestinians. And as Finkelstein observes, "Prospects after the interim period seem even dimmer. Although Israel does 'recognize Palestinian water rights in the West Bank,' these rights do *not* include the 'ownership of water,' which will be subject to the permanent status negotiations. . . . Indeed, Israel claims legal title to most of the West Bank water on the basis of 'historic usage.'"[48]

Israel thus divested itself of the burden and cost of the social welfare institutions and of the expense and function of a policing government in the territories but retained control of the Palestinian economy and matters directly related to economic development and growth. In other words, Israel retained the capacity to exploit the natural resources and the labor of the territories, obstruct their independent economic development and expansion, restrict the mobility of their goods, and direct the structure of their investments. And through all those structures of control Israel has also retained the capacity to use punitive economic measures against the autonomous Palestinian territories. Accordingly, the viability of sustained Palestinian economic growth and development under continuing Israeli dominion is nearly impossible.

Some Israeli intellectuals have described the "peace process" and the Israeli-Palestinian economic accords as "that of the old familiar transition known as 'decolonization.'"[49] As Yoav Peled remarks, "the outcome of decolonization has usually been neo-colonialism—that is, continued domination by the former rulers through mostly economic rather than mostly political means."[50] But in the case of the occupied West Bank and Gaza Strip, the Israelis, with the collaboration of the PLO, have set up a legitimized structure of domination over the Palestinian territories based on both economic *and* political means. Instead of decolonization, Israel has repackaged and extended old-fashioned predatory colonialism over the West Bank and Gaza Strip. It has excluded from all arrangements the diaspora Palestinians except for the well-capitalized expatriate bourgeoisie, which in turn is being encouraged by 'Arafat's PA to invest in the territories and in joint ventures on the border areas.

Other Israeli intellectuals are, we believe, more accurate in their assessment of the accords. Benvenisti, former deputy mayor of Jerusalem and a long-term analyst of Israeli colonization of the West Bank whose works have been published in a series of research reports, notes: "A perusal of hundreds of the Agreement's pages can leave no doubt who is the winner and the loser in this deal. By seeing through all the lofty phraseology, all the deliberate disinformation, hundreds of pettifogging sections, sub-sections, appendices and protocols, one can hardly not recognize that Israeli victory was absolute and Palestinian defeat abject."[51] Indeed an American scholar of the Arab and Palestinian-Israeli conflicts systematically compared the structure and terms of the Palestinian accords to the documents that created the Bantustans of South Africa and concluded "that Oslo is a veritable carbon copy of the Transkei (Bantustan) constitution."[52] Benvenisti draws the same comparison: "It goes without saying that 'cooperation' based on the current power relationship is no more than permanent Israeli domination in disguise, and the Palestinian self-rule is merely a euphemism for Bantustanization."[53]

The West Bank and Gaza Strip are resource-poor territories, and any hope for developing these areas and solving the enormous economic and social problems of the people there depends largely on the skills of the people and of its political leadership, the active economic and institutional support of the world community, and independence from Israel's suffocating embrace. It is unfortunate that except for the skills of the people, none of the other conditions is present.

Under the auspices of the PLO, Yusif Sayigh, a Palestinian economist and planner, headed a team that produced a comprehensive and ambitious plan for the development of an independent national Palestinian economy. The Palestinian Development Programme (PDP), as it was called, was based on the assumptions that the Palestinian Authority will "exercise the right of economic and social decision-making and the implementation of related decisions . . . that the Palestinians displaced in 1967 (numbering with descendants 650,000) are entitled to return to their homes . . . that the whole area of Palestine occupied in 1967 would return to Palestinian control."[54] The objectives of the PDP were important and noteworthy given the long-term, destructive, and predatory occupation. They included not only the "normal" objectives of development, such as the creation of (a vast number) of employment opportunities, extensive housing, improving and expanding the economic and social infrastructure, and the satisfaction of basic human needs, but also measures for the correction of distortions, dislocations, imbalances, and bottlenecks of the current (occupied) economy.[55] The PDP's point of departure was the development of the economic capacity to satisfy the internal demand for basic human needs in contrast to the currently more fashionable economic emphasis on open markets, deregulation, privatization, foreign investment, and export orientation.[56] Under this development plan, the role of the future Palestinian government in overcoming the Israeli-instituted economic deformities would be central.

Neither the assumptions of the PDP nor its proposals were promoted by the PLO or considered by Israel, the international donors, the World Bank, or the IMF. Indeed, despite World Bank exhortations that the Palestinians need to shift from "almost complete dependence on Israel, as at present, to interdependence with a range of economies, including Israel," the Oslo Accords and derivative agreements tie and subordinate the Palestinian economy to Israel's. "One consequence of this is that the Israeli enforced rupture in Palestinian trading relationships with Jordan and other Arab countries [during the occupation] will persist, dimming Palestinian prospects for future economic coordination with the large Arab market, as well as Palestinian prospects for balanced economic development in the broad community of nations."[57] The World Bank[58] and privately produced[59] development plans all support the basic thrust of the Israel-PLO economic accords, stress continued Palestinian economic linkage (and therefore dependence on and subordination) to Israel, stress open markets and export orientation,[60] and encourage ties to Israel-centered regional projects—policies that are not conducive to independent socioeconomic development and growth.

The protocols—with the active support of the Western powers and international institutions (the IMF, the World Bank, and the Paris Club)—allow Israel to establish the bases for using the captive and dependent Palestinian economy as a bridge through which to penetrate Arab markets (beginning with free trade and joint ventures and ending with economic integration).[61] There are, however, serious problems with the structure of these accords. The Israeli-Palestinian and Israeli-Jordanian economic agreements "give Israel a great deal of power in influencing the institutional framework of Arab economies, while allowing the Arabs no say in the economic affairs of Israel."[62] In any case, along with the Israeli-Palestinian arrangements the multilateral or regional economic plans and projects envision nothing more than a subordinate, exploitable, and dependent Palestinian economy, at best an Israeli colonial possession, at worst a Palestinian Bantustan.

The Politics of Implementation: Contradictions on the Ground

Since 1993 Israel and the PLO have negotiated several major agreements of implementation—the Paris protocols, the two Cairo Accords, and Oslo II. All negotiations were problematic, tortuous, long, and bitter. As a result, the implementation of the agreements was repeatedly delayed much beyond the time frame specified in the Declaration of Principles. The establishment of the PA in Gaza and Jericho was delayed nine months beyond the "withdrawal" date—actually the redeployment—of Israeli military forces. "Early empowerment" in the West Bank was to compensate for the delays of extending the second phase. Similarly, the redeployment from populated centers (except Jerusalem and Hebron) in the West Bank and the elections for the governing Legislative Council were also postponed for over a year. The redeployments from the six West Bank cities, however, were swiftly carried out by Israel in December just before the rescheduled date (January 1996) of the Palestinian Legislative Council elections in a transparent effort to boost 'Arafat's political popularity. This political objective was accomplished, as we see in a later section.

The disagreements between the PLO/PA and Israel derived from their differing conceptions of and aspirations for the resolution of the conflict and for the final, permanent status of the occupied territories. Israel's narrow, security-driven interpretation of the agreements as well as its bad-faith actions also came into play. The PLO/PA want to establish in the interim period the measures and conditions on the ground for eventual sovereign statehood, but Israel acts to prohibit that eventuality. The differing interpretations of the Declaration of Principles led to bitter arguments between the two parties, but the dismally uneven balance of power between them typically produced disadvantageous and humiliating protocols and accords for the Palestinians, agreements that have cast grave doubts on the possibility of extracting a sovereign Palestinian state out of, to use Khalidi's words again, "the womb of Oslo."

The PLO/PA repeatedly demonstrated, we believe, its incapacity for extricating from the Israelis a just and dignified solution to the Palestine question. This conclusion is all the more justified as we consider the developments on the ground. Despite the August 1992 assurances by Prime Minister Rabin of a "settlement freeze," Israel under the Labor Party increased the settler population by over 10 percent and confiscated more than 20 new square miles of Palestinian land (57 square miles if we include "closed military areas" and "nature reserves") between September 1993 and the May 1996 elections. "In annual terms (2.3 percent) this is higher than the 2.1 percent of the occupied territories which Israel has confiscated, on average, each year since 1967."[63] While the declaration specifies that neither party should do anything on the ground to prejudice the outcome of the "final status" negotiations, Israel continued to confiscate land and populate settlements, especially in and around East Jerusalem. "Since 1967, some 38,000 housing units have been built for Jews, with government subsidies, on confiscated Arab land, and a further 20,000 units are under construction or 'in the pipeline.'"[64] In addition to annexing the Palestinian side of the city of Jerusalem, with its 1967 municipal borders, Israel also annexed 24.5 square miles of the West Bank to create "greater Jerusalem," where much of the construction of new housing[65] has taken place since the signing of the Oslo Accords. And in Bethlehem, near Jerusalem, land confiscation increased in 1996 as Israel created a Jewish settlement.[66] According to Prime Minister Netanyahu, under the Labor government the number of Israeli settlers in the occupied territories grew from 96,000 to 145,000 from 1992 to 1996.[67]

Since the signing of the Oslo Accords, Israel's violations of the human rights of Palestinians in the West Bank continued. They included administrative arrests; ill treatment and torture of detainees; extrajudicial killings by undercover military units (death squads), especially in the Gaza Strip; house demolitions; more severe restrictions of movement (than even before); and varied forms of collective punishment.[68] Also since the signing of the Declaration of Principles, Israel closed the borders between the West Bank and Gaza Strip and Israel to Palestinian workers at least six times, ostensibly for security reasons.[69]

Each closure reduced the number of Palestinian workers allowed to seek employment in Israel. Indeed prior to the intifada, 180,000 Palestinian workers (including 80,000 from Gaza) were employed in Israel. After the 1991 Gulf War, the number declined to 100,000 workers. Following the signing of the declaration, the repeated closures of the borders reduced the number further—to a total of 45,000, with 16,000 from Gaza in 1995. In 1996, as we detail in Chapter 8, the "internal closure" in the wake of the suicide bombings by Hamas militants practically shut down all labor movement by Palestinians into Israel. This policy of reducing Palestinian labor employed in Israel and replacing it with foreign guest workers (by October 1994 Israel had imported around 59,000 foreign workers from Eastern Europe and Southeast Asia), what Rabin called "separation" of the two populations, is justified by security concerns. According to the Israeli peace bloc, however, "separation is the exact Hebrew translation for the South African term Apartheid."[70]

Unemployment in the Gaza Strip reached 50 percent and in the West Bank around 35 percent,[71] and much higher (at least 60 percent and 40 percent, respectively) in 1996 because of near total border closure. As a result of this policy and the commensurate inability of the Palestinian Authority to relieve the problem of unemployment in the West Bank and Gaza Strip, income from labor has declined steeply, from $920 million in 1992 to $400 million in 1994.[72] The figure continued to drop through 1996. The repeated and increasingly longer closure of the Israeli borders to Palestinian goods and labor, the lack of or delay in investment by international donors, and the reluctance of private diaspora Palestinian and Arab capital to enter the unstable environment of the autonomous areas all led to dramatic economic downturn since the Oslo Accords were signed.

The small additions of workers employed in the PLO/PA (as bureaucrats and police and security forces of the authority), most of whom were repatriates with 'Arafat, did not solve the local dilemma of unemployment and economic hardship. Since the establishment of the Palestinian Authority in July 1994, the cost of living has soared by 25 percent and living standards have fallen precipitously.[73] In an opinion poll taken after the creation of the authority, 44 percent of respondents believed their standard of living had declined, 45 percent reported no change, and only 10 percent said their situations had improved.[74] Thus in place of the economic improvement expected by the Palestinians and promised by all parties promoting and justifying the peace process and the Declaration of Principles, the Palestinian population, especially of the Gaza Strip, has experienced actual pauperization—an obvious source of social and political discontent. An illustration of this discontent is the riots that broke out at the Erez (Gaza Strip–Israel) border crossing in July 1994 between Palestinian workers seeking employment in Israel and the Israeli army; two workers were killed and over seventy-five wounded. The riots were characterized by the media as "a battle for a loaf of bread" by an "enraged proletariat."[75]

Only a minuscule amount out of the total of $2.4 billion promised by international donors over a five-year period trickled into the autonomous territories in the first year: less than $60 million of the $570 million pledged for that year. The Palestinian Authority spent the bulk on salaries, especially of the police and the security forces, and not on development projects. International aid has not arrived either in the requisite and promised amounts or invested in projects that would directly benefit the people of the autonomous and occupied territories. Such failure is typically blamed on both the donors and the PLO/PA. 'Arafat has reportedly been unwilling (and perhaps unable) to establish a financial agency infused with sufficient transparency and accountability to satisfy the demands of the donors and managers (the World Bank and the IMF) of the aid funds. Further, he has refused to delegate any authority over financial matters and has set up competing agencies for economic planning and development (the Palestine Economic Council for Development and Reconstruction, PECDAR, actually proposed and established by the World Bank and the IMF in order to create accountability and transparency, and the Planning Ministry), neither of which has clear authority.

All this has fostered confusion and reluctance on the part of donors. These same factors may also have kept the wealthy diaspora Palestinian bourgeoisie from investing in the autonomous areas. "The Palestinian business community has failed its people. . . . They established PADICO (the Palestine Development and Investment Co., Ltd.), that has done so very little until today. . . . The big fish among them are taking the back seat as Arafat's business associates make deals with the Israeli business community, with little reward for the Palestinian economy."[76] George Abed identifies the bottlenecks in the PA administration:

Little has been done to elaborate the legal and regulatory environment necessary to stimulate private investment, and the development program that could
have begun to be implemented as early as October or November (1993) has
not gotten off the ground . . . in the critical area of fiscal administration—that
is the management of public finances—which simply collapsed with the departure of the Israelis due to total Palestinian lack of preparation. Tax revenues
could not be collected and public expenditures could not be effected.[77]

'Arafat was reluctant "to permit the establishment of modern institutions
with the kinds of built-in checks and balances, controls, audits, etc. that
would undermine his personal control."[78] As a result, two years after the
establishment of the PA, few modern, credible institutions of governance
have been established in the PA by the 'Arafat regime. Instead, the old "in-
flated and creaky political machinery of the PLO has been grafted onto a
feeble governmental structure in the [West Bank and Gaza] and, with most
of the available funds redirected to satisfy this machinery's considerable
consumption appetite, the PA has transformed itself into a non-productive,
rentier regime clearly standing in the way of genuine social and economic
development."[79]

The dilemma of proletarianized, jobless Palestinians is not limited to the
individuals themselves; it impacts as well on their large dependent families
and the whole of society. Long used and exploited by Israel during the occupation, Palestinian workers became both a political and security liability
for Israel following the 1991 Gulf War. This fact coincided with the process
of liberalization and privatization of Israel's evolving economy, which was
therefore developing different labor needs. Accordingly, after that war Israel embarked on a new policy, intensified and rationalized since the various accords were signed. It hoped that the new strategy would solve the
two dilemmas simultaneously: replacing cheap Palestinian workers inside
Israel with foreign guest workers and enlarging the productive base, especially of the Gaza Strip, in order to "restore [Palestinian] consumption capacity without encouraging competitive development."[80]

Israel began to facilitate the development of "industrial parks" on the
northern border area of the Gaza Strip modeled on the *maquiladora* parks
of northern Mexico. Since then, but more so since the signing of the Declaration of Principles, "Israel has been quietly building 'pockets of infrastructure' adjacent to the territories. Capital will be invested by joint Israeli,
Palestinian and foreign ventures, but tied to the main contractors in Israel
and directed to labor-intensive industries such as food-processing, textiles
and furniture-making."[81] The main attraction for such investments is the
large mass of available and un-unionized Palestinian labor in Gaza, which
can be paid far lower wages than Israeli workers, receive few or no benefits,
and can be used or discarded as the Israeli market demands. In the West
Bank, "in a settlement just outside Jenin, one of the towns covered by Oslo

II, Israel recently approved an expansion project for five new factories, with land provided free to investors, who also got substantial tax breaks."[82]

These maquiladora-type factories and the absence of serious economic investment on the ground in the autonomous territories are far from the development plans of both Yusif Sayigh and the World Bank. In general, as Abed concluded, "The Palestinian economy would essentially remain severely handicapped and underdeveloped, its infrastructure in a state of disrepair, or at least inadequacy, unemployment high and growth rates minimal. . . . Given the dim prospects for the emigration of Palestinians to anywhere, social tension (will likely) rise in the [West Bank and Gaza Strip] as a result of the absence of tangible improvements in the life of the population."[83] Without immediate, rapid, deliberate, and systematic action by the PA to break the crippling shackles constraining West Bank and Gaza Strip economic development, the Palestinian territories are doomed to the status of being fragmented Bantustans for Israel, at least for the short and medium terms.

The Palestinian Authority: Structure and Dynamics

In 1995, a year after his triumphant entry into Gaza, 'Arafat was a diminished leader, a "faded icon [who] is asked what's he done lately."[84] What 'Arafat has done lately is to build a power base, an authoritarian regime composed of an extensive bureaucracy, security courts, and competing and overlapping security apparatuses and a police force, all under his individual control. The police force alone numbered over 19,000 by the end of the first year in the Gaza Strip, while only 6,000 teachers were employed for a population of nearly 1 million. The police force reached 30,000 members when the PA authority was extended into the six cities of the West Bank in late 1995.[85] Although more than twenty-five ministries were created, power is extraordinarily centralized in the hands of 'Arafat, who has tight control of all decisions, large and small. "There is the sheer lack of accountability of a movement which, at last count, placed no less than 60 semi-governmental functions under the sole prerogative of one man. Arafat decides on everything from the modalities of donors' aid programmes to who in Gaza receives a telephone line."[86] He is executive administrator, patron, legislator, and judge all in one.

Despite the election of a Legislative Council in January 1996, the 'Arafat regime made no credible attempt to establish the basic modern system of governance: separated, rationalized, and accountable executive, legislative, and judicial institutions. A proposed constitutional charter 'Arafat commissioned before the Gaza and Jericho First Agreement for the Palestinian Interim Self-Governing Authority—a draft Basic Law[87]—had been revised five times by early 1997 and has not yet been adopted officially. The unsuccessful constitutional attempt had provisions that were too strong on civil liberties and on separation of powers for 'Arafat's blessing, according to two analysts.[88]

'Arafat's autocratic style is helped by a chaotic legal structure composed of contradictory, inconsistent, and incomplete statutes and orders left over from the Ottoman and Egyptian rule in the Gaza Strip, Jordanian rule in the West Bank, and the Israeli military occupation. In the absence of a clear regulatory and legal environment and an established rule of law, the Palestinian people are at the mercy and whim of those in charge. No formal legal recourse for the population exists. As a result, corruption, malfeasance, and arbitrariness are widespread in the unrationalized institutions of the PA.[89] This is hardly an environment conducive to political stability (except perhaps through heavy-handed repression), the mobilization of the strongly needed expatriate private Palestinian capital and expert talent, or provision of aid by international donors. It is, however, a political situation that seems to meet with the Israeli and U.S. governments' approval, as the 'Arafat regime is capable of stifling dissent to the "peace accords" and suppressing resistance (violent, as in the case of Hamas and Al-Jihad al-Islami, or nonviolent) to the continuing occupation. Indeed these two governments have rarely if ever condemned the PA's record on human rights violations documented by Middle East Watch, Amnesty International, and other groups.

The evolving character of the increasingly autocratic 'Arafat regime of the PLO/PA depends on two factors. The first is the nature of the powers of the Legislative Council and of the electoral system that Israel and the PLO/PA have agreed to, and the second is the attitude and action of the Palestinian people subject to that regime. Of great significance to democracy in the Palestinian territories are the jurisdiction and powers of the Legislative Council and its relationship to the executive authority. We have seen above that the Legislative Council's powers are severely circumscribed. It is clear from the Oslo II agreement (and the regime-inspired proposal for a Palestinian constitution) that the head of the executive authority is simultaneously the head of the council, indicating little separation of political powers. Indeed the elected council and 'Arafat, as the elected president of the executive authority, clashed a number of times over questions of policy, powers and procedures, and substance. And given Israel's security-driven interpretation of the Declaration of Principles and successive agreements, 'Arafat's regime was allowed to create a strong internal security system that acts as an enforcer. Externally dependent, an authoritarian regime has emerged in place in the West Bank and Gaza Strip.

In our view, democracy, civil liberties, and the rule of law are not possible in a limited autonomous rentier regime under occupation. Sovereignty and independence are prerequisites for democracy. Further, the nature of the electoral system, the conduct of elections, and the political culture are also important conditions of democracy. Elsewhere we have argued that electoral regimes embedded in authoritarian state structures, as exist currently in many Middle Eastern countries, are not equivalent to democracy.[90] Mouin Rabbani, an analyst of Palestinian politics, describes 'Arafat's regime as an "elected autocracy [where] democracy is permitted only to the extent it respects autocracy."[91]

Democracy is not merely a process but also a political culture where the rule of law prevails and a climate of public confidence and trust in the political process and the leaders exists. Thomas Melia delineated four general indicators of the political climate that are conducive to meaningful elections and democracy: the separation of the state and the military; the degree of political openness and tolerance of opposition to the state; status and rights of women; and the integrity of public institutions.[92] The latter should operate independently of the state but lend credibility and legitimacy to state action and policy because they diffuse political power throughout society and stabilize the political process. We believe another factor, not identified by Melia, is a politically conscious and active constituency that perceives the political process as fair, clean (uncorrupt), and rational.

On all these indicators, the 'Arafat regime is dismally deficient. The regime does not separate the state from the military (police); it *is* the military. It has combined the Palestinian civil, political, and military societies into one—a sure formula for authoritarianism. It is not open and tolerates neither opposition nor a free press, and it intimidates and suppresses critics. Indeed it has been trying to co-opt and control, if not eliminate, all opposition, secular and Islamic. Similar to political tactics it used in Lebanon, 'Arafat's regime has established parties and movements in the autonomous areas as cosmetic opposition that not only parallels and delegitimizes the actual opposition groups but also confuses the public. The regime's security courts are secretive, have violated Palestinian human rights, and have created a climate of fear, not of tolerance and the rule of law. Further, a number of Palestinian women's groups have expressed their grievances concerning the authority's shortcomings, including those in the drafts of the Basic Law, on women's issues.

Accordingly, after decades of struggle and an intense and exhausting intifada, the Palestinian people inside the occupied territories (and in the diaspora) have become alienated and cynical about the conduct of Palestinian politics and the current leadership. The chances the Palestinians of the West Bank and Gaza Strip will have to build democracy in their society will depend on the social forces arrayed for and against it. It is quite clear that 'Arafat and the PA have greater interest in state building and monopoly of the public political, economic, and social institutions than in establishing democratic, transparent, and accountable public agencies subject to the rule of law and guaranteeing an independent civil society. The Palestinian nongovernmental organizations (NGOs), which, as we have seen earlier, played such a pivotal role in the intifada, have been starved financially and manipulated by 'Arafat's PA regime.[93] In all the above, 'Arafat is supported not only by the extensive security apparatuses but also by his political faction, the repatriated and local Fateh operatives who are anxious to reap the rewards (in jobs, positions, contracts, etc.) of loyalty to 'Arafat and the Oslo agreements.

Generally speaking, three important and powerful social classes—the landlords, the mercantile capitalists, and the national and emergent comprador bourgeoisie—have not typically been enamored of democracy unless it serves their interests and is under their control. In the West Bank and Gaza Strip, 'Arafat has ingratiated himself with these important and economically powerful social groups, and they have become supportive of his regime. Many members of these classes ran for the Legislative Council elections and failed. But many old and new PA cabinet appointees, for example, are members of the families and clans belonging to these elite social classes.[94] There seems to be an emergent ruling class, an alliance of local elites with 'Arafat's security officers, especially those of the police forces and senior PA administrators. This alliance is much more interested in order, stability, and business deals than it is in democracy and the rule of law. Such a ruling social configuration is essentially antidemocratic. In short, by Melia's criteria, 'Arafat's PA regime is far from democratic; the political climate he has created and the powerful social forces already in control are not conducive to developing genuine Palestinian democracy in the near term.

The Legislative Council Elections

Contradictory and dubious results of many an opinion poll taken in the West Bank and Gaza Strip do not provide a clear, reliable, or valid picture of the pattern and distribution of political attitudes or popular sentiment of the people. Nevertheless, they do indicate West Bank and Gaza Strip Palestinian willingness to participate in the election process[95] and also ambiguous and dissatisfied feelings toward the PA, which has so far failed them. The urgency and intensity of the debates and the accompanying sentiments, not limited to the West Bank and Gaza Strip Palestinians, reflected a "widely held conviction that free and democratic elections would make up for many of the deficiencies of the Oslo and Cairo agreements."[96]

Eighty-six percent of the sample in a preelection survey supported direct elections of all Legislative Council members, while 9 percent supported appointment of council members by the PLO and an additional 3 percent preferred their appointment by the various political groups in a manner similar to the way in which the PNC was formed.[97] Various people and political groups saw elections in the West Bank and Gaza Strip as having one of three principal functions: first, lending legitimacy to the Oslo Accords and derivative agreements; second, providing legitimacy to the Palestinian Authority, a central act of nation building; third, an important means to trigger democracy and the process of democratization. Many others, however, saw the elections merely as they believed 'Arafat viewed them: a procedure to legitimize and consolidate his power and policies.

The significant thing about the Palestinian elections in January 20, 1996, is that they were held at all and without serious interference from Israel or the PA. The tacit coalition of opposition groups (Hamas, the PFLP, the DFLP, and other lesser ones) deliberately boycotted the elections, a form of protest and opposition to the 'Arafat regime and the terms of the Declaration of Principles. They fielded no official candidates. And yet despite calls from all these opposition groups to all Palestinians in the West Bank and Gaza Strip to boycott the elections, official results certified that 86 percent of the Gaza Strip and 68 percent of the West Bank electorate went to the polls, an impressive turnout that showed the degree of political mobilization of the Palestinians and "a clear commitment by the Palestinian people to the democratic state and the rule of law," as Hanan 'Ashrawi, one of the candidates, said.[98] The difference between turnouts in the Gaza Strip and the West Bank was caused by Israeli intimidation (documented by international and local election observers, including former U.S. president Jimmy Carter) in Jerusalem (where only 40 percent of the eligible voters ventured to the polling stations) and Hebron (where the ratio was also low). Although charges and allegations of fraud and vote-rigging were made by several candidates and observers,[99] overall the elections were judged fair and clean.

In a parallel election, 'Arafat, running for the post of president of the Palestinian Authority, won by 87.1 percent of the vote against the only opponent, West Bank social activist and political leader Samiha Khalil. The structure and dynamics of the campaign (including control of the media and the press) guaranteed an 'Arafat victory. Nonetheless, the result of the presidential election was a personal vindication of 'Arafat. It showed that despite all the criticism and bitter denouncements, 'Arafat was still the symbol of Palestinian nationalism, at least for the majority of the West Bank and Gaza Strip Palestinians.

> Despite giving him low marks for his management of the negotiations with Israel (30.7 percent said it was good while 26 percent said it was poor) and of the Palestinian economy (24.3 good, 22.5 poor), and his method of decision-making (36.5 good, 22.5 poor)—Arafat was still considered by 60.9 percent of the sample to be a symbol of the Palestinian cause. . . . 39.4 considered him the most trustworthy Palestinian personality.[100]

As everyone expected, the Legislative Council emerged from the election campaign with a strong majority in support of 'Arafat. Fifty of the eighty-eight seats were won by Fateh or Fateh-supported candidates; one was won by the Fida Party, a pro-'Arafat and a pro-Oslo splinter group from the DFLP; and the remaining thirty-seven by independents. Other parties that ran candidates, especially the PPP, won no seats at all. Of the independents a few were known to be supporters of the opposition groups but had not received their blessing. Many were critics of the Declaration of Principles and 'Arafat's leadership style. They included especially Haidar 'Abdul-Shafi, leader of the Palestinian negotiating team in the Washington rounds of Israeli-Palestinian negotiations; Hanan 'Ashrawi, spokeswoman of that delegation (later "co-opted" to become minister of higher education in the 'Arafat cabinet); 'Abdul-Jawad Saleh, a former nationalist mayor of the West Bank town of El-Bireh (who also joined the cabinet); and others. Some "independent" Fateh candidates ran and won in spite of being stricken from the official Fateh list created by 'Arafat; one of the most prominent was Salah Ta'amari. The elected Fateh representatives are a mix of traditional local business and intifada leaders and repatriated activists with nationalist credentials, though most were loyal to 'Arafat.

In short, the majority of the candidates who won election to the Legislative Council were 'Arafat clients, loyalists, and pro-Oslo people. And thus, "The election campaign . . . ended with a deepening feeling of an emerging ruling elite, whose economic interests are tied with Israel."[101] Since its election, the Legislative Council took several important steps toward its internal organization. It elected a speaker, adopted certain standing orders, formed committees, and elected committee officers. However, the legal standing of the council's work and the physical surroundings in which it operates are not auspicious: Israel challenges council members' immunity, and the facility in which the council meets is totally inadequate. Council members and committees have no staffs and therefore have no assistance in the drafting or reviewing legislation. The council also has no independent resource base or research unit. Its hope to act as an independent branch of the Palestinian government, to practice an oversight function of the Palestinian Authority, and to control the PA budget are constantly challenged and rejected by both Israel and 'Arafat, the head of the executive branch of the PA. Lacking a budget to run its own affairs, the council is seeking the assistance of the Palestinian NGOs in its efforts to conduct its formal business. Power is not shared in the PA; it (and the purse strings) is in the hands of the ra'ees, 'Arafat.

Irrespective of the election results, reports of popular attitudes toward the regime are indicative of a reemergent political culture long asserted and valued by the Palestinian national liberation movement and the intifada. For example, an article in the *New York Times* assessing the one-year anniversary of self-rule quoted a Nablus citizen as saying: "I pay taxes, and I have the right to ask the authority how it teaches my children, what kind of hospital treatment it gives and whether it provides social security." Another was quoted as saying, "You can't feed your children with a flag or a picture of Arafat. . . . The flag is in my heart, but the priority now is factories, hospitals, better schools. If Arafat performs well, I'll elect him. If he doesn't, he won't get my vote."[102] As we discussed in the previous chapter, Palestinians, long under oppressive occupation, had built up a social structure made up of a network of autonomous social service organizations both as an alternative to the unresponsive and deliberately negligent Israeli authorities and as a means to mobilize opposition to the occupation. This rich experience and the political culture associated with it are bound to reemerge at some conjuncture renewed and vigorous, but henceforth possibly in opposition to the 'Arafat regime's autocracy as well as Israeli repression.

'Arafat probably won a legislature that would act in support of his pro-Oslo policies or at least serve as a rubber stamp for his regime; this, along with his control of the purse and the absence of a basic law or constitution, undoubtedly reinforces his authoritarian rule. It is, after all, constrained physically by the occupation authorities and legally by Israel under the terms of the Oslo agreements, as we have noted above. Nonetheless, we believe that in the long term the process of elections—even under such dubious conditions—will eventually plant the seeds of the idea of democracy, which will become the legitimate mechanism for effecting change in both leaders and policy. While this may become true in the future for the Palestinians inside the West Bank and Gaza Strip, it will not change the disenfranchisement of the diaspora communities.

The election of a Legislative Council in the West Bank and Gaza Strip neither created a legitimate independent body that could regulate the lives and affairs of a segment of the Palestinians still in their homeland under nominal autonomy nor produced a mechanism for effecting a just and lasting solution to the Palestine problem. If anything, it set up a dualistic structure of Palestinian representation and complicated the relationship between those in the homeland and those in the diaspora. "Today, Palestine is firmly locked in a transitional phase. It is trapped between its two councils: the Legislative Council and the Palestine National Council. . . . Both are far from being the legitimate representatives of the Palestinian people as a whole."[103] The elections of a Legislative Council may have affirmed and contributed further to the fragmentation of the Palestinian people and its destiny and thus to the political crisis that enveloped it as a result of the Oslo Accords.

Palestinian Public Opinion

Two years after the signing of the Declaration of Principles, one year after the establishment of the PA in the Gaza Strip and the Jericho area and shortly after the signing of the Oslo II agreement, Palestinian political discourse shifted focus. The emphasis went from an exclusive concern with the declaration, its shortcomings, legitimacy, and meaning for the Palestinian people to a political debate centered more on three broad areas: the content of the subsequent agreements, the process and the results of the implementation of those agreements, and the performance in office of 'Arafat and the PA.

The gist of the debate is that the agreements on implementation of the declaration and the results on the ground tended to confirm the position of those who were initially skeptical, critical, or opposed to the agreement.[104] The subsequent agreements were humiliating; the resultant arrangements and the treatment of Palestinians by the Israelis clearly betrayed Israel's bad faith in negotiations and its lack of desire for a historic resolution of the conflict and reconciliation with its victims: The process was carried out in the manner, style, and tone of a victor dictating terms to the vanquished. Palestinian negotiators were negotiating under the assumption that Israel is an occupying power engaged in transferring eventual sovereignty to them, while Israel was dealing with Palestinian "empowerment" at best as an internal civil rights issue without any rationale for sovereignty—hence the repeated disagreements, delays, and breakdowns and the feelings of discouragement, frustration, and even rancor on the part of the negotiators and the Palestinian public. These sentiments increased further as a result of the procedures of implementation Israel chose to pursue, and further still after the ascension to power of the right-wing Likud Party, with its more deliberately hostile and demeaning conduct toward the Palestinians.

Such feelings were reinforced by other actions taken by the Israelis after the signing of the Oslo Accords. In summary, they include continuing land confiscation, expansion of settlements, and persisting draconian security measures and violations of Palestinian human rights. For example, after initial release of about 5,000 out of 11,000 Palestinian political prisoners, Israel administratively detained 2,000 more after the signing of the Declaration of Principles, bringing the 1995 total to 6,000–7,000. A hunger strike declared by the political prisoners in Israeli jails in the summer of 1995 elicited tremendous popular support from the Palestinian public—including confrontations with the Israeli military reminiscent of the days of the intifada—and forced the hands of the Palestinian and Israeli authorities to hurry the long-delayed second-phase negotiations for the expansion of Palestinian autonomy into the West Bank, the redeployment of the Israeli military, the holding of Palestinian elections, and other issues. But the Oslo II agreements allowed the release only of certain categories and a limited number of political prisoners, and barely a week after Oslo II was signed, Israel held up the promised release of all women prisoners.

In the new Palestinian political discourse, the performance of the PA has come under extensive criticism from opponents and supporters alike. Such criticism of the whole regime typically derived from 'Arafat's autocratic style. Critics point to the improvised and chaotic manner in which the PA assumed power; established the economic and financial authorities to receive and manage aid from international donors (who are still skeptical of these authorities and commissions); and created the governing, legal, and social service institutions and its failure to build a political culture of tolerance and respect for the rule of law, human rights, and democracy.

The manner of appointments to the PA also came under criticism because its basis has been favoritism, loyalty to 'Arafat, and nepotism. Power as a result has flowed to Fateh loyalists, 'Arafat's political faction and power base, and local economic and social elites. Such appointments, critics believe, are counter to the goals of the efficiency and effectiveness of the PA institutions and to rational and accountable institution building in general, practices so desperately needed to make the transition to self-rule and eventual statehood. The highly centralized, personalized, and indeed arbitrary manner of decisionmaking by 'Arafat and his loyal and dependent lieutenants is encouraged by the absence in the PA of any mechanisms of oversight or checks and balances on its power and therefore by the lack of accountability on its part. The official oversight institutions of the PLO have been deliberately marginalized by 'Arafat and have therefore become nonfunctioning. Furthermore, a minority in the elected Legislative Council has shown the will to be critical and ask for accountability and oversight but has not yet been able to institutionalize that important role.

Polls in 1995 indicate that West Bank and Gaza Strip Palestinians have little faith in the integrity and performance of the PA's public institutions. Only 40.5 percent of those sampled indicated as "good" their evaluation of the PA, 48 percent said the same of health institutions, 29 percent of PEC-DAR, 39 percent of the Preventive Security Agency, and 23 percent of the tax authority. The educational institutions, however, were given a vote of confidence of 65 percent.[105] The "popularity" of the police fell from 72 percent in 1994 to 50 percent in 1995.[106]

The security forces of the PA, which received a hero's welcome upon their entry into the Gaza Strip, have since lost much respect and have become suspect to many Gazans and other Palestinians. In the years since the establishment of the PA, 'Arafat set up several (the reported number is nine) secret service security agencies, all of which compete with one another in the service of 'Arafat's regime and intimidate his opponents. The Palestinian security forces have been accused of human rights violations, political repression, and abuse of power.[107] They have suppressed political dissent and opposition to the occupation, not only by independent secular critics in the press and elsewhere (for example, Edward Said's books have been confiscated from West Bank bookstores and their sale prohibited everywhere) but also by Hamas and Al-Jihad al-Islami, particularly after the acts of violence they perpetrated against Israeli military and civilian targets. Clashes between Palestinian security forces and Hamas supporters led to thirteen fatalities and scores of casualties in a major confrontation in November 1994. "At the heart of relations between the PNA and the opposition lies an essential contradiction: The authority is bound ... to provide security and not to endanger the Israeli presence, while the opposition insists on its legitimate right to combat the remaining forms of occupation and resist the continued existence of Israeli settlements."[108]

'Arafat's PA regime and the Palestinian security forces are typically viewed by Palestinians inside the territories and in the diaspora as little more than Israel's enforcers and collaborators with the Israeli occupation authorities.[109] In October 1996, in the wake of the tunnel opening along the foundations of Al-Haram al-Sharif, Palestinian police returned fire against Israeli soldiers and border guards and were rehabilitated in the eyes of the populace. "The most immediate gain for the PLO leader in the confrontations' aftermath has been his enhanced stature among Palestinians. Polls ... show that 51 percent believe he has strengthened his leadership and a colossal 85 percent approve of the PNA security forces. This is quite a reversal from August (1996), when Palestinians took to the streets in Nablus and Tulkarm to protest at 'Arafat's governance in the self-rule areas and at his security forces' brutality."[110] It is clear that the popularity and legitimacy of 'Arafat and the Palestinian security forces are bound directly to their nationalist credentials in standing up to Israel.

The popularity and legitimacy of 'Arafat and his regime fluctuate greatly. The initial euphoria upon his return faded rapidly and reached a low point after the November 1994 clashes between the regime's security forces and Hamas activists and supporters. These clashes and the continuing conflict with the Islamic and other secular nationalist groups derive not only from 'Arafat's security commitment to Israel but also from the regime's efforts to establish exclusive authority over the West Bank cities and the Gaza Strip. The intra-Palestinian power struggle in the Gaza Strip coincided with Israeli and U.S. pressure on 'Arafat to control, if not eliminate, violent resistance to Israeli occupation.

Instead of establishing a "national authority," as a 1974 PNC resolution specified, to mobilize the Palestinians to carry on the struggle to end the occupation, 'Arafat's regime sought to end the resistance and act as Israel's enforcer/protector in the autonomous and occupied territories. Thus the Palestinian political division over the Declaration of Principles quickly emerged in the Gaza Strip between 'Arafat's PA regime on one side and Hamas and Al-Jihad al-Islami (who together oppose the Oslo Accords and who reportedly command 20–40 percent of popular support) on the other. In the years since the Oslo Accords were signed, this created political tension and instability in the autonomous areas, as did the severe economic crisis and autocracy of 'Arafat himself. This conflict intensified to a climax in early 1996 in the wake of the February-March Islamic suicide bombings inside Israel. Arafat's swift repression (roundup and incarceration of suspected Islamic activists) earned him praise from Israel and the United States but failed to solve both the social and political dilemmas he faces, which may have become more problematic with the election of a right-wing (Likud) government in Israel in May 1996. The PA conflict with Hamas and the other Islamic groups has pushed many activists underground.

The secular opposition is fragmented and ineffective, as is the reportedly large "silent majority" of discontented, passive, and politically alienated people. Yet the public is decidedly happy with the process of ending the oppressive Israeli occupation, even though the end result of the flawed peace process does not favor Palestinian independence. Opinion polling in the West Bank and Gaza has recently emerged as a regular activity of two research and opinion polling organizations: the Center for Palestine Research and Studies (CPRS) of Nablus and the Jerusalem Media and Communication Center (JMCC). The polls they conduct are often methodologically flawed, and therefore the validity of their survey results is somewhat dubious.[111] Their survey instruments are too crudely constructed to warrant anything greater than cautious inferences to the entire population. That said, the polls indicate declining support for the peace process: from the 65 percent support for the negotiations in 1993, to 39 percent in December 1994 and 14 percent in February 1995. Indeed in the latter poll 81 percent supported halting the negotiations altogether.[112]

Little if any celebration accompanied or followed the signing of the Oslo II agreement, despite the promise of Israeli military "withdrawal" from the six major cities of the West Bank and the end of direct Israeli intervention in everyday Palestinian life. But there was jubilation in the six cities when the Israeli military finally withdrew from them in late 1995, one month before the Palestinian elections. The West Bank and Gaza Strip reactions to Oslo II were characterized by journalists as full of anger and frozen rage over the lack of achievements but mixed with feelings of resignation to the defeat. Given Israel's overwhelming power, many felt that there was no alternative. In the diaspora, Palestinian outrage at and animosity toward the dismal agreement were aggravated by political impotence. The statement of a Fateh leader in Hebron perhaps sums up the widespread sentiment: "The settlers in Hebron live in five buildings. . . . With this agreement, they get a district. What we get is the occupation."[113]

The Oslo Accords have become less the path to independence, a better life, and dignity for the Palestinians of the occupied territories and more the core of the contemporary Palestinian dilemma, especially with the victory of the Israeli right-wing coalition in the 1996 elections. As one resident of the village of Nahaleen in the West Bank said in an interview in the wake of the tunnel upheaval:

But take it [the Oslo Accord] and compare it to our hopes the day that the two great leaders shook hands, . . . the day we believed we would have safe land, a good economy, and unquestioned dignity, and our own state. No, the big situation is worse since Oslo. Mix the truth of our lives with the hopes of our lives and you get an emotion that smells to me like gunpowder, which, as you know, can explode.

We have been hoping for an entire generation. The younger people here have never felt the wings of freedom. They know only the burden of humiliation.[114]

Notes

1. See N. G. Finkelstein, "Whither the 'Peace Process'?" paper presented at Georgetown and American Universities, Washington, D.C., April 24 and 25, 1996, 21.

2. N. Aruri, *The Obstruction of Peace: The U.S., Israel and the Palestinians* (Monroe, ME: Common Courage Press, 1995), 193–218; see also H. Ashrawi, *This Side of Peace* (New York: Simon and Schuster, 1995).

3. E. Said, *The Politics of Dispossession: The Struggle for Palestinian Self-Determination, 1969–1994* (New York: Pantheon, 1994), xxxii.

4. See B. Gellman, "West Bank Pact Eases Way for Palestinian Statehood: New Entity Still Limited by Israel—'For Now,'" *Washington Post,* September 27, 1995, A1.

5. S. K. Farsoun, "Palestine and America's Imperial Imperative," *Middle East International,* August 7, 1992, 16–17.

6. See Y. Peled, "From Zionism to Capitalism," *Middle East Report* 194/195 (May-June/July-August 1995): 13; see also S. Cohen, "Justice in Transition," *Middle East Report* 194/195 (May-June/July-August 1995): 2–5.

7. In a speech at the Jabalya refugee camp in the Gaza Strip upon his return to Palestinian soil in accordance with the Oslo agreements, Arafat said, "I know many of you here think Oslo is a bad agreement. It is a bad agreement. But it's the best we can get in the worst situation." Quotation in G. Usher, *Palestine in Crisis: The Struggle for Peace and Political Independence* (London: Pluto Press, 1995), 1.

8. These kinds of arguments were typically used by black African leaders who consented to the creation of Bantustans in South Africa's apartheid system. See Finkelstein, "Whither the 'Peace Process'?" 16–17, 19–20.

9. A. Khalidi, "The Palestinians: Current Dilemmas, Future Challenges," *Journal of Palestinian Studies* 24, 2 (Winter 1995): 6–7 (emphasis in the original).

10. This conclusion of no alternative but to support the declaration is also reached by another prominent Arab intellectual, Samir Amin. Although Amin criticizes the accords extensively, stating that "the Declaration of Principles was no more than a plan for establishing a Bantustan in the former Israeli occupied territories," he concludes: "History informs us that agreements evolve and are subject to interpretation, and that their contents depend on developments in the balance of power. The Declaration of Principles is no exception. Therefore I urge that we concentrate our struggle on a sincere, sober and serious implementation of the agree-

ment which would force the Israelis to make necessary concessions." S. Amin, "After Gaza and Jericho: The New Palestinian-Middle Eastern Problem," *Beirut Review* 8 (Fall 1994): 115.

11. Said, *The Politics of Dispossession*, xxxvii.

12. See B. Dajani, "The September 1993 Israeli-PLO Documents: A Textual Analysis," *Journal of Palestine Studies* 23, 3 (Spring 1994): 5–23.

13. Said, *The Politics of Dispossession*, xxxiv.

14. L. Drake, "Between the Lines: A Textual Analysis of the Gaza-Jericho Agreement," *Arab Studies Quarterly* 16, 4 (Fall 1994): 32.

15. Several tens of thousands of Palestinians did return to Gaza and Jericho largely as part of Arafat's PA regime security forces and bureaucracy. A few of those deported by Israel during the occupation (such as Hanna Nasir, president of Bir Zeit University, and Abdul-Jawad Saleh, former mayor of the town of El-Bireh) were allowed to return to the West Bank.

16. These include UN Security Council Resolutions 252, 267, 271, 298, 476, and 474. Explicit reference to Jerusalem is also frequently made in resolutions affirming the illegality of Israeli settlements in the occupied territories.

17. See UN Security Council Resolutions 446 and 452.

18. G. Aronson, "Historic Israeli-PLO Accord Leaves Settlements Intact," *Report on Israeli Settlement in the Occupied Territories* 4, 4 (July 1994): 1.

19. It appears that Israel's vision and intent is to preserve the settlements connected and under Israeli jurisdiction in the "final status" arrangements. See G. Aronson, "'Final Status' to Preserve Settlements," *Report on Israeli Settlement in the Occupied Territories* 5, 3 (May 1995): 1.

20. Quoting a senior Israeli military officer. G. Aronson, "New Roads Create an Asphalt Revolution," *Report on Israeli Settlement in the Occupied Territories* 5, 3 (May 1995): 7.

21. Israel, Ministry of Foreign Affairs, *Israeli-Palestinian Interim Agreement on the West Bank and Gaza Strip*, September 28, 1995, accessible on the Internet through the Israeli Information Service Gopher, ask@israel-info.gov.il.

22. Finkelstein, "Whither the 'Peace Process'?" 2.

23. See C. Maksoud, "Peace Process or Puppet Show?" *Foreign Policy* 100 (Fall 1995): 117–124.

24. B. Gellman, "Israel, Palestinians Reach Accord on Pullout, Elections in West Bank," *Washington Post*, September 25, 1995, A16.

25. UN officials in Lebanon said that the "situation [for Palestinians] is deteriorating. The Lebanese government is limiting our operations for purely political reasons. The [UNRWA] agency is not allowed to build new clinics and schools." J. Lancaster, "Palestinian Refugees in Lebanon Find Little Hope in Peace," *Washington Post*, July 8, 1995, A16. See also media reports on the expulsion of Palestinians (numbering an estimated 30,000) from Libya; G. Henderson, "Mass Expulsions Continue," *Middle East International*, October 6, 1995, 9. Lebanon, where many of the expellees are legal refugees, has placed severe and disabling restrictions on their return.

26. M. Rishmawi, "The Actions of the Palestinian Authority Under the Gaza/Jericho Agreements," in *The Palestine National Authority: A Critical Appraisal* (Washington, DC: Center for Policy Analysis on Palestine, 1995), 3–8.

27. J. Singer, "The Declaration of Principles on Interim Self-Government Arrangements, Some Legal Aspects," *Justice* (February 1994): 4–13.

28. D. Makofsky et al, "PM: Oslo II Is 'Blow to Greater Israel,'" *Jerusalem Post,* week ending August 26, 1995.

29. L. Andoni, "Hebron—The Danger of a Precedent," *Middle East International,* February 7, 1997, 17.

30. "Hebron Agreement Sets Timetable for Further Redeployment," *Report on Israeli Settlement in the Occupied Territories* 7, 2 (March-April 1997): 7.

31. Chapter 1, article I, section 5 of the agreement.

32. M. Rabbani, "Palestinian Authority, Israeli Rule: From Transitional to Permanent Arrangement," *Middle East Report* 201 (October-December 1996): 5.

33. E. W. Said, "The Mirage of Peace," *Nation,* October 16, 1995, 413.

34. Ibid.

35. Finkelstein, "Whither the 'Peace Process'?" 4.

36. Ibid., 13.

37. Annex II, article III, section 2. As Said notes, "No parallel proscription on the Israeli side" exists that prohibits Israeli racists from being Knesset members; *The Mirage of Peace,* 414.

38. See annex II, "Protocol Concerning Elections," of the Oslo II agreement, 75–92.

39. See annex III, "Protocol Concerning Civil Affairs"; annex V, "Protocol on Economic Relations"; and annex VI, "Protocol Concerning Israeli-Palestinian Programs," of the Oslo II agreement.

40. See the text of the agreement's annexes.

41. Article IX.1.a–b of the August 24, 1994, agreement, also known as "early empowerment." For a fuller discussion, see N. H. Aruri, "Early Empowerment: The Burden not the Responsibility," *Journal of Palestine Studies* 24, 2 (Winter 1995): 37.

42. S. Elmusa and M. El-Jaafari, "Power and Trade: The Israeli-Palestinian Economic Protocol," *Journal of Palestine Studies* 24, 2 (Winter 1995): 14–32.

43. *Ha-Aretz,* February 14, 1994. Cited in E. Murphy, "Stacking the Deck: The Economics of the Israel-PLO Accords," *Middle East Report* 194/195 (May-June/July August 1995): 38.

44. G. Abed, "Developing the Palestinian Economy," *Journal of Palestine Studies* 23, 4 (Summer 1994): 41–51.

45. R. Owen, "Establishing a Viable Palestinian Economy," *Beirut Review* 8 (Fall 1994): 48–49.

46. S. Roy, *The Gaza Strip: The Political Economy of De-development* (Washington, DC: Institute for Palestine Studies, 1995).

47. G. T. Abed, *The Palestinian Economy: Studies in Development Under Prolonged Occupation* (London: Routledge, 1988). See also World Bank, *Developing the Occupied Territories: An Investment in Peace,* 7 volumes (Washington, DC: World Bank, 1993).

48. Finkelstein, "Whither the 'Peace Process'?" 5. See also Chomsky, *World Orders: Old and New* (New York: Columbia University Press, 1994), 210, cited in ibid.

49. Cohen, "Justice in Transition," 4. See also Peled, "From Zionism to Capitalism," 14.

50. Peled, "From Zionism to Capitalism," 14.

51. M. Benvenisti, "An Agreement of Surrender," *Ha-Aretz,* May 12, 1994. Translated by I. Shahak in *From the Hebrew Press,* June 1994.

52. Finkelstein, "Whither the 'Peace Process'?" 15.

53. M. Benvenisti, *Intimate Enemies: Jews and Arabs in a Shared Land* (Berkeley: University of California Press, 1995), 232.

54. Y. Sayigh, *Programme for Development of the Palestinian National Economy for the Years 1994–2000, Executive Summary* (Tunis: PLO, 1993), 20–21.

55. Ibid., 23–24.

56. See a summary of the Palestinian debate on this issue in Usher, *Palestine in Crisis*, 36–40.

57. M. Jenin, "Economic Wedlock: Israel to Keep Upper Hand," *Breaking the Siege, the Newsletter of the Middle East Justice Network* 6, 2 (June-July 1994): 6.

58. World Bank, *Developing the Occupied Territories*.

59. Institute for Social and Economic Policy in the Middle East, John F. Kennedy School of Government, Harvard University, *Securing Peace in the Middle East: Project on Economic Transition* (Cambridge: Harvard University Press, 1993).

60. See W. Freedmen, "An Export Promotion Scheme for Palestine," *Graduate Review* 1, 6 (1994): 34–45.

61. Usher, *Palestine in Crisis*, 41. See also E. H. Tuma, "The Peace Negotiations, Economic Cooperation and Stability in the Middle East," *Beirut Review* 8 (Fall 1994): 3–20; and I. Diwan and M. Walton, "Palestine Between Israel and Jordan: The Economics of an Uneasy Triangle," *Beirut Review* 8 (Fall 1994): 21–44.

62. Tuma, "The Peace Negotiations, Economic Cooperation and Stability in the Middle East," 6.

63. P. Ogram, "Settlement Expansion," *Middle East Report* 194/195 (May-June/July-August 1995): 17.

64. Ibid.

65. See "Construction Escalates," *Report on Israeli Settlement in the Occupied Territories* 5, 5 (September 1995): 5.

66. M. Meehan, "Land Confiscations Increase as Israelis Impose Jewish Settlement on Bethlehem," *Washington Report on Middle East Affairs* 15, 2 (July 1996): 13–14.

67. D. Neff, "Netanyahu Gets the Royal Treatment in Washington," *Middle East International,* July 19, 1996, 5.

68. B'Tselem (Israeli Information Center for Human Rights in the Occupied Territories), September and November 1994 reports. See also Human Rights Watch/Middle East, *Torture and Ill-Treatment: Israel's Interrogation of Palestinians from the Occupied Territories* (New York: Human Rights Watch, 1994).

69. The closures occurred especially after the suicide bombings and other attacks inside Israel and in the occupied territories.

70. See their statement in *Ha-Aretz*, February 2, 1995. Cited in G. Usher, "Palestinian Trade Unions and the Struggle for Independence," *Middle East Report* 194/195 (May-June/July-August 1995): 21.

71. G. Abed, "The Political Economy of Development in the West Bank and Gaza Strip," paper delivered at the Workshop on Strategic Visions for the Middle East and North Africa, Economic Research Forum, Gammarth, Tunisia, June 9–11, 1995, 7.

72. Usher, *Palestine in Crisis*, 57.

73. Usher, "Palestinian Trade Unions and the Struggle for Independence," 21. See also B. Gellman, quoting the Norwegian social scientists (who were pivotal to the Oslo connection) and General Danny Rothschild, recently retired as military coor-

dinator for the occupied territories; "Palestinians Vent Their Ire over Arafat," *Washington Post,* February 27, 1995, A15.

74. Center for Palestine Research and Studies, Nablus (West Bank), "Palestinian Public Opinion Poll III," September 1995.

75. Gellman, "Palestinians Vent Their Ire over Arafat," A15.

76. "Palestinian Business: A Failure," *Issues: Perspectives on Middle East and World Affairs* 5, 1 (June 1996): 1, 13.

77. Abed, "Developing the Palestinian Economy," 44.

78. Ibid., 45.

79. Abed, "The Political Economy of Development in the West Bank and Gaza Strip," 3.

80. Murphy, "Stacking the Deck," 36.

81. Usher, "Palestinian Trade Unions and the Struggle for Independence," 21.

82. Said, "The Mirage of Peace," 416.

83. Abed, "The Political Economy of Development in the West Bank and Gaza Strip," 7–8.

84. J. Greenberg, "Faded Icon Is Asked What's He Done Lately," *New York Times,* June 30, 1995, A1.

85. G. Usher, "The Politics of Internal Security in Palestine," *Middle East International,* March 1, 1996, 15.

86. Usher, *Palestine in Crisis,* 81.

87. Ibid., 44–46.

88. N. H. Aruri and J. J. Carroll, "A New Palestinian Charter," *Journal of Palestine Studies* 23 , 4 (Summer 1994): 5–17.

89. Abed, "The Political Economy of Development in the West Bank and Gaza Strip."

90. See S. K. Farsoun and C. Zacharia, "Class, Economic Change and Democratization in the Arab World," in R. Brynen, B. Korany, and P. Noble, eds., *Political Liberalization and Democratization in the Arab World,* vol. 1 (Boulder, CO: Lynne Rienner, 1995), 261–280.

91. Rabbani, "Palestinian Authority, Israeli Rule," 6.

92. T. Melia, "Elections in Emerging Democracies," in *Palestinian Elections* (Washington, DC: Center for Policy Analysis on Palestine, 1995): 12–17.

93. "A Story of Manipulation, Containing the Palestinian NGOs," *Issues: Perspectives on Middle East and World Affairs* 5, 1 (June 1996): 2–3, 14.

94. R. Brynen, "The Dynamics of Palestinian Elite Formation," *Journal of Palestine Studies* 24, 3 (Spring 1995): 31–43.

95. C. E. Zacharia, "Public Opinions of West Bank and Gaza Strip Palestinians Toward Participation in Elections," photocopy, American University, Washington, DC, 1995, 10.

96. Abu-Amr, "Report from Palestine," 46.

97. Center for Policy Analysis on Palestine (Washington, DC), *Newsletter* 3, 5 (Fall 1995): 5.

98. Quoted in G. Usher, "The Message from the Palestinian Electorate," *Middle East International,* February 2, 1996, 3.

99. K. M. Amaryeh, "Allegations of Vote-rigging," *Middle East International,* February 2, 1996, 4.

100. Jerusalem Media and Communication Center Press Service, *Poll: One Year of Autonomy* (Jerusalem, 1996), [1].

101. L. Andoni, "A New Era," *Middle East International,* February 2, 1996, 4.

102. Greenberg, "Faded Icon Is Asked What's He Done Lately," A6.

103. "Palestine in Limbo: Entrapped by Councils," *Issues: Perspectives on Middle East and World Affairs* 4, 12 (April-May 1996): 1.

104. The discussion in the next two paragraphs is based on Abu-Amr, "Report from Palestine."

105. Jerusalem Media and Communication Center Press Service, "Poll: One Year of Autonomy" (1996), [4], table 5; figures rounded to nearest decimal.

106. Ibid., [1].

107. See Amnesty International, *Trial at Midnight: Secret, Summary, Unfair Trials in Gaza* (London: Amnesty International, 1995); Amnesty International, *Human Rights in the Gaza Strip and Jericho Under Palestinian Self-Rule* 6, 10 (September 1994). See also Gaza Center for Rights and Law (Affiliate of the International Commission of Jurists—Geneva), *Monthly Report* (May 1994 and June/July 1994); B. Gellman, "Palestinian Secret Force Wields Power in West Bank, Force Accused of 'Gross' Rights Violations," *Washington Post,* August 28, 1995, A1, A18; and G. Usher, "Elections Under Scrutiny," *Middle East International,* February 16, 1996, 7.

108. Usher, "Elections Under Scrutiny," 43.

109. See E. Said, "Symbols Versus Substance: A Year After the Declaration of Principles," *Journal of Palestine Studies* 24, 2 (Winter 1995): 61.

110. G. Usher, "The Palestinians' Hand Strengthens Against Israel," *Middle East International,* October 25, 1996, 3.

111. Zacharia, "Public Opinions of West Bank and Gaza Strip Palestinians," 23.

112. L. Dabdoub, "Palestinian Public Opinion Polls on the Peace Process," *Palestine-Israel: Journal of Politics, Economics and Culture* 5 (Winter 1995): 63.

113. G. Usher, "The Taba Agreement—Peace or Defeat?" *Middle East International,* October 6, 1995, 4.

114. H. Winternitz, "Village of Deeper Despair, Peace Has Made Life Worse in the West Bank Town Where I Lived," *Washington Post,* October 6, 1996, C4.

EIGHT

Epilogue: Whither Palestine and the Palestinians?

The Palestinian-Israeli conflict passed through four distinct phases. The first emerged with the process of Zionist settler colonialism, which started in the late nineteenth century but intensified greatly after WWI during the British Mandate (1921–1948). Palestinian resistance to European Jewish colonization, settlement, immigration, and the British Mandate was best symbolized by the great Palestinian revolt of 1936–1939 against British authorities and then again by the internal (Palestinian-Jewish/Israeli) war of 1947–1948. This phase ended with the destruction and dismemberment of Palestine and the dispossession and dispersal of its people.

In the second phase the Palestinian-Israeli conflict was "Arabized" into the Arab-Israeli state conflict, which culminated in the 1967 war in a swift defeat of the armies of the nationalist Arab states that had promised to liberate Palestine. The 1967 defeat plunged Arab nationalism into a political-ideological crisis: a no-war–no-peace situation with Israel, a compromise with the conservative monarchical regimes of the oil-rich Arabian peninsula, and accommodation with the Western powers protecting them and Israel. Thus the "Arabization" of the Palestinian-Israeli conflict failed to liberate Palestine or resolve the Palestine question. It did, however, lead to the emergence of a radical, Palestinian-controlled PLO. The radical Palestinians promised not only the liberation of Palestine but also social revolution through people's armed struggle. But they were quickly crushed by Jordan in 1970–1971.

In the October 1973 war against Israel, Egypt and Syria fell back on conventional military means in an attempt to correct the strategic imbalance between Israel and the nationalist Arab states. This campaign was only partially successful. Thereafter, the Arab states, with the support of the Soviet Union, became willing to negotiate a political settlement, but Israel and its Western supporters remained intransigent.[1] The latter also rejected the PLO as the representative of the Palestinian people, consistently portraying it as a terrorist organization dedicated to Israel's destruction. During this phase Israel and the West dismissed PLO peace proposals out of hand. As Said noted, "None of the Palestinian positions taken since the 1970s—on a two-state solution, on mutual recognition, on the imperatives for peaceful negotiations—has ever been reported [in the West] with requisite care or accuracy."[2]

Instead of seeking peace according to the internationally acknowledged formula of land for peace, Israel embarked on a program of colonizing and absorbing the West Bank and Gaza Strip, the remaining parts of historic Arab Palestine. The possibility of a comprehensive political settlement and just peace was effectively ruled out in 1977 with the open-door policy of the Sadat regime and Egypt's separate peace treaty with Israel. The 1979 Egyptian-Israeli peace treaty not only removed Egypt, the strongest Arab country, from the Arab-Israeli conflict but altered significantly the strategic balance between Israel and the other Arab states.

This imbalance invited aggressive Israeli expansionism in the West Bank and Gaza and the Golan Heights and military adventurism focused on Lebanon. Israel not only intervened in internal Lebanese affairs but also sought to destroy the PLO, which was headquartered there.[3] These efforts culminated in the 1982 Israeli invasion of Lebanon, the siege of Beirut, and the negotiated exit of the PLO and it military forces from the city. During this period Israel also formally annexed "greater" Jerusalem (East Jerusalem and an area expanded around the city in the West Bank) and the Golan Heights and significantly intensified its colonization and settlement of the West Bank and Gaza Strip.

Also during the 1980s, the decline in oil revenues; the sharp rise of Arab state indebtedness; the profound economic, social, and political-ideological transformation of the eastern Arab world (especially the surge of political Islam); and the Iraq-Iran war diverted Arab attention from the Palestine question and the Palestinian people and hastened the eclipse of the PLO (which had shifted its base to Tunis). These developments, signaling Arab state disengagement from the Arab-Israeli conflict, reflected and may even have aided a more serious political development: the erosion of popular public Arab support for the cause of Palestine. In short, this change in the political culture of the Arab peoples—perhaps commensurate with the demise of Arab nationalism—increasingly isolated the Palestinians and the PLO.

These same eventualities exacerbated the horrendous conditions of Palestinians under occupation in the West Bank and Gaza Strip. Within a month of the Arab summit meeting in 1987, however, a spectacular intifada marked the third major phase of the Palestinian-Israeli struggle. The intifada allowed the Palestinian people, including the PLO, to regain self-confidence, to galvanize the far-flung diaspora communities into renewed political activism, and to reassert Palestinian rights before a rapt international audience. In a dramatic sense the intifada re-Palestinianized the conflict that had so long been Arabized. As important, it exposed the limits of Israeli power and the arrogance, brutality, and racism of its occupation.

The intifada "finally extracted a response from world public opinion as it brought to light the enormity of the moral and material suffering inflicted on the Palestinian people under Israeli occupation."[4] Said remarked that "the Palestinians began to acquire in 1988 the irrevocable status of a people dispossessed and under a brutal military occupation in international consciousness, a status consolidated by the Palestine National Council meeting held in Algiers later that year."[5] At that meeting the PLO officially recognized Israel and voted to participate in the peace process. By 1990, U.S. public opinion began to shift: 45 percent of those polled by Gallup favored Palestinian self-determination in contrast to 24 percent who did not.[6]

The intifada not only revitalized the Palestinian question on the international and regional levels but also tipped the balance of power locally, inside Israel and the occupied territories. The intifada raised the issue of the political, economic, and social cost of the occupation for Israel. As a result, the Likud government participated in the Madrid peace conference in 1991, and Labor won the 1992 Israeli elections on a peace platform of a negotiated settlement with the Arab states and the Palestinians.

In 1991 Israel unleashed a new type of counterinsurgency, what it called a "security offensive," against the intifada. It succeeded "in divesting the uprising of its mass character, turning it instead into the private property of rival bands of armed 'strike forces.'"[7] The intifada began to wane because of the massive and unrelenting measures by Israel, the Israeli and Western financial and economic blockade, and the loss of Arab financial and political support. This increasingly untenable situation for the Palestinians in the occupied territories, in combination with the failure of the PLO to relieve if not end the occupation, led to the rise, especially in Gaza, of Hamas and the more extremist al-Jihad al-Islami,[8] which began to challenge the legitimacy and leadership of the PLO and 'Arafat.

Arab economic and political support of the Palestinians never returned to the level of the 1970s despite the popularity of the intifada and the end of the Iraq-Iran war in 1988. The PLO under 'Arafat's direction established closer relations with militarily strong Iraq. But in the 1991 Gulf War the U.S.-led military alliance destroyed Iraq's forces and the country's infrastructure, devastated its economy, and turned the politically weak oil-exporting states of the Arabian peninsula into U.S. protectorates. The PLO policy of opposition to U.S. military intervention in the Iraq-Kuwait crisis prompted Arab oil-states to end their support for 'Arafat, the PLO, and Palestinian social service institutions. 'Arafat's stand on the Gulf conflict "cost the organization $120 million in annual donations from Saudi Arabia, Kuwait and Iraq. Confiscations of Palestinian deposits in Kuwaiti banks, plus the loss of other revenues, brought PLO forfeits from the Gulf states in the years 1991–1993 to around $10 billion."[9]

The cessation of aid from the oil-exporting Gulf states precipitated the disintegration of all PLO institutions. As thousands of functionaries were laid off, the social, welfare, and educational services to the Palestinian refugees were suspended. The Arab governments and many of their citizens quickly turned hostile to the Palestinians as individuals and as communities living among them. Indeed the large Palestinian communities in Kuwait (about 350,000–400,000 people) and to a lesser extent in other Gulf states were expelled. Only a fraction (between 25,000 to 50,000) of those who had lived in Kuwait since the 1950s were allowed to remain. Palestinian activism in the post–Gulf War period in the Gulf states was constrained. In Lebanon severe restrictions were imposed on Palestinian residents, the chilly relationship between the Syrian government and 'Arafat's PLO put a freeze on mobilization of the Palestinian community in Syria, and loyalists to King Hussein expressed their suspicion of the Palestinians and the PLO in Jordan. The PLO was thus profoundly isolated and weakened as never before in its history.[10]

The Palestinian Political Crisis

It should be clear by now that the sudden, unexpected agreement between Israel and the PLO and the signing of the Declaration of Principles by 'Arafat plunged the PLO and the whole Palestinian people into a momentous political crisis. The subsequent agreements to the declaration placed the PLO/PA and most of the Palestinian people into a political and economic bind that further intensified the crisis. The shock and stunned disbelief that greeted announcement of the Oslo Accords quickly turned into four diversified reactions. It thus created new political fault lines related less to ideological considerations than issues of substance and process.[11]

The first reaction was enthusiastic support from those who believed that the agreements were a historic breakthrough that would lead to Israeli military withdrawal from the occupied territories and self-determination by the end of the interim period. Palestinians who reacted in this manner were small in number: those in the PLO bureaucracy; most of the PLO functionaries and diplomats; most of 'Arafat's supporters, allies, clients, and dependents in Fateh, the PLO, and the Fida Party (the Palestinian Democratic Union); and probably others, mainly small Palestinian businesspeople and professionals, formerly resident in the Gulf Arab states.

The second tendency was conditional approval: Some Palestinians saw in the agreement essential progress, although they viewed it as far from satisfactory. Adherents of this view included important elements of the Palestine People's Party and wide sectors, perhaps a plurality, of the Palestinian people in the West Bank and the Gaza Strip. This group was most interested in ridding the occupied territories of the repressive Israeli troops and finding some socioeconomic relief and normalcy in the promised economic aid.

The third response, by those who long supported peaceful resolution of the Israeli-Palestinian conflict, was to see the accord as thoroughly flawed and potentially fatal for Palestinian national aspirations and survival as a people. The adherents of this view were outraged at the enormous concessions of Palestinian rights that 'Arafat made without consultation, public debate, or legitimate formal approval. 'Arafat's secretive, individualistic, and unconstitutional style of negotiating the accords and securing "official" approval of them from the truncated, 'Arafat-dependent rump PLO bodies—not including the PNC—of highly questionable legitimacy appalled almost all Palestinians. This group saw the accords as controversial substantive agreements that shattered Palestinian consensus and political unity. Above all, this constituency was afraid that the Declaration of Principles, which disregarded international law and United Nations resolutions on Palestine, undermined the internationally recognized and codified rights of the Palestinian people. This group was large, especially but not only among the diaspora Palestinians, and it included prominent independent and long active PLO figures, some of whom resigned from the Executive Committee of the PLO over the agreement. Among them were Haidar 'Abdul-Shafi, head of the Palestinian delegation in the Madrid peace process and the Washington negotiations; Mahmoud Darwish,[12] the renowned Palestinian poet laureate; Shafiq al-Hout, the PLO representative in Lebanon and a member of the Executive Committee of the original PLO; Farouq Qaddoumi, the PLO foreign minister; Edward Said and Naseer Aruri, prominent Palestinian American academics and intellectuals; and many others. This political tendency had no organizational structure or a single voice, although it has had extensive popular support.

Finally, the "rejectionists" saw the accords as high treason, capitulation to the enemy, a violation of the Palestinian national consensus and principles of the national covenant or PLO charter and PNC resolutions. They believed the agreements would never lead to independence and statehood. This group included those of both the Right and the Left in the Palestinian political spectrum: Hamas and Al-Jihad al-Islami on the right and the PFLP, the DFLP, and a score of other minor parties on the left. This view also had significant support both inside the occupied territories and in the diaspora, especially in the refugee camps. It should be pointed out, however, that they did not reject a negotiated settlement; rather, like the previous group, they were against these particularly flawed and capitulationist agreements.

Except for the euphoric few around 'Arafat, most Palestinians expressed disbelief at the Declaration of Principles and anger, frustration, and hostil-

ity toward 'Arafat and his inner circle; intense feelings and incendiary attitudes threatened to flare up into intra-Palestinian violence and civil war.
However, leaders of nearly all political groups and many other prominent
figures spoke out and issued public pacts against the possibility of fratri-
cide. Thus while many stated their intention of resisting or undoing the
agreement, intra-Palestinian political violence was avoided except for intermittent clashes between the PA's official Palestinian security forces and
Hamas in Gaza after the establishment there of the Palestinian Authority.

In September 1993, shortly after the signing of the Oslo Accords, 'Arafat
called on his people to "reject violence and terrorism and return to ordinary life."[13] This call "amounted to the abandonment of any strategy of
nationalist mobilization or resistance in the territories."[14] It was a call to
end the intifada without formally saying so. With no reciprocal Israeli
cease-fire gesture made, this was another unilateral Palestinian concession.

Also shortly after the signing of the accords, the more right-wing and
hard-line Israeli settlers escalated their provocations. This climaxed in the
massacre of twenty-nine Palestinian Muslims prostrate in prayer in Hebron's Mosque of Ibrahim by Baruch Goldstein, a Hebron area settler and
a major in the Israeli army. The occupied territories were in ferment, and
threats of revenge were expressed frequently. This tension-filled situation
and international condemnation of the massacre characterized the period
during which the PLO negotiated the first set of implementation agreements, the Cairo Accords. It gave 'Arafat political leverage, but he missed
the opportunity to renegotiate the terms of the earlier declaration to include the specific issue of settlements then rather than later in the "final status" negotiations. Instead, "in his haste to get the Palestinian National Authority (PNA) installed in Gaza and Jericho, Arafat granted the Israelis
concessions on 'security' far more sweeping than anything specified in the
[Declaration of Principles]."[15]

In 1994 'Arafat returned to Gaza to set up the Palestinian Authority in
accordance with the terms of the Oslo Accords. The jubilation of the Gaza
people upon his entry was genuine, as they expressed the joy of freedom
from harsh Israeli control. Through a large police force (agreed to in the accords), 'Arafat set about imposing order and his authority on a restive population and a chaotic situation and terminating the active resistance to the
continuing Israeli occupation. The long grassroots political and armed
struggle was not to end but to be mobilized in support of the emerging
Palestinian Authority regime. Against his opponents, especially Hamas,
'Arafat utilized his tried-and-true political tactics of negotiations to build a
consensus and failing that, co-optation, infiltration, and force. These tactics
failed to resolve the disappointment and discontent of the great majority of
the Palestinians with the accords, 'Arafat, and the PLO. The political lines
and divisions were drawn, and the crisis persisted.

The Disorganized Opposition

Four years after the 1993 signing of the Declaration of Principles, three years after the establishment of the PA in the Gaza Strip and Jericho, and two years after its extension to six of the eight cities of the West Bank, Palestinian divisions in 1997 were just as sharp. But the anticipated political battle with the opposition never quite developed. Indeed the opposition to the Palestinian-Israeli "peace process," which went forward with new and disadvantageous implementation agreements for the Palestinians, has done little. The secular Palestinian left and radical nationalists led by the PFLP and the DFLP are based in Damascus. Their immediate and sharpest response to the Oslo Accords was rhetorical condemnation of the accords and the "liquidationist" leadership (of 'Arafat and his supporters) and withdrawal from all the agencies of the PLO. They attempted to organize a "rejectionist" coalition composed of themselves, Saiqa, Hamas, and other smaller groups, but they could not agree on organizational matters (Hamas insisted on the lion's share of the seats and votes) and accomplished little beyond rhetorical stands.

It appeared that the specific objectives of the secularists and Hamas differed substantially. While the former wanted to reform and revive the PLO and its institutions and to eliminate the "surrenderist" and "liquidationist" 'Arafat leadership, the latter was ambivalent and stood firm in its refusal to stand under the PLO umbrella. The official PLO opposition was thus reactive, weak, disorganized, paralyzed, and underfunded. It has not yet formulated a comprehensive or coherent political program or organizational structure to advance its aspirations. It principally argued for guarding the old PLO political agenda and the national consensus that had existed between 1968 and 1993.

After the initial shock of the Oslo Accords and the installation of the PA, the secular leftist opposition began a more pragmatic approach to the new political realities. It sought to strengthen the West Bank and Gaza Strip institutions and to work for their democratization. However, dissension in relations between the "internal" (West Bank and Gaza) cadres and "external" (diaspora) leadership emerged. Furthermore, according to the opinion polls, support for these groups declined sharply in the West Bank and Gaza Strip, although it does not appear to have dropped off in the diaspora communities. Within the diaspora communities, the leftists and nationalists carried on with business as usual despite the alarm of their rhetoric about the threatened destiny of the cause. In short, "Since Oslo, opposition politics has been marked by theoretical poverty and organizational paralysis."[16]

The only serious opposition to both the Declaration of Principles and 'Arafat's regime is Hamas and Al-Jihad al-Islami, which are principally limited to the Gaza Strip. Their attacks against the occupation troops and Israeli civilians inside Israel have been branded by most of the international media and those controlled by 'Arafat's regime as terrorist actions against peace. Their power base in the Gaza Strip is relatively strong and represents, after the years of PA rule, a continuing albeit attenuated challenge to the regime's authority and legitimacy. But despite the political and violent confrontations in Gaza, the PA-Hamas conflict has settled into mutual accommodation. Although Hamas is the only serious threat to the PLO-Israeli arrangements, its impact has neither stopped nor modified the march of events. Thus the Palestinian political spectrum seems to consist of "quite a large group of silent and disappointed Palestinians, a second group of ['Arafat] loyalists, a third group waiting around to see if things will get better for them, and, lastly, a group opposing the process and Arafat who can't seem to get together."[17]

Popular Disillusionment

The disaffected Palestinian majority has become disillusioned, demoralized, politically paralyzed, and unable to mount any significant action to change conditions on the ground in the occupied territories or internationally. This situation reflects the deepening crisis in the Palestinian national movement. This crisis also produced widespread political cynicism and depoliticization and, among some, desperation and profound hopelessness. In the hapless slums of Gaza, many angry young men have volunteered for suicide missions against the Israelis. Many (including former Fateh militants) rallied to the cause of Hamas not out of religious conviction as true believers but because Hamas emerged as the only group to resist the truly unjust and disappointing turn of events. "We are at a stage where the old Palestinian movement is dying, and a new movement is not created yet," says Mustapha Barghouthi, who heads the Union of Palestinian Medical Relief Committees in the West Bank and Gaza Strip.[18]

And yet in their bleak social, economic, and political situation the Palestinian people have made efforts not only to redefine the nature of Palestinian national identity and consciousness but also to address emergent social issues. The slim hope of renewal among Palestinian progressives derives from the new contradictions that have arisen over the shape and structure of Palestinian society—"issues long delayed by a movement preoccupied by the confrontation with Israel. Women, for instance, have been organizing against what they perceive to be capitulation by the secular parties to Islamist conservatives on 'personal status' issues. Non-governmental organizations (NGOs) from differing political tendencies are coming together to campaign for democratic and civil rights."[19]

Expressive of this latter tendency are two political efforts in the West Bank and Gaza Strip: the "democratic building movement" led by Haidar

'Abdul-Shafi and the Third Force led by a coalition of independents and certain party activists (from the PPP, PFLP, DFLP, and others).[20] Both movements see the contemporary Palestinian political terrain monopolized by 'Arafat and his PA on one side and the Islamists on the other. Both movements also believe that the majority of the Palestinian public—the proverbial silent majority—tends to be secular, democratic, and supportive of the idea of Palestinian sovereignty and unhappy with 'Arafat's unprincipled concessions to Israel and his role as Israel's enforcer. They are confident that this silent majority, including the multiplicity of NGOs, the intellectuals, unions, women's groups, and other economic and cultural organizations in cities, villages, and refugee camps, will be responsive to the proposed alternative: a broad movement that would break the political monopoly of 'Arafat's regime and the religious opposition.[21]

Most of these social service and cultural organizations were the popular groups that mobilized the Palestinian people against Israeli occupation during the intifada. At that time they were morally, politically, and financially supported by the legitimate PLO and Arab and international donors. Currently, however, they are constrained, undermined, and financially starved by Israel, the PA/PLO, and the formerly generous Arab and international donors.[22] Worse yet, as Naseer Aruri argues, the PA itself has "ruptured the moral fabric of [West Bank and Gaza Strip] society and rendered the grassroots structures and pluralist political culture, built during 20 years of anti-occupation resistance, relics of the past. The norms of voluntarism and the associational values, the self-help projects, are being steadily overwhelmed by inertia, bureaucratization and opposition."[23]

Among the diaspora Palestinians, little in the form of opposition to 'Arafat's policies exists beyond passive antagonism, disaffection, anger, and rhetoric. Diaspora Palestinians are politically rudderless and isolated in the different and disconnected communities. The demise of the PLO institutions all but eliminated the transnational connectedness of the refugee and other diaspora communities. Independent groups have attempted to start initiatives to organize the diaspora communities and give them a political voice. By early 1997 not much had come of these efforts. The most promising is an independent ad hoc grouping of Palestinian intellectuals and others from the United States, Jordan, Lebanon, Syria, and Egypt who have called for a gathering of diaspora Palestinians, the "Conference of 'Return' and Self-Determination," to reassert internationally recognized and codified Palestinian diaspora rights and to voice their interests and concerns. This call not only received support from many Palestinians in the West Bank and Gaza Strip and in the diaspora but also among prominent individual nationalist and leftist Arabs, Arab human rights organizations, and other groups. Whether this initiative will succeed in rallying the diaspora communities remains to be seen.

The Institutional Crisis:
The Representation Dilemma

The accords between the PLO and Israel triggered not only a political crisis but also an institutional one. It raised the question of the representativeness, legitimacy, and credibility of the PLO, its institutions, and its leadership. With the creation of the Palestinian Authority, with limited civil and police powers over the population centers of the West Bank and the Gaza Strip, the relationship between the PLO and the PA became an issue. Just as confounding for all Palestinians was the election of a Legislative Council in the autonomy areas in January 1996, which raised questions of institutional legitimacy and representativeness and of the council's relationship to the existing PNC. Adding further to the dilemma is that the Legislative Council is an elected body, in contrast to the largely appointive character of the PNC. The PA and the council, legitimate as they may be in the eyes of the West Bank and Gaza Strip Palestinians (and much of the rest of the world), in no way could speak for or represent the diaspora communities. While the Legislative Council may have become the institution that articulates the will and aspirations of three-quarters of a million voters in the West Bank and the Gaza Strip, who represents the 4.5 million diaspora Palestinians? Indeed which institution is to authorize and ratify the "final status" agreements? Compounding this dilemma is the behavior of 'Arafat, who continued to hold onto the supreme official powers of both institutions: the PLO and the PA.

Of specific relevance to the questions of representation and legitimacy was 'Arafat's formal promise (in response to an Israeli and a U.S. government demand) in the Oslo I and II Accords to amend the 1968 national charter of the PLO. 'Arafat, as head of the PLO, had not called a meeting of the PNC since 1991. He ignored it and seemed to be unconcerned with its marginalization except for the promise to Israel to amend the PLO charter. He was thus faced with the dilemma that the Legislative Council cannot amend that charter—it has no jurisdiction—nor can his PA regime unilaterally rescind the national covenant of all Palestinians. Such amendment became all the more urgent as the 1996 Israeli elections heated up and the Labor Party under Prime Minister Peres, 'Arafat's "peace partner," in a difficult election campaign, wanted a political "achievement" with which to impress the Israeli electorate. Accordingly, the acting head of the PNC, an 'Arafat appointee and loyalist, suddenly called for a PNC meeting (the twenty-first session), which was held in Gaza in late April 1996.[24]

When the PNC [meetings] started in Gaza there were 448 members in attendance, including 110 recently returned from the diaspora. By the time the session closed on 25 April, there were 630 members, most of them appointed by

'Arafat as the PNC proceeded over its four days. The session devoted specifically to amending the Charter . . . lasted just over two hours, with most of that time taken by debate over procedures . . . rather than the political meaning of the changes themselves.[25]

Many of PNC members of the former loyal opposition (the different nationalist and leftist organizations and independents) either did not come to Gaza or, if they came, refused to participate in voting they considered an orchestrated charade. Through typical ways, "less by winning a majority for the changes in the Charter than by manufacturing a majority via patronage, procedural *diktat* and filibuster,"[26] 'Arafat got a large majority (504 members)[27] to vote for amendment of the charter and to remand it to the legal committee for drafting a new charter.[28] What made all this even more outrageous for most Palestinians, their Lebanese supporters, and other Arab sympathizers was that 'Arafat held the meeting, ensured passage of such a major political concession (in return for little), and presented the "political gift" to prime minister and candidate Shimon Peres while Israel was mercilessly punishing the Lebanese people and destroying strategic infrastructure of Lebanon during a savage assault (Operation Grapes of Wrath) on that hapless country. Thus with a quick show of hands, the 'Arafat-controlled 1996 PNC dropped its claim to Palestine and did not replace it with an alternative national covenant to direct the Palestinian negotiators in the "final status" negotiations.

The 1996 PNC meeting in Gaza effectively eliminated the existing but moribund PLO Executive Committee, which was anchored in the long-held national consensus and composed of representatives of the major feda'iyyin groups and political parties and some independents. 'Arafat replaced it with a new Executive Committee made up of his allies and loyalists, a rubber-stamp group. Long fearing a formal vote of no confidence or serious organizational division or collapse, 'Arafat had shied away from most of the official institutions of the liberation movement, especially the PNC. In the context of the disarray of the opposition, however, 'Arafat executed a white coup d'état over both the PNC and the PLO Executive Committee and reasserted his authority over the long-established and legitimate institution of the Palestinian diaspora. The PLO; its Executive Committee; and its legislative council, the PNC, became controlled institutions of the 'Arafat regime, the PA. The status of the diaspora communities in the varied Arab host countries suddenly emerged as a politically contentious and divisive issue for them, the PLO/PA, and the host countries. And the national political consensus has been destroyed; organizations such as the PFLP and DFLP have been effectively disenfranchised. Shortly after these developments, the PFLP, itself in disarray, formally withdrew from the PLO. The diaspora is without a collective or organized voice, perhaps for the first time since 1948.

"Final Status" Negotiations and Likud Israel

"Final status" negotiations over the occupied territories between Israel and the PLO/PA formally opened on schedule in early May in the Egyptian resort of Taba and adjourned quickly until after the Israeli elections of May 29, 1996. The pro forma meeting was largely ceremonial and accomplished little beyond holding the meeting on schedule and showing the continuing interest of the two parties to carry on the "peace process" in accordance with the Oslo Accords. This meeting took place in an extremely charged political environment within Israel itself and involving Israel and the PA on one side and Hamas and the Islamic movement on the other.

In Israel a right-wing Jewish religious militant, Yigal Amir, assassinated Prime Minister Yitzhak Rabin on November 4, 1995, and plunged the country into a short-term political crisis. Foreign Minister Peres took over the position of prime minister and promised to continue along the path of Rabin. However, despite the agreements and security cooperation between Israel and the PLO/PA, Israel kept up its underground war against Hamas. Israel's security forces, for example, assassinated the top Hamas political leader in Malta. In the course of such attacks and retaliations, Hamas in February-March 1996 launched a series of suicide bombings inside Israel. The civilian death toll was high (fifty-eight dead and more than 200 wounded), and the political reaction, both in Israel and internationally, was extremely strong. Accordingly, the Peres government called on 'Arafat to "crack down" heavily on Hamas and its supporters and itself initiated measures to prohibit entry of Palestinians from the territories to work in Israel.

'Arafat's PA security forces arrested nearly 1,000 Palestinians suspected of links to Hamas. In the Gaza Strip, they raided and confiscated materials and resources from more than thirty educational, medical, and other welfare institutions and took control of fifty-nine mosques. While 'Arafat received kudos from Peres and U.S. president Clinton for his suppression of the Islamic militants, Israel proceeded to impose the tightest closure of the territories in its twenty-nine years of occupation. Not only were Palestinians prohibited from entering Israel, but the Israeli army imposed what the Israelis called "internal closure" on the autonomous population centers of the West Bank and Gaza Strip: For nearly two weeks following the March 4, 1996, suicide attack in Tel Aviv, the Peres government placed the 1.3 million Palestinians of the West Bank under wholesale curfew, with all movement between the "autonomous" towns and villages completely prohibited. Israel was able to do this because under the terms of the Oslo II agreement, which transferred authority over the population centers to the PA, it retained control of the roads and infrastructure outside those population centers. In Gaza the Israeli army sliced the strip in two and set up check points that choked movement and economic life.

Although this total curfew was slowly lifted by Israel—with the promise of total lifting after the elections—the economic and social toll on the occupied territories was catastrophic. In addition to the 40,000 or so workers who were denied entry into Israel, 80 percent of the Palestinian labor force of the territories was prevented access to their jobs. "Daily losses to the Palestinian economy were approximately $6 million."[29] Indeed, Nabil Sha'ath, minister of planning and international cooperation in the PA, cited a World Bank estimate of $800 million loss to the Palestinian economy in three months as a result of the Israeli closures. And while the Palestinian national per capita income declined in 1994 by 8 percent compared to the year before, between 1994 and 1996 it fell by 19–22 percent.[30] Others, such as the Deputy Minister of the Economy, said the damage is rather incalculable as it threatened both investments and business confidence. All exports and imports to and from (and therefore via) Israel were terminated, causing severe shortages in basic foods, medical supplies and raw materials.

Even after the easing of the total closure, enhanced Israeli security procedures "cut the number of trucks crossing from a pre-closure rate of 400 to 40 a day."[31] A bread famine was averted only because of the emergency measures that UNRWA and the Palestinian Authority instituted. According to the PA Ministry of Health, the "internal closure" led to the shutting down of 245 health clinics because of medical shortages. Several people, including an infant, died as a result of unattended medical emergencies. Additionally, Prime Minister Peres's government reimposed from the pre-Oslo era a series of punitive security measures, including administrative detentions, blowing up houses of suspects, and closing down of welfare agencies and educational institutions. Finally, Peres approved the building of a buffer zone (2 kilometers wide along a 350-kilometer border area) to separate large segments of the West Bank from Israel.

The swift Israeli military closure and control of the autonomous Palestinian population cantons—an action that would have provoked, at the very least, extensive civil unrest and popular resistance during the intifada—elicited no armed or popular resistance on the part of the Palestinians. But this closure occurred in coordination with the Palestinian security forces who basically stepped aside as the Israelis swept through. The only centers they did not enter, but closed off tightly, were the six "autonomous" cities of the West Bank. There and in the Gaza areas, the PA itself imposed a heavy security mantle. In the wake of these events, the mood among the Palestinians in the territories has "swung back, not so much in support of Hamas, but against the peace process and its exclusivist privileging of Israel's security."[32] Palestinian support for the PA plummeted. Rabbani noted:

> In contrast to most Palestinian exiles, who from the outset rejected the [Declaration of Principles] because it relegated them to the furthest margins of the Is-

raeli-Palestinian equation, reassessment of this agreement within the occupied territories has been a slower and more complex process. Ever so gradually, appeals for the faithful implementation and proper stewardship of the [declaration] are giving way to demands for its fundamental reconsideration.[33]

Indeed, as he also noted, "the belief [among Palestinians of the West Bank and Gaza Strip] that no agreement at all would have been preferable to the present arrangements is gaining ground."[34]

And so has the pendulum of antipathy toward the "peace process" also swung in Israel. After the suicide bombings in early 1996, the public mood increasingly favored the hard-line right-wing political coalition (Likud and religious parties). The pro-peace sentiment that had surged and become politically powerful in Israel after the assassination of Prime Minister Rabin had thus waned and nearly disappeared by the May 29, 1996, elections. As a result, Netanyahu, the rightist leader of the Likud, was elected prime minister over Peres of the Labor Party, the principal architect of the accords with the PLO.

The victory of Netanyahu and the Likud-led coalition in Israel introduced a potentially problematic political situation not only in the Palestinian context but also throughout the Middle East, not least because of his campaign and postelection victory rhetoric. Netanyahu's five "nos" (no to a Palestinian state, no to a Palestinian East Jerusalem, no to withdrawal from Hebron as scheduled, no to an end of Israeli settlement in the occupied territories, and no to withdrawal from the Golan Heights in return for a peace treaty with Syria) were a direct rejection of the terms of negotiations largely based on UN Security Council Resolutions 242 and 338 (the land for peace formula), the Madrid Middle East peace conference, the Oslo Accords, and the "peace process." Netanyahu's recidivist reinterpretation of the terms of the "peace process" from "land for peace" to "peace for peace" or "peace with security" is "for those who with minimal knowledge of Israeli political semantics, . . . an unmistakable euphemism for retaining the occupied Arab land, including much of the West Bank, the Golan Heights and, of course, East Jerusalem."[35] This posture by the new Israeli leader and the rightist cabinet he assembled cast serious doubt on the potential for resumption of the "peace process," especially the "final status" negotiations, between Israel and the PLO/PA.[36] Negotiations between the Israeli government of Netanyahu and the Palestinian Authority of 'Arafat have lurched from crisis to crisis. And despite international intervention, especially by the U.S. government, including President Clinton himself, to defuse the tension and bridge the differences, the talks have generated greater ill will among the Palestinians (and some Israelis) and uncertainty about the destiny of the "peace process," especially the "final status" negotiations. The eventual independence of Palestine and the Palestinians is more than ever in doubt.

Netanyahu's actions spoke even louder than his rhetoric. The opening of an archaeological tunnel along the foundations of al-Haram al-Sharif in Jerusalem and the deliberate humiliation of 'Arafat triggered a popular political upheaval in September 1996 that quickly escalated into armed and bloody conflict between Israeli occupation troops and the Palestinian police. The stonewalling on the Hebron deployment was followed in early 1997 by the building of a new Jewish settlement on Jabal Abu Ghuneim in Palestinian East Jerusalem, which led to another uprising in March 1997 that was characterized by tactics perfected during the intifada. In short, the Likud victory that put into power a hard-line Israeli leadership articulating intransigent positions, coupled with an Israel-PLO/PA peace process already viewed as unjust, unfair, and economically devastating by the majority of the Palestinian people, has sharpened further the internal Palestinian political crisis and raised doubts about a just or honorable political solution to the Palestine problem.

Palestinian Destiny

The Palestinian people now face a number of serious historic challenges whose resolution will determine their destiny as a people and the fate of their country. These challenges are of two types: immediate dilemmas and longer-term predicaments. In the political sphere, the immediate dilemmas include finding a credible, rational, and legitimate political process for decisionmaking that would involve and satisfy most political groups and tendencies, including Hamas and the radicals, and the mass of the "silent majority," both internal to the autonomous areas and in the diaspora. Also important is establishing legitimate democratic institutions, political participation processes, and a climate of tolerance, free expression, and free assembly. Reforming and reconstructing the political, legal, and social service agencies and institutions are also essential to deliver needed aid to the West Bank and Gaza Strip and diaspora Palestinians. Central to the Palestinian political dilemma is the restructuring of the relationship between the PLO and the PA, whereby the PA exists as the agency of self-rule in the West Bank and Gaza Strip, while a reinvigorated, legitimate, and functioning PLO (or successor organization) and its institutions reemerge as the political framework and representative of *all* Palestinians, not just those in the occupied territories.

In the economic sphere, the dilemmas include rationalizing development planning and investment in order to generate needed jobs; creating a legal and rational regulatory environment for the orderly conduct of economic and financial activity; and building the physical infrastructure. Above all the Palestinians leadership must describe a vision of the future society—humane, free, democratic, based on the rule of law, and socially just—that would capture the imagination and energies of the people in order to translate that vision into specific political, economic, social, and legal institutions and practice. However, even assuming enormous goodwill and cooperation on the part of the Israelis—assumptions that were untrue in the past, given that Israel's interpretations of the Oslo Accords were always restrictive and, with the Likud Party in power, are currently more suspect— these are tremendously demanding challenges for the Palestinian people and the ineffectual or incapable PLO/PA. Now, therefore, is the time to resist on the ground the rapid Israeli appropriation and absorption of East Jerusalem and other Palestinian areas and the increase of Israeli settlers. This is no doubt an echo of the pre-Nakbah challenges that faced the Palestinians of the mandate period.

The longer-term challenges facing the Palestinians are even more daunting. They can be grouped into several categories:

1. determining the future status of the Palestinian diaspora communities, which comprise about 55–60 percent of the Palestinian people (the most important challenge in direct human terms);
2. rebuilding the integrity of the Palestinians as a people who must now construct, assert, and maintain a new transnational political and cultural identity, reconnecting and organizing the separated and isolated diaspora communities, already transformed by widely varied circumstances, experiences, and social histories;
3. redefining the nature of the relationships between Palestinians in the homeland and those in the diaspora;
4. redefining and remolding the character, structure, and goals of their transnational political organization;
5. planning for long-range economic development; and
6. consolidating democracy and the rule of law in a socially just society.

As have many other critics before us, we believe a careful reading of the texts of the Declaration of Principles, its annexes, and the derivative Cairo, Paris, and Oslo II Accords indicates clearly that they provide only for a limited Palestinian administration—for a fraction of the Palestinian people on a fraction of its land—and do not envision the building of an independent Palestinian state in the future. And because these agreements envision neither political nor economic independence for the Palestinian territories, such independence is not possible through the current "peace process." We therefore believe that in the context of such an imbalance of power between the politically weak Palestinian Authority and a strong Israel, the Declaration of Principles will *not* lead to Palestinian self-determination and independent statehood or to the restoration of or compensation for the internationally codified rights of the Palestinian diaspora.

What, then, would be the character of the emergent Palestinian entity? Gone are the days of struggle for the revolutionary liberation of Palestine during which the Palestinian intellectuals and political leaders had the luxury of imagining a liberated, progressive, democratic, and socially just future Palestine. That dream and that option are now destroyed as much by the erstwhile Palestinian leadership of the PLO as by the enemies of Palestine and the Palestinian people—Israeli, American, European, and Arab. We believe that the so-called peace process, specifically, the implementation of the Oslo-inspired agreements, will create on the ground in the occupied territories—with the consent of 'Arafat's PA regime—a permanent reality of fragmented, subjugated, exploited, miniature Palestinian cantons under Israeli-style apartheid. Israel has already legitimately established this form of colonialism, in which it has invested enormous resources, economic interests, and political capital and for which it has garnered international, Arab, and official PLO/PA support. Little if any evidence suggests that Israel will in the "final status" negotiations abandon such a privileged, profitable, controlled, and legitimate colonial structure and grant independent Palestinian statehood or repatriation of the diaspora.[37] At best Israel may in the future allow 'Arafat and his regime to *call* this colonized, politically and economically controlled entity a "state" and grant it cosmetic symbols of statehood—a flag, a token army and perhaps a navy, an airline, and foreign missions—but it will be effectively devoid of sovereignty, freedom, self-determination, and dignity. It will be a client state, a dependent state, a symbolic state that would not satisfy the needs and aspirations of the Palestinian people.[38]

If in this analysis of the nature of the emergent Palestinian entity, we made no direct mention of the Palestinians of the diaspora, it is because they have not only been disenfranchised by the 'Arafat regime but also largely abandoned to their own destinies. The probable future of the diaspora Palestinians is foreshadowed in the misfortunes and misery of the Palestinians expelled from Libya in 1995. Neither the Palestinian Authority, which is constrained by the Israel-PLO agreements, nor Lebanon, Egypt, or other Arab states (except Syria) were willing to take in any of the expelled Palestinians, who were stranded for a long time in camps on the Libyan-Egyptian desert frontier and in ferryboats in Cypriot harbors. Resolution of the latter case took weeks; the former were still stranded on a strip of land on the Egyptian-Libyan border in early 1997.

In the accords that may emerge from the "final status" negotiations, if they resume, we expect at best a small symbolic group of Palestinian refugees may be allowed to exercise their right of return, while the majority will be given symbolic compensation and "naturalized"—a process labeled tawtin in Arabic—as residents in some Arab countries. There they will become second-class citizens (if they are lucky) or subjugated, disadvantaged, and exploitable minorities (if they are not). They could well become another group of *"bedoons"* (literally, "without"), like those who are official Kuwaiti residents but who have no citizenship and few or no civil rights.

Any reparations, symbolic or otherwise, from Israel will likely be folded into the international aid and paid directly to the PLO/PA. The political result of the tawtin in Arab and other countries of the Palestinian diaspora communities will be "Armenianization," not the Kurdization or Kurdistanization in several neighboring states, as some intellectuals have suggested. For except in Jordan, the Palestinian exiles will not have the critical population and geographic mass, as the Kurds have in Turkey and Iraq, which would give them some political leverage in their host countries. Instead, we believe, they will more likely become fearful minorities as the Armenian refugee communities were in the countries of their refuge after WWI.

In debates taking place inside the occupied territories among some Palestinian intellectuals about the future of the occupied Palestinian territories, two possible scenarios are being proposed. 'Azmi Bishara, an intellectual teaching in Bir Zeit University in the West Bank city of Ramallah, names the two possibilities within the first scenario: "the Bantustan plan or the binational option."[39] Given that the Israelis want only a Jewish state, and given the structure and content of all the Oslo Accords and the elaborate integration and subordination of all of historic Palestine into Israel's political economy, the first scenario (the Bantustan plan) is that of two peoples (Israeli and Palestinian) living under *one*—Israeli—sovereignty. Under this plan the Palestinians of the West Bank and the Gaza Strip would—unlike the so-called Israeli Arabs (the Palestinians citizens of Israel)—have only civil autonomy, but like them they would become controlled, economically disadvantaged residents of greater Israel. They could commute to work in the lesser Israeli jobs but return at night to townshiplike communities of their own. Even the right-wing Likud is not antithetical to this possible outcome. In the binational option, Israel/Palestine would presumably become a democratic and not just a Jewish state, where the two ethnic nationalities would retain their cultural identity and eventually coexist in harmony in an integrated economy and single sovereignty. This option seems unlikely to us, much as it may superficially resemble the "secular democratic state" imagined by the Palestinian revolutionaries of the 1960s.

The second scenario being debated is a bit more optimistic. In the longer term, the Palestinian elections may, perhaps after several rounds, produce an increasingly autonomous Palestinian Council—autonomous from both Israel and the 'Arafat-type regime—that will establish a new model of intra-Palestinian politics and will draw the West Bank and the Gaza Strip away from Israel's octopuslike grip toward a confederation with Jordan. Of course this option is the old Jordanian option long preferred by earlier Israeli governments and U.S. administrations. Jordanian dominion over the occupied territories or a Jordanian-Israeli condominium is indeed possible in the medium to long term, especially as 'Arafat's PA regime is unable to cope with the domestic dilemmas of the West Bank and Gaza Strip and squanders much of the foreign aid upon which it so desperately depends. After more than two full years, its record of diplomacy, economic policy and practice, and programs of social service to its people do not augur well for the future. It may therefore waste all of its political and economic capital and succumb to either Jordanian control or dual Jordanian-Israeli condominium. Should this happen, the economically subordinated Palestinian territories would likely remain poor and exploitable civil autonomy areas of a confederation.

More likely in our judgment is a Palestinian future of fragmented cantons in parts of the original homeland, the people enjoying fewer political and civil rights than the Palestinians of Israel or those of Jordan. This would likely be coupled with the Armenianization of the diaspora communities. If this occurs, it will be a tragic outcome for a people that has struggled and sacrificed so much for so long. To rephrase a famous statement made by Prime Minister Churchill at the conclusion of the Battle of Britain, never have so many sacrificed so much for so little. The short and the medium terms are unbelievably bleak for Palestine and the Palestinians.

However, we do not believe that the Palestinian struggle will end with the full implementation of the Oslo Accords. Despite the capitulation of 'Arafat and the PLO and the imposition of a new Israeli order over Palestine, the Palestinians, who have consistently rejected defeat and shown themselves to be resilient, will continue the struggle in other forms in the emergent Middle Eastern realities. The Palestinians' destiny, in the final analysis, is in their own hands. The Palestinians may need another intifada, now not only against the repackaged Israeli occupation but also against the 'Arafat regime, "because not only are we [Palestinians] still fighting the Israeli occupation, but in fact we are fighting an enforcer of the occupation—namely the PLO—which has the distinction of being the first national liberation movement in history to keep an occupying power in place."[40]

In our judgment, it would therefore be a mistake to assume that once established, the new Palestinian order under Israeli dominion would remain unchanged. The region as well as the world is in an era of profound transformation. The global, regional, and local balances of power may well shift to give the Palestinians new and different opportunities to pursue their struggle for an equitable, just, and lasting peace with the Israelis. Finally, we believe that the failure to establish a just peace through which the Palestinian people will restore its inalienable rights will lead to the unraveling of the Declaration of Principles and derivative agreements and to future conflict in the region. It is not the end of Palestinian history.

Notes

1. See N. Aruri, *The Obstruction of Peace: The U.S., Israel and the Palestinians* (Monroe, ME: Common Courage Press, 1995); see also N. Chomsky, *World Orders: Old and New* (New York: Columbia University Press, 1994); and N. G. Finkelstein, *Image and Reality of the Israel-Palestine Conflict* (London: Verso, 1995).

2. E. W. Said, *The Politics of Dispossession: The Struggle for Palestinian Self-Determination, 1969–1994* (New York: Pantheon, 1994), xxvi. See studies of earlier Israeli rejectionism: E. Berger, *Peace for Palestine: First Lost Opportunity* (Gainesville: University Press of Florida, 1993).

3. The Israeli attack on the PLO was largely to blunt its "peace offensive." See the analysis of Finkelstein, *Image and Reality of the Israel-Palestine Conflict*, especially ch. 6.

4. S. Amin, "After Gaza and Jericho: The New Palestinian–Middle Eastern Problem," *Beirut Review* 8 (Fall 1994): 115.

5. Said, *The Politics of Dispossession*, xx.

6. *Journal of Palestine Studies* (Winter 1990): 75–86. Earlier U.S. public opinion on the question of Palestine is analyzed in F. Moughrabi, "American Public Opinion and the Palestine Question," occasional paper 4 (Washington, DC: International Center for Research and Public Policy, 1986).

7. G. Usher, *Palestine in Crisis: The Struggle for Peace and Political Independence* (London: Pluto Press, 1995), 5.

8. Z. Abu-Amr, *Islamic Fundamentalism in the West Bank and Gaza* (Bloomington: Indiana University Press, 1994).

9. Usher, *Palestine in Crisis*, 1.

10. Former secretary of state Henry Kissinger reports that when he met 'Arafat, he asked him "why the Israelis should trust him. 'Because the Saudis have cut us off,' he replied, 'the Jordanians are trying to weaken us and the Syrians are seeking to dominate us.'" H. Kissinger, "Retooling the Process for Peace," *Washington Post*, July 1, 1996.

11. M. Rabbani, "'Gaza-Jericho First': The Palestinian Debate," *Middle East International*, September 24, 1993, 16–17.

12. Darwish later attenuated his opposition and made a visit to Gaza. See *Mideast Mirror*, June 13, 1995.

13. Usher, *Palestine in Crisis*, 15.

14. Ibid.

15. Ibid., 23.

16. Ibid., 50.

17. E. W. Said, "Symbols Versus Substance: A Year After the Declaration of Principles," *Journal of Palestine Studies* 24, 2 (Winter 1995): 61.

18. Cited in D. Connell, "Palestine on the Edge, Crisis in the National Movement," *Middle East Report* 194/195 (May-June/July-August 1995): 7.

19. Ibid.

20. The "Founding Declaration of the Palestinian Democratic Building Movement," was distributed at a talk by Abdul-Shafi at the Center for Policy Analysis on Palestine, Washington, D.C., June 1995. An unofficial statement of the Third Force was distributed by fax July 1995.

21. N. H. Aruri, "The Serious Challenges Facing Palestinian Society," *Middle East International*, August 25, 1995, 17. See also T. Aruri, "Some Features of Palestinian Political Life and Its Future," paper presented at a workshop, Muwaten Institute, Jerusalem, August 8, 1995; and T. Aruri, "Some Expected Political Consequences from Establishing an Elected Palestinian Council," paper presented at a workshop of the Palestinian People's Party, August 18, 1995.

22. "A Story of Manipulation, Containing the Palestinian NGOs," *Issues: Perspectives on Middle East and World Affairs* 5, 1 (June 1996): 2–3, 14.

23. Aruri, "The Serious Challenges Facing Palestinian Society," 17.

24. Critics of 'Arafat argued that the choice of Gaza as the site of the PNC meeting was deliberate because 'Arafat knew that much of the opposition (especially the radicals) would not be able or willing to come to Gaza, which in effect has remained under ultimate Israeli control. Visitors have to be approved and allowed entry by Israeli authorities.

25. G. Usher, "The Charter and the Future of Palestinian Politics," *Middle East International,* May 10, 1996, 17.

26. Ibid.

27. For reasons why they supported the charter amendment, see L. Andoni, "Amending the Charter Means the Demise of the PLO," *Middle East International,* May 24, 1996, 17.

28. "For many of the Legislative Council members (who are *ex officio* PNC members) the PNC was viewed as little less than their own disenfranchisement, since their elected status still appears to carry no more weight on the PNC than that of their leader's patronage." Usher, "The Charter and the Future of Palestinian Politics," 17.

29. G. Usher, "Closures, Cantons and the Palestinian Covenant," *Middle East Report* 199 (April-June 1996): 35.

30. N. Nasser, "Sha'ath Estimates Palestinian Economic Losses at $800 Million in Three Months," *Al-Hayat* (London), June 12, 1996, 10.

31. Usher, "Closures, Cantons and the Palestinian Covenant," 35.

32. Ibid., 37.

33. M. Rabbani, "Palestinian Authority, Israeli Rule: From Transitional to Permanent Arrangement," *Middle East Report* 201 (October-December 1996): 2.

34. Ibid., 6.

35. K. M. Amayreh, "Why Netanyahu Is Bad News for the Peace Process," *Middle East International,* July 19, 1996, 16.

36. See especially D. Neff, "Netanyahu Gets the Royal Treatment in Washington"; M. Jansen, "The Peace of the Sword"; G. Usher, "The Demand for 'Reciprocity'"; L. Andoni, "Dismay in Gaza"; K. M. Amayreh, "More Settlements Planned," and "Why Netanyahu Is Bad News for the Peace Process," all in *Middle East International,* July 19, 1996.

37. See the Likud-Labor agreement on permanent status: G. Aronson, "The Beilin-Eitan Agreement on Permanent Status and Its True Antecedents," *Report on Israeli Settlement in the Occupied Territories* 7, 2 (March-April 1997): 1, 7.

38. See the compelling analogy to the creation of Transkei in apartheid South Africa made by N. G. Finkelstein, "Whither the 'Peace Process'?" paper presented at Georgetown and American Universities, Washington, D.C., April 24 and 25, 1996, 14–17.

39. A. Bishara, "Only Two Alternatives Remain: The Bantustan Plan or the Bi-National Option," *News from Within* 11, 7 (July 1995): 14–17. See also a special issue of *Middle East Report* 201 (October-December 1996), devoted to the theme "Israel and Palestine: Two States, Bantustans or Binationalism."

40. Said, "Symbols Versus Substance," 62.

Appendix 1:
UN Security Council
Resolution 242,
November 22, 1967

The Security Council,

Expressing its continuing concern with the grave situation in the Middle East;

Emphasizing the inadmissibility of the acquisition of territory by war and the need to work for a just and lasting peace in which every State in the area can live in security;

Emphasizing further that all Member states in their acceptance of the Charter of the United Nations have undertaken a commitment to act in accordance with Article 2 of the Charter;

1. Affirms that the fulfillment of Charter principles requires the establishment of a just and lasting peace in the Middle East which should include the application of both the following principles:

(i) Withdrawal of Israeli armed forces from territories occupied in the recent conflict;

(ii) Termination of all claims or states of belligerency and respect for and acknowledgment of the sovereignty, territorial integrity and political independence of every State in the area and their right to live in peace within secure and recognized boundaries free from threats or acts of force;

2. Affirms further the necessity

a) for guaranteeing freedom of navigation through international waterways in the area;

b) for achieving a just settlement of the refugee problem;

c) for guaranteeing the territorial inviolability and political independence of every State in the area, through measures including the establishment of demilitarized zones;

3. Requests the Secretary-General to designate a Special Representative to proceed to the Middle East to establish and maintain contacts with the States concerned in order to promote agreement and assist efforts to achieve a peaceful and accepted settlement in accordance with the provisions and principles in this resolution;

4. Requests the Secretary-General to report to the Security Council on the progress of the efforts of the Special Representative as soon as possible.

Appendix 2:
The Balfour Declaration

November 2, 1917

Dear Lord Rothschild,

I have much pleasure in conveying to you, on behalf of His Majesty's Government, the following declaration of sympathy with Jewish Zionist aspirations which has been submitted to and approved by the Cabinet.

"His Majesty's Government view with favour the establishment in Palestine of a national home for the Jewish people, and will use their best endeavours to facilitate the achievement of this object, it being clearly understood that nothing shall be done which may prejudice the civil and religious rights of existing non-Jewish communities in Palestine, or in any other country".

I should be grateful if you would bring the declaration to the knowledge of the Zionist Federation.

Yours sincerely,

Arthur James Balfour

Appendix 3:
McMahon-Hussein
Correspondence, 1915–1916

Ten letters passed between Sir Henry McMahon, British high commissioner in Cairo, and Sharif Hussein of Mecca from July 1915 to March 1916. Hussein offered Arab help in the war against the Turks if Britain would support the principle of an independent Arab state. The most important letter is that of October 24, 1915, from McMahon to Hussein:

... I regret that you should have received from my last letter the impression that I regarded the question of limits and boundaries with coldness and hesitation; such was not the case, but it appeared to me that the time had not yet come when that question could be discussed in a conclusive manner. I have realized, however, from your last letter that you regard this question as one of vital and urgent importance. I have, therefore, lost no time in informing the Government of Great Britain of the contents of your letter, and it is with great pleasure that I communicate to you on their behalf the following statement, which I am confident you will receive with satisfaction.

The two districts of Mersina and Alexandretta and portions of Syria lying to the west of the districts of Damascus, Homs, Hama and Aleppo cannot be said to be purely Arab, and should be excluded from the limits demanded.

With the above modifications, and without prejudice to our existing treaties with Arab chiefs, we accept those limits.

As for those regions lying within those frontiers wherein Great Britain is free to act without detriment to the interest of her ally, France, I am empowered in the name of the Government of Great Britain to give the following assurances and make the following reply to your letter:

(1) Subject to the above modifications, Great Britain is prepared to recognize and support the independence of the Arabs in all the regions within the limits demanded by the Sherif of Mecca.

(2) Great Britain will guarantee the Holy Places against all external aggression and will recognize their inviolability.

(3) When the situation admits, Great Britain will give to the Arabs her advice and will assist them to establish what may appear to be the most suitable forms of government in those various territories.

(4) On the other hand, it is understood that the Arabs have decided to seek the advice and guidance of Great Britain only, and that such European advisers and officials as may be required for the formation of a sound form of administration will be British.

(5) With regard to the vilayets of Baghdad and Basra, the Arabs will recognize that the established position and interests of Great Britain necessitate special administrative arrangements in order to secure these territories from foreign aggression, to promote the welfare of the local populations and to safeguard our mutual economic interests.

I am convinced that this declaration will assure you beyond all possible doubt of the sympathy of Great Britain towards the aspirations of her friends the Arabs and will result in a firm and lasting alliance, the immediate results of which will be the expulsion of the Turks from the Arab countries and the freeing of the Arab peoples from the Turkish yoke, which for so many years has pressed heavily upon them. . . .

Appendix 4:
Excerpts from the Report
of the King-Crane Commission,
August 30, 1919

Perhaps for fear of being confronted by recommendations from their own delegates that might conflict with official policy, both Britain and France declined to nominate members to a commission the Allies created to inform them of the wishes of the Arabs in Palestine. President Wilson appointed two Americans, Henry King and Charles Crane, whose subsequent findings were suppressed and kept secret for three years. Their report was not published until 1947.

If the strict terms of the Balfour Statement are adhered to—favoring 'the establishment in Palestine of a national home for the Jewish people, it being clearly understood that nothing shall be done which may prejudice the civil and religious rights of existing non-Jewish communities in Palestine'—it can hardly be doubted that the extreme Zionist program must be greatly modified. For 'a national home for the Jewish people' is not equivalent to making Palestine into a Jewish State; nor can the erection of such a Jewish State be accomplished without the gravest trespass upon 'civil and religious rights of existing non-Jewish communities in Palestine'. The fact came out repeatedly in the Commission's conference with Jewish representatives, that the Zionists looked forward to a practically complete dispossession of the present non-Jewish inhabitants of Palestine, by various forms of purchase.

In his address of July 4, 1918, President Wilson laid down the following principle as one of the four great 'ends for which the associated people of the world were fighting': 'The settlement of every question, whether of territory, of sovereignty, of economic arrangement, or of political relationship upon the basis of the free acceptance of that settlement by the people immediately concerned, and not upon the basis of the material interest or advantage of any other nation or people which may desire a different settlement for the sake of its own exterior influence or mastery.' If that principle is to rule, and so the wishes of Palestine's population are to be decisive as to what is to be done with Palestine—nearly nine-tenths of the whole—are emphatically against the entire Zionist program. The tables show that there was no one thing upon which the population of Palestine were more agreed than upon this. To subject a people so minded to unlimited Jewish immigration, and to steady financial and social pressure to surrender the land, would be a gross violation of the principle just quoted, and of the people's rights, though it kept within the forms of law.

No British officer consulted by the Commissioners believed that the Zionist program could be carried out except by the force of arms. That of itself is evidence of a strong sense of the injustice of the Zionist program, on the part of the non-Jewish populations of Palestine and Syria. Decisions, requiring armies to carry out, are sometimes necessary, but they are surely not gratuitously to be taken in the interests of a serious injustice. For the initial claim, often submitted by Zionist representatives, that they have a 'right' to Palestine, based on an occupation of two thousand years ago, can hardly be seriously considered.

Appendix 5:
UN General Assembly
Resolution 181 on
the Future Government
of Palestine, November 29, 1947
(The Partition Plan)

The General Assembly,

Having met in special session at the request of the mandatory Power to constitute and instruct a special committee to prepare for the consideration of the question of the future government of Palestine at the second regular session;

Having constituted a Special Committee and instructed it to investigate all questions and issues relevant to the problem of Palestine, and to prepare proposals for the solution of the problem, and

Having received and examined the report of the Special Committee (document A/364) including a number of unanimous recommendations and a plan of partition with economic union approved by the majority of a Special Committee;

Considers that the present situation in Palestine is one which is likely to impair the general welfare and friendly relations among nations;

Takes note of the declaration by the mandatory Power that it plans to complete its evacuation of Palestine by 1 August 1948;

Recommends to the United Kingdom, as the mandatory Power for Palestine, and to all other Members of the United Nations the adoption and implementation, with regard to the future government of Palestine, of the Plan of Partition with Economic Union set out below;

Request that:

a) The Security Council take the necessary measures as provided for in the plan for its implementation;

b) The Security Council consider, if circumstances during the transitional period require such consideration, whether the situation in Palestine constitutes a threat to the peace. If it decides that such a threat exists, and in order to maintain international peace and security, the Security Council should supplement the authorization of the General Assembly by taking measures, under Articles 39 and 41 of the Charter, to empower the United Nations Commission, as provided in this resolution, to exercise in Palestine the functions which are assigned to it by this resolution;

c) The Security Council determine as a threat to the peace, breach of the peace or act of aggression, in accordance with Article 39 of the Charter, any attempt to alter by force the settlement envisaged by this resolution;

d) The Trusteeship Council be informed of the responsibilities envisaged for it in this plan;

Calls upon the inhabitants of Palestine to take such steps as may be necessary on their part to put this plan into effect;

Appeals to all Governments and all peoples to refrain from taking any action which might hamper or delay the carrying out of these recommendations, and;

Authorizes the Secretary-General to reimburse travel and subsistence expenses of the members of the commission referred to in Part I, Section B, paragraph 1 below, on such basis and in such form as he may determine most appropriate in the circumstances, and to provide the commission with the necessary staff to assist in carrying out the functions assigned to the Commission by the General Assembly.

Authorizes the Secretary-General to draw from the Working Capital Fund a sum not to exceed $2,000,000 for the purposes set forth in the last paragraph of the resolution on the future government of Palestine.

At its hundred and twenty-eighth plenary meeting on 29 November 1947 the General Assembly, in accordance with the terms of the above resolution, elected the following members of the United Nations Commission on Palestine:

Bolivia, Czechoslovakia, Denmark, Panama and Philippines.

Appendix 6:
UN General Assembly Resolution 194, December 11, 1948 (The Right of Return)

The General Assembly,

Having considered further the situation in Palestine,

1. Expresses its deep appreciation of the progress achieved through the good offices of the late United Nations Mediator in promoting a peaceful adjustment of the future situation of Palestine, for which cause he sacrificed his life; and extends its thanks to the acting Mediator and his staff for their continued efforts and devotion to duty in Palestine;

2. Establishes a Conciliation Commission consisting of three States members of the United Nations which shall have the following functions:

a) To assume, in so far as it considers necessary in existing circumstances, the functions given to the United Nations Mediator on Palestine by resolution 186 (S-2) of the General Assembly of 14 May 1948;

b) To carry out the specific functions and directives given to it by the present resolution and such additional functions and directives as may be given to it by the General Assembly or by the Security Council;

c) To undertake, upon the request of the Security Council, any of the functions now assigned to the United Nations Mediator on Palestine or to the United Nations Truce Commission by resolutions of the Security Council; upon such request to the Conciliation Commission by the Security Council with respect to all the remaining functions of the United Nations Mediator on Palestine under Security Council resolutions, the office of the Mediator shall be terminated;

3. Decides that a Committee of the Assembly, consisting of China, France, the Union of Soviet Socialist Republics, the United Kingdom and the United States of America, shall present before the end of the first part of the present session of the General Assembly, for the approval of the Assembly, a proposal concerning the names of the three States which will constitute the Conciliation Commission;

4. Requests the Commission to begin its functions at once, with a view to the establishment of contact between the parties themselves and the Commission at the earliest possible date;

5. Calls upon the Governments and authorities concerned to extend the scope of the negotiations provided for in the Security Council's resolution of 16 November 1948 and to seek agreement by negotiations conducted either with the Conciliation Commission or directly, with a view to the final settlement of all questions outstanding between them;

6. Instructs the Conciliation Commission to take steps to assist the Governments and authorities concerned to achieve a final settlement of all questions outstanding between them;

7. Resolves that the Holy Places—including Nazareth—religious buildings and sites in Palestine should be protected and free access to them assured, in accordance with existing right and historical practices; that arrangements to this end should be under effective United Nations supervision, that the fourth regular session of the General Assembly in its detailed proposals for a permanent international regime for the territory of Jerusalem, should include recommendations concerning the Holy Places in that territory; that with regard to the Holy Places in the rest of Palestine the commission should call upon the political authorities of the areas concerned to give appropriate formal guarantees as to protection of the Holy Places and access to them; and that these undertakings should be presented to the General Assembly for approval;

8. Resolves that, in view of its association with three world religions the Jerusalem area, including the present municipality of Jerusalem plus the surrounding villages and towns, the most eastern of which shall be Abu Dis; the most southern, Bethlehem; the most western, Ein Karim (including also the built-up area of Motsa); and the most northern Shu'fat, should be accorded special and separate treatment from the rest of Palestine and should be placed under effective United Nations control;

Requests the Security Council to take further steps to ensure the demilitarization of Jerusalem at the earliest possible date;

Instructs the Commission to present to the fourth regular session of the General Assembly detailed proposals for a permanent international regime for the Jerusalem area which will provide for the maximum local autonomy for distinctive groups consistent with the special international status of the Jerusalem area;

The Conciliation Commission is authorized to appoint a United Nations representative, who shall co-operate with the local authorities with respect to the interim administration of the Jerusalem area;

9. Resolves that, pending agreement on more detailed arrangements among the Governments and authorities concerned, the freest possible access to Jerusalem by road, rail or air should be accorded to all inhabitants of Palestine;

10. Instructs the Conciliation Commission to seek arrangements among the Governments and authorities concerned which will facilitate the economic development of the area, including

arrangements for access to ports and airfields and the use of transportation and communication facilities;

11. Resolves that the refugees wishing to return to their homes and live at peace with their neighbors should be permitted to do so at the earliest practical date, and that compensation should be paid for the property of those choosing not to return and for loss of or damage to property which, under principles of international law or in equity, should be made good by the Governments or authorities responsible;

Instructs the Conciliation Commission to facilitate the repatriation, resettlement and economic and social rehabilitation of the refugees and the payment of compensation and to maintain close relations with the director of the United Nations Relief for Palestine Refugees and, through him, with the appropriate organs and agencies of the United Nations;

12. Authorizes the Conciliation Commission to appoint such subsidiary bodies and to employ such technical experts acting under its authority, as it may find necessary for the effective discharge of it functions and responsibilities under the present resolution;

The Conciliation Commission will have its official headquarters at Jerusalem. The Authorities will be responsible for taking all measures necessary to ensure the security of the Commission. The Secretary-General will provide a limited number of guards for the protection of the staff and premises of the Commission;

13. Instructs the Conciliation Commission to render progress reports periodically to the Secretary-General for transmission to the Security Council and to the Members of the United Nations;

14. Calls upon all Governments and authorities concerned to cooperate with the Conciliation Commission and to take all possible steps to assist in the implementation of the present resolution;

15. Requests the Secretary-General to provide the necessary staff and facilities and to make appropriate arrangements to provide the necessary funds required in carrying out the terms of the present resolution.

Appendix 7:
UN General Assembly
Resolution 3236,
November 22, 1974

The General Assembly,

Having considered the Question of Palestine,

Having heard the statement of the Palestine Liberation Organization, the representative of the Palestinian people,

Having also heard other statements made during the debate,

Deeply concerned that no just solution to the problem of Palestine has yet been achieved and recognizing the problem of Palestine continues to endanger international peace and security,

Recognizing that the Palestinian people is entitled to self-determination in accordance with the Charter of the United Nations,

Expressing its grave concern that the Palestinian people has been prevented from enjoying its inalienable rights, in particular its right to self-determination,

Guided by the purposes and principles of the Charter,

Recalling its relevant resolutions which affirm the right of the Palestinian people to self-determination,

1. Reaffirms the inalienable rights of the Palestinian people in Palestine, including:

a) The right to self-determination without external interference;

b) The right to national independence and sovereignty;

2. Reaffirms also the inalienable right of the Palestinians to return to their homes and property from which they have been displaced and uprooted, and calls for their return;

3. Emphasizes that full respect for and the realization of these inalienable rights of the Palestinian people are indispensable for the solution of the Question of Palestine;

4. Recognizes that the Palestinian people is a principal party in the establishment of a just and durable peace in the Middle East;

5. Further recognizes the right of the Palestinian people to regain its rights by all means in accordance with the purposes and principles of the Charter of the United Nations

6. Appeals to all States and international organizations to extend their support to the Palestinian people in its struggle to restore its rights, in accordance with the Charter;

7. Requests the Secretary-General to establish contacts with the Palestine Liberation Organization on all matters concerning the Question of Palestine;

8. Requests the Secretary-General to report to the General Assembly at its thirtieth session on the implementation of the present Resolution;

9. Decides to include the item "Question of Palestine" in the provisional agenda of its thirtieth session.

Appendix 8:
UN Security Council
Resolution 338,
October 22, 1973

The Security Council,

1. Calls upon all participants to the present fighting to cease all firing and terminate all military activity immediately, no later than 12 hours after the moment of the adoption of this decision, in the positions they now occupy;

2. Calls upon the parties concerned to start immediately after the cease-fire the implementation of Security Council Resolution 242 (1967) in all of its parts;

3. Decides that, immediately and concurrently with the cease-fire, negotiations start between the parties concerned under appropriate auspices aimed at establishing a just and durable peace in the Middle East.

Appendix 9:
Excerpts from the Declaration of Palestinian Independence, November 15, 1988

... Despite the historical injustice inflicted on the Palestinian Arab people resulting in their dispersion and depriving them of their right to self-determination, following upon UN General Assembly Resolution 181 (1947), which partitioned Palestine into two states, one Arab, one Jewish, yet it is this resolution that still provides those conditions of international legitimacy that ensure the right of the Palestinian Arab people to sovereignty ...

... Whereas the Palestinian people reaffirms most definitively its inalienable rights in the Land of it patrimony:

Now by virtue of natural, historic and legal rights, and the sacrifices of successive generations who gave of themselves in defence of the freedom and independence of their homeland;

In pursuance of Resolutions adopted by Arab Summit Conferences and relying on the authority bestowed by international legitimacy as embodied in the resolutions of the United Nations Organization since 1947;

And in exercise of the Palestinian Arab people of its rights to self-determination, political independence, and sovereignty over its territory;

The Palestine National Council, in the name of God, and in the name of the Palestinian Arab people; hereby proclaims the establishment of the State of Palestine on our Palestinian territory with its capital Holy Jerusalem (Al-Quds Ash-Sharif).

The state of Palestine is the state of Palestinians wherever they may be. The state is for them to enjoy in it their collective national and cultural identity, theirs to pursue in it a complete equality of rights. In it will be safeguarded their political and religious convictions and their human dignity by means of a parliamentary democratic system of governance, itself based on freedom of expression and the freedom to form parties. The rights of minorities will duly be respected by the majority, as minorities must abide by decisions of the majority. Governance will be based on principles of social justice, equality and non-discrimination in public rights of men or women, on grounds of race, religion, colour or sex under the aegis of a constitution which ensures the rule of law and independent judiciary. Thus shall these principles allow no departure from Palestine's age-old spiritual and civilizational heritage of tolerance and religious coexistence.

The State of Palestine is an Arab state, an integral and indivisible part of the Arab nation, at one with that nation in heritage and civilization, with it also in its aspiration for liberation, progress, democracy and unity. The State of Palestine affirms its obligation to abide by the Charter of the League of Arab States, whereby the coordination of the Arab states with each other shall be strengthened. It calls upon Arab compatriots to consolidate and enhance the emergence in reality of our state, to mobilize potential, and to intensify efforts whose goal is to end Israeli occupation.

The State of Palestine proclaims its commitment to the principles and purposes of the United Nations, and to the Universal Declaration of Human Rights. It proclaims its commitment as well to the principles and policies of the Non-Aligned Movement. . . .

. . . The State of Palestine herewith declares that it believes in the settlement of regional and international disputes by peaceful means, in accordance with the UN Charter and resolutions. Without prejudice to its natural right to defend its territorial integrity and independence, it therefore rejects the threat or use of force, violence and terrorism against its territorial integrity or political independence, as it also rejects their use against the territorial integrity of other states. . . .

Appendix 10:
The Stockholm Statement,
December 7, 1988

The text of the joint PLO–American Jewish delegation statement, presented by Swedish foreign minister Stern Anderson:

The Palestinian National Council met in Algiers from November 12 to 15, 1988, and announced the declaration of independence which proclaimed the state of Palestine and issued a political statement.

The following explanation was given by the representatives of the PLO of certain important points in the Palestinian declaration of independence and the political statement adopted by the PNC in Algiers.

Affirming the principle incorporated in those UN resolutions which call for a two-state solution of Israel and Palestine, the PNC:

1. Agreed to enter into peace negotiations at an international conference under the auspices of the UN with the participation of the permanent members of the Security Council and the PLO as the sole legitimate representative of the Palestinian people, on equal footing with the other parties to the conflict; such an international conference is to be held on the basis of UN resolutions 242 and 338 and the right of the Palestinian people of self-determination, without external interference, as provided in the UN Charter, including the right to an independent state, which conference should resolve the Palestinian problem in all aspects;

2. Established the independent state of Palestine and accepted the existence of Israel as a state in the region;

3. Declared its rejection and condemnation of terrorism in all its forms, including state terrorism;

4. Called for a solution to the Palestinian refugee problem in accordance with international law and practices and relevant UN resolutions (including right of return or compensation).

The American personalities strongly supported and applauded the Palestinian declaration of independence and the political statement adopted in Algiers, and felt there was no further impediment to a direct dialogue between the United States Government and the PLO.

Appendix 11: The Palestinian Peace Initiative, December 13, 1988

Excerpts from the speech by Yasser Arafat to the UN General Assembly in Geneva.
In my capacity as Chairman of the PLO Executive Committee, presently assuming the functions of the provisional government of the State of Palestine, I therefore present the following Palestinian peace initiative:

First: That a serious effort be made to convene, under the supervision of the Secretary General of the United Nations, the preparatory Committee of the international conference for peace in the Middle East . . . to pave the way for the convening of the international conference, which commands universal support except from the government of Israel.

Second: . . . that actions be undertaken to place our occupied Palestinian land under temporary United Nations supervision, and that international forces be deployed there to protect our people and, at the same time, to supervise the withdrawal of the Israeli forces from our country.

Third: The PLO will seek a comprehensive settlement among the parties concerned in the Arab-Israeli conflict, including the State of Palestine, Israel and other neighbors, within the framework of the international conference for peace in the Middle East on the basis of Resolutions 242 and 338 and so as to guarantee equality and the balance of interests, especially our people's rights to live in freedom, national independence, and respect the right to exist in peace and security for all.

If these principles are endorsed at the international conference, we will have come a long way toward a just settlement, and this will enable us to reach agreement on all security and peace arrangements. . . .

I come to you in the name of my people, offering my hand so that we can make true peace, peace based on justice.

I ask the leaders of Israel to come here under the sponsorship of the United Nations so that, together, we can forge that peace. . . .

And here, I would address myself specifically to the Israeli people in all their parties and forces, and especially to the advocates of democracy and peace among them. I say to them: 'Come let us make peace. Cast away fear and intimidation. Leave behind the spectre of the wars that have raged continuously for the past 40 years'.

Appendix 12:
UN Security Council
Resolution 298 on Jerusalem,
September 25, 1971

The Security Council,

Recalling its resolutions 252 (1968) of 21 May 1968, and 267 (1969) of 3 July 1969, and the earlier General Assembly resolution 2253 (RS-V) and 2254 (RS-V) of 4 and 14 July 1967, concerning measures and actions by Israel designed to change the status of the Israeli-occupied section of Jerusalem,

Having considered the letter of the Permanent Representative of Jordan on this situation in Jerusalem and the reports of the Secretary-General, and having heard the statements of the parties concerned in the questions,

Recalling the principle that acquisition of territory by military conquest is inadmissible,

Noting with concern the non-compliance of Israel with the above-mentioned resolutions,

Noting with concern also that since the adoption of the above-mentioned resolutions Israel has taken further measures designed to change the status and character of the occupied section of Jerusalem;

1. Reaffirms its resolution 252 (1968) and 267 (1969);

2. Deplores the failure of Israel to respect the previous resolutions adopted by the United Nations concerning measures and actions by Israel purporting to affect the status of the City of Jerusalem;

3. Confirms in the clearest possible terms that all legislative and administrative actions taken by Israel to change the status of the City of Jerusalem, including expropriation of land and properties, transfer of populations and legislation aimed at the incorporation of the occupied section, are totally invalid and cannot change the status;

4. Urgently calls upon Israel to rescind all previous measures and actions and to take no further steps in the occupied section of Jerusalem which may purport to change the status of the City, or which would prejudice the rights of the inhabitants and the interests of the international community, or a just and lasting peace;

5. Requests the Security-General, in consultation with the President of the Security Council and using such instrumentalities as he may choose, including a representative or a mission, to report to the Council as appropriate and in any event within 60 days on the implementation of the present resolution.

Appendix 13:
Article 27 of the Charter of the Islamic Resistance Movement (HAMAS)

[On the] Palestine Liberation Organization
Article 27

The Palestine Liberation Organization is closest of the close to the Islamic Resistance Movement, in that it is the father, the brother, the relative, or friend; and does the Muslim offend his father, brother, relative, or friend? Our nation is one, plight is one, destiny is one, and our enemy is the same, being affected by the situation that surrounded the formation of the organization (PLO) and the chaotic ideologies that overwhelm the Arab world due to the ideological invasion that befell the Arab world since the defeat of the Crusades and the ongoing consolidation of orientalism, missionary work, and imperialism. The organization (PLO) adopted the idea of a secular state, and as such we considered it.

Secularist ideology is in total contradiction to religious ideologies, and it is upon ideology that positions, actions, and decisions are made. From here, with our respect for the Palestine Liberation Organization and what it might become, and not understanding its role in the Arab-Israeli struggle, we cannot exchange the current status and future of Islam in Palestine to adopt the secular ideology because the Islamic nature of the Palestinian issue is part and parcel of our *din* (ideology and way of life) and whosoever neglects part of his *din* is surely lost.

And who turns away from the religion of Abraham but such as debase their souls with folly?
Sura 2: Baqara: 130

When the Palestine Liberation Organization adopts Islam as its system of life, we will be its soldiers and the firewood of its fire, which will burn the enemies. Until this happens, and we ask Allah that it be soon, the position of the Islamic Resistance Movement toward the Palestine Liberation Organization is the position of a son toward his father, and the brother toward his brother, and the relative toward his relative. He will be hurt if a thorn pricks him; he supports him in confronting the enemy and wishes guidance from him.

Your brother, your brother he who has no brother is like one going to battle without weapons.

And know that your cousin is like your wings; and does the falcon fly without wings?

Appendix 14:
Palestine National
Council Statement,
September 28, 1991

The following are the salient points of the political statement issued by the twentieth PNC after its September 23–28, 1991, meeting in Algiers:

Premises: In keeping with the 1988 Palestinian peace initiative and international and Arab legality, the PLO dealt positively and actively with all ideas, proposals and international peace initiatives based on international legitimacy. It welcomed the positive elements in the declaration of President George Bush, and the positions taken by the EC, the Soviet Union, the Non-Aligned nations and other international parties.

The PLO has welcomed current peace efforts and responded to them positively, including the call by Presidents Bush and Gorbachev for a peace conference to resolve the conflict in the Middle East.

It believes that the success of efforts to convene the peace conference require continued work with the other parties to achieve the following premises:

1) That the peace conference be based on international legitimacy and resolutions, including UN Security Council Resolutions 242 and 338, and on a commitment to their implementation, in a manner securing complete Israeli withdrawal from the occupied Arab and Palestinian territories—including Jerusalem—and fulfillment of the principle of land for peace and the national and political rights of the Palestinian people.

2) A reaffirmation that Jerusalem is an integral part of the occupied Palestinian territory, to which all that applies to the rest of the occupied territories under UN resolutions is also applicable.

3) That a cessation of settlement in the occupied territories, including Jerusalem, is indispensable to start the peace process. International guarantees should be provided in this respect.

4) That the PLO, in its capacity as sole legitimate representative of the Palestinian people, has the right to form the Palestinian delegation from inside and outside the occupied territories, including Jerusalem, and to formulate a framework for [the

delegation's] participation in the peacemaking that upholds [the PLO's] authority in this context.

5) That Arab positions are coordinated in a manner that ensures a comprehensive settlement and rules out separate solutions, in keeping with Arab summit resolutions.

6) Guaranteeing that all stages of the solution are linked and bound to lead to a final and comprehensive settlement in keeping with the resolutions of international legitimacy.

Aims: On the basis of these aforementioned peacemaking premises, the PLO aims to achieve the following:

1) To secure the Palestinian people's right to self-determination which would also ensure its right to freedom and national independence.

2) Total Israeli withdrawal from the Palestinian and Arab territories occupied in 1967, including Jerusalem.

3) A solution, in accordance with UN Resolutions, particularly General Assembly Resolution 194, to the problem of Palestinian refugees who were uprooted from their land by force and coercion.

4) The need for any transitional arrangements to incorporate our people's right to sovereignty over all its land, water, natural resources and political and economic affairs.

5) The provision of international protection to the Palestinian people in preparation for its exercise of its right to self-determination.

6) The provision of full guarantees for action to remove the existing settlements, which are considered illegal under the resolutions of international legitimacy, including Security Council Resolution 465.

The PNC instructs the Executive Committee to continue its current efforts to achieve the best conditions that can ensure success for the peace process in accordance with PNC resolutions, and to report the results to the Central Council for it to take a final decision in the light of the supreme national interests of our people.

The PLO, which in the past period has made every possible effort to advance the peace process, hopes that other parties, particularly the United States and the Soviet Union, will in turn strive to remove the obstacles raised by Israel before the current political process, leaving open the option of recourse to the Security Council to seek the implementation of resolutions of international legitimacy.

Glossary

Ahl al-Kitab. "People of the Book" (the Bible). A reference to Christians and Jews.

al-Ard. Land.

al-'Ard. The honor of the women in a family.

al-Ard al-Muqaddasah. The Holy Land.

Aradi Sultaniyya. Sultanic lands or state land during the Ottoman era.

Arz-i Filistin. Turkish for "land of Palestine."

Ashraf. The Islamic Arab "nobility," descendants of the Prophet Muhammad or his early companions.

A'yan. Political and economic notables.

Ba'ath Party. An Arab nationalist political movement and party that sought unity of the Arab World and the liberation of Palestine.

Balfour Declaration. The declaration by the imperial British government in 1917 of its support for the establishment in Palestine of a national home for the Jewish people.

Barrakiyat. Refugee camp dwellings made up of corrugated iron, tin, wood, or other materials.

Bayan (pl. *bayanat*). Communiqué issued by the leaders of the intifada to direct its action.

Bayt al-Maqdis. The Holy Abode, the city of Jerusalem.

al-Buraq. The winged stallion upon which the Prophet Muhammad ascended to heaven from a rock in Jerusalem and returned to earth.

Canaanites. Ancient people of Palestine, first mentioned in the Tell al-Amarna archaeological finds of 1500 B.C.

Corpus separatum. Literally, separate entity: the international status (independent from the Arab and Jewish states in Palestine) that Jerusalem and Bethlehem would come under according to the 1947 UN partition plan for Palestine.

Corvée labor. Forced labor.

al-Dakhel. Inside; a reference to the area inside historic Palestine where the Palestinians are still resident.

Dalet. Hebrew for the name of the plan for a Jewish-Zionist campaign of terror and conquest to capture the territory of Palestine in the 1947–1948 internal war.

Declaration of Principles. The Israel-PLO agreements to resolve the conflict between them. Also called the Oslo Accords.

al-Defa'a. Defense; the name of a Palestinian newspaper during the period of the British Mandate.

Dhimmah. Conscience. Ahl al-Dhimmah were the people of conscience, the protected minorities of Christians and Jews during the Arab Islamic caliphates, A.D. 632–1258.

Dibs. Molasses made from carob.

Durra. Maize.

Emin. A salaried Turkish tax collector.

Emir. A prince or powerful local ruler.

Fada'il al-Quds. The eulogizing literature of Jerusalem during the Crusades.

Fallah (pl. *fallahin*). Peasant. Also transliterated as *fellah*.

Fard (Turkish *ferde*). Individual. Also used to denote a capitation tax.

Fasa'il. Guerrilla bands of the 1936–1939 Palestinian Arab revolt against the British. Also used to describe the various guerrilla groups that made up the PLO.

Fateh. Conquest or opening; a reverse acronym for the Palestine National Liberation Movement (often transliterated as Fatah, al-Fatah, or Fath). One of the earliest, largest, and dominant political-guerrilla groups constituting the PLO. It has been led by Yasser 'Arafat since 1968.

Fatwa (pl. *fatawa*). Legal religious opinion.

Faz'a. Spontaneous mobilization of support of neighboring villages or communities against British attacks during the 1936–1939 Palestinian Arab revolt.

Feda'iyyin. Self-sacrificers (also transliterated as *fedayeen*); the name Palestinians give to guerrilla fighters or groups.

Fida. A small DFLP splinter group that supports the Oslo Accords.

Filastinuna. "Our Palestine," the name of the underground publication of Fateh early in its clandestine period in the 1950s.

Futuwwa. A youth group that fought during the 1947–1948 Jewish-Palestinian conflict inside Palestine.

Ghor. The rift valley of the Jordan River.

al-Ghourba. Estrangement; a term used by Palestinians to refer to their diaspora.

Haganah. The official Jewish forces during the mandate period in Palestine.

Hajj. The pilgrimage to Mecca. Also a title for one who has performed the hajj.

Hamas. Literally, zeal or enthusiasm; an Arabic acronym for the Islamic Resistance Movement, based largely in the Gaza Strip.

Hamula. Patrilineal lineage or clan.

Hanafi. One of the four schools of Islamic jurisprudence.

Harakat al-Muqawama al-Filastiniyya. Palestinian Resistance Movement.

Harakat al-Tahrir al-Islami. Islamic Liberation Movement, whose acronym is Hamas.

Harakat al-Tahrir al-Watani al-Filastini. Palestine National Liberation Movement.

al-Haram al-Sharif. The Noble Sanctuary (or Temple Mount) in Jerusalem, where the two holy Islamic mosques of Al-Aqsa and Dome of the Rock are located.

Hatt-i Humayun. Turkish for imperial rescript, a second reform decree in the nineteenth century.

Hatt-i Sherif of Gulhane. The first royal edict of Ottoman reform, issued in 1839.

Hawakir (sing. *hakourah*). Small plots of productive land.

Hawiyya. Identity card.

Histadrut. Jewish labor federation established in 1920 in Palestine.

Hizb al-Watan al-Uthmani. Ottoman Patriotic Party.

Hovevei Zion. Lovers of Zion, a Zionist movement.

al-Ikhwan al-Muslimin. The Muslim Brotherhood, a political Islamic movement.

Ikhwan al-Qassam. Brothers of al-Qassam, the martyred leader of the Palestinian Arab revolt against the British mandate authorities between 1936 and 1939.

Innana 'ai'doun (or *Innana raji'oun*). Arabic for "We shall return," the phrase that became the slogan expressing diaspora Palestinians' desire to return home to Palestine.

Intifada. The Palestinian uprising against Israeli occupation of the West Bank and the Gaza Strip.

Irgun Z'vai Leumi. A Jewish Zionist underground terrorist organization during the 1940s led by Menachem Begin, later (1977–1982) prime minister of Israel.

Istiqlal Party. Independence Party.

Jam'iyyat al-Shabiba al-Nabulsiyya. Nablus Youth Society.

Jaysh al-Inqath. Army of Salvation, an Arab volunteer force that fought the Jewish Zionist militias in the 1947–1948 Jewish-Palestinian war.

Jihad. Struggle; often interpreted as armed struggle in defense of Islam or Islamic society and institutions.

al-Jihad al-Islami. Islamic Jihad, a radical Islamic political movement anchored largely in the Gaza Strip.

al-Jihad al-Muqaddas. Holy Struggle, a volunteer force in the Jewish-Palestinian war of 1947–1948.

Jund Filastin. Military district of Palestine under Muslim Arab rule.

Kaffiyya. The traditional Arab checkered headdress, worn by the youthful activists and militants of the intifada.

Al-Karameh. The name of the refugee camp and village in East Jordan in which an Israeli military force fought a pitched battle against Palestinian guerrillas in 1968. It marked a turning point in the political rise and surfacing (from clandestine status) of the Palestinian guerrilla (feda'iyyin) movement. *Karameh* in Arabic means "dignity."

Al-Karmel. Mount Carmel, near the city of Haifa; also the name of a Palestinian newspaper during the period of the British Mandate.

Kha'in. Traitor.

Al-Khalil. Hebron.

Khan. Turkish for an inn for travelers and their animals.

al-Kharej. Outside; a reference to any area outside Palestine where refugees live.

Kibbutz. An agricultural cooperative Jewish settlement in Palestine.

Kiyan. Entity; a political organization or jurisdiction.

Lohamei Herut Yisrael (Lehi). A Jewish Zionist underground terrorist organization during the 1940s. Also known as the Stern Gang after its founder, Abraham Stern.

Ma'arakat al-massir. The battle of destiny against Israel.

Madaniyyin (sing. *madani*). Urbanites or city dwellers.

Maghreb. The Arab west, or north Africa.

Majlis (pl. *majalis*). Local or village council.

al-Manfa. Exile; a reference to the Palestinian diaspora.

Maqam. A sacred sanctuary, usually the tomb of a *wali,* or popular saint.

Mashreq. The Arab east, or Arab Asia and Egypt.

al-Masjed al-Aqsa. Al-Aqsa mosque on al-Haram al-Sharif in Jerusalem.

Metayer. Tenant farmer.

Millet. Religious sect; collectively taxed by the Ottomans.

Muhajjarin. Displaced persons, a reference to camp dwellers who sought shelter in other secure camps or settlements during the Lebanese civil war.

Muharram. One of the months in the Islamic calendar. Also the name of a decree issued by Ottoman authorities in the nineteenth century that consolidated European financial control over the Ottoman Empire.

Mukhtar. Village selectman or mayor, a representative of the Turkish authorities.

Mulk. Also transliterated as *milk*. Private property.

Muqata'aji. Feudal lord/tax farmer.

al-Muqawama. Resistance; short name for the Palestinian Resistance Movement.

Musha'a. Communal land in Palestine during the nineteenth and the first half of the twentieth centuries.

Mustabaheen. An unprotected group open to repression, killings, and pogroms. It is used to describe the status of the Palestinians in Lebanon since the mid-1980s.

Mutafa'il. Optimist.

Mutasariffiyya. An administrative subdistrict during the Ottoman period.

al-Mutasha'il. An Arabic neologism meaning "pessoptimist," one who is simultaneously a pessimist and an optimist.

Mutasha'im. Pessimist.

Nabi Musa. The Prophet Moses, a popular *wali,* or saint, recognized throughout Palestine.

Nabi Saleh. The Prophet Saleh, a popular *wali,* or saint, recognized throughout Palestine.

al-Nahda al-Orthodoksiyya. The orthodox renaissance in the first decade of the nineteenth century.

Nahiya. During the Ottoman period, a small administrative subdistrict composed of several villages.

Najjadah. Youth group that fought during the 1947–1948 Jewish-Palestinian conflict.

al-Nakbah. Catastrophe or disaster; the term that Palestinians use to refer to the destruction of their society in 1948.

Naqib. Elected leader of the *ashraf* "nobility" in urban nineteenth-century Palestine.

Oslo Accords. The agreements, officially labeled the Declaration of Principles, negotiated between Israel and the PLO in secret meetings in Oslo in 1993.

Qadi. Court judge.

Qa'id. Leader; specifically, leader of a guerrilla band of the 1936–1939 Palestinian Arab revolt against the British.

Qays. One of the lineage-based traditional political factions in Palestine and the Arab east.

Qilli. An alkaline powder, a raw material crucial for the production of soap.

al-Qiyada al-Wataniyya al-Muwahhada li-l Intifada. Unified National Leadership of the Uprising (UNLU).

Qubbat al-Sakhra. The holy mosque of the Dome of the Rock.

Al-Quds. Literally, "the Holy," the city of Jerusalem.

Ra'ees. Head, the title the Israel-PLO accords settled on for Yasser 'Arafat. 'Arafat and the Palestinian negotiators wanted to use the title "president," while the Israelis wanted him to use the title "chairman."

Sabr. Cactus bush that has become a national symbol for the West Bank and Gaza Strip Palestinians under occupation. The term also means "patience," "perseverance."

Salam. Nineteenth-century Arabic term for futures purchase (not to be confused with current usage, in which the term means "peace").

Samedin (or *samedoun*). Steadfast (people).

Sanjak. An administrative subdistrict of an Ottoman governorate.

al-Sha'ab al-Filastini. The Palestinian People.

Sha'abi. Poor residential areas or slums.

Shabab. Young men, a term that refers to the youthful activists and militants of the intifada.

Shari'a. Islamic law.

Shaykh. Tribal leader, religious cleric, or dignitary.

Shi'a. One of the two great sects of Islam. The Shi'a are the partisans of Ali, cousin and son-in-law of the Prophet Muhammad.

Sultan. King or sovereign.

Sumoud. Perseverance.

Sunni. The largest and dominant orthodox sect of Islam.

Tabu (**Turkish** *tapu*). Land registration law.

Tanzimat. The administrative and economic reforms within the Ottoman Empire during the middle of the nineteenth century.

Tawtin. Naturalization and settlement of Palestinian refugees in the Arab host countries.

Tempelgesellschaft. Association of Templars, an offshoot of a Protestant Pietistic movement in the German kingdom of Württemberg that established several colonies in Palestine during the nineteenth century.

Tha'ir. Rebel in the 1936–1939 Palestinian Arab revolt against the British.

'Ulama. Islamic theologians.

Umma. Nation or community.

'Urf. Customary law.

Vali (**Arabic** *wali*). Literally, guardian; Turkish term used for both the governor of a large administrative district and an Islamic saint.

Waqf (**pl** *awqaf*). Tax-free religious endowment.

Watan. Homeland.

Wilaya. Governorate.

Wujaha. Political and economic notables.

Yaman. One of the lineage-based factional political divisions that cut across the whole country and the region.

Yishuv. The Jewish settler-immigrant community in Palestine.

Zakat. Islamic obligation of almsgiving.

Selected Bibliography

Books and Dissertations

Abboushi, W. *The Unmaking of Palestine* (Brattleboro: Amana Books, 1990).

Abcarius, M. F. *Palestine Through the Fog of Propaganda* (London: Hutchinson, 1946).

Abed, G. T., ed. *The Palestinian Economy: Studies in Development Under Prolonged Occupation* (London: Routledge, 1988).

Abu, Iyad with Eric Rouleau. *My Home, My Land* (New York: Times Books, 1981).

Abu-Amr, Z. *Islamic Fundamentalism in the West Bank and Gaza* (Bloomington: Indiana University Press, 1994).

Abu El-Haj, N. "Excavating the Land, Creating the Homeland: Archaeology, the State and the Making of History in Modern Jewish Nationalism." Ph.D. dissertation, Duke University, 1995.

Abu-Ghazaleh, A. *Arab Cultural Nationalism in Palestine* (Beirut: Institute for Palestine Studies, 1973).

Abu-Lughod, I., ed. *The Transformation of Palestine* (Evanston, IL: Northwestern University Press, 1971).

'Allush, N. *Arab Resistance in Palestine (1917–1948)* (in Arabic) (Beirut: Dar al-Tali'a, 1975).

Amin, S. *The Arab World Today* (London: Zed, 1978).

Anderson, B. *Imagined Communities: Reflections on the Origin and Spread of Nationalism* (New York: Verso, 1991).

Antonius, G. *The Arab Awakening: The Story of the Arab National Movement* (New York: Capricorn Books, 1965).

al-'Arif, 'A. *History of Gaza* (in Arabic) (Al-Quds: Matba'at Dar al-Aytam al-Islamiyya, 1943).

Aronson, G. *Creating Facts: Israel, Palestinians and the West Bank* (Washington, DC: Institute for Palestine Studies, 1987).

Aruri, N. H. *Jordan: A Study in Political Development, 1921–1965* (The Hague: Nijhoff, 1972).

_____. *The Obstruction of Peace: The U.S., Israel and the Palestinians* (Monroe, ME: Common Courage Press, 1995).

_____, ed. *Occupation: Israel over Palestine*, 2nd ed. (Belmont, MA: Association of Arab-American University Graduates, 1989).

_____, ed. *Palestinian Resistance to the Israeli Occupation* (Wilmette, IL: Medina University Press, 1970).

Ashrawi, H. *This Side of Peace* (New York: Simon and Schuster, 1995).

Awad, A. *Introduction to the Modern History of Palestine, 1831–1914* (in Arabic) (Beirut: Arab Institution for Studies and Publishing, 1983).

Ayyoub, S. M. *The Class Structure of Palestinians in Lebanon* (in Arabic) (Beirut: Beirut Arab University, 1978).

Badran, N. *Education and Modernization in Palestinian Arab Society* (in Arabic) (Beirut: PLO Research Center, 1978).

Barghouthi, O. and K. Tawtah. *History of Palestine* (in Arabic) (Jerusalem, 1923).

Benvenisti, M. *Intimate Enemies: Jews and Arabs in a Shared Land* (Berkeley: University of California Press, 1995).

_____. *1986 Report: Demographic, Economic, Legal, Social, and Political Developments in the West Bank* (Boulder, CO: Westview Press, 1986).

_____. *1987 Report: Demographic, Economic, Legal, Social, and Political Developments in the West Bank* (Boulder, CO: Westview Press, 1987).

_____ with Z. Abu-Zayed and D. Rubinstein. *The West Bank Handbook: A Political Lexicon* (Boulder, CO: Westview Press, 1986).

Berger, E. *Peace for Palestine: First Lost Opportunity* (Gainesville: University Press of Florida, 1993).

Bethell, N. *The Palestine Triangle: The Struggle Between the British, the Jews and the Arabs, 1935–48* (London: Andre Deutsch, 1979).

Bowersock, G. W. *Roman Arabia* (Cambridge: Harvard University Press, 1983).

Brand, L. A. *Palestinians in the Arab World* (New York: Columbia University Press, 1988).

Bromley, S. *American Hegemony and World Oil* (University Park: Pennsylvania State University Press, 1991).

Brynen, R., ed. *Echoes of the Intifada: Regional Repercussions of the Palestinian-Israeli Conflict* (Boulder, CO: Westview Press, 1991).

_____. *Sanctuary and Survival: The PLO in Lebanon* (Boulder, CO: Westview Press, 1990).

Budeiri, M. *The Palestine Communist Party, 1919–1948* (London: Ithaca Press, 1979).

Buheiry, M., ed. *Intellectual Life in the Arab East: 1890–1939* (Beirut: American University of Beirut Press, 1981).

Carnoy, M. *The State and Political Theory* (Princeton, NJ: Princeton University Press, 1984).

Chomsky, N. *Deterring Democracy* (New York: Vintage, 1992).

_____. *The Fateful Triangle: The United States, Israel and the Palestinians* (Boston: South End Press, 1983).

_____. *World Orders: Old and New* (New York: Columbia University Press, 1994).

Cobban, H. *The Palestinian Liberation Organization: People, Power and Politics* (Cambridge: Cambridge University Press, 1984).

Cohen, A. *Economic Life in Ottoman Jerusalem* (Cambridge: Cambridge University Press, 1989).

_____. *Palestine in the 18th Century* (Jerusalem: Magnes Press, 1973).

_____ and G. Baer, eds. *Egypt and Palestine—A Millennium of Association (868–1948)* (New York: St. Martin's Press, 1984).

_____ and B. L. Lewis. *Population and Revenue in the Towns of Palestine in the Sixteenth Century* (Princeton, NJ: Princeton University Press, 1978).

Cooley, J. K. *Green March, Black September: The Story of the Palestinian Arabs* (London: Frank Cass, 1973).

Dajani, S. R. *Eyes Without Country: Searching for a Palestinian Strategy of Liberation* (Philadelphia: Temple University Press, 1994).

Dodd, P. and H. Barakat. *River Without Bridges: A Study of the Exodus of the 1967 Palestinian Arab Refugees* (Beirut: Institute for Palestine Studies, 1969).

Doumani, B. B. "Merchants, Socioeconomic Change and the State in Ottoman Palestine: The Nablus Region, 1800–1860." Ph.D. dissertation, Georgetown University, 1990.

_____. *Rediscovering Palestine: Merchants and Peasants in Jabal Nablus, 1700–1900* (Berkeley: University of California Press, 1995).

Esco Foundation for Palestine. *Palestine: A Study of Jewish, Arab, and British Policies*, vols. 1 and 2 (New Haven: Yale University Press, 1947).

Finkelstein, N. G. *Image and Reality of the Israel-Palestine Conflict* (London: Verso, 1995).

_____. *The Rise and Fall of Palestine* (Minneapolis: University of Minnesota Press, 1996).

Finn, J. *Stirring Times*, 2 vols. (London: C. Kegan Paul, 1978).

Flapan, S. *The Birth of Israel: Myths and Realities* (New York: Pantheon, 1987).

Frischwasser-Ra'anan, H. *The Frontiers of a Nation: A Re-examination of the Forces Which Created the Palestine Mandate and Determined Its Territorial Shape* (London: Batchworth Press, 1955).

Ghabra, S. *The Palestinians in Kuwait: The Family and Politics of Survival* (Boulder, CO: Westview Press, 1987).

Gibb, H.A.R., trans. *The Damascus Chronicle of the Crusades* (London: Luzac, 1932).

_____ and H. Bowen. *Islamic Society and the West*, vols. 1 and 2 (Oxford: Oxford University Press, 1950, 1957).

Gilbar, G. G., ed. *Ottoman Palestine, 1800–1914: Studies in Economic and Social History* (Leiden: E. J. Brill, 1990).

Glubb, J. B. *A Soldier with the Arabs* (London: Hodder & Stoughton, 1957).

Graham-Brown, S. *Education, Repression and Liberation: Palestinians* (London: World University Service UK, 1984).

Gramsci, A. *Selections from Prison Notebooks* (New York: International Publishers, 1971).

Granott, A. *The Land System in Palestine*, translated by M. Sinion (London: Eyre and Spottiswoode, 1952).

Gresh, A. *The PLO: The Struggle Within* (London: Zed, 1985).

Habiby, E. *The Secret Life of Saeed, the Illfated-Pessoptimist: A Palestinian Who Became a Citizen of Israel*, translated by S. K. Jayyussi and T. Le Gassick (New York: Vantage, 1982).

Hadawi, S. *Palestinian Rights and Losses in 1948: A Comprehensive Study* (London: Saqi Books, 1988).

Hagopian, E., ed. *Amal and the Palestinians: Understanding the Battle of the Camps* (Belmont, MA: Association of Arab-American University Graduates, 1985).

Haim, S. G., ed. *Arab Nationalism: An Anthology* (Berkeley: University of California Press, 1964).

Halevy, N. and R. Klinov-Malul. *The Economic Development of Israel* (New York: Praeger, 1968).

Al-Haq. *Punishing a Nation: Israeli Human Rights Violations During the Palestinian Uprising, December 1987–December 1988* (Boston: South End Press, 1989).

Harkabi, Y. *Fedayeen Action and Arab Strategy* (London: Institute for Strategic Studies, 1968).

Heiberg, M. and G. Ovensen. *Palestinian Society in Gaza, West Bank and Arab Jerusalem: A Survey of Living Conditions*, FAFO report 151 (Oslo: FAFO, 1993).

Heyd, U. *Ottoman Documents on Palestine 1552–1615* (Oxford: Oxford University Press, 1960).

Hiltermann, J. R. *Behind the Intifada: Labor and Women's Movements in the Occupied Territories* (Princeton, NJ: Princeton University Press, 1991).

Himadeh, S. B., ed. *Economic Organization of Palestine* (Beirut: American University of Beirut, 1938).

Hirst, D. *The Gun and the Olive Branch* (London: Futura, 1977).

Hitti, P. K. *History of Syria* (London: Macmillan, 1957).

Hourani, A. *Arabic Thought in the Liberal Age: 1798–1939* (Oxford: Oxford University Press, 1970).

_____. *A History of the Arab Peoples* (Cambridge: Harvard University Press, 1991).

_____. *A Vision of History* (Beirut: American University of Beirut, 1961).

_____, P. Khoury, and M. C. Wilson, eds. *The Modern Middle East: A Reader* (London: I. B. Tauris, 1993).

Hudson, M. C. *Arab Politics* (New Haven: Yale University Press, 1989).

_____, ed. *The Palestinians: New Directions* (Washington, DC: Center for Contemporary Arab Studies, Georgetown University, 1990).

Hurewitz, J. C. *The Struggle for Palestine* (New York: W. W. Norton, 1950).

al-Husseini, M. Y. *Socioeconomic Development in Arab Palestine* (in Arabic) (Jaffa: Al-Taher Bros., 1946).

Hyamson, A. M. *Palestine Under the Mandate, 1920–1948* (Westport, CT: Greenwood Press, 1950).

Institute for Social and Economic Policy in the Middle East, John F. Kennedy School of Government, Harvard University, *Securing Peace in the Middle East: Project on Economic Transition* (Cambridge: Harvard University Press, 1993).

Issawi, C., ed. *The Economic History of the Middle East, 1800–1914* (Chicago: University of Chicago Press, 1966).

Kanafani, G. *Men in the Sun*, translated by H. Kilpatrick (Washington, DC: Three Continents Press, 1991).

Kazziha, W. *Palestine in the Arab Dilemma* (New York: Barnes and Noble, 1979).

_____. *Revolutionary Transformation in the Arab World: Habash and His Comrades from Nationalism to Marxism* (London: Charles Knight, 1975).

Kerr, M. H. *The Arab Cold War* (New York: Oxford University Press, 1971).

Khalaf, I. *Politics in Palestine* (Albany: State University of New York Press, 1991).

Khalaf, S. and P. Kongstad. *Hamra of Beirut: A Case of Rapid Urbanization* (Leiden: E. J. Brill, 1973).

Khalidi, R. *Under Siege: PLO Decision-making in the 1982 War* (New York: Columbia University Press, 1986).

_____ and C. Mansour, eds. *Palestine and the Gulf* (Beirut: Institute for Palestine Studies, 1982).

Khalidi, T., ed. *Land Tenure and Social Transformation in the Middle East* (Beirut: American University of Beirut, 1984).

Khalidi, W., ed. *All That Remains: The Palestinian Villages Occupied and Depopulated by Israel in 1948* (Washington, DC: Institute for Palestine Studies, 1992).

_____. *Before Their Diaspora: A Photographic History of the Palestinians, 1876–1948* (Washington, DC: Institute for Palestine Studies, 1984).

_____. *From Haven to Conquest: Readings in Zionism and the Palestine Problem Until 1948* (Beirut: Institute for Palestine Studies, 1971).

Khouri, E. *Palestinian Statistics* (Beirut: PLO Research Center, 1979).

Khouri, F. J. *The Arab Israeli Dilemma*, 3rd ed.(Syracuse: Syracuse University Press, 1985).

Khoury, Y. *Arab Press in Palestine: 1876–1948* (in Arabic) (Beirut: Institute for Palestine Studies, 1976).

Kimmerling, B. *Zionism and Territory* (Berkeley: Institute of International Studies, University of California, 1983).

_____ and J. Migdal. *Palestinians: The Making of a People* (New York: Free Press, 1993).

Krogh, P. F. and M. C. McDavid, eds. *Palestinians Under Occupation: Prospects for the Future* (Washington, DC: Center for Contemporary Arab Studies, Georgetown University, 1989).

Kushner, D., ed. *Palestine in the Late Ottoman Period: Political, Social and Economic Transformation* (Jerusalem: Yad Izhak Ben Zvi, 1986).

Kurd Ali, M. *The Book of al-Sham's Ways* (in Arabic) (Damascus: Maktabat al-Nuri, 1983).

Lehn, W. and U. Davis. *The Jewish National Fund* (London: Kegan Paul International, 1988).

Le Strange, G. *Palestine Under the Moslems* (London: A. P. Watt, 1890).

Lewis, B. L. *The Middle East and the West* (Bloomington: Indiana University Press, 1964).

Lockman, Z. and J. Beinin, eds. *Intifada: The Palestinian Uprising Against Israeli Occupation* (Boston: South End Press, 1989).

Luciani, G., ed. *The Arab State* (Berkeley: University of California Press, 1990).

Lustick, I. S., ed. *The Conflict with Israel in Arab Politics and Society* (New York: Garland, 1994).

_____. *From Wars Toward Peace in the Arab-Israeli Conflict 1969–1993* (New York: Garland, 1994).

Lutsky, V. *Modern History of the Arab Countries* (Moscow: Progress House, 1971).

Mallison, W. T. and S. V. Mallison, *The Palestine Problem in International Law and World Order* (New York: Longman, 1986).

Mandel, N. *The Arabs and Zionism Before World War I* (Berkeley: University of California Press, 1976).

Ma'oz, M. *Ottoman Reform in Syria and Palestine, 1840–1861: The Impact of the Tanzimat on Politics and Society* (Oxford: Oxford University Press, 1968).

_____, ed. *Studies on Palestine During the Ottoman Period* (Jerusalem: Magnes Press, 1975).

Mattar, P. *The Mufti of Jerusalem* (New York: Columbia University Press, 1992).

Migdal, J. S., ed. *Palestinian Society and Politics* (Princeton, NJ: Princeton University Press, 1980).

Miller, Y. N. *Government and Society in Rural Palestine, 1920–1948* (Austin: University of Texas Press, 1985).

Morris, B. *The Birth of the Palestine Refugee Problem, 1947–1949* (Cambridge: Cambridge University Press, 1987).

_____. *1948 and After* (New York: Oxford University Press, 1990).

Muslih, M. Y. *The Origins of Palestinian Nationalism* (New York: Columbia University Press, 1988).

Naff, T. and R. Owen, eds. *Studies in Eighteenth Century Islamic History* (Carbondale: Southern Illinois University Press, 1977).

Nakhleh, N. and E. Zureik, eds. *The Sociology of the Palestinians* (London: Croom Helm, 1980).

Nassar, J. R. *The Palestine Liberation Organization* (New York: Praeger, 1991).

_____ and R. Heacock, eds. *Intifada: Palestine at the Crossroads* (New York: Praeger, 1990).

Nathan, R. A., O. Gass, and D. Creamer. *Palestine: Problem and Promise* (Washington, DC: Middle East Institute, 1946).

Nazzal, N. *The Palestinian Exodus from Galilee* (Beirut: Institute for Palestine Studies, 1978).

al-Nimr, I. *History of Jabal Nablus and al-Balqa* (in Arabic) (Nablus: N.p., 1937; reprinted 1961).

Norton, A. R. *Amal and the Shi'a: Struggle for the Soul of Lebanon* (Austin: University of Texas Press, 1987).

_____ and M. H. Greenberg, eds. *The International Relations of the Palestine Liberation Organization* (Carbondale: Southern Illinois University Press, 1989).

Ovensen, G. *Responding to Change, Trends in Palestinian Household Economy*, FAFO report 166 (Oslo: FAFO, 1994).

Owen, R. *The Middle East in the World Economy, 1800–1914* (London: Methuen, 1981).

_____, ed. *Studies in the Economic History of Palestine in the Nineteenth and Twentieth Centuries* (Carbondale: Southern Illinois University Press, 1982).

Palumbo, M. *The Palestinian Catastrophe: The 1948 Expulsion of a People from Their Homeland* (London: Quartet Books, 1987).

Peretz, D. *Intifada: The Palestinian Uprising* (Boulder, CO: Westview Press, 1990).

_____. *Israel and the Palestinian Arabs* (Washington, DC: Middle East Institute, 1958).

Peteet, J. *Gender in Crisis: Women and the Palestinian Resistance Movement* (New York: Columbia University Press, 1991).

Petran, T. *The Struggle over Lebanon* (New York: Monthly Review Press, 1987).

Polk, W. E. and R. L. Chambers, eds. *Beginnings of Modernization in the Middle East* (Chicago: University of Chicago Press, 1968).

Porath, Y. *The Emergence of the Palestinian Arab National Movement, 1918–1929* (London: Frank Cass, 1974).

_____. *The Palestinian Arab National Movement, from Riots to Rebellion* (London: Frank Cass, 1977).

Quandt, W. B., F. Jabber, and A. M. Lesch. *The Politics of Palestinian Nationalism* (Berkeley: University of California Press, 1973).

Qubain, F. *Crisis in Lebanon* (Washington, DC: Middle East Institute, 1961).

al-Ramini, A. *Nablus in the Nineteenth Century* (in Arabic) (Amman: Dar al-Sha'ab, 1979).

El-Rayyes, R. N. and D. Nahhas. *Guerrillas for Palestine: A Study of the Palestinian Commando Organizations* (Beirut: An-Nahar Press, 1974).

Roy, S. *The Gaza Strip: The Political Economy of De-development* (Washington, DC: Institute for Palestine Studies, 1995).

Rubenberg, C. *The Palestine Liberation Organization: Its Institutional Infrastructure* (Belmont, MA: Institute for Arab Studies, 1983).

Rubin, B. *Revolution Until Victory? The Politics and History of the PLO* (Cambridge: Harvard University Press, 1994).

Runciman, S. *History of the Crusades* (Cambridge: Cambridge University Press, 1952).

Rustum, A. J. *The Royal Archives of Egypt and the Disturbances in Palestine, 1834* (Beirut: American University of Beirut, 1938).

Said, E. W. with photographs by Jean Mohr. *After the Last Sky* (London: Faber and Faber, 1986).

_____. *Orientalism* (New York: Pantheon, 1978).

_____. *Peace and Its Discontents: Essays on Palestine in the Middle East Peace Process* (New York: Vintage, 1995).

_____. *The Politics of Dispossession: The Struggle for Palestinian Self-Determination, 1969–1994* (New York: Pantheon, 1994).

_____. *The Question of Palestine* (New York: Vintage, 1980).

_____ and C. Hitchens, eds. *Blaming the Victims* (London: Verso, 1988).

Sayigh, R. *Palestinians: From Peasants to Revolutionaries* (London: Zed, 1979).

_____. *Too Many Enemies: The Palestinian Experience in Lebanon* (London: Zed, 1994).

Schölch, A. *Palestine in Transformation, 1856–1882: Studies in Social, Economic and Political Development,* translated by W. C. Young and M. C. Gerrity (Washington, DC: Institute for Palestine Studies, 1993).

Seikaly, M. *Haifa: Transformation of an Arab Society, 1918–1939* (London: I. B. Tauris, 1995).

Semyonov, M. and N. L. Epstein. *Hewers of Wood and Drawers of Water: Noncitizen Arabs in the Israeli Labor Market,* report number 13 (New York: Cornell International Industrial and Labor Relations, 1987).

Shafir, G. *Land, Labor and the Origins of Israeli-Palestinian Conflict, 1882–1914* (Cambridge: Cambridge University Press, 1989).

Sharabi, H. *Arab Intellectuals and the West: The Formative Years, 1875–1914* (Baltimore: Johns Hopkins University Press, 1970).

_____. *Governments and Politics of the Middle East in the Twentieth Century* (Princeton, NJ: Van Nostrand, 1962).

Shipler, D. *Arab and Jew: Wounded Spirits in a Promised Land* (New York: Penguin, 1987).

Shlaim, A. *Collusion Across the Jordan: King Abdullah, the Zionist Movement, and the Partition of Palestine* (New York: Columbia University Press, 1988).

_____. *The Politics of Partition: King Abdullah, the Zionists and Palestine, 1921–1951* (New York: Columbia University Press, 1990).

Smith, B. J. *The Roots of Separatism in Palestine, British Economic Policy, 1920–1929* (Syracuse: Syracuse University Press, 1993).

Smith, C. D. *Palestine and the Arab-Israeli Conflict* (New York: St. Martin's Press, 1988).

Smith, P. A. *Palestine and the Palestinians, 1876–1983* (New York: St. Martin's Press, 1984).

Stein, K. W. *The Land Question in Palestine* (Chapel Hill: University of North Carolina Press, 1984).

Stoyanovsky, J. *The Mandate for Palestine: A Contribution to the Theory and Practice of International Mandates* (Westport, CT: Hyperion Press, 1976).

Swedenburg, T. R. *Memories of Revolt: The 1936–1939 Rebellion and the Palestinian National Past* (Minneapolis: University of Minnesota Press, 1995).

Szerezewski, R. *Essays on the Structure of the Jewish Economy in Palestine and Israel* (Jerusalem: Maurice Falk Institute, 1968).

Tibawi, A. L. *Arab Education in Mandatory Palestine: A Study of Three Decades of British Administration* (London: Luzac, 1956).

Turki, F. *The Disinherited, Journal of a Palestinian Exile* (New York: Monthly Review Press, 1972).

Usher, G. *Palestine in Crisis: The Struggle for Peace and Political Independence* (London: Pluto Press, 1995).

Vital, D. *The Origins of Zionism* (Oxford: Oxford University Press, 1975).

Wallach, J. and J. Wallach. *The New Palestinians: The Emerging Generation of Leaders* (Rocklin, CA: Prima Publishers, 1992).

Warriner, D. *Land and Poverty in the Middle East* (London: Royal Institute of International Affairs, 1948).

Zureik, E. *The Palestinians in Israel: A Study in Internal Colonialism* (London: Routledge & Kegan Paul, 1979).

Documents and Reports

Amnesty International. *Human Rights in the Gaza Strip and Jericho Under Palestinian Self-Rule* 6, 10 (September 1994).

_____. *Trial at Midnight: Secret, Summary, Unfair Trials in Gaza* (London: Amnesty International, 1995).

Anglo-American Committee of Inquiry. *A Survey of Palestine*, vol. 1 (1945–1946; reprint, Washington, DC: Institute for Palestine Studies, 1991).

Barron, J. B. *Palestine: Report and General Abstracts of the Census of 1922* (Jerusalem: Government of Palestine, 1923).

B'Tselem (Israeli Information Center for Human Rights in the Occupied Territories). September and November 1994 reports.

Center for Palestine Research and Studies, Nablus (West Bank). "Palestinian Public Opinion Poll III," September 1995.

Economic Intelligence Unit. *Israel/The Occupied Territories, 1993–94* (London: Economic Intelligence Unit, 1994).

Elmusa, S. S. *The Water Issue and the Palestinian-Israeli Conflict* (Washington, DC: Center for Policy Analysis on Palestine, 1993).

Facts and Figures About the Palestinians (Washington, DC: Center for Policy Analysis on Palestine, 1993).

Foundation for Middle East Peace. *Report on Israeli Settlement in the Occupied Territories* 5, 5 (September 1995).

Gaza Center for Rights and Law (Affiliate of the International Commission of Jurists, Geneva). *Monthly Report*, May 1994; June/July 1994.

Hope Simpson, John. *Palestine, Report on Immigration, Land Settlement and Development* [the Hope Simpson report] (London: His Majesty's Stationery Office, 1930).

Human Rights Watch/Middle East. *Torture and Ill-Treatment: Israel's Interrogation of Palestinians from the Occupied Territories* (New York: Human Rights Watch, 1994).

Israel, Ministry of Foreign Affairs. *Israeli-Palestinian Interim Agreement on the West Bank and Gaza Strip*, September 28, 1995. Accessible on the Internet through the Israel Information Service Gopher, ask@israel-info.gov.il.

Kossaifi, G. F. *The Palestinian Refugees and the Right of Return* (Washington, DC: Center for Policy Analysis on Palestine, 1996).

Kubursi, A. *Palestinian Losses in 1948: The Quest for Precision* (Washington, DC: Center for Policy Analysis on Palestine, 1996).

Lesch, A. M. "The Palestinian Uprising—Causes and Consequences." UFSI report 1 (Washington, DC: Universities Field Staff International, 1988-1989).

Palestine. *Statistical Abstract of Palestine, 1944–1945* (Jerusalem: Government of Palestine, 1946).

Palestine Human Rights Information Center, Jerusalem/Washington. *The Washington Report on Middle East Affairs* 13, 1 (June 1994).

Sayigh, Y. *Programme for Development of the Palestinian National Economy for the Years 1994–2000, Executive Summary* (Tunis: PLO, 1993).

United Nations. *The Origins and Evolution of the Palestine Problem, 1917–1988* (New York: United Nations, 1990).

_____. *Report of the Commissioner-General of the UNRWA in the Near East, 1 July 1992–30 June 1993* (New York: United Nations, 1994).

United Nations Commission for Western Asia. *Statistical Abstract of the Study on the Economic and Social Situation and Potential of the Palestinian Arab People in the Region of Western Asia* (New York: United Nations, 1983).

United Nations Conference on Trade and Development. "The Palestinian Financial Sector Under Israeli Occupation," UNCTAD/ST/SEU/3, Geneva, July 8, 1987.

_____. "Prospects for Sustained Development of the Palestinian Economy in the West Bank and Gaza Strip," UNCTAD/DSD/SEU/2, Geneva, September 27, 1993.

El-Uteibi, Y. J. and M. Amous. "Jordanian Returnees Profile." Photocopy, Returnees Compensation Center, the Hashemite Charity Organization, Geneva, 1993.

World Bank. *Developing the Occupied Territories: An Investment in Peace*, 7 vols. (Washington, DC: World Bank, 1993).

Journal Articles, Conference Papers, and Other Sources

Abed, G. T. "Developing the Palestinian Economy." *Journal of Palestine Studies* 23, 4 (Summer 1994): 41–51.

_____. "The Political Economy of Development in the West Bank and Gaza Strip." Paper delivered at the Workshop on Strategic Visions for the Middle East and North Africa, Economic Research Forum, Gammarth, Tunisia, June 9–11, 1995.

Abu-Amr, Z. "Hamas: A Historical and Political Background." *Journal of Palestine Studies* 22, 4 (Summer 1993): 5–19.

_____ "Report from Palestine." *Journal of Palestine Studies* 24, 2 (Winter 1995): 40–47.

AbuKhalil, A. "The Palestinian-Shi'ite War in Lebanon." *Third World Affairs* (1988): 77–89.

Abu-Lughod, I. "Educating a Community in Exile: The Palestinian Experience." *Journal of Palestine Studies* 2, 3 (Spring 1973).

Abu-Lughod, J. L. "The Demographic Transformation of Palestine: Relevance for Planning Palestine Open University," in *Palestine Open University Feasibility Study*, part 2 (Paris: UNESCO, 1980), 1–91, i–xxii.

_____. "Palestinians: Exiles at Home and Abroad." *Current Sociology* 36 (Summer 1988): 61–69.

Amin, S. "After Gaza and Jericho: The New Palestinian-Middle Eastern Problem." *Beirut Review* 8 (Fall 1994): 113–120.

Aronson, G. "'Final Status' to Preserve Settlements." *Report on Israeli Settlement in the Occupied Territories* 5, 3 (May 1995).

_____. "Historic Israeli-PLO Accord Leaves Settlements Intact." *Report on Israeli Settlement in the Occupied Territories* 4, 4 (July 1994).

Aruri, N. H. "Early Empowerment: The Burden not the Responsibility." *Journal of Palestine Studies* 24, 2 (Winter 1995): 33–39.

_____ and J. J. Carroll. "A New Palestinian Charter." *Journal of Palestine Studies* 23, 4 (Summer 1994): 5–17.

Aruri, T. "Some Expected Political Consequences from Establishing an Elected Palestinian Council." Paper presented at a workshop of the Palestinian People's Party, August 18, 1995.

_____. "Some Features of Palestinian Political Life and Its Future." Paper presented at a workshop, Muwaten Institute, Jerusalem, August 8, 1995.

Asad, T. "Anthropological Texts and Ideological Problems: An Analysis of Cohen on Arab Border Villages in Israel." *Review of Middle East Studies* 1 (1975): 1–40.

Badran, N. "The Means of Survival: Education and the Palestinian Community, 1948–67." *Journal of Palestine Studies* 9, 4 (Summer 1980): 44–74.

_____. "The Palestinian Countryside Before World War I" (in Arabic). *Palestine Affairs* 7 (March 1972).

Barkan, O. L. "The Price Revolution of the Sixteenth Century: A Turning Point in the Economic History of the Near East." *International Journal of Middle East Studies* 6 (January 1975): 3–28.

Ben-Arieh, Y. "The Growth of Jerusalem in the Nineteenth Century." *Annals of the Association of American Geographers* 65 (1975).

Bishara, A. "Only Two Alternatives Remain: The Bantustan Plan or the Bi-National Option." *News from Within*, 11, 7 (July 1995): 14–17.

Bowersock, G. W. "Palestine: Ancient History and Modern Politics." *Journal of Palestine Studies* 14, 4 (Summer 1985): 49–57.

Brynen, R. "The Dynamics of Palestinian Elite Formation." *Journal of Palestine Studies* 24, 3 (Spring 1995): 31–43.

Buheiry, M. "The Agricultural Exports of Southern Palestine, 1885–1914." *Journal of Palestine Studies* 10, 4 (Summer 1981): 61–81.

Caradon, Lord. "The Palestinians: Their Place in the Middle East." Paper presented at the annual conference of the Middle East Institute, Washington, D.C., September 30–October 1, 1977.

Childers, E. "The Other Exodus." *Spectator*, May 12, 1961.

Cockburn, A. "Why Say No?" *Nation*, October 4, 1993, 342–343.

Cohen, S. "Justice in Transition." *Middle East Report* 194/195 (May-June/July-August 1995): 2–5.

Connell, D. "Palestine on the Edge, Crisis in the National Movement." *Middle East Report* 194/195 (May-June/July-August 1995): 6–9.

Dabdoub, L. "Palestinian Public Opinion Polls on the Peace Process." *Palestine-Israel: Journal of Politics, Economics and Culture* 5 (Winter 1995): 60–63.

Dajani, B. "The September 1993 Israeli-PLO Documents: A Textual Analysis." *Journal of Palestine Studies* 23, 3 (Spring 1994): 5–23.

Dehter, A. "How Expensive Are West Bank Settlements?" *The West Bank Data Project* (Jerusalem: Jerusalem Post, 1987) III.

Diwan, I. and M. Walton. "Palestine Between Israel and Jordan: The Economics of an Uneasy Triangle." *Beirut Review* 8 (Fall 1994): 21–43.

Doumani, B. B. "The Political Economy of Population Counts in Ottoman Palestine: Nablus Circa 1850." *International Journal of Middle East Studies* 26, 1 (February 1994): 1–17.

Drake, L. "Between the Lines: A Textual Analysis of the Gaza-Jericho Agreement." *Arab Studies Quarterly* 16, 4 (Fall 1994): 1–36.

Dumper, M. T. "Jerusalem's Infrastructure: Is Annexation Irreversible?" *Journal of Palestine Studies* 22, 3 (Spring 1993): 78–95.

Elmusa, S. and M. El-Jaafari. "Power and Trade: The Israeli-Palestinian Economic Protocol." *Journal of Palestine Studies* 24, 2 (Winter 1995): 14–32.

Erakat, S. "Preparation for Elections." In *Palestinian Elections* (Washington, DC: Center for Policy Analysis on Palestine, 1995).

Farsoun, S. K. "Oil, State and Social Structure in the Middle East." *Arab Studies Quarterly* 10, 2 (Spring 1988): 155–175.

_____ and W. Carroll. "The Civil War in Lebanon: Sect, Class, and Imperialism." *Monthly Review* 28, 2 (June 1976): 12–37.

_____ and J. M. Landis. "Structures of Resistance and the 'War of Position': A Case Study of the Palestinian Uprising." *Arab Studies Quarterly* 11, 4 (Fall 1989): 59–86.

_____ and R. B. Wingerter. "The Palestinians in Lebanon." *SAIS Review* 3 (Winter 1981/1982): 93–106.

_____ and C. Zacharia. "Class, Economic Change and Democratization in the Arab World." In R. Brynen, B. Korany, and P. Noble, eds., *Political Liberalization and Democratization in the Arab World*, vol. 1 (Boulder, CO: Lynne Rienner, 1995).

Finkelstein, N. G. "Whither the 'Peace Process'?" Paper presented at Georgetown and American Universities, Washington, D.C., April 24 and 25, 1996.

Freedmen, W. "An Export Promotion Scheme for Palestine." *Graduate Review* 1, 6 (American University) 1994: 34–45.

Gerber, H. "Modernization in Nineteenth Century Palestine: the Role of Foreign Trade." *Middle Eastern Studies* 18 (July 1982): 250–264.

Halevi, N. "The Political Economy of Absorptive Capacity: Growth and Cycles in Jewish Palestine Under the British Mandate." *Middle Eastern Studies* 19 (October 1983): 456–469.

Hijjawi, S. "The Palestinians in Lebanon" (in Arabic). *Journal of the Center for Palestinian Studies* (Baghdad) 22 (May-June 1977).

Hoexter, M. "The Role of Qays and Yaman Factions in Local Political Divisions: Jabal Nablus Compared with the Judean Hills in the First Half of the Nineteenth Century." *Asian and African Studies* 9 (Fall 1973): 249–311.

al-Hout, B. N. "The Palestinian Political Elite During the Mandate Period." *Journal of Palestine Studies* 9, 1 (Autumn 1979): 85–111.

Hudson, M. C. "The Palestinian Arab Resistance Movement: Its Significance in the Middle East Crisis." *Middle East Journal* 23, 3 (Summer 1969).

Jabber, F. "The Arab Regimes and the Palestinian Revolution." *Journal of Palestine Studies* 2, 2 (Winter 1973): 79–101.

Jenin, J. "Economic Wedlock: Israel to Keep Upper Hand." *Breaking the Siege, the Newsletter of the Middle East Justice Network* 6, 2 (June-July 1994).

Khalidi, A. "The Palestinians: Current Dilemmas, Future Challenges." *Journal of Palestine Studies* 24, 2 (Winter 1995): 5–13.

Khalidi, R. "A Palestinian View of the Accord with Israel." *Current History* 93, 580 (February 1994): 62–66.

_____. "The Role of the Press in the Early Arab Reaction to Zionism." *Peuples Méditerranéens/Mediterranean Peoples*, July-September 1982.

Khalidi, T. "Palestinian Historiography: 1900–1948." *Journal of Palestine Studies* 10, 3 (Spring 1981): 59–76.

Khalidi, W. "Plan Dalet: The Zionist Masterplan for the Conquest of Palestine, 1948." *Middle East Forum* (November 1961): 22–28.

Kimmerling, B. "Sociology, Ideology and Nation Building: The Palestinians in Israeli Sociology." *American Sociological Review* 57 (August 1992): 446–460.

Maksoud, C. "Peace Process or Puppet Show?" *Foreign Policy* 100 (Fall 1995): 117–124.

Mandell, J. "Gaza: Israel's Soweto." *Middle East Report* 136/137 (October-December 1985): 7–19, 58.

McTague, J. J. Jr. "The British Military Administration in Palestine, 1917–1920." *Journal of Palestine Studies* 7, 3 (Spring 1978): 55–76.

Metzer, J. "Economic Structure and National Goals—The Jewish National Home in Interwar Palestine." *Journal of Economic History* 38 (March 1978): 101–119.

_____. "Fiscal Incidence and Resource Transfer Between Jews and Arabs in Mandatory Palestine." *Research in Economic History* 7 (1982): 87–132.

Moughrabi, F. "American Public Opinion and the Palestine Question." Occasional paper 4 (Washington, DC: International Center for Research and Public Policy, 1986).

Murphy, E. "Stacking the Deck: The Economics of the Israel-PLO Accords." *Middle East Report* 194/195 (May-June/July-August 1995): 35–38.

Nakhleh, K. "Anthropological and Sociological Studies on the Arabs in Israel: A Critique." *Journal of Palestine Studies* 6, 4 (Summer 1977): 41–70.

Ogram, P. "Settlement Expansion." *Middle East Report* 194/195 (May-June/July-August 1995): 17.

Owen, R. "Establishing a Viable Palestinian Economy." *Beirut Review* 8 (Fall 1994): 45–57.

Peled, Y. "From Zionism to Capitalism." *Middle East Report* 194/195 (May-June/July-August 1995): 13–17.

Rabbani, M. "Palestinian Authority, Israeli Rule: From Transitional to Permanent Arrangement." *Middle East Report* 201 (October-December 1996): 2–6.

Reilly, J. "The Peasantry of Late Ottoman Palestine." *Journal of Palestine Studies* 10, 4 (Summer 1981): 82–97.

Rishmawi, M. "The Actions of the Palestinian Authority Under the Gaza/Jericho Agreements." *The Palestine National Authority: A Critical Appraisal* (Washington, DC: Center for Policy Analysis on Palestine, 1995).

Ryan, S. "The West Bank and Gaza: Political Consequences of the Intifada." *Middle East Report* 74 (January 1979): 3–8.

Said, E. W. "The Mirage of Peace." *Nation,* October 16, 1995, 413–420.

_____. "Symbols Versus Substance: A Year After the Declaration of Principles." *Journal of Palestine Studies* 24, 2 (Winter 1995): 60–72.

Schölch, A. "Britain in Palestine, 1838–1882: The Roots of the Balfour Policy." *Journal of Palestine Studies* 22, 1 (Autumn 1992).

al-Sharif, M. "A Contribution to the Study of the Process of the Emergence of the Arab Labor Movement in Palestine" (in Arabic) *Samed al-Iqtisadi* 26 (July 1980).

_____ and N. Badran. "Emergence and Evolution of the Palestinian Working Class" (in Arabic). *Samed al-Iqtisadi* 27 (April 1981).

Shlaim, A. "The Founding of Israel." *Commentary* 89 (February 1990).

Singer, J. "The Declaration of Principles on Interim Self-Government Arrangements, Some Legal Aspects." *Justice* (February 1994): 4–13.

Tamari, S. "The Palestinian Demand for Independence Cannot Be Postponed Indefinitely." *MERIP Reports* 100–101 (October-December 1981): 28–35.

Teveth, S. "Charging Israel with Original Sin." *Commentary* 88 (September 1989): 24–33.

_____. "The Palestine Arab Refugee Problem and Its Origins." *Middle Eastern Studies* 26 (April 1990): 214–249.

Tuma, E. H. "The Peace Negotiations, Economic Cooperation and Stability in the Middle East." *Beirut Review* 8 (Fall 1994): 3–20.

Usher, G. "Closures, Cantons and the Palestinian Covenant." *Middle East Report* 199 (April-June 1996): 33–37.

_____. "Palestinian Trade Unions and the Struggle for Independence." *Middle East Report* 194/195 (May-June/July-August, 1995): 20–24.

Wenger, M. "The Money Tree: US Aid to Israel." *Middle East Report* 164/165 (May-August 1990): 12–13.

Wing, A. K. "Legitimacy and Coercion: Legal Traditions and Legal Rules During the Intifada." *Middle East Policy* 2, 2 (1993): 87–103.

Zacharia, C. E. "Public Opinions of West Bank and Gaza Strip Palestinians Toward Participation in Elections." Department of Sociology, American University, 1995.

Zahlan, A. B. and E. Hagopian. "Palestine's Arab Population." *Journal of Palestine Studies* 3, 4 (Summer 1974): 32–73.

_____ and R. S. Zahlan. "The Palestinian Future: Education and Manpower." *Journal of Palestine Studies* 6, 4 (Summer 1977): 103–112.

Zureik, E. "Toward a Sociology of the Palestinians." *Journal of Palestine Studies* 7, 4 (Summer 1977): 3–16.

About the Book and Authors

Following the historic Oslo Accords between the PLO and Israel, the future status of the Palestinian population living under Israeli occupation since 1967 has taken center stage. Effectively negotiated out of the agreement is the right of return or of compensation for almost four million Palestinians in exile. This book argues that because these Accords formally sever the Palestinians' historical claims from the present, it is crucial to understand the larger historical and ideological context in which the claims arose.

In this broad and richly textured analysis, the authors examine the social, economic, and political development of the people of Palestine from the nineteenth century to the present. The book opens with an overview of the question of Palestine and Palestine's place in regional and global history. Subsequent chapters analyze Palestinian society before and after its catastrophic destruction, the division of Palestine, and the dispersal of its people in 1948. Next, the book explores the forces and constraints affecting the formation of Palestinian national identity, as embodied in popular institutions, the PLO, resistance movements, and the Palestinian uprising against Israeli occupation. The final chapter considers the prospects for Palestinian self-determination and statehood despite the limitations imposed by the Oslo Accords, as well as Palestine's future viability.

Samih K. Farsoun is professor of sociology at American University. **Christina E. Zacharia** is a Ph.D. candidate in the Department of Sociology at American University.

Index